International Energy and Poverty

T0300443

Around 2.8 billion people globally, also known as the "Other Third" or "Energy Poor," have little or no access to beneficial energy that meets their needs for cooking, heating, water, sanitation, illumination, transportation, or basic mechanical power. This book uniquely integrates the hitherto segmented and fragmented approaches to the challenge of access to energy. It provides theoretical, philosophical, and practical analysis of energy for the low energy (non-hydrocarbon based) Other Third of the world, and how the unmet needs of the Energy Poor might be satisfied. It comprehensively addresses the range of issues relating to energy justice and energy access for all, including appropriate sustainable energy technologies (ASETs).

The book breaks new ground by crafting a unified and cohesive framework for analysis and action that explains the factual and socio-political phenomenon of the Energy Poor, and demonstrates why clean energy is a primary determinant of their human progress.

This is a must-read for all scholars, students, professionals, and policymakers working on energy policy, poverty, and sustainable energy technologies.

Lakshman Guruswamy is Nicholas Doman Professor of International Environmental Law at the University of Colorado at Boulder, USA.

Routledge Studies in Energy Policy

Our Energy Future
Socioeconomic Implications and Policy Options for Rural America
Edited by Done E. Albrecht

Energy Security and Natural Gas Markets in Europe
Lessons from the EU and the USA
Tim Boersma

International Energy Policy
The emerging contours
Edited by Lakshman Guruswamy

For further details please visit the series page on the Routledge website:
http://www.routledge.com/books/series/RSIEP/

International Energy and Poverty

The emerging contours

Edited by Lakshman Guruswamy

with Elizabeth Neville

Routledge
Taylor & Francis Group

LONDON AND NEW YORK

earthscan
from Routledge

First published 2016
by Routledge
2 Park Square, Milton Park, Abingdon, Oxfordshire OX14 4RN

and by Routledge
711 Third Avenue, New York, NY 10017

First issued in paperback 2017

Routledge is an imprint of the Taylor & Francis Group, an informa business

British Library Cataloguing-in-Publication Data
A catalogue record for this book is available from the British Library

Library of Congress Cataloging-in-Publication Data
International energy and poverty : the emerging contours / [edited by] Lakshman Guruswamy, with Elizabeth Neville.
pages cm
Includes bibliographical references and index.
1. Power resources--Economic aspects--Developing countries. 2. Energy development--Developing countries. 3. Poverty--Developing countries. 4. Economic development--Developing countries. I. Guruswamy, Lakshman D., 1939-
HD9502.D4421585 2016
333.7909172'4--dc23
2015010686

ISBN 13: 978-1-138-05582-7 (pbk)
ISBN 13: 978-1-138-79231-9 (hbk)

Typeset in Goudy
by Saxon Graphics Ltd, Derby

Contents

Acknowledgments

We are beholden to Sean Owens for his diligence, perspicacity, and dedication. This book could not have been completed without him. We are also indebted to, and greatly appreciative of Diana Avelis for her invaluable word processing and indexing skills.

A major part of this book was written and edited in the idyllic and inspiring environs of the William S. Richardson School of Law in Honolulu. We are grateful to Dean Avi Soifer, Associate Dean Denise Antolini, and David Forman, Director of the Environmental Program, for favoring Lakshman with a Distinguished Visitorship. The warmth and collegiality of the faculty, and staff, made the visit even more memorable.

Jane Thompson, Research Librarian, is one of the most valuable assets of the University of Colorado, School of Law. We are very grateful for her invaluable help.

Finally, Lakshman is indebted to the University of Colorado, School of Law, for granting him sabbatical leave during the Fall of 2014. A major part of this book was completed during this sabbatical leave.

Lakshman Guruswamy
Elizabeth Neville

Figures and tables

Figures

Tables

Dedication

This book is dedicated to Dr. Kandeh Yumkella, the extraordinary and awe-inspiring United Nations Under-Secretary-General, Special Representative of the Secretary-General Sustainable Energy for All, Chief Executive Officer Sustainable Energy for All Initiative, and Chairman of UN Energy. Dr. Yumkella has predominantly been responsible for drawing attention to the plight of the Energy Poor. The world is deeply indebted to him for his unremitting focus on this forgotten third of the world. His vision, dedication, and pursuit of sustainable energy have illuminated the path of decision makers the world over.

Contributors

Editor

Lakshman Guruswamy was born in Sri Lanka, and is the Nicholas Doman Professor of International Environmental Law at the University of Colorado at Boulder. He is a recognized expert in International Environmental and Energy Law, and is widely published in books, and legal and scientific journals in international energy and environmental law. Lakshman is an invited speaker in scholarly venues across the world, and his present scholarship is focused on access to energy for the Other Third of the world.

Contributors

Jason B. Aamodt is the Assistant Dean for online legal education at the University of Tulsa College of Law where he teaches international environmental law and water law, while administering the online programs. Aamodt is published in numerous journals and book chapters on sustainable development, and water law. He is the founding member of the Indian and Environmental Law Center, a mid-western law firm specializing in water rights, land damages, Indian law, and toxic tort litigation. He earned his JD from the University of Tulsa, and a BS in Chemistry from the State University of New York.

Harold Annegarn is the Director: Annegarn Environmental Research [AER] (Pty) Ltd, Johannesburg; and Professor, Department of Geography, Environmental Management & Energy Studies: University of Johannesburg, Johannesburg.

E. Christian Brugger is the J. Francis Cardinal Stafford Professor of Moral Theology at St. John Vianney Theological Seminary in Denver, Colorado. He has Master's degrees in Moral Theology and Philosophy from Seton Hall, Harvard and Oxford Universities, and a Ph.D. in Christian Ethics from Oxford. He has published over 200 articles in scholarly and popular periodicals on topics in bioethics, sexual ethics, natural law theory, and psychology. He lives on a farm in Evergreen, Colorado, with his wife and five children.

Kristen A. Carpenter is a Professor of Law and Associate Dean for Research at the University of Colorado Law School, where she teaches Property, American Indian Law, and related courses. Her research and advocacy activities focus on the rights of indigenous peoples vis-à-vis land, culture, and religion, both in the United States and elsewhere around the world. She obtained her AB at Dartmouth College and her JD at Harvard Law School.

Joy S. Clancy is a Reader (Associate Professor) in Development Studies specializing in Technology Transfer, at the University of Twente, The Netherlands. Her research has focused, for more than 25 years, on small scale energy systems for developing countries, and the role that energy plays for small businesses and the potential it offers entrepreneurs through the provision of a new infrastructure service. Gender and energy has been an important factor addressed in this research.

Vincent Doyle currently works for Concern Universal in Malawi where he has lived for more than five years. He possesses almost 20 years' experience in project management, rural livelihoods, food security, vocational training, income generation, sustainable energy, organizational learning, and other areas.

Soma Dutta is Programme Coordinator with ENERGIA, the international network on Gender and Sustainable Energy. She works on cross-cutting issues of gender, poverty and development in the context of energy access and on efforts that contribute to women's economic empowerment through energy access. In the area of energy access, Soma has supported policy makers, practitioners, governments, NGOs and international organizations in project planning; socio-economic, institutional and policy analysis; and capacity building. Soma is Indian, with degrees in Economics (Bachelor's from the University of Delhi) and Rural Management (Master's from the Institute of Rural Management, Anand, India).

Blake M. Feamster is an attorney at the Widdows Law Firm, focusing on litigation and family law. Ms. Feamster graduated from the University of Tulsa College of Law, and earned distinction in her classes relating to International Law and Development.

Carmen G. Gonzalez is a Professor of Law at Seattle University School of Law, who has published widely in the areas of international environmental law and environmental justice. She was a Fulbright Scholar in Argentina, a US Supreme Court Fellow, and a Visiting Fellow at the Lauterpacht Centre for International Law at the University of Cambridge in the United Kingdom. Her book, *International Environmental Law and the Global South*, will be published by Cambridge University Press in 2015. She holds a BA from Yale University and a JD from Harvard Law School.

Katrin Harvey is the Management and Development Officer of the Renewable Energy and Energy Efficiency Partnership (REEEP), where she is in charge of the Director General's office, as well as all matters pertaining to REEEP's governance and coordination with partner organizations. She holds a Master's degree in English and American Studies, and a second Master's degree in International Development Studies, both from the University of Vienna.

Martin Hiller has been Director General of the Renewable Energy Energy Efficiency Partnership (REEEP) since December 2011. He has over 20 years of experience in environmental issues and sustainability, policy, specialized policy communications and campaigns, and in-depth knowledge of climate change and energy policy. Under his leadership, REEEP has sharpened its focus as a catalyst for up-scaling clean energy business models. Prior to joining REEEP, Martin had a distinguished career with the World Wide Fund for Nature (WWF).

Matt Hulse is a professional electrical, computer, and software systems engineer with diverse experience in embedded devices and digital communication technologies, who has worked in aerospace engineering, imaging science, telecommunications, energy and electrical engineering, and information technology. He possesses extensive knowledge of photovoltaic systems, radio engineering, networking, and telecommunication protocols. His specialization is in energy and communication infrastructure in developing communities and emerging markets. His work spans several countries and disciplines within industry, public sector and non-profits.

Jacquelyn Amour Jampolsky was the first graduate to receive a simultaneous JD and PhD degree from the University of Colorado, Boulder, from the Law School and the Department of Environmental Studies. She came to Colorado after receiving her BS in Conservation and Resource Studies from the University of California, Berkeley in 2008. She has worked with the Native American Rights Fund, North American Tribal governments, rural Indigenous communities in Ecuador and Peru, and urban squatter communities in Brazil. She currently serves as the David H. Getches American Indian and Natural Resources Law Fellow for the Getches-Wilkinson Center for Natural Resources, Energy, and the Environment at the University of Colorado, Boulder.

Karim-Aly S. Kassam is International Professor of Environmental and Indigenous Studies in the Department of Natural Resources and the American Indian Program at the College of Agriculture and Life Sciences, Cornell University. His research focuses on the complex connectivity of human and environmental relations, addressing indigenous ways of knowing, food sovereignty, sustainable livelihoods, and climate change. He holds a PhD in Natural Resource Policy and Management from Cornell University (USA), an MSc in Social Policy and Planning in Developing Countries from the London School of Economics (UK), an MPhil in Islamic Studies from the University of Cambridge (UK), and a BA in Economics from the University of Calgary (Canada).

Stephen Katsaros is an inventor, mechanical engineer, and US patent agent. In 2010, he invented a simple, portable solar light bulb with the potential to revolutionize life for the Energy Poor. Five months after his first sketch, Steve launched Nokero, a for-profit company with a mission to provide affordable solar technology solutions for off-grid communities around the world. Stephen has a BS in Mechanical Engineering (BSME) from Purdue University, is a patent agent registered with the US Patent and Trademark Office, won the Collegiate Inventors Competition in 1995, and was awarded the 2012 Outstanding Mechanical Engineer Award from Purdue University; Nokero won the Patents for Humanity award from the United States Patent and Trademark Office.

Murodbek Laldjebaev is a PhD candidate at the Department of Natural Resources, Cornell University, and a research fellow at the University of Central Asia. His research interests span the areas of energy security, energy sovereignty, energy poverty, water resources management, food sovereignty, and energy–water–food nexus. Murodbek has a Master's in Public Policy from the National University of Singapore, and a Bachelor's degree in English Language from Khorog State University, Tajikistan. He has worked in teacher education in rural Tajikistan, consulted with the World Bank on pre-service education, and worked for the Ministry of Economic Development of Trade on Tajikistan's accession to the WTO.

Martin Lugmayr is a Sustainable Energy Expert at UNIDO Energy Branch. Mr. Lugmayr coordinates the Global Network of Regional Sustainable Energy Centers. He works closely with SIDS DOCK, SPC, CARICOM on the creation of regional centres for SIDS. Before, the UNIDO expert was based in Cape Verde and assisted in the establishment of the ECOWAS Centre for Renewable Energy and Energy Efficiency (ECREEE) and its technical program. A number of years, he managed the energy program of the Austrian Development Agency (ADA) and worked on international energy-development policy at the Development Cooperation Department of the Austrian Ministry for Foreign Affairs, as well as the Global Forum on Sustainable Energy (GFSE). He holds an MSc degree in renewable energy technologies and an MA in political science.

Arjun Makhijani is President of the Institute for Energy and Environmental Research in Takoma Park, Maryland. He earned his Ph.D. from the Department of Electrical Engineering and Computer Sciences at the University of California, Berkeley in 1972, specializing in nuclear fusion, and his Bachelor of Engineering (Electrical) from the University of Bombay (1965). A recognized authority on energy issues, He is the author and co-author of numerous reports and books on energy and environment related issues. He has served as a consultant on energy issues to many institutions, including the United Nations Development Programme, the Food and Agriculture Organization, and the United Nations Environment Programme.

Margaret Njirambo Matinga is an independent consultant whose work is centered on energy poverty in sub-Sahara Africa (SSA) with a special focus on household energy. She explores the interface between technology and society with a view to obtaining an understanding of why household members do things the way they do, and what factors facilitate inertia as well as change. She has authored a number of scholarly articles on energy poverty, indoor air pollution, gender equity and access to energy. She is a member of the African Research on Energy Policy Network (AFREPREN), Household Energy Network (HEDON) and the International Network on Gender and Energy (ENERGIA). She holds a degree in Mechanical Engineering from the University of Malawi and an MSc in Engineering from the University of Cape Town.

Amy Meyer graduated from the University of Colorado, Boulder, in 2013 with a degree in Environmental Studies and Ecology/Evolutionary Biology. She has worked with a number of environmentally oriented organizations, including the Breakthrough Institute, Natural Capitalism Solutions, SustainUS, and the University of Colorado Law's Center for Energy and Environmental Security. Currently Ms. Meyer works as an energy efficiency consultant for Navigant Consulting, Inc.

Alois P. Mhlanga is an Industrial Development Officer at UNIDO Energy Branch. Mr. Mhlanga has over 17 years' experience in the renewable energy and climate change field. He currently manages UNIDO's projects on renewable energy in Africa and Asia. He is responsible for flagship programmes such as the design and creation of the ECOWAS Centre for Renewable Energy and Energy Efficiency. Before joining UNIDO, Mr. Mhlanga was a Renewable Energy Expert in the African Development Bank managing a vast portfolio of renewable energy and sustainable energy investment projects across Africa. Before that, he was the principal sustainable energy expert at the Southern Center for Energy and Environment and a part-time lecture in the Master of Renewable Energy programme at the University of Zimbabwe.

Nthabiseng Mohlakoana is a post-doctoral researcher on Energy, Gender, and Development at the University of Twente, The Netherlands. She has 15 years of experience in research focusing on energy use by low-income urban and rural households, energy policy implementation analysis and gender and energy research. Nthabiseng completed her PhD at the Twente Centre for Studies in Technology and Sustainable Development at the University of Twente. She raised funds for the network to work on gender mainstreaming of energy policies and strategies, especially those affecting the low-income areas of South Africa.

Pradeep Monga is Director and Special Representative of the Director General on Energy at the United Nations Industrial Development Organization (UNIDO) in Vienna, Austria. In this capacity he leads the energy and environment related work at the international agency. In addition to his regular duties, he represents UNIDO at high-level meetings on energy and environment. He has presented several technical papers at over 40 international seminars/workshops and has co-authored three books. In addition, he holds a certificate in Advanced Organizational Management from Harvard Business School. He is both a Fulbright and Humphrey scholar.

Melissa F. Moore-Pachucki is a practicing attorney, specializing in civil and commercial litigation. Her practice also involves litigation concerning energy and environmental matters. She earned her Juris Doctorate from the University of Tulsa College of Law in 2014, graduating with highest honors. She also received an M.A. in Composition and Rhetoric in 2009. She served as Articles Editor for the nationally published *Energy Law Journal*, which is affiliated with the Energy Bar Association. She remains active in Energy and Environmental Policy in her region.

Ved P. Nanda is the Evans University Professor, and Thompson G. Marsh Professor of Law at the University of Denver. He has authored or co-authored 22 books in the various fields of international law and over 180 chapters and major law review articles, and has been a Distinguished Visiting Professor and Scholar at a number of universities in the United States and abroad. In addition to his scholarly achievements, he is significantly involved in the global international law community, and has served as President of many international scholarly and professional organizations, and is the recipient of awards from many countries.

Elizabeth Neville is an attorney focused on domestic and international environmental law. She has a career interest in the intersection between law, anthropogenic pollution, wildlife conservation, development, and poverty issues. Prior to working as the Editorial Coordinator for this book, she worked with a number of NGOs including Refugees International Japan, the Center for Biological Diversity, and the Animal Welfare Institute. She earned her JD at the University of Colorado Law School and her BA in English with a Writing and Rhetoric emphasis at Pepperdine University. She currently resides on her home island of St. Croix and works as a law clerk to Judge Robert Molloy of the Superior Court of the Virgin Islands.

Ana Victoria Rojas is a sustainable development specialist with 15 years of experience working with policy makers, program practitioners, international organizations, NGOs and grassroots level organizations in Latin America, Asia, Africa and Europe. She has a background in environmental law, graduating from the University of Costa Rica (Law Bach. and Lic. degree in Law) in 2001 and pursuing her M.Sc. on Environmental Management, at the Vrije Universiteit Amsterdam (2003–2004). Ana has built her expertise as a sustainable development specialist working on climate change, energy, poverty, gender and sustainable development sectors. She has worked for CEDARENA, in Costa Rica, BothENDS and ETC Foundation/ENERGIA in the Netherlands.

Ana combines her current position as energy task leader for IUCN's Global Gender Office with the provision of technical support to gender and mitigation pilot projects in the Mekong region.

Mark Safty holds the Wirth Chair in Sustainable Development at the University of Colorado in Denver. He is also an Adjunct Professor in Law at the University of Colorado in Boulder. He is a partner of the large law firm of Holland and Hart. Since the late 1990s, Mr. Safty has focused his practice on development, construction, financing and M&A activity in the renewable energy industry. He is listed in The Best Lawyers in America for project finance law.

Benjamin K. Sovacool is Director of the Danish Center for Energy Technologies and a Professor of Business and Social Sciences at Aarhus University. He is also Associate Professor of Law at Vermont Law School and Director of the Energy Security and Justice Program at their Institute for Energy and the Environment, as well as the Editor-in-Chief of the peer-reviewed international journal *Energy Research & Social Science*. He is the author of more than 300 refereed articles, book chapters, and reports on energy and climate topics. He received his PhD in Science and Technology Studies from the Virginia Polytechnic Institute & State University in Blacksburg, Virginia.

Sarah Revi Sterling is the founder and director of the first Information and Communication Technology for Development (ICTD) professional Master's program in the United States, a program that places equal emphasis on technology, methodology, and development studies. She also consults extensively for the United Nations, development agencies and high technology companies interested in utilizing technology for societal benefit. Previously, Sarah worked at Microsoft for ten years where she spearheaded Microsoft Research's efforts in gender equity in computer science. She has served on the leading gender and technology boards, and testified before the US Congress about the need for more women in the technical workforce.

David I. Stern is a Professor in the Crawford School of Policy at The Australian National University. He is an energy and environmental economist, whose research focuses on the role of energy in growth and development and environmental impacts including climate change. He is an associate editor of *Ecological Economics* and was a lead author for the chapter on Drivers, Trends, and Mitigation in Working Group III's contribution to the IPCC's 5th Assessment Report.

Simon Trace took up his appointment as CEO of Practical Action in 2005. He has been associated with this development NGO during a period of strong growth and rising international recognition for its work, particularly in the area of the environment and energy. Simon's career has principally been in community development, in the fields of soil and water conservation or water and sanitation, and he has spent time with a number of agencies, including periods of secondment to CARE and UNICEF. Prior to joining Practical Action, Simon was Strategic Development Director for the UK NGO WaterAid.

Doug Vilsack is the Executive Director of the Posner Center for International Development (www.posnercenter.org) in Denver, Colorado, a shared workspace for international development organizations that engages over 100 tenants and members. He is also the founder and Board Chair of Elephant Energy (www.elephantenergy.org), a social venture that distributes small scale renewable energy technologies in southern Africa and the Navajo Nation in the USA.

Anoja Wickramasinghe is an Emeritus Professor of Geography, University of Peradeniya, Sri Lanka. Anoja began her career as a geographer, and secured a Msc. in Natural Resource Management and a PhD in Forest Ecology from the University of Sheffield, UK. She has significantly contributed to the field of energy poverty as a researcher, policy analyst, gender activist, and a trainer. She coordinates the National Network on Gender, Energy and Environment, and works as the focal point for ENERGIA International Network.

Kandeh K. Yumkella is United Nations Under-Secretary-General, the Special Representative of the Secretary-General for Sustainable Energy for All (SE4All), and CEO of the SE4All Initiative. He is also the Chairman of UN-Energy, and a two-term former Director General of the United Nations Industrial Development Organization (UNIDO). Prior to working for UNIDO, he was the Minister for Trade, Industry and State Enterprises of the Republic of Sierra Leone from 1994–1995. From 1987–1996, he held various academic positions at Michigan State University and the University of Illinois.

Andreas Zahner is Senior Project Manager at the Renewable Energy and Energy Efficiency Partnership (REEEP). He develops and manages clean energy interventions that lead to market transformation. He has more than 15 years of experience working on environmental issues, climate change and renewable energy. Andreas holds a Master's degree in Ecology and obtained his MSc in Renewable Energy and Energy Efficiency at the Vienna University of Technology.

Foreword

Kandeh K. Yumkella

Providing sustainable energy for all is one of the world's greatest challenges. Energy is critical for socio-economic development; it powers human progress, from job generation to economic competitiveness, from strengthening security to empowering women. It is the great integrator that cuts across all sectors and lies at the heart of all countries' core interests. However, the benefits of modern energy are yet to be enjoyed by all.

Everyone needs access to modern energy sources to manage their everyday lives and to thrive economically. Considerable progress has been made in the last decade, yet in spite of rapid strides made by a few countries, more than a billion people today lack access to reliable, affordable and clean electricity. Many more rely on traditional sources of energy, such as coal, wood or animal waste for cooking and heating. The indoor air pollution caused by such fuels causes 4.3 million premature deaths every year, mainly women and children.

The Sustainable Energy for All initiative, launched by Secretary-General Ban Ki-moon, highlights the fact that we can provide the energy that is so crucial for economic growth and development, while at the same time safeguarding the planet by curbing the greenhouse gas emissions that cause climate change. In meeting the initiative's three global targets of ensuring universal access to modern energy, doubling the global rate of improvement in energy efficiency and doubling the share of renewables in the global energy mix – all by 2030 – we will end energy poverty and reduce energy-related carbon dioxide emissions.

These three objectives are mutually reinforcing. Increasingly, affordable renewable energy technologies are bringing modern energy services to rural communities where extension of the conventional electric power grid would be prohibitively expensive and impractical. More efficient devices for lighting and other uses require less energy and thus reduce the amount of power needed to support them. Increased efficiency in the production and use of electricity relieves strained power grids, allowing them to stretch further to reach more households and businesses.

It is therefore my pleasure to write the foreword for this comprehensive book, which takes an interdisciplinary approach to the relationship between energy and poverty. The authors explore a wide range of issues of direct relevance to the work of Sustainable Energy for All, from energy justice to energy security, from

economics to technology, from political and market reform to the legal
underpinnings of an energy revolution.

This book is essential reading for students, academics, policymakers, business
leaders and all those who are interested in exploring the conceptual framework
for addressing the needs of the world's Energy Poor. As a reader, you have a
role to play. So do governments, multilateral organizations, the private sector
and civil society. Through this multi-stakeholder partnership, we must all
ensure that policy, investment and on-the-ground action go hand in hand for
the good of all.

Kandeh K. Yumkella
United Nations Under-Secretary-General
Special Representative of the Secretary-General
Sustainable Energy for All
Chief Executive Officer
Sustainable Energy for All Initiative

Introduction

Lakshman Guruswamy

Energy poverty

> Energy is the golden thread that connects economic growth, increased social
> equity, and an environment that allows the world to thrive... Sustainable energy
> for all is an investment in our collective future. Universal energy access, increasing
> the use of renewable energy, improved energy efficiency and addressing the nexus
> between energy and health, women, food, water and other development issues are
> at the heart of all countries' core interest, which must be deeply integrated in the
> development agenda.
>
> United Nations "Decade of Sustainability for All," 2014

Globally, around 2.8 billion people (the "Other Third" or "Energy Poor" [EP])
have little or no access to beneficial energy to meet their basic human needs,
including cooking, heating, water, sanitation, illumination, transportation,
and basic mechanical power (World Bank 2014). This dearth of energy affects
their households, their chances of making a living whether by way of agriculture,
industry, or crafts, and the hospitals and schools serving their communities.
More than 95 percent of the Energy Poor live either in sub-Saharan Africa or
developing Asia, predominantly (84 percent) in rural areas (International
Energy Agency 2014).

A disturbingly large swath of humanity is caught in a time warp. They rely on
biomass-generated fire as their principal source of energy. These fires are made by
burning animal dung, waste, crop residues, rotted wood, other forms of harmful
biomass, or raw coal. Smoke from the fire used for cooking leads to 4.3 million
premature deaths from respiratory infection every year, primarily of women and
children (World Health Organization 2014).

Women are traditionally responsible for cooking and child care in the home,
and they spend more time inhaling the polluted air that is trapped indoors. Thus,
women and children have the highest exposure to indoor air pollution and suffer
more than anyone from these negative health effects (Global Alliance for Clean
Cookstoves 2012). Specifically, the risk for child pneumonia increases 2.3 times
in homes that burn solid fuels for cooking, and women are about twice as likely
to be afflicted with chronic pulmonary disease than men in homes using solid

fuels (Legros et al. 2009). Beyond suffering adverse health effects, women and children are also disproportionately affected by the time constraints needed for collecting fuel. Women are burdened with the majority of the work to collect fuel, which can present other serious risks such as an increased chance of being raped, as occurred in the refugee camps of Darfur (Darfur Cookstoves 2010).

The EP also lack access to lighting. Lighting is essential to human progress and without it "mankind would be comparatively inactive about one-half of its lifetime" (Luckiesh 1920). The scorching sun and withering temperatures in the LDCs prevent agricultural labor during the daytime and reduce productivity, and the absence of artificial lights severely impedes working at night. Without lighting it is not possible for students to do homework after nightfall. The absence of lighting creates physical insecurity, particularly for women and children, while venturing out in the darkness, and almost entirely prevents commercial activity after dark. Almost 500 million people rely on kerosene for illumination (Lam et al. 2012). The hazards of kerosene, such as fires, explosions, and poisonings resulting from children ingesting it, are extensively documented, and children and women are disproportionately affected (Peck 2011). There is evidence implicating kerosene with other ailments including the impairing of lung functions, asthma, cancer, and tuberculosis (Lam et al. 2012). The use of kerosene and candles is costly. Households often spend 10 to 25 percent of their income on kerosene. Over $36 billion is spent on kerosene annually, $10 billion of which is spent in sub-Saharan Africa (*The Economist* 2012).

The lack of motive power for pumping water for domestic and agricultural use, plowing fields, transport, metal works, and agro-processing (such as grinding food), thwarts any livelihoods requiring energy. Generating income through small businesses requires energy to transport and distribute goods and services to markets, and for telecommunications. Even the most rudimentary forms of rural agriculture require energy for water pumping, irrigation, plowing, harvesting, milling, grinding, and processing food. Water treatment plants that provide safe drinking water for communities and schools require energy; this is highly problematic given that polluted drinking water causes 3.5 million deaths per year, largely among children (United Nations Water 2012). The lack of energy impairs hospitals and schools. Hospitals need energy for refrigerating vital medications and vaccinations. Education calls for energy for lighting and heating of schools, and a lack of energy for illumination prevents women and children from studying at night and makes life dangerous after dark. In sum, the lack of energy access faced by the Energy Poor greatly inhibits their ability to live safe and productive lives, and, more broadly, it inhibits the ability of civilizations to develop and eradicate poverty.

Several books have been written about sustainable energy for high-energy (hydrocarbon based) societies of developed countries, as well as the advanced (industrializing) developing countries such as India and China. However, there is a conspicuous absence of books dealing with energy for the low energy (non-carbon based) Other Third of the world, and how the unmet needs of the Energy Poor might be satisfied. This book seeks to fill that absence by providing a comprehensive discourse on the nature of energy poverty and conceptual and practical strategies for its eradication.

Content preview

This volume consists of an introduction, twenty chapters, which fall within four conceptual parts, and a conclusion. Part 1 offers an overview of the "phenomenon of the energy poor." Part 2 examines appropriate "conceptual foundations" for addressing energy poverty. Part 3, "Assessing the various challenges," focuses on a variety of barriers to eliminating energy poverty, while Part 4 "The way forward," discusses in detail some practical strategies, including Affordable/ Appropriate Sustainable Energy Technologies (ASETs), for addressing the needs of the Energy Poor. Finally, the conclusion will seek to weave these various threads and offer an integrated perspective on access to energy for the Other Third or Energy Poor.

The examination of the "phenomenon of the Energy Poor," begins with Chapter 1, in which Dr. David Stern inquires whether energy is a primary determinant of economic progress. He reviews mainstream economic models and analysis that overlook the importance of energy in economic growth, and he compares them to those of ecological economics that emphasize the primacy of energy. This chapter demonstrates that, depending on its availability and access, energy plays a key role in economic growth. But, this role is diminished where energy is abundant and cheap.

While the burdens of energy poverty affect all of the Other Third, lack of energy access disproportionately disadvantages certain members of low energy civilizations. In Chapter 2, Dr. Joy Clancy and co-authors examine the most pressing women's energy poverty issues, and illustrate how the burdens caused by lack of access to energy fall most heavily on women, effectively leading to the infliction of silent violence on women and children. Dr. Clancy argues that, for energy poverty to be alleviated and this silent violence to cease, women must be empowered to make choices about energy, and the energy sector must be willing to make necessary changes.

Chapter 3 focuses on how lack of access to energy has affected indigenous peoples. Although they constitute roughly 4.5 percent of the global population, indigenous peoples account for about 10 percent of the world's poor. They suffer from higher poverty, lower education, and a greater incidence of disease and discrimination than other minorities. They are also disproportionately vulnerable to the effects of climate change. This chapter discusses the extent to which this conflicts with human rights norms, and examines practical steps for empowering indigenous peoples.

Part 2, "Conceptual foundations," begins with Chapter 4 on energy justice, by Dr. Lakshman Guruswamy. He delineates the existence and extent of energy poverty, and how the lack of beneficial energy prevents and negates development. He then offers a definition of justice that applies to international societies. He relies on John Rawls and the duty of assistance to "burdened societies," which he equates with the Energy Poor. In Chapter 5, Dr. Christian Brugger raises and answers the question of whether there is a "right" to energy. He argues that there is a right to energy, that it is a natural right, and that it correlates to a duty to render its proper object. He then clarifies the concept of what a "right to energy" contains (i.e., the object or *res* being rendered), and seeks to identify who possesses the correlative duty to render the *res* (i.e., to make energy accessible to those who need it).

While international law may not currently contain a "right" to energy as articulated by Dr. Brugger, expressions of distributive justice pervade international agreements and discourse. Chapter 6 examines sustainable development (SD) as the foundational premise of international energy and environmental law. Professor Ved Nanda explains SD and how it is being politically institutionalized in the Sustainable Development Goals and a plethora of significant international instruments.

In Chapter 7, Murodbek Laldjebaev, Dr. Benjamin Sovacool, and Dr. Karim-Aly Kassam examine the idea of energy security and how it is interlinked with poverty and energy sovereignty. "Energy insecurity" refers to the human insecurity of the Other Third of the world arising from the absence of clean energy for cooking, illumination, water, sanitation, and motive power. The authors argue that this insecurity is linked to the Energy Poor's lack of energy sovereignty, a concept that is concerned with decision-making and enabling people to follow certain energy use patterns. This chapter explores these concepts and posits implications for contemporary energy analysis and policy-making.

In Chapter 8, Professor Carmen Gonzalez discusses why the adverse impacts of energy poverty on the natural environment render this issue universal and crucial to all nations. Based on the concepts of climate debt and climate justice, this chapter argues that the modest sums required to combat energy poverty will simultaneously address a host of serious, universally relevant environmental and human rights challenges.

Part 3, "Assessing the various challenges," examines political, economic, and behavioral challenges confronting access to energy, as well as challenges related to measuring access for differing needs.

In Chapter 9, Mark Safty examines the project finance (PF) framework for assessing barriers to development projects that aim to provide energy infrastructure. PF provides a system for understanding, prioritizing, classifying, and mitigating the effects of the barriers. Safty explains some of the commonly identified categories of barriers, asserts that this set of barriers is overly broad, and then focuses on a risk assessment framework to analyze and discuss the barriers in the context of PF.

Even when financing for ASETs, and other technologies, is available, other challenges often prevent their implementation. Chapter 10 by Dr. Matinga et al. discusses "behavioral challenges" to energy access for the Other Third. Even when presented with good information, some among the Energy Poor may choose to continue doing what they have long been accustomed to doing, like using biomass fires although cookstoves are made available to them. The reasons for their reluctance to change can range from tradition to taste, cost, and expense, or the fear of the new.

Another major challenge to alleviating energy poverty lies in how to tailor the solutions to the unique needs and challenges faced by different communities. In Chapter 11, Simon Trace explains that access to energy, and measures or metrics for determining if people have obtained access, depends on whether it is required for household use, productive enterprise, or community needs. This chapter evaluates metrics or measures for determining whether access to energy has or has not been secured.

Part 4, "The way forward," presents practical and innovative solutions to these challenges. In Chapter 12, Dr. Pradeep Monga reviews the challenges in providing electricity in the 15-nation Economic Community of West African States (ECOWAS) that constitutes a third of the population of sub-Saharan Africa. In light of the cost of running the electric grid to the rural and peri-urban parts of these countries, achieving Sustainable Energy for All by 2030 faces formidable obstacles. Therefore, he advocates that decentralized solutions should be pursued in parallel with grid-based electricity, and illustrates how this might be done.

In Chapter 13, Martin Hiller et al. propose an imaginative solution to address both the economic challenges that face improving energy access, and global environmental issues, generally. The Green Climate Fund (GCF) is a fund created by the United Nations Framework Convention on Climate Change to transfer money from the developed to the developing world for the adaptation and mitigation of GHGs and climate change. Hiller et al. argue that using the money to bring clean energy access to the Energy Poor offers an important avenue to reduce both energy poverty and global warming.

In Chapter 14, Jason Aamodt and Blake M. Feamster begin by establishing that access to energy has been equated with access to electricity, but the daunting additional costs of electricity, and the time required to implement full access to electricity – 30 years, realistically – will shunt the Energy Poor into limbo unless interim measures are taken to provide intermediate energy. Beneficial energy based on appropriate sustainable energy technologies (ASETs) can provide such intermediate energy.

The difficulties of globalizing ASETs is one of the most pressing issues inhibiting the wide use of ASETs as providers of intermediate energy. In Chapter 15, Stephen Katsaros and Elizabeth Neville assert that while ASETs have global potential, they are not being disseminated or distributed in the millions of units necessary to have an impact on the Energy Poor. This chapter addresses specific issues pertaining to the type of ASET enterprise that will best promote sustainable development in underdeveloped areas, along with questions about the start up and continued financing of ASET enterprises.

Chapter 16 discusses energy for rural women, examining the situation of Sri Lanka's rural women as a case study. Rural women are critical agents of development and contribute significantly to the rural and national economy of Sri Lanka. This chapter examines the predicament of rural women and the extent to which they are being offered access to energy. In doing so, this chapter considers national laws, policies, and other measures, both state and non-state, and whether they facilitate access to energy for the rural poor. Dr. Anoja Wickramasinghe then presents suggestions for future decisions and actions that might better ensure energy access for the rural poor.

Energy poverty remains a pressing global issue, and some entities that have pioneered in providing access to energy may provide positive examples for future endeavors. In Chapter 17, Doug Vilsack uses the case study of his organization, Elephant Energy, to demonstrate entrepreneurial solutions for energy access. Elephant Energy, a nonprofit organization, provides intermediate means of energy access through ASETs until those in rural areas of Namibia are able to connect to the electric grid. Namibia and Elephant Energy illustrate the answers to the problem of energy access, such as why "leapfrogging" (jumping directly from energy poverty to electricity) is not a feasible option, how ASETs provide an intermediate solution, and what important benefits are gained through energy access. Furthermore, Elephant Energy provides a profitable method of furnishing ASETs. This chapter emphasizes that energy access is a problem that can be solved, at least in part, through local entrepreneurship.

One of the essential features of ASETs is that the technology required already exists within the target community. In Chapter 18, Arjun Makhijani discusses improvements that can be made to the use of draft animals, a prevalent existing source of energy for much of the Other Third, and a prime example of this ASET feature. Draft animals are the primary source of motive power (mechanical energy) for agriculture in Asia, as well as parts of Africa and Latin America. This chapter explores some of the issues arising from draft power in providing motive power for the Energy Poor. These issues include the potential for better productivity by using improved harnesses, yokes, and animal care. Additionally, this chapter addresses methane emissions from draft animals; how the land is used for food crops, fuel, wood, and grazing; and gender considerations.

Growing fields of technology can beneficially intersect with ASETs to foster development and energy access; the intersection between Information and Communication Technology (ICT) and other ASETs illustrates this well. In Chapter 19, authors Sarah Revi Starling and Matt Hulse begin by establishing that ICT is inextricably related to energy and enables modern technology to be used by 6.2 billion mobile subscribers. This chapter explores some interfaces between ICT and access to energy. Globally, a number of energy sources ranging from solar, biofuel, stove heat, and car batteries already apply innovative uses of ICT. They operate within white space-based networks, educational technologies, and remote monitoring systems. These are in addition to the thousands of banking, agriculture, and health applications. However, there are reports that many ICT interventions do not enjoy adoption because the community appropriates and even diverts electricity for other uses besides the intended ICT effort. Such adverse outcomes can be mitigated by the use of ICT to manage energy systems, and this chapter provides many examples of the intersections of ICT and ASETs that are emerging in both developing and developed communities.

The eradication of energy poverty will almost certainly require the adoption of some laws on the national level. In Chapter 20, Dr. Lakshman Guruswamy presents the case for using model laws, and provides model laws (with commentaries) for developed and developing countries for the installation of clean cookstoves. One set of model laws is intended for use by developing countries, and the other is for developed countries. A model law is a legislative text recommended to states for enactment as part of their national law. There are compelling reasons, addressed in this chapter, as to why national legal responses to the problem of indoor air pollution should and can provide answers to this global problem. The draft model laws are blueprints for providing access to energy using law to generate private and public action.

Finally, the conclusion to this volume elaborates upon and synthesizes some of the concepts and themes traversed by the authors of this volume. The conclusion posits that energy poverty cannot be solved in a fragmented manner; rather, this complex issue of global importance will require collaboration and thoughtful action by all stakeholders: those in policy, law, and business, with maximum participation by the Energy Poor, themselves.

References

Darfur Cookstoves. 2010. *Darfur Cookstove Projects Overview.* Accessed February 20, 2015. http://cookstoves.lbl.gov/darfur-archives/.

Global Alliance for Clean Cookstoves. 2012. "Clean cookstoves can save lives and empower women." Accessed January 11, 2014. http://cleancookstoves.org/impact-areas/women/.

International Energy Agency. 2014. "About energy poverty." Accessed September 12, 2014. www.iea.org/topics/energypoverty/.

Lam, N., K. Smith, A. Gautier, and M. Bates. 2012. "Kerosene: a review of household uses and their hazards in low and middle income countries." *Journal of Toxicology and Environmental Health* 15(6): 396–432. doi: 10.1080/10937404.2012.710134.

Legros, Gwénaëlle, Ines Havet, Nigel Bruce, and Sophie Bonjour. 2009. *The Energy Access Situation in Developing Countries: A Review Focusing on Least Developed Countries and Sub Saharan Africa.* New York: United Nations Development Programme: Environment and Energy Group, and World Health Organization.

Luckiesh, Matthew. 1920. *Artificial Light: Its Influence Upon Civilization*, 8th edn. New York: Library of Alexandria.

Peck, M. 2011. "Epidemiology of burns throughout the world, Part 1: distribution and risk factors." *Burns* 37(7): 1087–1100. doi: 10.1016/j.burns.2011.06.005.

The Economist. 2012. "Solar lighting: lighting the way." September 1. Accessed September 12, 2014. www.economist.com/node/21560983.

United Nations. 2014. *Decade of Sustainability for All 2014–2024.* Accessed September 12, 2014. www.se4all.org/decade/.

United Nations Water. 2012. "Water quality." Accessed September 12, 2014. www.unwater.org/topics/water-quality/en/.World Bank. 2014. "Energy overview." Accessed September 12, 2014. www.worldbank.org/en/topic/energy/overview#1.

World Health Organization. 2014. "Household air pollution and health." Accessed September 12, 2014. www.who.int/mediacentre/factsheets/fs292/en/.

Part 1

The phenomenon of the Energy Poor

1 The role of energy in economic growth

David I. Stern

Introduction

Researchers differ on the importance of energy in economic growth and development. Toman and Jemelkova (2003) argue that most of the literature on energy and economic development discusses how development affects energy use rather than the reverse. The principal mainstream economic growth models do not include energy (Aghion and Howitt 2009), though macroeconomics pays significant attention to the impact of oil prices on economic activity in the short run (Hamilton 2009). Resource economists have developed models that incorporate the role of resources, including energy, in the growth process, but these ideas have not been integrated into the core economic models and theories. Ecological economists, on the other hand, often ascribe to energy the central role in economic growth (e.g., Hall et al. 2003). Obviously energy is used to produce goods and services, but is it an important driver of economic growth and development? This chapter attempts to answer this question by surveying the literature and synthesizing its more relevant strands.

We cannot understand the role of energy in economic growth without first understanding the role of energy in production. Therefore, I first review basic physical principles and economic concepts that define the role of energy in economic production. The mainstream theory of economic growth is reviewed next. I then discuss ecological economics in the third section. The fourth section presents a simple model that synthesizes mainstream and ecological economics views. Penultimately, I review the empirical evidence on the causal link between energy and growth. The final section of the chapter presents some discussion and conclusions on the role of energy in economic growth.

Energy as a production input

Physical laws describe the operating constraints of economic systems (Boulding 1966; Ayres and Kneese 1969). Conservation of mass means that, to obtain a given production output, greater or equal quantities of materials must be used as inputs, and the production process results in residuals or waste (Ayres and Kneese 1969). Additionally, production requires energy to carry out work to convert materials into desired products and to transport raw materials, goods, and people. The second law of thermodynamics (the entropy law) implies that energy cannot be reused and there are limits to how much energy efficiency can be improved. As a result, energy is always an essential production input (Stern 1997a) and continuous supplies of energy are needed to maintain existing levels of economic activity as well as to grow and develop the economy. Before being used in the production of goods and services, energy and matter must be captured from the environment, and large quantities of energy must be invested to obtain a given amount of net energy (Hall et al. 1986). Before the Industrial Revolution, economies depended on energy from agricultural crops and wood as well as a smaller amount of wind and water power, all of which are directly dependent on the sun. This is still largely the case in rural areas of less developed countries. While solar energy is abundant and inexhaustible, it is very diffuse compared to concentrated fossil fuels. This is why the shift to fossil fuels in the Industrial Revolution released the prevailing constraints on energy supply and, therefore, on production and growth (Wrigley 1988).

Resources in the mainstream theory of economic growth

Despite the facts laid out above, most mainstream economic growth models regard technological change as the primary driver of growth and disregard energy or other resources (Aghion and Howitt 2009). Aghion and Howitt's (2009) textbook on economic growth does discuss growth and the environment but only in a chapter near the end of the book. Acemoglu's (2008) textbook does not cover the topic at all. There has been some analysis of the potential for resources to constrain growth in the journal literature but it has mostly been contained within the sub-field of environmental and resource economics.

Robert Solow, who developed the best-known mainstream economic growth model (Solow 1956), in later work introduced non-renewable resources – which could represent fossil or nuclear fuels – into a mainstream economic model (Solow 1974). He showed that sustainability – or the ability of a nation to support a constant level of economic production indefinitely – is achievable under certain institutional and technical conditions. First, even though Solow assumed that resources are essential to production, his model allows the level of production to be maintained with infinitesimally small amounts of these resources as long as enough capital – machines and buildings – is available. Second, policymakers must set policies and make decisions that give equal weight to the well-being of individuals regardless of when they happen to live.

If, instead of Solow's characterization of the policymaker, we introduce a free market economy into Solow's (1974) model, the resources are eventually exhausted and the economy completely collapses (Stiglitz 1974a). Dasgupta and Heal (1979) showed that if instead of a free market economy we have a policymaker who tries to make optimal decisions for society but discounts the future at any constant rate,[1] then again the natural resource endowment is eventually depleted and the economy collapses. Hartwick (1977, 1995) showed that, if as in the Solow (1974) model, sustainability is technically feasible, a constant level of consumption can be achieved by investing all the rents from the non-renewable resources in other forms of capital, which in turn can substitute for exhausted resources. It is difficult to apply this rule in practice, as the rents and capital must be valued at prices that are compatible with sustainability (Asheim 1994; Stern 1997b; Asheim et al. 2003). Such prices are unknowable given that we have poor understanding of the costs of current environmental damage and resource depletion or of the future development of technology.

In addition to the substitution of capital for resources, technological change might permit continued growth or at least constant consumption in the face of a finite resource base. Solow (1974) did not allow for increases in productivity. Stiglitz (1974b) introduced technological change into this model and showed that under certain technical conditions, technological progress will allow consumption to grow over time. Technological change might enable sustainability even if resources must be used in finite quantities, which is much more realistic for energy given the laws of thermodynamics. But once again, technical feasibility does not guarantee sustainability. Depending on preferences for current versus future consumption, technological change might instead result in faster depletion of the resource (Smulders 2005).

The ecological economics approach

A prominent tradition in ecological economics, known as the biophysical economics approach (Hall et al. 1986), is based on thermodynamics as discussed above (Georgescu-Roegen 1971; Costanza 1980; Cleveland et al. 1984; Hall et al. 1986; Hall et al. 2003; Ayres and Warr 2005, 2009; Murphy and Hall 2010). Ecological economists usually argue that substitution between capital and resources can only play a limited role in mitigating the scarcity of resources (Stern 1997a). Furthermore, some ecological economists downplay the role of technological change in economic growth, arguing that growth is a result of either increased energy use or innovations allowing the more productive use of energy (Cleveland et al. 1984; Hall et al.1986; Hall et al. 2003). Therefore, in this view, increased energy use is the main or only cause of economic growth.

In this approach, value is derived from the action of energy that is directed by capital and labor. Energy flows into the economy from fossil fuels and the sun. In some biophysical economic models, geological constraints fix the rate of energy extraction so that the flow rather than the stock can be considered as the primary input to production (Gever et al. 1986). Capital and labor are considered as intermediate inputs that are created and maintained by the primary input of energy and flows of matter. The level of the flows is computed in terms of the embodied energy use associated with them. Prices of goods should then ideally be determined by their embodied energy cost (Hannon 1973) – a normative energy theory of value – or are seen as actually being correlated with energy cost (Costanza 1980) – a positive energy theory of value (Common 1995). This theory – like the Marxian paradigm – must then explain how labor, capital, etc. end up receiving part of the surplus. Energy surplus must be appropriated by the owners of labor, capital, and land (Costanza 1980; Gever et al. 1986; Hall et al. 1986; Kaufmann 1987) with the actual distribution of the surplus determined by relative bargaining power.

However, because the quality of resources and technology do affect the amount of energy needed to produce goods and services, it is difficult to argue for a model where energy use alone explains the level of production. For example, the quality of resources such as oil reservoirs is critical in determining the energy required to extract and process fuels. As an oil reservoir is depleted, the energy needed to extract oil increases. On the positive side, improved geophysical knowledge and techniques can increase the extent to which oil can be extracted for a given energy cost. Odum's energy approach (Brown and Herendeen 1996) and the framework developed by Costanza (1980) address the resource quality issue by including the solar and geological energy embodied in natural resource inputs in indicators of total embodied energy. An alternative approach is to measure material and energy inputs on the common basis of their exergy[2] (Ayres et al. 1998; Ukidwe and Bakshi 2007).

However, both approaches seem too reductionist. For example, other services provided by nature such as nutrient recycling, the provision of clean air and water, pollination, and the climate system, that make economic production – and life itself – possible should also then be accounted for. Georgescu-Roegen (1971) formulated a more flexible approach with a variety of different types of production inputs. The neo-Ricardian models developed by Perrings (1987) and O'Connor (1993) also allow any number of inputs while complying with thermodynamic and mass-balance constraints.

A key concept in biophysical economics is energy return on investment (EROI), which is the ratio of useful energy produced by an energy supply system to the amount of energy invested in extracting that energy. Lower quality energy resources have lower EROIs. Biophysical economists argue that the more energy that is required to extract energy, the less energy is available for other uses and the poorer an economy will be. In this view, the increase in EROI allowed by the switch from biomass to fossil fuels enabled the Industrial Revolution and the period of modern economic growth that followed it (Hall et al. 1986).

Thus, declining EROI would threaten not just growth but overall economic output and, therefore, sustainability. Murphy and Hall (2010) document EROI for many energy sources, arguing that it is declining over time. Wind and direct solar energy have more favorable EROIs than biomass fuels, but worse than most fossil fuels. However, unlike fossil fuels, the EROI of these energy sources tends to improve over time with innovation (Kubiszewski et al. 2010). Declining EROI could be mitigated by substituting other inputs for energy or by improving the efficiency with which energy is used. However, biophysical economists argue that both these processes have limits.

Substitution can occur *within* a category of similar production inputs – for example between different fuels – and *between* different categories of inputs – for example between energy and machines. There is also a distinction to be made between substitution at the micro level – for example, within a single engineering process or at a single firm – and at the macro level, i.e., in the economy as a whole.

The long-run pattern of energy use in industrial economies has been dominated by substitutions from wood and animal power to coal, oil, natural gas, and primary electricity (see Figure 1.1) (Hall et al. 1986; Smil 1991). Meta-analysis of existing studies of interfuel substitution suggests that the long-run substitution possibilities at the level of the industrial sector as a whole are good. But there seems to be less substitutability at the macro level (Stern 2012).

Ecological economists emphasize the importance of limits to inter-category substitution; in particular, the substitution of manufactured capital for resources including energy (Costanza and Daly 1992). Thermodynamic limits can be approximated by a production function with an elasticity of substitution significantly below one (Stern 1997a).[3] A meta-analysis of the existing empirical literature finds that the elasticity of substitution between capital and energy is less than one (Koetse et al. 2008).

In addition to this microeconomic limit to substitution, there may also be macroeconomic limits to substitution. The construction, operation, and maintenance of tools, machines, and factories require a flow of materials and energy. Similarly, the humans that direct manufactured capital consume energy and materials. Thus, producing more of the "substitute" for energy – manufactured capital – requires more of the thing that it is supposed to substitute for. This again limits potential substitutability (Cleveland et al. 1984).

The mainstream economic argument that technological change can overcome limited substitutability would be more convincing if technological change were really something different from substitution. Changes in technology occur when new techniques are developed. However, these new techniques represent the

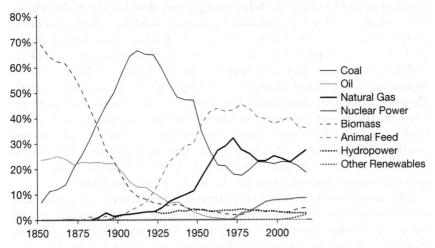

Figure 1.1 Composition of US primary energy input 1850–2013

Source: Energy Information Administration 2014

substitution of knowledge for other inputs. The knowledge is embodied in improved capital goods and more skilled workers and managers. But there are still thermodynamic restrictions on the extent to which energy and material flows can be reduced in this way. Although knowledge is non-rival in use, it must be used in conjunction with the other inputs, such as energy, and the productivity of knowledge is limited by the available quantities of those inputs.

Synthesis: unified models of energy and growth

As we have seen, most mainstream growth models ignore energy though some mainstream economists investigate whether limited energy or other resources could be a constraint on growth. By contrast, ecological economists posit a central role for energy in driving growth and point to the switch from traditional energy sources to fossil fuels as the cause of the Industrial Revolution. But they argue that limits to substitutability and/or technological change might restrict or reverse growth in the future. Can these two approaches be integrated into a unified model of energy and growth that provides a satisfactory explanation of the long-run history of the economy?

As a first step to integrating the different approaches, Stern and Kander (2012) modify Solow's original growth model (Solow 1956) by adding an energy input that is imperfectly substitutable with capital and labor. The model also breaks down technological change into those innovations that directly increase the productivity of energy – energy-augmenting technical change – and those that increase the productivity of labor – labor-augmenting technical change.[4]

In Solow's (1956) model, as long as there is technological change the economy can grow. In Stern and Kander's model, depending on the availability of energy and the nature of technological change, energy can be either a constraint on growth or an enabler of growth. When energy is very abundant the model behaves very similarly to Solow's original model and energy neither constrains nor drives growth.[5] But when energy is relatively scarce, the level of output depends on the level of energy supply and the level of energy-augmenting technology. Technological change that only improves the productivity of labor – "labor-augmenting technological change" – no longer results in economic growth. Therefore, in the pre-industrial era when energy was scarce, the level of output was determined by the supply of energy and the level of energy-augmenting technology. Until the Industrial Revolution, output per capita was generally low and economic growth was not sustained (Maddison 2001). After the Industrial Revolution, as energy became more and more abundant, the long-run behavior of the model economy becomes more and more like the Solow (1956) growth model.

Why assume that the elasticity of substitution between energy and capital-labor is less than one? First, the share of energy in production costs fell over time in both Britain and Sweden, countries for which we have data from 1800 till the present (Figure 1.2). When the elasticity of substitution is one, this is not possible – cost shares must be constant in the long run. The extent of the fall from 45 percent of total production costs in Sweden in 1800 to close to 10 percent of GDP today

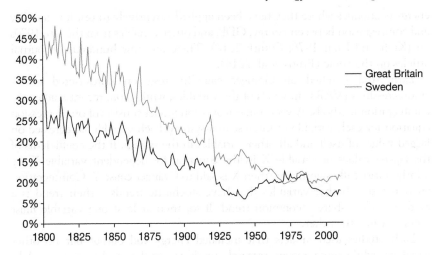

Figure 1.2 Share of energy in total production costs: Britain and Sweden 1800–2009

Source: Gentuilaite et al. 2015

appears to rule out structural change as the explanation either. Second, the ecological economics literature and empirical evidence discussed above also indicate that the elasticity of substitution between capital and energy is less than one.

Stern and Kander (2012) show that this model can simulate the observed features of the Swedish economy in the last two centuries reasonably well including the fall in the cost share of energy and the decline in energy intensity over time. Stern and Kander find that increases in energy use and energy-augmenting technological change were the main contributors to economic growth in the nineteenth and early twentieth centuries but in the second half of the twentieth century labor-augmenting technological change became the main driver of growth in income per capita as it is in the Solow (1956) growth model.

If this model is a reasonable representation of reality, then mainstream economists are not so wrong to ignore the role of energy in economic growth in developed economies where energy is abundant but their models may have limited applicability to both earlier historical periods and possibly to today's developing countries. However, in the long run, energy supply or energy productivity must continue to increase or eventually energy will again begin to constrain economic growth.

Empirical testing of the causal relationship between energy and growth

Two methods for testing for causality among time series variables are Granger causality tests and cointegration analysis (Granger 1969; Engle and Granger 1987). Hendry and Juselius (2000) discuss the application of these methods to energy economics where they have been applied extensively to test for causality and cointegration between energy, GDP, and other variables from the late 1970s on (Kraft and Kraft 1978; Ozturk 2010). There are now hundreds of journal articles on this topic (Bruns et al. 2014).

Early studies relied on Granger causality tests on unrestricted vector autoregressions (VARs) in levels of the variables, while more recent studies use cointegration methods. A vector autoregression model consists of one regression equation for each variable of interest in a system. Each variable is regressed on lagged values of itself and all other variables in the system. If the coefficients of the lagged values of variable X in the equation for dependent variable Y are jointly statistically significant, then X is said to Granger cause Y. Cointegration analysis tests whether variables that have stochastic trends – their trend is a random walk – share a common trend. If so, then at least one variable must Granger cause the other.

Early studies used models that included energy and output but no other variables, while more recent research tends to employ multivariate models. Ignoring other relevant variables can generate spurious causality findings. The most common additional variables used are capital and labor or energy prices. A third way to differentiate among models is whether energy is measured in standard heat units or whether a method is used to account for differences in quality among fuels.

The results of early studies that tested for Granger causality using a bivariate model were generally inconclusive (Stern 1993). Stern tested for Granger causality in the US in a multivariate setting using a vector autoregression (VAR) model of GDP, capital and labor inputs, and a Divisia index of quality-adjusted energy use in place of the usual heat equivalent of energy use. When both the multivariate approach and quality-adjusted energy index were employed, energy use was found to Granger cause GDP.

Yu and Jin (1992) conducted the first cointegration study of the energy–GDP relationship using the bivariate approach. Stern (2000) estimated a dynamic cointegration model for GDP, quality weighted energy, labor, and capital. The analysis showed that there is a cointegrating relation between the four variables and, depending on the version of the model used, found that energy Granger causes GDP or that there is mutual causation between energy and GDP. Some subsequent research appeared to confirm these findings using other measures of energy quality (Warr and Ayres 2010) or data for other countries (Oh and Lee 2004; Ghali and El-Sakka 2004) and panels of many countries (Lee and Chang 2008; Lee et al. 2008).

Bruns et al. (2014) carried out a meta-analysis of 75 single country Granger causality and cointegration studies comprising more than 500 tests of causality in each direction. They found that most seemingly statistically significant results in the literature are probably the result of statistical biases that occur in models that use short time series of data – "overfitting bias" – or the result of the selection for publication of statistically significant results – "publication bias". The most robust findings in the literature are that growth causes energy use when energy prices are controlled for in the underlying studies. Using a panel cointegration model of GDP, energy use, and energy prices for 26 OECD countries (1978–2005), Costantini and Martini (2010) also found that in the long run GDP growth drives energy use and energy prices though in the short run energy prices cause GDP and energy use, and energy use and GDP are mutually causative.

However, Bruns et al. (2014) found that studies that control for capital do not find a genuine effect of energy on growth or vice versa. But they had too small a number of studies that used quality-adjusted energy to test whether there was a genuine relationship between energy and growth when this measure of energy use was employed. So, their findings do not necessarily contradict the previous research by Stern and others reviewed above.

Discussion and conclusions

In conclusion, theory and empirical evidence indicate that energy use and output are tightly coupled and that energy availability plays a key role in enabling growth. However, greater availability of energy, technical progress, and the employment of higher quality fuels, has led over time to a decrease in energy use per dollar, and the diminishing of energy used per unit of output. These developments, while reducing the impact of energy resources on the output of the economy and economic growth, have not significantly detracted from the underlying importance of energy. The current low price of energy reflects that energy has low marginal productivity because of this heavy use. But if energy use was significantly curtailed its importance would again become more apparent. Despite attempts by mainstream economists to show that sustainability is possible even when energy is provided by non-renewable resources, their results are not applicable in the real world because of both the laws of thermodynamics and the nature of actual political and economic institutions. Economies will eventually need to transition to renewable energy sources or nuclear fusion if it ever were to be economically viable. The flow of renewable energy from the sun (or geothermal energy from Earth) is, of course, fixed. Sustainability is possible with a renewable energy flow but growth is limited.

On the other hand, there is still ambiguity on the nature of the causal relationship between energy and growth. The large literature on energy–GDP causality is plagued by statistical biases. The most robust relationship in the data is that GDP causes energy use when energy prices are controlled for – in other words, an energy demand function. But there is some evidence that energy use causes GDP too, if energy quality is taken into account and other inputs to production are controlled for. The effect of energy on GDP is likely to be smaller than the effect of GDP on energy and hence harder to detect. As this survey shows, there is clearly much scope for further research to better understand the role of energy in growth.

Acknowledgements

I thank Ruta Gentvilaite, Astrid Kander, and Paul Warde for making available the energy cost share data for Britain and Sweden (in Figure 1.2). Sean Owens did a fantastic job of editing my original overly long submission and Shuang Liu provided helpful comments.

Notes

1   The discount rate is the annual percentage rate at which people reduce their valuation of future payoffs.
2   In thermodynamics, the exergy of energy is the energy that is available to do work (Perrot 1998).
3   We can classify inputs as good or poor substitutes using the elasticity of substitution, which can take values from zero to infinity (Stern 2011). Good and poor substitutes have elasticities of substitution of greater than and less than one, respectively. Technically, the elasticity of substitution between two production inputs is given by the percentage change in the ratio in which they are used in response to a 1 percent change in the ratio of their two prices. In Solow's (1974) model discussed above the elasticity of substitution is one – the so-called Cobb-Douglas production function. This means that resources are essential, but that production could be sustained even with infinitesimally small resource inputs. An elasticity of substitution greater than one means that resources are not essential to production and an elasticity substitution of less than one means that finite quantities of resources must be used. Only the latter is compatible with the laws of thermodynamics.
4   More precisely, input-augmenting technical change increases the effective amount of the production input that it augments. So, for example, an energy-augmenting technological change of 2 percent has the same impact on output as increasing the use of energy by 2 percent. Unless the elasticity of substitution between labor and energy is zero, this will also increase the productivity of labor just as if there was 2 percent more energy per worker than before.
5   This applies equally to abundant physical energy or to abundant effective energy where effective energy is the product of the quantity of energy and the state of energy-augmenting technology.

References

Acemoglu, D. 2008. *Introduction to Economic Growth*. Princeton NJ: Princeton University Press.

Aghion, P. and Howitt, P. 2009. *The Economics of Growth*. Cambridge, MA: MIT Press.

Asheim, G. B. 1994. "Net national product as an indicator of sustainability." *Scandinavian Journal of Economics* 96: 257–265.

Asheim, G. B., Buchholz, W., and Withagen, C. 2003. "The Hartwick rule: myths and facts." *Environmental and Resource Economics* 25: 129–150.

Ayres, R. U. and Kneese, A. V. 1969. "Production, consumption and externalities." *American Economic Review* 59: 282–297.

Ayres, R. U. and Warr, B. 2005. "Accounting for growth: the role of physical work." *Structural Change and Economic Dynamics* 16: 181–209.

——2009. *The Economic Growth Engine: How Energy and Work Drive Material Prosperity*. Cheltenham: Edward Elgar.

Ayres, R. U., Ayres, L. W., and Martinás, K. 1998. "Exergy, waste accounting, and life-cycle analysis." *Energy* 23(5): 355–363.

Boulding, K. 1966. "The economics of the coming spaceship Earth." In *Environmental Quality in a Growing Economy*, edited by H. Jarett. Baltimore: Johns Hopkins University Press.

Brown, M. T. and Herendeen, R. A. 1996. "Embodied energy analysis and emergy analysis: a comparative view." *Ecological Economics* 19: 219–236.

Bruns, S. B., Gross, C., and Stern, D. I. 2014. "Is there really Granger causality between energy use and output?" *Energy Journal* 35(4): 101–134.

Cleveland, C. J., Costanza, R., Hall, C. A. S., and Kaufmann, R. K. 1984. "Energy and the U.S. economy: a biophysical perspective." *Science* 225: 890–897.

Common, M. S. 1995. *Sustainability and Policy: Limits to Economics*. Melbourne: Cambridge University Press.

Costantini, V. and Martini, C. 2010. "The causality between energy consumption and economic growth: a multi-sectoral analysis using non-stationary cointegrated panel data." *Energy Economics* 32: 591–603.

Costanza, R. 1980. "Embodied energy and economic valuation." *Science* 210: 1219–1224.

Costanza, R. and Daly, H. E. 1992. "Natural capital and sustainable development." *Conservation Biology* 6: 37–46.

Dasgupta, P. S. and Heal, G. M. 1979. *Economic Theory and Exhaustible Resources*. Cambridge: Cambridge University Press.

Energy Information Administration. 2014. *Monthly Energy Review, May 2014*. DOE/EIA-0035(2014/05). Washington, DC: Department of Energy.

Engle, R. E. and Granger, C. W. J. 1987. "Cointegration and error-correction: representation, estimation, and testing." *Econometrica* 55: 251–276.

Gentvilaite, R., Kander, A. and Warde, P. 2015. "The role of energy quality in shaping long-term energy intensity in Europe." *Energies* 8(1): 133–153.

Georgescu-Roegen, N. 1971. *The Entropy Law and the Economic Process*. Cambridge, MA: Harvard University Press.

Gever, J., Kaufmann, R. K., Skole, D., and Vörösmarty, C. 1986. *Beyond Oil: The Threat to Food and Fuel in the Coming Decades*. Cambridge, MA: Ballinger.

Ghali, K. H. and El-Sakka, M. I. T. 2004. "Energy use and output growth in Canada: a multivariate cointegration analysis." *Energy Economics* 26: 225–238.

Granger, C. W. J. 1969. "Investigating causal relations by econometric models and cross-spectral methods." *Econometrica* 37: 424–438.

Hall, C. A. S., Cleveland, C. J., and Kaufmann, R. K. 1986. *Energy and Resource Quality: The Ecology of the Economic Process*. New York: Wiley Interscience.

Hall, C. A. S., Tharakan, P., Hallock, J., Cleveland, C., and Jefferson, M. 2003. "Hydrocarbons and the evolution of human culture." *Nature* 426: 318–322.

Hamilton, J. D. 2009. "Causes and consequences of the oil shock of 2007–08." *Brookings Papers on Economic Activity* 2009(1): 215–261.

Hannon, B. 1973. "An energy standard of value." *Annals of the American Academy* 410: 139–153.

Hartwick, J. M. 1977. "Intergenerational equity and the investing of rents from exhaustible resources." *American Economic Review* 66: 972–974.

——1995. "Constant consumption paths in open economies with exhaustible resources." *Review of International Economics* 3: 275–283.

Hendry, D. F., and Juselius, K. 2000. "Explaining cointegration analysis: Part 1." *Energy Journal* 21(1): 1–42.

Kaufmann, R. K. 1987. "Biophysical and Marxist economics: learning from each other." *Ecological Modelling* 38: 91–105.

Koetse, M. J., de Groot, H. L. F., and Florax, R. J. G. M. 2008. "Capital-energy substitution and shifts in factor demand: a meta-analysis." *Energy Economics* 30: 2236–2251.

Kraft, J. and Kraft, A. 1978. "On the relationship between energy and GNP." *Journal of Energy and Development* 3: 401–403.

Kubiszewski, I., Cleveland, C. J., and Endres, P. K. 2010. "Meta-analysis of net energy return for wind power systems." *Renewable Energy* 35: 218–225.

Lee, C.-C. and Chang, C.-P. 2008. "Energy consumption and economic growth in Asian economies: a more comprehensive analysis using panel data." *Resource and Energy Economics* 30(1): 50–65.

Lee, C.-C., Chang, C.-P., and Chen, P.-F. 2008. "Energy-income causality in OECD countries revisited: the key role of capital stock." *Energy Economics* 30: 2359–2373.

Maddison, A. 2001. *The World Economy: A Millennial Perspective*. Paris: OECD.

Murphy D. J. and Hall, C. A. S. 2010. "Year in review – EROI or energy return on (energy) invested." *Annals of the New York Academy of Sciences* 1185: 102–118.

O'Connor, M. P. 1993. "Entropic irreversibility and uncontrolled technological change in the economy and environment." *Journal of Evolutionary Economics* 34: 285–315.

Oh, W. and Lee, K. 2004. "Causal relationship between energy consumption and GDP revisited: the case of Korea 1970–1999." *Energy Economics* 26: 51–59.

Ozturk, I. 2010. "A literature survey on energy-growth nexus." *Energy Policy* 38: 340–349.

Perrings, C. A. 1987. *Economy and Environment: A Theoretical Essay on the Interdependence of Economic and Environmental Systems*. Cambridge: Cambridge University Press.

Perrot, P. 1998. *A to Z of Thermodynamics*. Oxford: Oxford University Press.

Smil, V. 1991. *General Energetics Energy in the Biosphere and Civilization*. New York: John Wiley.

Smulders, S. 2005. "Endogenous technical change, natural resources and growth." In *Scarcity and Growth in the New Millennium*, edited by R. Ayres, D. Simpson, and M. Toman. Washington, DC: Resources for the Future.

Solow, R. M. 1956. "A contribution to the theory of economic growth." *Quarterly Journal of Economics* 70: 65–94.

——1974. "Intergenerational equity and exhaustible resources." *Review of Economic Studies* 41: 29–46.

Stern, D. I. 1993. "Energy use and economic growth in the USA, a multivariate approach." *Energy Economics* 15: 137–150.

——1997a. "Limits to substitution and irreversibility in production and consumption: a neoclassical interpretation of ecological economics." *Ecological Economics* 21: 197–215.

——1997b. "The capital theory approach to sustainability: a critical appraisal." *Journal of Economic Issues* 31: 145–173.

——2000. "A multivariate cointegration analysis of the role of energy in the U.S. macroeconomy." *Energy Economics* 22: 267–283.

——2011. "Elasticities of substitution and complementarity." *Journal of Productivity Analysis* 36(1): 79–89.

——2012. "Interfuel substitution: a meta-analysis." *Journal of Economic Surveys* 26: 307–331.

Stern, D. I. and Kander, A. 2012. "The role of energy in the Industrial Revolution and modern economic growth." *Energy Journal* 33(3): 125–152.

Stiglitz, J. E. 1974a. "Growth with exhaustible natural resources: the competitive economy." *Review of Economic Studies* 41: 139–152.

——1974b. "Growth with exhaustible natural resources: efficient and optimal growth paths." *Review of Economic Studies* 41: 123–138.

Toman, M. A. and Jemelkova, B. 2003. "Energy and economic development: an assessment of the state of knowledge." *Energy Journal* 24(4): 93–112.

Ukidwe, N. U. and Bakshi, B. R. 2007. "Industrial and ecological cumulative exergy consumption of the United States via the 1997 input–output benchmark model." *Energy* 32: 1560–1592.

Warr, B. and Ayres, R. U. 2010. "Evidence of causality between the quantity and quality of energy consumption and economic growth." *Energy* 35: 1688–1693.

Wrigley, E. A. 1988. *Continuity, Chance, and Change: The Character of the Industrial Revolution in England.* Cambridge: Cambridge University Press.

Yu, E. S. H. and Jin, J. C. 1992. "Cointegration tests of energy consumption, income, and employment." *Resources and Energy* 14: 259–266.

2 The predicament of women

Joy S. Clancy, Soma Dutta,
Nthabiseng Mohlakoana, Ana Victoria Rojas,
and Margaret Njirambo Matinga

Introduction: why a focus on women when we talk about energy poverty?

Two assumptions underlie assertions about energy and poverty: firstly, that the poor form a homogeneous group; and secondly, that the poor will benefit equally from energy interventions. Work on poverty has increasingly recognized that the poor are not homogeneous. Indeed, the poor have multiple identities differentiated in terms of a number of social characteristics including gender. The poor vary not only in terms of the extent of their poverty but also their reasons for being poor. The processes through which people become poor have a distinct gender dimension (Narayan 1999). For men, unemployment and illness (which can be linked) are common reasons for entering poverty. For women, divorce, widowhood, and desertion are cited reasons. The routes out of poverty for women and men are different due to their different assets. Women tend to be more disadvantaged than men in similar circumstances; for example, women's access and control over assets such as land, cash, and credit is more limited than men's. Women's technical skills are often less than men's; for example, compared to men, women's reading levels are lower and they have less experience with hardware (WDR 2012).

These differences in women's and men's assets mean that interventions promoting energy access aimed to help the poor are likely to benefit men differently from women, in part due to their different capacities to respond and partly because they have different needs linked to the socially determined division of labor between women and men. In general, women tend to have a greater range of tasks and responsibilities than men. These differences in socially determined roles and responsibilities for women and men, comprising their gender roles, have implications for their capacity to participate in activities such as meetings and to take on opportunities (e.g. income-generating projects) since these are additional tasks to the daily routine to sustain the household. Participation in such processes as well as equitable outcomes are made more complex because women generally wield less influence over decisions and exercise less control over their own lives and resources – both at the household and community levels – than men (Moser 1993); this includes the acquisition of energy technologies. Women are generally "time poor" (see below) which affects their capacity to respond to interventions, including those to promote energy access, designed to reduce poverty.

Poor households use less energy per household than wealthier ones in absolute terms. Water is less likely to be boiled for drinking and other hygiene purposes, increasing the likelihood of water-borne diseases. This differentiation in energy use related to household economic status has led to the recognition of an energy dimension of poverty: energy poverty. Energy poverty has been defined as the absence of sufficient choice in accessing adequate, affordable, reliable, high quality, safe and environmentally benign, energy services to support economic and human development (Reddy 2000).

However, both women and men experience energy poverty, albeit differently due to their different demands and capacity to respond, so why does so much of the discussion around "gender and energy" seem to focus on women? Of the 1.3 billion people who live in poverty, approximately 70 percent are women (Jato 2004: 1). Approximately one-quarter of the households in rural areas are headed by women (UN 2000).[1] Many of these women are more disadvantaged than men in similar circumstances. As pointed out above, women generally have fewer assets and less experience with hardware. This means that when making interventions to improve energy access to help people move out of poverty, the ability of women to respond is more restricted than it is for men; accordingly, special elements need to be included in projects and programs to address these gender differences to ensure that anyone who wishes to participate and benefit is not excluded due to the lack of assets and skills. Another reason for a greater focus on women is that in their households, energy provision is generally their responsibility; in short, energy is women's business.

This chapter examines women's most pressing energy poverty issues and how energy access can help women and men out of energy poverty. However, this chapter does not, and cannot, leave men completely out of the picture. Since they generally make the decisions about energy in the household and about energy policy, they play an important role in reducing women's energy poverty issues.

Women's most challenging energy poverty issues

The two most challenging energy poverty issues for women are related to the forms of energy they use to accomplish everyday tasks to provide for their families. In poor households, there is a reliance on poor quality fuels, primarily woody biomass and kerosene, usually using traditional technologies such as the three stone fire for cooking and water boiling and wick lamps and candles for lighting. Women also rely heavily on their own physical effort with little help by way of labor-saving equipment. Biomass collection to meet a household's energy needs is the burden (physically and metaphorically) of women and girls. In rural areas, it can mean spending several hours a day collecting fuelwood loads of 20 kg or more (FAO 2006). In urban areas, meeting family fuel needs can entail juggling tight household incomes in order to buy charcoal or kerosene; increased fuel prices result in less money for food and other essential items thus increasing household vulnerability.

Improved access to modern forms of energy, such as electricity, liquefied petroleum gas (LPG), and technologies such as more efficient wood stoves, can help reduce women's burdens and free up their time for other opportunities. Yet energy interventions are not reaching sufficiently large numbers of women to make major differences. This can be attributed in part to women's lack of influence of decisions within the household and over energy policy. This lack of voice can be considered a third challenge related to women's energy poverty. This section provides a brief overview of these three issues from a gender perspective:[2] time poverty and drudgery, health and safety, and women's empowerment.

Time poverty and drudgery

Time poverty can be conceptualized as the condition in which an individual does not have enough time for rest and leisure after taking into account the time spent in productive and reproductive work. Time poverty has been increasingly recognized as a dimension of poverty (Blackden and Wodon 2006). A person who is time poor is not able to allocate sufficient time for important activities, and is therefore forced to make difficult trade-offs (Bardasi and Wodon 2006). Women are particularly time poor and the associated drudgery of their daily tasks are mainly fulfilled through their own physical labor. This type of work has implications for their health, and indirectly, the well-being of their children and families. Time poverty also reduces opportunities for income generation, and women are more likely to be affected by this constraint than men.

Women generally have a longer working day than men. For example, in Sri Lanka women get up earlier and are awake for 16 hours or more, of which 13 hours are for work, compared with ten for men (Massé and Samaranayake 2002). Women carry, on their heads, about four times as much in volume as men, primarily water, firewood, and crops for grinding (Blackden and Wodon 2006). In urban areas, much time can be expended waiting in line for water from public standpipes. Processing staple foods, such as grain grinding, is a time-consuming manual task performed daily by women. Micro hydro plants powering grain mills in Nepal reduced women's workload from at least two hours of hand processing to around half an hour with mechanization (Mahat 2004).

It is generally assumed that women are the main fuelwood collectors; however, men tend to take over responsibility when the fuelwood supply close to the household decreases (Cooke et al. 2008), when greater amounts of physical capital and machinery are required to harvest fuelwood, or in urban areas (Blackden and Wodon 2006). Access to affordable modern energy services can reduce both time and effort by increasing efficiency and productivity, thus improving well-being and freeing up time for leisure and rest. Time spent on fetching water can be significantly reduced through a piped water supply. Men and women use the time saved differently. Men are more likely to use it for recreation and leisure, while women tend to use the time for housework and child care, as well as for resting, socializing, watching TV, and not necessarily for income-generating activities (Matly 2003).

Health and safety

A healthy and strong body is crucial to well-being (Narayan 1999). Sufficient good quality food, clean water, and a clean environment can be seen as fundamental to good health. There are close linkages between good health and energy use, as well as the quality of health and energy services available.

The use of biomass fuels has considerable implications for health. A substantial body of evidence and data shows links between negative aspects of health and indoor air pollution (IAP)[3] caused by the use of biomass-based fuels in traditional cookstoves in poorly ventilated cooking spaces. Two million premature deaths can be attributed to traditional cooking practices (WHO 2014). It appears that women bear the heaviest burden due to their high exposure to IAP. Illnesses from indoor pollution alone result in more deaths of women and children annually than those from HIV/AIDS, malaria, tuberculosis, and malnutrition combined (Lim et al. 2010). Less well recognized is that men's mortality risk increases when exposure to IAP combines with other health issues due to spending time in the kitchen as part of family social and meal times. Depending on culture, boys or girls will spend more time in the kitchen, and hence siblings will have different exposure levels.[4]

In 2010, 287,000 women died of complications from pregnancy and childbirth (WHO et al. 2012); many of these deaths could probably have been averted if the clinics had electricity. Based on an analysis of publicly available data from 11 sub-Saharan African countries it is estimated that on average 26 percent of health care facilities have access to electricity (Adair-Rohani et al. 2013). This lack of electricity causes serious deficiencies in primary health care services, such as basic lighting, vaccine storage, and essential equipment (i.e. for sterilization).

Women and men may suffer skeletal damage from carrying heavy loads, such as fuelwood. Women may be exposed to sexual and other forms of violence when carrying out their daily survival tasks including participation in the gendered fuel chain, carrying water, and staple food preparation.[5] Street lighting can help women to feel confident to go out after dark since illumination reduces the opportunities for gender-based violence (Doleac and Sanders 2012). However, it might take time for women to take advantage of the opportunity that street lighting offers since social norms and values can take time to adjust after the introduction of new technologies (Kelkar and Nathan 2007).

Lack of empowerment

The manner in which women and men behave within their gender roles is largely shaped by societal norms, the accepted standards of behavior shared by a particular society. Along with these roles come certain rights and obligations for women and men based on cooperation and support, although there can be conflict over use of household resources. These social arrangements determine who does what, who gets to consume what, and who makes what decisions. In most societies, men have more power than women to make decisions about, and exercise control over, not only their own bodies, lives, and resources, but also those of other family members. The balance of power between men and women defines the relationship between them (referred to as gender relations). The effects of differences in power operate at all levels in society: household, community, organizational, national, and international. In making decisions about energy access, men often prioritize their own interests over the needs of women, for example, a man might opt to buy a radio in preference to a fuel efficient stove which would benefit women (Meikle 2004; Danielsen 2012). Giving women influence (or power) over decisions can be achieved by the processes collectively known as "empowerment."[6]

Women participating in income-generating opportunities can gain increased control over their lives through their economic empowerment. Implicit in this concept is that women possess the skills, assets, and ability to exercise agency to achieve their goals. Evidence suggests that access to electricity enables women to enter the labor market. The electric rice cooker has been credited as one of the labor-saving devices that enabled large numbers of Japanese women to enter the labor market (Shioda 1994). A study in rural South Africa found that, within five years of access to grid electricity, there was a significant substitution of wood by electricity for cooking (Dinkelman 2008). Over the same period, women's employment increased 13.5 percent, but there was no effect on male employment. Nevertheless, economic empowerment of women must be meaningful, in the sense that work must be rewarding in terms of financial rewards and self-fulfillment as well as leading to positive transformations in their lives and in gender relations.

It cannot be assumed that freeing women's time from domestic chores necessarily leads to their economic empowerment. For example, a study in the United States found that, between 1930 and 1960, "household electrification had no immediate impact on female employment, but is associated with increased school attendance, particularly among teenage daughters" (Lewis 2014).

How energy access can help

Access to affordable energy services is an essential prerequisite for achieving economic growth and poverty reduction. At the micro-level, energy access can play in combating poverty through: (i) improved health; (ii) increased productivity and new opportunities for additional income; (iii) reduced labor and time spent on household activities (World Bank 1996; World Bank 2000; UNDP 2006). These categories are linked; for example, the reduced time spent on backbreaking physical labor allows the body time to recuperate. The use of biomass for cooking contributes significantly to indoor air pollution, and the shortage of biomass can lead to a reduction in boiled water, which has implications for the spread of water-borne diseases as well as general hygiene. Here, energy interventions can include the promotion of cleaner combustion through access to modern energy, such as electricity or LPG, and improved cookstoves. In rural areas, increases in household income can be achieved through improved agricultural production with mechanization using diesel engines and electricity. Mechanization can bring women other benefits: the reduction of drudgery, corresponding positive health effects, and the saving of time. In Mali, women reported saving two and a half hours a day on processing grains (Porcaro and Takada 2005) and girls' scholastic achievements are reported to be measurably higher after the introduction of village level mechanical power for grinding, pumping, and threshing services (UNDP 2004).

This section examines three ways that ending energy poverty can transform the lives of men and women: First, improvements in quality of life – the very basis of development; second, the role energy access plays in women's economic empowerment; and, finally, how energy access contributes to women's increased agency and voice.

Improved quality of life

Modern energy services can contribute significantly to people's quality of life, firstly by bringing improvements in well-being, due to increased time for rest and reduced physical effort, and secondly by increasing opportunities that can accrue for income generation, which can be used to further improve well-being.

Most of the evidence relating to energy access and improved quality of life focuses on electricity. For rural dwellers, at least in China, the main benefit for having access to electricity is for improvement in the quality of life – not necessarily for productive purposes (IDS 2003). In rural areas of Bhutan, electricity was found to encourage more young people to remain in the villages – although for poor households urban migration remained a survival strategy. Electric light has been found to reduce petty crime and electric fences to stop animals damaging crops. These benefits accrued to both electrified and non-electrified households (Asian Development Bank 2010). Villagers reported a feeling of increased self-esteem or no longer being neglected by the government.

Electricity has transformed village social life in the evenings and at festival time. There is more option to socialize after dark and work is finished. Family members now come home for festivals so social ties are maintained. In Zanzibar before electricity, men spent their evening hours outside the home with their male friends; after households had access to electricity, the men were more inclined to spend their evenings watching TV at home (Winther 2008). Such change in behavior was considered to increase family cohesion.

While there are concerns that extending the working day through electric light could increase women's workload, it appears that women value the flexibility good quality light allows for managing their time, as tasks can be carried out when best fits within the day (Winther 2008).

Increased economic empowerment

Improved and sustainable energy services can increase employment and income-generating opportunities for women and empower them economically. In developing countries, a large number of women work in micro/small-scale enterprises (MSEs), an important part of their livelihood and coping strategy. These MSEs exist mostly in the informal sector and often are based in the home to allow women to combine income-generating tasks with household duties (Kooijman-van Dijk and Clancy 2010).

There is a gender dimension to the nature of enterprises women and men use for their livelihoods, which then lead to different requirements for energy needs (Practical Action 2012). Women's enterprises are in sectors closely related to traditional female roles such as cooking, hairdressing, washing clothes, and tailoring. These are often heat-intensive (food processing), labor-intensive, and/or light intensive (home-based industries with work in evenings). Men tend to work with heavy electric appliances such as in welding and carpentry.

A shift to better energy services can contribute to increased profitability. In rural Brazil, self-employed women with access to electricity have been found to have an income double that of women who do not have access (O'Dell et al. 2014). However, access to finance, natural and human resources, and technology are also determining factors in the establishment of enterprises. Women face an additional set of barriers as compared to men. These barriers are related to ownership and control over productive resources; exclusion and marginalization regarding decision-making; illiteracy; and lack of exposure, information, and training. The informal nature of many women's enterprises is linked to problems of access to credit, equipment, and other support services (Dutta and Clancy 2005).

Encouraging women to sell energy products and lead energy enterprises can contribute to their economic and social empowerment. A growing number of energy enterprises have begun to engage women as sales representatives in order to reach consumers at the base of the pyramid with electricity and cooking solutions. Examples include sale of solar lights and mobile phone chargers (Solar Sister in Africa and SEWA in India), sale of clean energy products in largely women-run Tech Kiosks and Tech Agents (by Kopernik Solutions in Indonesia) (ENERGIA 2015), and women building biogas digesters and managing biogas construction companies (Centre for Rural Technology in Nepal) (Biogas Sector Partnership Nepal 2009). Women help ensure that energy products reflect the priorities of women users, thereby increasing the likelihood of adoption and use. Through their informal networks, they can reach remote and poor customers.

Increased agency and voice

Women's empowerment can be gained by participation in processes such as energy projects, which build self-confidence, self-awareness, and assertiveness. Through empowerment, women gain the ability to make effective choices and to transform those choices into desired outcomes. The extent to which an individual is able to exercise her or his agency determines, amongst other things, the ability to have a "voice" – that is, to contribute to and influence decision-making in households, communities, and broader society. Through agency and voice, women can ensure that energy policy meets their needs and that they can participate in energy sector initiatives and opportunities. A study in rural South Africa found that women were able to use their income (from social security payments) to buy electrical items (Matinga 2011); this contrasts with a study in Zanzibar where women had access to fewer appliances, which in part was attributed to women in Zanzibar having limited financial independence and decision-making power (Winther 2005).

Skutsch has questioned whether energy technologies are able to empower women (2005). The evidence is mixed. There are many examples of increased women's empowerment by participating in energy projects (ENERIGA 2006). For example, in the Solomon Islands women were given responsibility for the financial management of a village hydro scheme through which they gained men's respect and encouragement to take up new initiatives (Bryce and Soo 2004). Alternatively, studies in China, Sri Lanka, and Indonesia showed that electrification did not result in greater voice for women in community affairs (Ramani and Heijndermans 2003). However, such transformations may require an external agent to enable women's participation. For example, access to positive images and stories shown on television has changed women's (and to some extent men's) perceptions of gender roles and relations: women gain the confidence to challenge male authority (Standal 2008).

At the community level, increased participation by women on village project committees, which are structures usually dominated by men, should not be seen as an automatic route to increased voice or indication that women will be able to use their voice effectively. Women's participation can encounter a considerable degree of resistance, due to men's perception that women's gain may be their loss (World Bank 2005). There is evidence to suggest that women members must form at least 25 percent of project committees to influence women's effective participation (Agarwal 2010).

Women's empowerment through energy projects (either by being participants or beneficiaries) is possible, but it is not automatic and cannot be assumed. Changes in gender relations, manifested in women's increased agency and voice, are taking place but often at a pace slower than the time frame for post-intervention evaluation (Clancy et al. 2011).

Engendering energy policy

Women and men experience energy poverty in different ways, and they are affected by climate change in different ways linked to their gender roles. Regarding energy policy interventions, policy-makers do not generally recognize the existence of gender needs in energy services, and as a consequence, women's energy needs tend to be marginalized in policy documents (Mensah-Kutin 2006). Climate change initiatives where funds are available to promote energy access present a similar situation. A review of the Clean Development Mechanism concluded that only 5 of the 3864 projects listed in 2012 included gender considerations (UNFCCC 2012).

It is assumed that energy policies benefit women and men equally, so energy planning is implemented in a gender-neutral way. In reality, energy planning is gender-*blind*, and it fails to recognize that needs of men and women are different (Clancy and Feenstra 2006). Such an approach misses issues that are of relevance to women. For example, a policy to promote the use of electricity by small enterprises neglects the fact that many of women's traditional income-generating activities use process heat (Woroniuk and Schalkwyk 1998) for which electricity is not the cheapest option. In contrast, a more gender-aware policy would promote energy forms more compatible with process heat generation, such as LPG (Karlsson 2003).

Two linked factors may explain why energy policy is gender-blind: women's social position and the attitude of energy institutions to gender issues (Clancy and Feenstra 2006). Gender relations indicate that men tend to dominate decision-making within households, in communities and organizations. Policy-makers tend to be men and energy institutions and organizations, both in the public and private sector, as well as civil society (including NGOs dealing with energy), tend to be male-dominated, particularly in the professional posts. Male-dominated structures result in men talking to men about energy issues. Women are universally under-represented in political decision-making bodies at the international, national, and local level.[7] As a consequence, the forums where the energy issues are identified and potential solutions are proposed tend to have an inadvertent male bias. Policy responses prioritize men's issues (for example, the need for irrigation pumps) whereas women's issues (for example, the need for drinking water) are overlooked. Gender issues appear not to be a high priority in the energy sector despite the existence of gender policies at the national level, based on international accords such as the Beijing Platform for Action.[8]

Experience shows that there is a general lack of awareness amongst policy-makers that women and men have different energy needs, and this can be attributed to the lack of sex-disaggregated data related to energy (Clancy 2011). The availability of good data is the basis of planning. If there's no data, then there is no visibility of problems and issues to create the interest necessary for policy-makers to take action. When data is collected, it tends to be from the head of the household, who is generally assumed to be a man. However, this lack of understanding of the gender issues in energy access is not unique to the energy sector, but among gender specialists, there appears to be a failure to understand the nature of the energy sector and its relevance to women. This is despite the fact that, in developing countries, energy at the micro-level is "women's business." In one sense, this lack of gender specialists' engagement in the energy sector is surprising since the Beijing Platform for Action calls for mainstreaming gender in all sectors.

Gender mainstreaming is a strategy that aims to re-organize, improve, develop, and evaluate policy-making processes to incorporate gender at all levels and stages in the policy process. This approach calls for transparency in the policy-making and implementation processes, in order for both women and men to be involved. This includes considering the difficulties women may face in being able to participate in informal settlements in urban areas or in remote rural areas where, as a consequence of lack of access to modern energy, they also cannot access services such as cell phones, the internet, and media services. Women may require capacity-building to enable them to participate in such dialogues in a meaningful way. Men also need to create space to give women voice.

Concluding remarks

In this chapter we have reviewed the gender dimension of energy poverty, particularly how energy poverty impacts on poor women and men. The use of biomass is one of the main characteristics of energy poverty. The fuel quality is low, and when burnt, it gives off quantities of smoke and particulates that are recognized as negatively affecting health. Biomass collection also negatively affects health through the physical drudgery involved, and it affects women disproportionately to men. The time spent collecting fuel means less time for women to pursue other livelihood activities. Women are also responsible for a number of other survival tasks needed to sustain the household such as water collection, food processing, and cooking. Many of these tasks are demanding in terms of both human energy and time.

It would be incorrect to view women as passive victims of biomass use. Women have responded to fuelwood shortages by adopting management strategies to conserve fuel: they shorten cooking times, explore less fuel-intensive cooking and food processing methods, cook fewer meals, serve cold leftovers, change the types of food eaten, and purchase other fuels. Women are important managers of natural resources and also producers of biomass fuels. They make rational decisions about which resources to use and how to use them.

This chapter has demonstrated that one of the reasons for this continued reliance on biomass and women's labor relates to gender relations. At all levels in society, men make the decisions about energy. At the household level, these decisions involve which energy forms and technologies to buy. At the policy level, the decisions are about which interventions to promote. Women have limited voice in these decisions.

If gender aspects of energy poverty are to be addressed, two major transformations have to take place. Firstly, women have to be empowered to make choices about energy. Enabling choice is linked to issues of poverty alleviation, including access to income-generating activities. However, empowerment will require more than financial improvements. Women must be able to act upon the energy choices open to them, and their scope for this type of action is linked to decision-making within households. Such a shift in decision-making requires women's social and political empowerment. It means men have to change as well. Energy can play a role. Access to electricity allows men to take on tasks that do not infringe on their ideas of masculinity such as ironing and preparing snacks and drinks (Winther 2008).

Secondly, addressing gender issues of energy poverty will require changes on the energy supply-side. The energy sector must be responsive by providing, at affordable prices, equipment using modern energy forms that reduce the drudgery of women's labor. These changes also require business models that recognize women's role in the energy value chain as consumers (with particular income patterns), as role models, and as entrepreneurs who can, in some circumstances, be better positioned than their male counterparts to sell to other female consumers. The challenge to the energy profession is evident. There are plenty of good examples to draw on, such as the World Bank's Lighting Africa, ENERGIA's Women's Economic Empowerment (WEE) Programme, and the Global Alliance for Clean Cookstoves, which show firstly that when you target women for energy access, not only do they benefit but also their families do as well and secondly that women have a positive role to play in making energy poverty history.

Notes

1   There are significant variations in the percentage between regions and within regions. In part, this is due to difficulties in defining what constitutes a "head of household" so there is a lack of consistency between surveys. This figure should therefore be taken as indicative.
2   A gender perspective analyzes situations from the standpoint of differences between women and men based on their social relations, that is, on the basis of gender. Such an analysis recognizes that these relations are not static but change over time and they are shaped by power within the household and society at large. The balance of this power generally lies with men. The consequences of gender relations include the difference in capacity of women and men to respond to energy poverty and society's responses (that is the political will to develop appropriate policies) to ensure gender equitable outcomes in moving women and men out of energy poverty.
3   Indoor air pollution (IAP) is the smoke emitted when burning solid fuels, such as coal and biomass, which is considered to contain many health-damaging pollutants, including particulate matter (PM), carbon monoxide (CO), sulphur oxides, nitrogen oxides, aldehydes, benzene, and polyaromatic compounds (Smith 1987 cited in Bruce et al. 2006). IAP exposure is linked to a range of medical conditions including cardiovascular disease, low birth-weights and perinatal mortality, eye diseases including cataracts and blindness, asthma, increased risks of maternal depression, nasopharyngeal and lung cancers, nutritional deficiencies including anaemia and stunted growth, and the exacerbation of the effects of HIV/AIDS (World Bank 2012).
4   For instance, acute respiratory infections incidence for boys is said to be higher than that for girls in India (Mishra 2004 cited in World Bank 2012, 62).
5   See Matinga (2010) for a review of the literature.
6   Empowerment of women is defined in the 1995 Beijing Platform for Action as giving women greater equality with men in terms of the division of labor, creating more and better life chances for women and giving them greater control over their bodies.
7   Although more recently women have held posts as Minister of Energy, for example, in Zambia, South Africa, Uganda, and Botswana.
8   The Beijing Platform for Action is the resolution adopted at the end of the United Nations Fourth World Conference on Women held in Beijing, 4–15 September 1995.

References

Adair-Rohani, H., K. Zukor, S. Bonjour, S. Wilburn, A. Kuesel, R. Hebert, et al. 2013. "Limited electricity access in health facilities of sub-Saharan Africa: a systematic review of data on electricity access, sources, and reliability." *Global Health: Science and Practice* 1(2): 249–261.

Agarwal, B. 2010. "Does women's proportional strength affect their participation? Governing local forests in South Asia." *World Development* 38(1): 98–112.

Asian Development Bank. 2010. *Asian Development Bank's Assistance for Rural Electrification in Bhutan – Does Electrification Improve the Quality of Rural Life?* Impact Evaluation Study No. 26194. Manila: Independent Evaluation Department, Asian Development Bank.

Bardasi, E. and Q. Wodon. 2006. "Measuring time poverty and analyzing its determinants: concepts and application to Guinea" in C.M. Blackden and Q. Wodon (eds) (2006) *Gender, Time Use, and Poverty in Sub-Saharan Africa.* World Bank Working Paper No. 73. Washington, DC: The World Bank.

Biogas Sector Partnership Nepal. 2009. *Gender Mainstreaming in the Biogas Support Programme, Nepal.* Leusden: ENERGIA.

Blackden, C.M. and Q. Wodon (eds). 2006. *Gender, Time Use, and Poverty in Sub-Saharan Africa.* World Bank Working Paper No. 73. Washington, DC: The World Bank.

Bruce, N., Rehfuess, E., Mehta, S., Hutton, G., and Smith, K. 2006. "Indoor air pollution," in Jamison, D.T., Breman, J.G., Measham, A.R., Alleyne, G., Claeson, M., Evans, D.B., Jha, P., Mills, A., and Musgrove, P. (eds) *Disease Control Priorities in Developing Countries.* Washington, DC: The World Bank.

Bryce, D. and C.C. Soo. 2004. "Bulelavata women speak," *ENERGIA News,* 6(2): 19–20.

Clancy, J.S. 2011. *Swimming in the Mainstream: Energia's Experiences with Engendering Energy Policy.* Discussion paper prepared for ENERGIA.

Clancy J.S. and Marielle Feenstra. 2006. *How to Engender Energy Policy.* Technical Paper prepared for ENERGIA.

Clancy, J.S., M. Matinga, S. Oparaocha, and T. Winther. 2011. *Gender Equity in Access to and Benefits from Modern Energy and Improved Energy Technologies.* Background Paper for World Development Report 2012. ENERGIA/Norad/World Bank.

Cooke, P., W.F. Hyde, and G. Köhlin. 2008. "Fuelwood, forests and community management – evidence from household studies." *Environment and Development Economics* 13: 103–135.

Danielsen, K. 2012. *Gender Equality, Women's Rights and Access to Energy Services.* February. Ministry of Foreign Affairs of Denmark.

Dinkelman, T. 2008. *The Effects of Rural Electrification on Employment: New Evidence from South Africa.* Report 08-653. Ann Arbor, Michigan: Population Studies Center, University of Michigan.

Doleac, J.L. and N.J. Sanders. 2012. *Under the Cover of Darkness: Using Daylight Saving Time to Measure How Ambient Light Influences Criminal Behavior.* SIEPR Discussion Paper No. 12-004. Stanford, California: Stanford University.

Dutta, S. and J.S. Clancy. 2005. "Women and Productive Uses of Energy: Some light on a shadowy area." UNDP Meeting on Productive Uses of Renewable Energy, Bangkok, Thailand, 9–11 May.

ENERGIA. 2006. *From the Millennium Development Goals: Towards a Gender-Sensitive Energy Policy Research and Practice: Empirical Evidence and Case Studies.* Synthesis

Report for Department for International Development (DFID) KaR research project R8346 "Gender as a Key Variable in Energy Interventions."

ENERGIA. 2014. "Women's economic empowerment." *ENERGIA News* 15(1): 19–25.

FAO. 2006. *Technology for Agriculture. Labour Saving Technologies and Practices Decision Support Tool.* Rome: Food and Agricultural Organization (FAO).

IDS. 2003. *Energy, Poverty Gender: A Review of the Evidence and Case Studies in Rural China.* Washington DC: The World Bank.

Jato, M.N. 2004. *Gender-Responsive Programming for Poverty Reduction.* Addis Ababa: United Nations Population Fund (UNPFA).

Karlsson, G.V. 2003. *Government Policies to Meet the Energy Needs of Women and Rural Communities.* UNDP Energy and Women Project. New York: United Nations Development Programme.

Kelkar, G. and D. Nathan. 2007. *Testing of Gender Tools for Energy Projects in India.* Report for ENERGIA. Leusden: ENERGIA.

Kooijman-van Dijk, A.L. and J.S. Clancy. 2010. "Enabling access to sustainable energy: a synthesis of research findings in Bolivia, Tanzania and Vietnam," *Energy for Sustainable Development* 14: 14–21.

Lewis, J. 2014. "Short-run and long-run effects of household electrification." Paper presented at Economic History Workshop, Queen's University, Kingston, Ontario, Canada, April 25, 2014. Accessed January 3, 2015. www.econ.queensu.ca/files/other/Lewis%20electrification_SR_LR.pdf.

Lim, Stephen S. et al. 2010. "A comparative risk assessment of burden of disease and injury attributable to 67 risk factors and risk factor clusters in 21 regions 1990–2010: a systematic analysis for the global burden of disease study 2010." *The Lancet* 380, no. 9859 (December 15, 2010): 2224–2260.

Mahat, I. 2004. "Implementation of alternative energy technologies in Nepal: towards the achievement of sustainable livelihoods." *Energy for Sustainable Development* 8(2): 9–16.

Massé, R and M.R. Samaranayake. 2002. "EnPoGen study in Sri Lanka." *ENERGIA News* 5 (3): 14–16.

Matinga, M.N. 2010. "We grow up with it: an ethnographic study of the experiences, perceptions and responses to the health impacts of energy acquisition and use in rural South Africa." PhD diss., University of Twente, The Netherlands.

Matinga, M.N. 2011. "A socio-cultural perspective on transformation of gender roles and relations, and non-change in energy-health perceptions following electrification in rural South Africa." Case study for World Development Report 2012. ENERGIA/Norad/World Bank.

Matly, M. 2003. *Rural Electrification in Indonesia and Sri Lanka: From Social Analysis to Reform of the Power Sector.* ASTAE EnPoGen Project. Washington DC: The World Bank.

Meikle, S. 2004. *A Study of the Impact of Energy Use on Poor Urban Women and Girls' Livelihoods in Arusha, Tanzania.* London: University College London.

Mensah-Kutin, R. 2006. *Gender and Energy in Africa: Regional Initiatives and Challenges in Promoting Gender and Energy.* Leusden: ENERGIA.

Moser, C.O.N. 1993. *Gender Planning and Development: Theory, Practice and Training.* London: Routledge.

Narayan, D. 1999. *Can Anyone Hear Us?: Voices From 47 Countries.* Washington DC: The World Bank.

O'Dell, Kathleen, Sophia Peters, and Kate Wharton. 2014. *Women, Energy, and Economic Empowerment: Applying a Gender Lens to Amplify the Impact of Energy Access.* Westlake, Texas: Deloitte University Press.

Porcaro, J. and M. Takada (eds). 2005. *Achieving the Millennium Development Goals: The Role of Energy Services.* New York: United Nations Development Program.

Practical Action. 2012. *Poor People's Energy Outlook 2012: Energy for Earning a Living.* Practical Action Publishing: Rugby, UK.

Ramani, K.V. and E. Heijndermans. 2003. *Energy, Poverty and Gender: A Synthesis.* Washington DC: The World Bank.

Reddy, A.K.N. 2000. 'Energy and social issues', in United Nations Development Programme, United Nations Department of Economic and Social Affairs and World Energy Council. *World Energy Assessment,* UNDP: New York.

Shioda, S. 1994. "Innovation and change in the rapid economic growth period." In M. Nakamura (ed). *Technology Change and Female Labour in Japan.* Tokyo and New York: United Nations University Press.

Skutsch, M.M. 2005. "Gender analysis for energy projects and programmes." *J. Energy for Sustainable Development* IX(1): 37–52.

Smith, K.R. 1987. *Biofuels, Air Pollution, and Health: A Global Review.* New York: Plenum Press.

Standal, K. 2008. "Giving light and hope in rural Afghanistan: the impact of Norwegian Church Aid's barefoot approach on women beneficiaries." Master's thesis, University of Oslo.

UN. 2000. *The World's Women, 2000: Trends and Statistics.* New York: United Nations.

UNDP. 2004. *Reducing Rural Poverty through Increased Access to Energy Services: A Review of the Multifunctional Platform Project in Mali.* New York: United Nations Development Programme.

UNDP. 2006. *Expanding Access to Modern Energy Services: Replicating, Scaling Up and Mainstreaming at the Local Level.* New York: United Nations Development Programme.

United Nations Framework Convention on Climate Change (UNFCCC). 2012. *Benefits of the Clean Development Mechanism.* Accessed November 3, 2014. https://cdm.unfccc.int/about/dev_ben/ABC_2012.pdf.

WDR. 2012. *World Development Report 2012: Gender and Development.* World Bank: Washington DC.

Winther, T. 2005. "Rising electricity consumption: driving forces and consequences. The case of rural Zanzibar." ECEEE 2007 Summer Study: 1835–1845. Oslo: European Council for an Energy Efficient Economy.

Winther, T. 2008. *The Impact of Electricity: Development, Desires and Dilemmas.* Oxford: Berghahn Books.

World Bank. 1996. *Rural Energy and Development: Improving Energy Supplies for Two Billion People.* Washington DC: The World Bank.

World Bank. 2000. *Energy Services for the World's Poor.* Washington DC: The World Bank.

World Bank. 2005. *Gender-Responsive Social Analysis: A Guidance Note. Incorporating Social Dimensions into Bank-Supported Projects.* Washington DC: Social Development Department, The World Bank.

World Bank. 2012. *State of the Clean Cooking Energy Sector in Sub-Saharan Africa.* Washingto, DC: The World Bank.

World Health Organization. 2014. *WHO Guidelines for Indoor Air Quality: Household Fuel Combustion.* Geneva: World Health Organization (WHO).

World Health Organization, UNICEF, UNFPA and The World Bank. 2012. *Trends in Maternal Mortality: 1990–2010*. Geneva: World Health Organization (WHO).

Woroniuk, B. and J. Schalkwyk. 1998. *Energy Policy and Equality between Women and Men*. SIDA Equality Prompt #9. Stockholm: Sweden International Development Cooperation.

3 Indigenous peoples

From energy poverty to energy empowerment

Kristen A. Carpenter and
Jacquelyn Amour Jampolsky

Introduction

There are approximately 370 million indigenous people in the world, belonging to 5,000 different groups, in 90 countries worldwide. Although indigenous peoples share in some common struggles associated with energy poverty, it is important to note the vast differences across communities. Indigenous peoples around the world are dealing with different state regimes and laws, from those that recognize and respect their status as self-governing entities to those that deny their separate existence altogether. Moreover, indigenous peoples differ widely with respect to their social organization, religions, and subsistence activities, and legal, political, and economic circumstances. Many indigenous people live in rural communities, while others may live in densely urbanized settings. Some have access to electricity and running water, and others do not. In the United States alone, there are 566 federally recognized Indian tribes, some of which hold great tracts of land, rich with oil, gas, timber, minerals, as well as water, fish, and other wildlife, while others have small land bases reliant on casino gambling and financial lending for economic development. Some American Indians live in reservation communities that are highly networked with wireless access to the Internet, while others live in traditional villages that still do not have running water or electricity, in part out of respect for customary life ways. In short, the topic of indigenous peoples and their experiences with energy canvasses a very wide group of people with different experiences.

However, on a global scale, indigenous peoples share in some similar sociocultural, historical, legal, and political struggles. First, the relationship of many indigenous peoples with their homelands is sacred in nature, and aspects of the natural world are deeply tied not only to economic development and self-governance, but also to identity, religion, and culture. As the land sustains the people, so too do the people have an obligation to sustain the land; and the particular ways in which tribes express this relationship, through ceremonies, subsistence, laws, and customs, gives rise to traditional tribal identities. Some tribal people will say, for example, that their survival – whether as Navajo or Cherokees, Quechua or Maya – is deeply tied to an ongoing relationship of reciprocity with their traditional lands. To the extent that energy development and access implicate indigenous peoples' relationship with the land where they live, these are issues that affect cultural and social realities, as much as economics and politics (Royster et al. 2013).

Second, energy poverty disproportionately affects indigenous peoples relative to other groups. Even though indigenous peoples account for about 5 percent of the global population, they account for 10 percent of people living in abject poverty (World Bank 2010). As S. James Anaya, former Special Rapporteur for Indigenous Peoples Rights, has explained, "[i]n both industrial and less-developed countries in which indigenous peoples live, the indigenous sectors almost invariably are on the lowest rung of the socioeconomic ladder, and they exist at the margins of power" (Anaya 2004, 4). Many communities are located on traditional lands outside the connectivity of the grid and are forced to use traditional forms of energy – such as biomass and biofuels – characteristic of many of the energy oppressed poor (EOP) (Guruswamy 2004).

Furthermore, indigenous peoples are disproportionately affected by global climate change (United Nations Human Rights Council 2009, 28). Many indigenous peoples live in environmentally sensitive regions and maintain a heightened dependence on their land, which leads to increased socio-ecological vulnerability. This scenario is exacerbated by the fact that much of the world's conventional energy reserves are located in indigenous territories. It is common for large extractive industries to operate 50 percent or more of their operations on indigenous lands (First Peoples Worldwide 2013, 11), and in the United States alone, at least 10 percent of all domestic energy resources are located on reservations (Tanana and Ruple 2012, 2).

These contemporary circumstances have their origins in the conquest and colonization of indigenous peoples and territories. Historically, indigenous peoples have been widely dispossessed of their lands and resources, relocated to disparate geographies, and left without access to mainstream energy sources. In instances where indigenous peoples have been able to hold onto territories rich with resources, governments and private actors have often exploited these resources for the benefit of the energy needs of the industrialized world. As one advocacy group, the Indigenous Environmental Network, explains,

> Indigenous peoples have disproportionately suffered impacts due to the production and use of energy resources – coal mining, uranium mining, oil and gas extraction, coal bed methane, nuclear power and hydropower development – yet are among those who benefit least from these energy developments.
>
> (Global Justice Ecology Project 2015)

Thus the energy situation of indigenous peoples generally reflects historical and ongoing exploitation, inequality, and poverty.

Today however, many indigenous peoples are looking at energy, whether traditional or in renewables, as an important way to address basic needs and promote community economic development. They want to develop on their own terms and in a way that they have not been able to in the past and are increasingly engaging in the international human rights framework to do so. International human rights law recognizes indigenous peoples' individual and collective rights to self-determination, non-discrimination, and equality in political, economic, cultural, and other matters (Carpenter and Riley 2014). Instruments ranging from the International Labour Organisation Convention 169 (1989) (ILO 169), a binding treaty entered into by twenty states, to the United Nations Declaration on the Rights of Indigenous Peoples (2007) (UNDRIP), a non-binding declaration of the United Nations General Assembly adopted by 144 states, recognize that indigenous peoples have rights to land, natural resources, and economic development (Anaya 2009). Pursuant to the UNDRIP, indigenous peoples have broad rights to culture, religion, and education, to participate in national lawmaking that affects them, to provide "free, prior, and informed consent" to critical measures, and to receive restitution for violations of property, governance, and other rights.

As indigenous peoples continue to participate in the human rights movement and assert self-determination over their lands and resources, in some cases they have been able to advocate for energy development that advances access, economic self-sufficiency, and environmental sustainability. Recognizing significant differences among indigenous peoples, this chapter begins to map a shift from energy poverty to energy empowerment. The first section surveys several non-exhaustive examples from around the world and then the second section describes developments in the United States specifically.

From energy poverty to energy empowerment around the world

There are dozens of cases illustrating the disempowerment and devastation of indigenous peoples at the hands of players in the extractive industries. In the case of the Lubicon Lake Band of Cree Indians, for example, Canada allowed the province of Alberta to grant oil and gas leases within the Band's aboriginal territory, bringing about devastating destruction and poverty to the community.[1] Air and water pollution from extraction ruined subsistence hunting and fishing habitats and had deleterious impacts on the community's health, including claims before the United Nations Human Rights Committee that miscarriages, stillbirths, and abnormal births increased from "near zero to near 100 per cent" between 1987 and 1990.[2] The Human Rights Committee found that Canada, by allowing activities that threatened the way of life and culture of the Band, violated the Band's rights to culture provided by Article 27 of the International Covenant on Civil and Political Rights.[3] Ongoing environmental, political, and financial problems persist in the community today.[4]

The Lubicon Band is, unfortunately, only one of many indigenous groups worldwide that has suffered violations of human rights connected to the activities of extractive industries. For example, there have been devastating environmental and social effects on indigenous peoples in the Ecuadorian

Amazon caused by botched petroleum development from willful discharges, numerous spills, and other harms (Kimerling 2007). In Nigeria, oil development has infamously brought about devastating work conditions, environmental damage, and human rights violations, at the hands of colluding government and corporate parties, with significant impacts on indigenous peoples in the Niger Delta (Foster 2012; Konne 2014).

Harmful energy development on indigenous lands for the benefit of non-indigenous people is not limited to the extractive industries. Renewable energy development, especially in the case of mega-dams, may also threaten indigenous peoples. In the Xingu basin of the Brazilian Amazon, indigenous peoples have been fighting the construction of the Belo Monte Dam for more than thirty years (Jampolsky 2012, 242; Hernández-Truyol 2014). Belo Monte would not only physically displace between 20,000–40,000 people, but it would flood the "Big Bend," the cultural birthplace of civilization for the people of the Xingu (Jampolsky 2012, 245). Although the dam would add more than 11,000 MW of carbon-free energy to the grid, there is no evidence that any of the energy would be diverted to the indigenous people of the Xingu (Jampolsky 2012, 244).

In Kuala Lumpur, Malaysia, indigenous peoples are currently threatened by a hydroelectric power project that would strip their customary lands of timber and inundate them with water, without consultation or consent. When the people of Long Kesseh recently refused to abandon their lands or disperse from the site, they faced intimidation by government and private parties (Lee 2014). These types of cases are common around the world (Colchester 2000).

> A conservative estimate of the number of people displaced by dams in the past fifty years is 50–60 million people … The overwhelming majority of these displaced people have been poor and politically powerless, and a disproportionately large number of them are members of indigenous communities.
>
> (Fisher 1999)

In some cases, indigenous communities have utilized international tribunals to combat energy poverty and exploitation to hold states and industry accountable. For example, the Inter-American Court of Human Rights (IACHR) recently ruled in *The Kichwa Peoples of the Sarayaku community and its members v. Ecuador*[5] that the Ecuadorian government had failed to properly consult with the Kichwa people during a ten-year period of environmentally unsound oil exploration, leading to violations of the right to property and accompanying rights to personal life, culture, and personal integrity, as provided in the American Convention on Human Rights.[6] In an opinion also referencing the provisions of ILO 169 on the right of consultation, the IACHR called for the payment of $1.4M in damages, the removal of hazardous materials from the territory of the Sarayaku people, and the adoption of measures for consultation and participation going forward (Alvaro 2014). As Amnesty International has explained, the *Sarayaku* opinion "establishes in detail how consultation should be undertaken: in good faith, through culturally appropriate procedures that are aimed at reaching consent." It further stands for the proposition that "exploration or extraction of natural resources cannot be done at the expense of an indigenous community's means of physical or cultural survival on their own land" (Amnesty International 2012).

In some instances, indigenous peoples have made explicit that they will not come to the table for new negotiations with states and industry until harms from past projects have been remedied. Peru has recently declared more than one "state of emergency" when communities experienced severe contamination at the hands of oil development. Invoking international human rights standards, local communities have said that they will not come to the table regarding current and future activities in the northern Amazon until the government and companies start to redress forty years of "legacy issues associated with the project (such as environmental remediation measures in polluted areas, land titling, and compensation for land use and violation of land rights) before initiating a new consultation" (Greenspan 2014).

Reports prepared by the United Nations, as well as the best-practices documents of scholars, non-governmental organizations, industry associations, and corporations themselves, increasingly recognize the application of human rights standards to development activities (United Nations Office of the High Commissioner for Human Rights 2012; Blecher et al. 2014). More specifically, the United Nations Special Rapporteur's Report on Extractive Industries and Indigenous Peoples sets forth various legal instruments and cases pertaining to energy development affecting indigenous peoples (Anaya 2013). The report describes that while the preferred alternative is for indigenous peoples to develop natural resources through their own enterprises and initiatives, consistent with self-determination norms, the standard scenario is for third parties to develop indigenous peoples' natural resources. In the standard scenario, states and companies must obtain the "free, prior and informed consent" (FPIC) of indigenous peoples to development activities affecting them. This principle of FPIC must be construed alongside with other human rights provisions including indigenous peoples' rights to be free from violence, reprisals, and coercion; rights to participation, self-determination, property, culture, religion, and non-discrimination; rights to health and physical well-being; and the right of indigenous peoples to set and pursue their own priorities for development, with respect for traditional practices of self-governance and customary laws on land use (Anaya 2013).

Accordingly, indigenous peoples are using the human rights framework to forge new partnerships with corporate developers to improve the energy paradigm for indigenous peoples (Henderson 2013). As recognition of indigenous rights becomes increasingly more common, meaningful partnerships will be necessary for extractive industries to mitigate risk by addressing community needs (Davis 2013; First Peoples Worldwide 2013). Consistent with human rights norms, some commentators have suggested better revenue-sharing models or that indigenous peoples form their own companies to develop such resources (James-Eluyode 2012; Konne 2014). These models must be evaluated with attention to the relevant domestic legal, political, social, and economic situations of the indigenous peoples, states, industries, and resources involved. Despite persistent challenges in implementing these agreements, new conversations and cooperative models between indigenous peoples, governments, and industry suggests a shift from energy exploitation towards energy empowerment for indigenous peoples.

For many indigenous peoples cooperative agreements for equitable development and improved energy access on indigenous lands may not be feasible – for lack of capital, political clout, or appropriate natural resources. In these cases, indigenous communities may be particularly well suited for other types of partnerships that encourage the adoption of appropriate sustainable energy technologies (ASETs) as means to combat energy poverty within their own communities (Guruswamy 2011, 141).

Consider the energy issues facing four indigenous Quechua communities living in the province of Puno in the Peruvian Andes. The community members live more than two hours from the closest town of Ayaviri at around 13,000 feet in elevation, where resources are scarce and connectivity to the grid is unavailable.[7] The community members are almost exclusively ranchers and therefore use cow dung as their only source of fuel for cooking, which causes indoor particulate pollution and leads to a wide range of health problems primarily affecting women and children (Partnership for the Relief of Energy Poverty 2010).[8] To combat this symptom of energy poverty on a small scale, the communities partnered with the two universities and a local non-governmental organization named Caritas to develop a more efficient cookstove for the community members in order to reduce indoor particulate pollution and overall fuel use. Although it is difficult to gauge the "success" of projects like this, it demonstrates how indigenous communities are engaging in energy empowerment without entering into large-scale and capital-intensive infrastructural development (see Chapter 17 of this book).

Despite the general trend towards energy empowerment, be it through new partnerships to disseminate ASETs or large-scale development partnerships, indigenous peoples continue to face major challenges with respect to energy access and development in their communities. These challenges plague poor and industrialized countries alike, where tribes in the US continue to find social and legal barriers slowing progress. The next section briefly catalogs the legal history and current moment of tribal energy issues in the United States.

From energy poverty to energy empowerment in the United States

Federal Indian policy historically sought to remove tribes from their aboriginal territories to smaller tracts of land where they would relinquish subsistence life ways in favor of family farming. These practices, embodied in the policies of "assimilation" and "allotment," also opened up so-called surplus Indian lands to purchase by non-Indian governments and individuals. This history is significant with respect to energy poverty for indigenous peoples in the United States for two primary reasons. First, tribes have been overlooked in much of the energy infrastructure planning in the United States (United States Senate Comm. on

Indian Affairs 2009). As a result, many tribal communities in the United States cannot fulfill their basic energy needs because they are not connected to the grid and purchasing energy through local utilities is unaffordable. On the Navajo Reservation alone, at least 18,000 of the 48,000 households lack electricity (Tarasi et al. 2011, 265). Like many people suffering from energy poverty, the lack of electricity in Indian Country perpetuates other sociocultural and physical health problems. Given inadequate lighting, heating, refrigeration, for example, the alternatives for meeting basic needs are sometimes unhealthy ones, such as burning biomass or biofuels (Tarasi et al. 2011).

Second, federal Indian policy has created a complex body of laws that pose a series of obstacles for tribes seeking to remedy the energy gap on the reservation while simultaneously preventing them from meaningfully participating in development projects that may affect culturally significant lands outside of the reservation boundaries. This split regime forces tribes and developers alike into a tedious jurisdictional and regulatory framework that exacerbates common obstacles to energy development such as remote geographic location, poor infrastructure, and lack of access to capital (Kronk 2010, 467–469). Thus the problematic energy paradigm facing tribes in the United States mimics some of the challenges facing indigenous communities across the globe, while also demonstrating a unique legal and political paradigm for how tribes may seek energy empowerment in the future.

As Rebecca Tsosie (2009, 205) has noted,

> The history of energy development in Indian Country is complex, revealing successive episodes of federal policy designed to exploit energy resources on reservation lands for the benefit of the American population, and then shifting to a recognition of the Indian nations as sovereigns with the right to control mineral development on reservation lands.

Historical energy development on reservations occurred for many generations pursuant to development leases that the Secretary of the Interior negotiated for tribes under the Indian Mineral Leasing Act of 1938.[9] This arrangement gave the federal government, vis-à-vis the Secretary of the Interior, a lot of power, and an equal opportunity to abuse it. For example, in the disputes between Peabody Coal and the Navajo Nation, the Secretary famously entered into a long-term set of leases in which Peabody paid the Navajo royalties of 12.5 percent for its coal – when the going rate was 20 percent – amounting to damages that lower courts valued at $600M. The United States Supreme Court held that the Secretary had no enforceable duty to refrain from ex parte communications to the economic detriment of the tribe.[10] Today, energy development on reservation lands is primarily governed by four major statutes: the 1938 Indian Mineral Leasing Act, the 1982 Indian Mineral Development Act (considered together as the primary laws regarding mineral extraction),[11] the Indian Long-Term Leasing Act,[12] and the Indian Reorganization Act.[13] These statutes give tribes liberty to enter into their own leases and have better control over the type of development and tribal benefit for energy projects on tribal lands. Although subsequent legislation provides a better model for energy development on reservations, problems reflecting past federal policies persist (Royster et al. 2013).

Starting in the early 2000s, Congress has passed a series of laws in attempts to improve tribal access to energy and encourage development of domestic energy reserves on tribal lands. For example, in 2005, Congress enacted the Indian Tribal Energy Development and Self-Determination Act (EDSA).[14] The EDSA sought to promote economic growth through energy production and self-determination by establishing the Office of Indian Energy Policy and Programs in the Department of Energy (DOE) and setting up an Indian energy resource development program in the Department of the Interior. The EDSA requires that the DOE make financial and technical assistance available to tribes seeking to develop energy resources through grants, loans, training, and other support (Sullivan 2010, 828–829).

In addition to financial and technical assistance, the EDSA attempts to facilitate development legislatively by allowing certain tribes to "enter into a lease or business agreement for the purpose of energy resource development on tribal land" without requiring Secretarial approval otherwise required under federal law.[15] The purported idea behind the EDSA was to promote energy development on tribal lands by streamlining the bureaucratic process (Kronk 2012, 818). To qualify for the EDSA however, tribes must first enter into a Tribal Energy Resource Agreement, or TERA with the Secretary. Although TERAs grant authority to the tribe to review, approve, and manage leases, business agreements, and rights-of-way for energy development on tribal lands without the approval of the Secretary of the Interior, they also require tribal energy development decisions to comport with a myriad of federal mandates while absolving the federal government of all liability regarding development leases.[16] As a result, no tribe has entered into a TERA with the Secretary and the EDSA remains unutilized. Currently, the Senate Committee on Indian Affairs is attempting to revise the EDSA to make TERAs and funding more workable. However, "S. 1684 barely scratches the surface of outdated laws and regulations, bureaucratic regulatory and permitting processes, and insufficient federal staffing or expertise to implement those processes" (Kronk 2012, 820).

Despite the unresolved legislative challenges with respect to traditional energy development, the first decade of the new millennium marked a change in energy development in Indian Country. Ushering in a new national prerogative, the Obama administration responded to the increased risks of environmental and energy insecurity from dependency on foreign oil and other non-renewable energy generation by allocating billions of dollars to promote renewable energy generation on United States soil (Dreveskracht 2011, 28–29). The potential renewable generation in wind and solar alone is estimated at "535 billion kWh/ year of wind energy (equivalent to 14 percent of current US total annual energy generation) and 17,600 billion kWh/year of solar energy potential (equivalent to 4.5 times the total US electric generation in 2004)" (Tanana and Ruple 2012). Because at least 10 percent of all domestic energy resources are on Indian lands, tribes stand at the forefront of energy development in the United States (Tanana and Ruple 2012). While many reservations were originally granted to tribes as "left overs" viewed as undesirable to the federal government in the nineteenth century, now the potential for renewable generation in the United States relies on tribal lands.

The shift towards renewable energy generation in the United States has presented tribes with unprecedented opportunity for renewable energy development on the reservation, which has the potential not only to address local access to energy, but also to position tribes as energy producers. Increasingly tribes in the United States are seeking to participate in energy development and distribution on and off their reservations, addressing their own issues of access, economic needs, and sustainability in the process. The federal government supports various tribal renewable projects including geothermal, biomass, wind, and solar (United States Department of Energy 2013).

For example, many members of the Ute Mountain Ute Tribe of southwestern Colorado suffer from poverty and a lack of consistent access to electricity on the reservation. Utilizing the new political and legal energy framework, in 2012 the tribe secured a $72,176 grant from the Department of Energy to conduct a small-scale solar feasibility study on the reservation as part of the EDSA. The grant paid for the tribe to assess loads, connectivity, slope and exposure, environmental considerations, economic and benefit sharing, and other considerations to potentially construct a 1 to 2 MW maximum photovoltaic installation to offset the energy needs of the community of Towaoc, the capital of the Ute Mountain Ute reservation (Jampolsky 2014, 154). Additionally, the tribe is seeking to develop a commercial-scale solar farm on the reservation. In 2012 the Four Corners Power Plant near Fruitland, New Mexico shut down three of its five units, and the San Juan Generating Station near Farmington, New Mexico agreed to shut down two of its four units by 2017 (Thompson 2013). This has not only created a new demand for power no longer being generated in the region, but also opened up transmission space in existing Shiprock substation for easy connectivity to the grid. The Shiprock substation is less than five miles from the Ute Mountain Ute reservation boundary, and new space in the substation introduced the potential for energy produced on the reservation to be exported to markets in Arizona and California (Jampolsky 2014).

The Navajo Nation, arguably the most energy poor indigenous community in the United States, has become a leader in renewable energy generation to offset local energy needs, engage in economic development, and offset the harmful environmental effects of carbon and capital-intensive energy development (Greenhowe 2013, 287). With assistance from the DOE, the Navajo Nation has installed 272 individual solar photovoltaic systems for residents who lack electricity on the reservation (Kronk 2010, 464). The Tribe has also begun to invest in both small- and commercial-scale wind farms to bolster renewable energy generation to combat energy poverty in a way that is consistent with Navajo environmental ethics and spirituality (Tsosie 2009, 254). The Big Boquillas Wind Project will function as a tribally owned utility and provide 200

MW of power to the Navajo Reservation upon completion (Kaushik 2012). Additionally, the project will provide many needed jobs on the reservation dually aiding to combat energy poverty through economic development (Greenhowe 2013).

The Campo Band of Kumeyaay Indians and the Blackfeet Nation have developed similarly sized wind farms on their reservations. The Campo Band of Kumeyaay wind project powers 30,000 homes both on and off the reservation while offsetting approximately 110,000 tons of carbon emissions. Although these projects have been successful and there is

> tremendous potential for renewable energy development in Indian Country ... actual projects have been slow to materialize. This is due to a variety of obstacles ranging from overly complex and burdensome lease approval processes to difficult transmission access and ill-fitting financial incentives.

Large-scale projects are capital and time intensive, and therefore require complicated partnerships and financing agreements with governments or other non-tribal entities (Kronk 2010, 465–467).

Challenges that face indigenous communities engaging in energy development in the United States include internal social and cultural turmoil as well. Reports suggest that in the Bakken area of North Dakota, hydraulic fracturing has brought salt water leaks and natural gas fires (Brown 2013), allegations of political and financial corruption (Donovan 2014; LaDuke 2014), and the challenges of managing an influx of outside workers residing temporarily in rural communities (Murdoch 2013; Pember 2014). The media has described challenges experienced in other tribes with highly profitable development enterprises, including differing viewpoints and priorities within the community (Thompson 2010). In some communities, advocacy around sustainability includes an appeal to tribal law and human rights. The Navajo Nation Human Rights Commission recently opposed a federal bill to settle water rights in part because members of the community had not had the chance to provide "free, prior, and informed consent" to aspects of the bill, especially those involving Navajo Generating Station and the protection of water for use by subsistence herders (Navajo Nation Human Rights Commission 2012; Carpenter and Riley 2014).

The model emerging in the United States is one in which tribal governments are taking energy empowerment – with all of its benefits and challenges – into their own hands, with a focus on clean energy in many instances. Tribes are leveraging priorities and opportunities with the federal government, partnering with energy developers' own terms, and incorporating their own mineral development companies. For example, Missouri River Resources is a tribally chartered energy company that describes itself as "an independent energy development company that develops oil and gas resources for the benefit of the Three Affiliated Tribes" (Missouri River Resources 2013). Thus, despite the remaining challenges however, the success of some projects and general movement towards tribally run energy development demonstrates the general trend from energy poverty towards energy empowerment for tribes in the United States.

Conclusion

Indigenous peoples continue to face challenges with respect to energy access and development. Yet, indigenous peoples' participation in the international human rights movement worldwide, with its emphasis on self-determination, as well as the drive towards renewable energy in the United States specifically both suggest important steps in the path from energy poverty towards energy empowerment.

Notes

1 *Lubicon Lake Band v. Canada*, Communication No. 167/1984 (26 March 1990), U.N. Doc. Supp. No. 40 (A/45/40) at 1 (1990).
2 *Id.* at para. 29.5.
3 *Id.* at para. 30.
4 There are currently competing groups claiming to govern the community, each with its own website and description of historical and current events. Compare the website of the Lubicon Lake Nation, available at www.lubiconlakenation.ca/, with the website of the Lubicon Lake Band, available at www.lubiconlakeband.ca/about/.
5 Case 167/03, Report No. 62/04, Inter-Am. C.H.R., OEA/Ser.L/V/II.122 Doc. 5 rev. 1 at 308 (2004).
6 *Id.* at para. 341.
7 Information based from field research conducted by Jocelyn Jenks and Jacquelyn Amour Jampolsky in 2010 as volunteer policy analysts for the former Center for Energy and Environmental Security at the University of Colorado, Boulder, and subsequent studies (reports on file with author).
8 Manure comprises 100 percent of fuel for cooking (based on a 2010 Energy Needs Assessment surveying 200 community members) (reports on file with author).
9 25 U.S.C.A. § 396.
10 *US v. Navajo Nation*, 537 U.S. 488 (2003); *US v. Navajo Nation*, 556 U.S. 287 (2009).
11 25 U.S.C.A. §§ 2101–2108.
12 25 U.S.C.A. § 415; § 8.1.
13 25 U.S.C.A. §§ 461–479.
14 Pub. L. No. 109-58, tit. V, 119 Stat. 594, 763–779 (2005).
15 25 U.S.C. § 3504(a)(1).
16 25 U.S.C. § 3504(e)(6)(D)(ii).

References

Alvaro, Mercedes. 2014. "Ecuador minister to apologize publicly to indigenous people over oil project." *The Wall Street Journal Online*, September 30. Accessed February 28, 2015. http://online.wsj.com/articles/ecuador-minister-to-apologize-publicly-to-indigenous-people-over-oil-project-1412110097.

Amnesty International. 2012. "Ecuador: Inter-American Court ruling marks key victory for Indigenous Peoples." Accessed February 28, 2015. www.amnesty.org/en/news/ecuador-inter-american-court-ruling-marks-key-victory-indigenous-peoples-2012-07-26.

Anaya, S. James. 2004. *Indigenous Peoples in International Law*. 2nd edn. New York: Oxford University Press.

——2009. *International Human Rights and Indigenous Peoples*. New York: Aspen Publishers.

——2013. "Extractive industries and indigenous peoples. Report of the Special Rapporteur on the rights of indigenous peoples, James Anaya." Report to the Human Rights Council. A/HRC/24/41. Accessed February 28, 2015. http://unsr.jamesanaya.org/study/report-a-hrc-24-41-extractive-industries-and-indigenous-peoples-report-of-the-special-rapporteur-on-the-rights-of-indigenous-peoples.

Blecher, Lara, Nancy Kaymar Stafford, and Gretchen C. Bellamy. (eds.) 2014. *Corporate Responsibility for Human Rights Impacts: New Expectations and Paradigms*. Chicago, Illinois: American Bar Association Book Publishing.

Brown, Curt. 2013. "Taking a stand on their sacred land: keepers of the earth struggle to come to terms with North Dakota's oil boom." *Star Tribune*, date unlisted. Accessed February 28, 2015. www.startribune.com/local/233854981.html.

Carpenter, Kristen A. and Angela R. Riley. 2014. "Indigenous peoples and the jurisgenerative moment in human rights." *Cal. L. Rev.* 102: 173–234.

Colchester, Marcus. 2000. "Sharing power: dams, indigenous peoples, and ethnic minorities." *Report Prepared for World Commission on Dams Thematic Reviews*, Social Issues I.2. Accessed February 28, 2015. www.forestpeoples.org/sites/fpp/files/publication/2010/08/damsipsethnicminoritiesnov00eng.pdf.

Davis, Danielle C. 2013. "Land in the second decade: the evolution of indigenous property rights and the energy industry in the United States and Brazil." *Energy L. J.* 34: 667–686.

Donovan, Lauren. 2014. "Tribe sees election as the most significant." *Bismarck Tribune*, October 14. Accessed February 28, 2015. http://bismarcktribune.com/bakken/tribe-sees-election-as-the-most-significant/article_71941d8e-5423-11e4-b572-f7c174003c7c.html.

Dreveskracht, Ryan. 2011. "Native nation economic development via the implementation of solar projects: how to make them work." *Wash. & Lee L. Rev.* 68: 27–112.

First Peoples Worldwide. 2013. *Indigenous Rights Risk Report for the Extractive Industry (U.S.)*. Accessed February 28, 2015. www.firstpeoples.org/images/uploads/R1K Report2.pdf.

Fisher, William F. 1999. "Going under: indigenous peoples and the struggle against large dams." *Cultural Survival Quarterly* 23(3). Accessed February 28, 2015. www.culturalsurvival.org/publications/cultural-survival-quarterly/brazil/going-under-indigenous-peoples-and-struggle-against-.

Foster, George K. 2012. "Foreign investment and indigenous peoples: options for promoting equilibrium between economic development and indigenous rights." *Mich. J. Int'l L.* 33: 627–691.

Global Justice Ecology Project. 2015. *Statement on Indigenous Rights by the Indigenous Environmental Network*. Accessed April 29, 2015. http://globaljusticeecology.org/indigenous-peoples/

Greenhowe, Jada Scott. 2013. "Reservations please! Could energy development on Native American land be America's most valuable resource?" *Pitt. J. Envtl. Pub. Health L.* 7: 279–304.

Greenspan, Emily. 2014. "A new threat to Peru's Indigenous Peoples' Consultation Law: United Nations visit highlights importance of continued negotiation with indigenous peoples." *The Politics of Poverty: Ideas and Analysis from Oxfam's Policy Experts*, January

16. Accessed February 28, 2015. http://politicsofpoverty.oxfamamerica.org/2014/01/a-new-threat-to-perus-indigenous-peoples-consultation-law/.

Guruswamy, Lakshman. 2004. "Energy justice and sustainable development." *Colo. J. Int'l Envtl. L. & Pol'y* 21:231–276.

——2011. "Energy poverty." *Ann. Rev. Envt. & Resources* 36: 139–161.

Henderson, Chris. 2013. *Aboriginal Power: Clean Energy and the Future of Canada's First Peoples*. Erin, Ont.: Rainforest Editions.

Hernández-Truyol, Berta Esperanza. 2014. "Culture clashes: indigenous populations and globalization – the case of Belo Monte." *Seattle J. for Soc. Just.* 12: 775–820.

James-Eluyode, Jide. 2012. "Collective rights to lands and resources: exploring the comparative natural resource revenue allocation model of Native American tribes and Indigenous African tribes." *Ariz. J. Int'l & Comp. L.* 29: 177.

Jampolsky, Jacquelyn Amour. 2012. "Activism is the new black: demonstrating the benefits of celebrity activism through James Cameron's campaign against the Belo Monte Dam." 23 *Colo. J. Int'l Envtl. L. & Pol'y* 23: 227–256.

——2014. "Integrated resource management planning with the Ute Mountain Ute: property, place, and governable space." PhD diss., University of Colorado, Boulder (unpublished on file with the author).

Kaushik, Tara S. 2012. "Tribal lands: an emerging market for renewable energy development." *Renewable Energy World Online*, April 25. Accessed February 28, 2015. www.renewableenergyworld.com/rea/news/article/2012/04/tribal-lands-an-emerging-market-for-renewable-energy-development.

Kimerling, Judith. 2007. "Transnational operations, bi-national injustice: Chevrontexaco and Indigenous Huaorani and Kichwa in the Amazon Rainforest in Ecuador." *Am. Indian L. Rev.* 31: 445–503.

Konne, Barisere Rachel. 2014. "Inadequate monitoring and enforcement in the Nigerian oil industry: the case of Shell and Ogoniland." *Cornell Int'l L.J.* 47: 181–204.

Kronk, Elizabeth Ann. 2010. "Alternative energy development in Indian Country: lighting the way for the seventh generation." *Idaho L. Rev.* 46 :449–471.

——2012. "Tribal energy resource agreements: the unintended 'Great Mischief for Indian Energy Development' and the resulting need for reform." 29 *Pace Envtl. L. Rev.* 29: 811–859.

LaDuke, Winona. 2014. "Land thievery redux." *Indian Country Today*, October 10. Accessed February 28, 2015. http://indiancountrytodaymedianetwork.com/2014/10/10/land-thievery-redux-bakken-oil-leases-and-money-mismanagement-157271.

Lee, Tanya. 2014. *Attempt to Expel Indigenous Peoples from Proposed Baram Dam Site Denounced By Human Rights Group* (October 22). International Rivers Press Release. Accessed February 28, 2015. www.internationalrivers.org/resources/8430.

Missouri River Resources. 2013. "Home." Accessed February 28, 2015. www.missouririverresources.com/.

Murdoch, Sierra Crane. 2013. "On Indian land criminals can get away with almost anything." *The Atlantic*, February 22. Accessed February 28, 2015. www.theatlantic.com/national/archive/2013/02/on-indian-land-criminals-can-get-away-with-almost-anything/273391/.

Navajo Nation Human Rights Commission. 2012. *Resolution*. NNHRCMay-18-12. Accessed February 28, 2015. www.nnhrc.navajo-nsn.gov/docs/NewsRptResolution/Resolutions/NNHRCMAY-18-12.pdf.

Partnership for the Relief of Energy Poverty. 2010. *Ayavari, Peru | The Other Third*. Accessed February 28, 2015. www.colorado.edu/theotherthird/projects/ayaviri-peru.

Pember, Mary Annette. 2014. "Will Keystone XL pipeline pump sexual violence into South Dakota." *Indian Country Today*, January 27. Accessed February 28, 2015. http://indiancountrytodaymedianetwork.com/2014/01/27/will-keystone-xl-pipeline-pump-sexual-violence-south-dakota-153280.

Royster, Judith, Michael Blumm, and Elizabeth Ann Kronk. 2013. *Native American Natural Resources Law, Cases and Materials*. 3rd edn. Durham, NC: Carolina Academic Press.

Sullivan, Bethany. 2010. "Changing winds: reconfiguring the legal framework for renewable-energy development." *Ariz. L. Rev.* 52: 823–852.

Tanana, Heather, and John Ruple. 2012. "Energy development in Indian Country: working within the realm of Indian law and moving towards collaboration." *Utah Envtl. L. Rev.* 32:1–53.

Tarasi, David, Christian Alexander, Julie Nania, Bob Gregory, Naree Chan, and Doug Vilsack. 2011. "18,000 Americans without electricity: illuminating and solving the Navajo energy crisis." 22 *Colo. J. Int'l Envtl. L. & Pol'y* 22(2): 263–282.

Thompson, Jonathan. 2010. "The Ute Paradox – a small Colorado tribe takes control of its energy resources and becomes a billion-dollar corporation – but has it gone too far?" *High Country News*, July 12. Accessed February 28, 2015. www.hcn.org/issues/42.12/the-ute-paradox.

——2013. "Coal's gasping on the Colorado Plateau." *High Country News*, February 28. Accessed February 28, 2015. www.hcn.org/blogs/goat/coals-gasping-on-the-colorado-plateau.

Tsosie, Rebecca. 2009. "Climate change, sustainability and globalization: charting the future of indigenous environmental self-determination." *Envtl. & Energy L. & Pol'y J.* 4: 188–255.

United Nations Human Rights Council. 2009. Resolution 10/4, *Human Rights and Climate Change*. A/64/53 (March 25). Accessed February 28, 2015. http://undocs.org/A/64/53.

United Nations Office of the High Commissioner for Human Rights. 2012. *The Corporate Responsibility to Protect Human Rights: An Interpretive Guide*. Accessed February 28, 2015. www.ohchr.org/Documents/Publications/HR.PUB.12.2_En.pdf.

United States Department of Energy. 2013. *Tribal Energy Programs: Wind Turbines*. Accessed February 28, 2015. www1.eere.energy.gov/tribalenergy/guide/wind_turbines.html.

United States Senate Comm. on Indian Affairs. 2009. *Indian Energy and Energy Efficiency Concept Paper*. September 10. Accessed February 28, 2015. http://indian.senate.gov/issues/upload/Indian-Energy-and-Energy-Efficiency-Concept-Paper.pdf.

World Bank. 2010. *Indigenous Peoples – Indigenous Peoples Still Among Poorest in World, but Progress Reported in Some Countries*. Accessed February 28, 2015. http://go.worldbank.org/IEJYK3VL00.

Part 2
Conceptual foundations

4 Global energy justice

Lakshman Guruswamy

First, this chapter will delineate the existence and extent of energy poverty, and how the lack of beneficial energy prevents and negates development. Second, it offers a definition of justice that applies to international societies and institutions. Finally, this chapter will argue that global justice enjoins that energy poverty should be addressed through affordable sustainable energy technologies (ASETs).

Modern industrialized societies – the high energy world – are built upon the ubiquitous availability of energy for domestic, commercial, and industrial uses. Energy enables transportation, food production, information technology, national security, health care, cooking, lighting, mechanical power, chemical production, and general economic growth.

In stark contrast to this high energy world, nearly one-third of the world's population still lacks access to appropriate forms of energy adequate to meet their basic needs. Globally, around 2.8 billion people (the "Other Third" or "Energy Poor" [EP]) have little or no access to beneficial energy for: (a) cooking and heating; (b) clean water; (c) sanitation; (d) illumination; and (e) basic mechanical power essential for performing a variety of domestic and commercial functions.

More than 95 percent of the Energy Poor live either in sub-Saharan Africa or developing Asia, predominantly (84 percent) in rural areas, and they cannot be situated within simplistic sociopolitical divisions of the world, such as the WTO's categories of developing and developed countries. For example, there is a subset of nations within the developing world, called the least developed countries (LDCs). In 2009, the LDCs consisted of 48 countries and 767 million people located primarily in Africa and Asia. The LDCs have been officially identified by the UN as "least developed" in light of their low income (three-year average gross national income [GNI] per capita of less than US$992), weak human assets (low nutrition, high mortality, lack of school enrollment, and high illiteracy), high economic vulnerability, exposure to natural shocks and disasters, prevalence of trade shocks, economic smallness, and economic remoteness.[1] While 28 percent of people in developing countries lack access to electricity, the number in the LDCs is 79 percent (Legros et al. 2009, 10).

These LDCs may be contrasted to another subset of developing countries, sometimes called newly industrialized countries (NICs) or advanced developing countries, that have made tremendous economic strides in recent decades. This category includes the BRIC countries of Brazil, Russia, India, and China (Thompson 2014), South Africa, and the "Asian Tigers" of Taiwan, Singapore, Hong Kong, and South Korea (Barro 1998). It also includes Thailand, Indonesia, Malaysia, and the Philippines, which are following the trajectory of exceptional economic growth and rapid industrialization of the Asian Tigers and have consequently been dubbed "Tiger Cub Economies" (Makabenta 2014).

However, access to clean energy or electricity is not uniform within NICs. The EP are a significant population in NICs like India, and to a lesser extent China. The EP in these countries suffer from a dearth of energy in their households, are denied the chance of making a living whether by way of agriculture, industry, or crafts, and lack energy for their hospitals and schools serving their communities.

Cooking

A disturbingly large swath of humanity relies on biomass-generated fire as their principal source of energy. These fires are made by burning animal dung, waste, crop residues, rotted wood, other forms of harmful biomass, or raw coal. The smoke from biomass-fueled cookfires leads to the premature deaths by respiratory infection of 3.5 million people annually, primarily women and children. Moreover, in the LDCs, 715 million people rely on solid fuels, and only 74 million people – a mere 9 percent of the population – have access to electric, gas, or kerosene for cooking. Wood is by far the most important fuel, with 73 percent of the population in LDCs relying upon it for cooking (Legros et al. 2009).

The EP that rely on biomass fuel generally cook over an open fire, or with some other form of traditional stove. This process is exceedingly inefficient, as only about 18 percent of the energy from the fire transfers to the pot (Warwick and Doig 2004). Depending on the type of fuel and stove being used, indoor air pollution can contain a variety of dangerous pollutants, such as CO, nitrogen and sulfur oxides, formaldehyde, carcinogens, and small particulate matter (World Health Organization 2006, 10). The US Environmental Protection Agency (EPA) sets a limit of 150 micrograms per cubic meter for small particulates in the United States, yet WHO reports that a typical 24-hour mean level for homes burning biomass fuels is between 300 to 3,000 micrograms per cubic meter (World Health Organization 2006, 10). This results in pollution levels that are far more deadly in EP countries than the levels of atmospheric pollution allowed in developed nations. According to WHO, exposure to high concentrations of indoor air pollution presents one of the ten most important threats to public health worldwide, resulting in diseases such as pneumonia, chronic pulmonary disease, lung cancer, asthma, and acute respiratory infections (World Health Organization 2007).

Women and children are disproportionately affected by biomass cooking. Women are traditionally responsible for cooking and child care in the home, and they spend more time inhaling the polluted air that is trapped indoors. Thus, women and children have the highest exposure to indoor air pollution and suffer more than anyone from these negative health effects (Global Alliance for Clean Cookstoves 2012). Specifically, the risk for child pneumonia increases 2.3 times in homes that burn solid fuels for cooking, and women are about twice as likely to be afflicted with chronic pulmonary disease than men in homes using solid fuels (Legros et al. 2009). Beyond suffering adverse health effects, women and children are also disproportionately affected by the time constraints needed for collecting fuel. Women are burdened with the majority of the work to collect fuel, which can present other serious risks such increased chance of injury and sexual violence (Shannon 2011).

Research has identified emissions from the burning of biomass as a significant cause of anthropogenic global warming in the form of black carbon (Ramanathan and Carmichael 2008, 221; Service 2008). Once in the atmosphere black carbon can eventually make its way to polar ice. The presence of overlying black carbon may result in ice retaining more heat, leading to increased melting and further global warming. Reducing the generation of black carbon would reduce its negative effects on albedo, or reflectivity, of polar ice (Hansen and Nazarenko 2004, 428). Furthermore, unlike GHGs, ambient black carbon dissipates in a very short period of time. Thus, helping to move one-third of the global population away from biomass burning will have the effect of reducing global warming more immediately than merely reducing carbon dioxide emissions.

The dependence on biomass for cooking can be addressed in two ways. First, agricultural waste or animal dung can be converted to other useable forms of energy, for example using biogas digesters to create better fuels. Biodigesters are more fully discussed in Chapter 14 of this volume.

The other way to address indoor air pollution is to increase access to improved cookstoves. The Global Alliance for Clean Cookstoves is an initiative, led by the UN Foundation, supporting large-scale adoption of clean and safe household cooking solutions as a way to save lives, improve livelihoods, empower women, and reduce climate change emissions. The Alliance's founding partners have set a goal of enabling an additional 100 million homes to adopt clean and efficient stoves and fuels by 2020 (Global Alliance for Clean Cookstoves 2012).

Improved cookstoves can utilize a number of different fuel types, but in general are designed for efficient combustion and reduced particulate generation. According to the Alliance's website, clean cookstoves can cost anywhere from US$15–$150 depending on the model and region in which it is assembled, again demonstrating a relatively low cost–benefit ratio, and presenting a timely opportunity to address the needs of the EP.

Lighting

The EP also lack access to lighting. Lighting is essential to human progress and without it "mankind would be comparatively inactive about one-half of its lifetime" (Luckiesh 1920). The scorching sun and withering temperatures in the LDCs prevent agricultural labor during the daytime and reduce productivity, and the absence of artificial lights severely impedes working at night. Without lighting it is not possible for students to do homework after nightfall. The absence of lighting creates physical insecurity, particularly for women and children, while venturing out in the darkness, and almost entirely prevents commercial activity after dark. Almost 500 million people rely on kerosene for illumination (Lam et al. 2012). The hazards of kerosene, such as fires, explosions, and poisonings resulting from children ingesting it, are extensively documented, and children and women are disproportionately affected (Lam et al. 2012, 423; Peck 2011, 1096). There is evidence implicating kerosene with other ailments including the impairing of lung functions, asthma, cancer, and tuberculosis (Lam et al. 2012, 399–401, 412–423). The use of kerosene and candles is costly. Households often spend 10–25 percent of their income on kerosene (*The Economist* 2012, 14). Over US$36 billion is spent on kerosene annually, US$10 billion of which is spent in sub-Saharan Africa (*The Economist* 2012, 14). The use of solar lamps to address the lack of lighting is discussed in Chapter 15 of this volume.

Drinking water and sanitation

Lack of access to clean drinking water and sanitation are two interconnected, deadly issues facing the EP. Worldwide, approximately one in eight people – 748 million in total – lack access to safe water supplies (WHO/UNICEF 2014). While the MDG on sustainable access to drinking water was reached in 2010, with the threshold of 88 percent of the world's population having access to improved water sources reached, the sanitation MDG remains off track with only 64 percent of people having access to improved sanitation (short of the aim of 75 percent by 2015) (WHO/UNICEF 2014). For preventing diseases such as diarrhoea, tuberculosis, cholera, and other water-borne diseases, basic sanitation is just as important as fresh drinking water. Two and a half billion people lack access to improved sanitation, including one billion people who have no facilities at all (WHO/UNICEF 2014). As a result, 3.4 million people die from water-related disease each year; this number is nearly equivalent to the entire population of Los Angeles and many of these deaths are those of children (Prüss-Üstün et al. 2008, table 1). Other consequences from the lack of clean drinking water and basic sanitation include crop failure in irrigated fields, livestock death, and environmental damage. Energy is necessary to alleviate these problems by collecting, transporting, and distributing clean water, powering water treatment facilities, facilitating in-home water treatment (through boiling, for example), and constructing and powering sanitation facilities (International Energy Agency 2012). However, ASETs such as small-scale sustainable power grids and water transport mechanisms could help to remediate these issues.

Most of the 2.5 billion people without access to adequate sanitation, including the 1.2 billion people without any facilities at all, live in LDCs in rural Africa and Asia. Accordingly, lack of sanitation affects the EP in rural areas more dramatically than those in urban areas. However, the issue is becoming increasingly urban; of the 60 million people added to the world's towns and cities every year, most occupy impoverished slums and shanty-towns with no sanitation facilities (WSSCC 2008).

As with many other issues faced by the EP, children are intensely affected by lack of access to clean drinking water and sanitation facilities. Nearly one in five child deaths – about 1.5 million each year – are due to diarrhoea, which is often caused by unclean drinking water and inadequate sanitation facilities (WSSCC 2008). These deaths occur primarily in LDCs, and many of the children there who suffer from diarrhoea also suffer from acute malnutrition, a condition that is exacerbated by diarrhoea. Child diarrhoea is a serious global issue, as it painfully kills more young children than AIDS, malaria, and measles combined (WHO/ UNICEF 2009).

Energy is necessary to power water treatment and sanitation facilities to provide safe drinking water supplies and adequate sanitation facilities. Within the home, too, clean energy can provide people with the ability to boil water. While extending large-scale electricity grids to rural communities is often impracticable at the outset, decentralized mini grids based on solar, wind, and biomass-generated electricity comprise ASETs that can provide power to the EP for water treatment, sanitation facilities, and in-home water boiling (Visagie and Prasad 2006). Another example of an ASET that has been used to combat these issues is the implementation of "dry composting latrines" in Calchuapa, El Salvador. These latrines are fairly simple, inexpensive mechanisms that utilize sawdust in combination with human manure to produce a rich fertilizer that can be used on crops after six to eight months (Trees, Water & People 2015).

Though the MDG for access to clean drinking water has been reached, several factors indicate that the water crisis is going to worsen over time. Over the last century, water use grew more than twice as fast as the population, and this trend is predicted to continue (Zabarenko 2011). Population growth and urbanization are two factors stressing the global water supply. Additionally, as the effects of climate change intensify, the water cycle will change and water will become increasingly hard to come by, especially as rainfall is already irregular and water sources are already scarce in many LDCs (Bruckner 2012, 1). Accordingly, it is crucial that ASETs be implemented to reduce need for clean water and sanitation among the EP.

Mechanical power

According to the United Nations Development Programme, "[t]he 2.5 billion people without access to modern energy services still depend on unimproved versions of mechanical power equipment that inefficiently use human or animal power to meet their energy needs" (Bates et al. 2009, 2). Mechanical power refers to "the transmission of energy through a solid structure to impart motion, such as for pumping, pushing, and other similar needs" (Legros et al. 2009). In a practical sense, this means either using human and animal power, or "modern" energy sources such as wind, solar, gas, or electrical power to complete daily tasks. The energy services that stem from access to mechanical power include agriculture (irrigation, farming, and processing), water pumping, transportation, and small-scale industry (Bates et al. 2009, 2). Unfortunately, specific data quantifying exactly how many of the EP in the LDCs lack access to mechanical power is wanting, and as of 2009 only three LDCs had data to report on access to mechanical power (Bates et al. 2009, 3). It is clear, however, that access to mechanical power is a problem for the EP, and that it has begun to receive attention on the international energy agenda (Bates et al. 2009, 11–14).

For the EP, the inability to access modern forms of mechanical energy results in the use of inefficient human and animal power to satisfy their most basic needs. To have water for drinking, women (primarily) must perform the arduous task of walking to the natural source, and collecting it for use in the household. Depending on the season, in parts of Africa, this can require spending up to four hours per day collecting water. In Uganda, women spend an average of 660 hours per year (about a month's time) collecting water. Even a very simple ASET, such as a water pump, could drastically cut collection time. Less time spent collecting water will also aid development and gender equality by allowing women to spend the time saved on other productive activities – whether they be economic, educational, or domestic (Bates et al. 2009, 2).

While water pumps are widely used in parts of the developing world, they are most commonly operated through the use of human power (by either hand or foot) and, in many cases, by women and children. These pumps are physically demanding and time consuming. In some locations, it may be appropriate to employ windmill, water wheel, or photovoltaic solar technologies to ease the burden caused by manual pumping. Selecting an effective ASET-based pump for lifting potable water requires investigating the groundwater depth, water characteristics, capacity demand, preferred method of operation, and maintenance in the target region. Fortunately, there are numerous non-electric or fossil fuel based pumps that are up to the task (Stewart 2003).

Another example of how ASETs can be used to provide useful mechanical energy involves the method for processing grain. Before grain can be consumed or sold, the EP must dry it in the sun or with a handheld fan, and then grind it by hand or with a flail. Because post harvest processing is "arguably the main factor in helping farmers increase their income," simple technologies such as watermills could drastically cut the amount of physical labor needed, increase production, and improve both food security and profit margins for farmers (Watkins 2006). Although improving access to some basic services achieved through mechanical power can be addressed through expanding access to electricity, this energy deficit can also be addressed through non-electric, non-fossil fuel ASETs, such as hand operated grinding and pounding equipment.

The right to sustainable development and access to energy

The problem of access to energy relegates the EP to a life of desperation that affronts international concepts of justice and sustainable development (SD) which is more fully discussed in Chapter 6. The concept of SD was originally formulated by the World Commission on Sustainable Development, also known as the Brundtland Commission, as a distributional principle to address the needs of the world's poor while maintaining environmental integrity. SD mandates that global environmental protection must be pursued in tandem with economic and social development.

International law, as expressed particularly in the treaty titled *UN Framework Convention on Climate Change*[2] unequivocally institutionalizes SD. International law is the law governing relations between legally sovereign co-equal states and treaties are the primary way in which international law is created. Treaties are written agreements between two or more states, governed by international law, creating or restating legal rights and duties. The *Vienna Convention on the Law of Treaties*[3] deals comprehensively with questions concerning treaties which are also described as conventions, agreements, protocols, covenants, and pacts.

The UNFCCC is the most important and extensively adopted energy treaty, having obtained 194 instruments of ratification. Article 3(1) of the UNFCCC states that the Parties have a right to and should promote sustainable development, and that economic development is essential for adopting measures to address climate change, while Article 3(2) affirms that full consideration be given to the special circumstances of developing countries. Parties are required to protect the climate system on the basis of equity and in accordance with their common but differentiated responsibilities and respective capacities. The principle of common but differentiated responsibility, which is found in Principle 7 of the *Rio Declaration on Environment and Development* and conclusively embodied in Articles 3(1) and 4(1), affirms the responsibility of the developed country parties to take the lead in combating climate change and the adverse effects thereof (UN General Assembly 1992).

The UNFCCC coalesced with another widely accepted treaty, the *Convention on Biological Diversity* (CBD)[4] by forcefully and unequivocally expressing the developmental priority of SD. Article 4(7) of the UNFCCC and Article 20(4) of the CBD re-affirm in unison that parties "will take fully into account that economic and social development and poverty eradication are the first and overriding priorities of the developing country Parties." Specifically, therefore, energy poverty can only be addressed within a framework of distributive justice, as part of the overall right to economic and social development established by the foundational norm of SD.

In Chapter 6 of this book Professor Ved Nanda delineates the concept of sustainable development, and tracks the actions taken by the United Nations (UN) to address access to energy. The UN declared 2012 as the International Year of Sustainable Energy for All, and the entire decade as the Decade of Sustainable Energy for All (UN General Assembly 2011). Moreover, the UN announced a goal of universal, primarily electrical, energy access, by 2030 (United Nations 2011). World leaders at the UN Conference on Sustainable Development 2012, also called the Rio+20 CSD, endorsed the outcome document of the conference, containing these goals, entitled *The Future We Want* (UN General Assembly 2012). The Open Working Group (OWG), established by the Rio+20 CSD to better articulate its goals, submitted its report in July 2014 (UN General Assembly 2014). Among the 18 goals enumerated by the OWG is a stand-alone goal on energy (Goal number 7) calling for access to affordable, reliable, sustainable, and modern energy for all (UN General Assembly 2014). This energy has been understood as electricity.

John Rawls and sustainable development

John Rawls' foundational concept of international justice provides a moral justification for SD. Rawls discusses a "realistic utopia" grounded in sociopolitical, institutional, and psychological reality (Rawls 2001, 106). This section attempts to reconcile Rawls' ideas with present realities insofar as they apply to SD and the EP.

Rawls' "original position," a thought experiment expounded in *A Theory of Justice* and developed in numerous other works, envisioned a collection of negotiators from liberal democratic societies. The negotiators assembled behind a veil of ignorance, shorn of any knowledge that might be the basis of self-interested bias – such as knowledge of their gender, wealth, race, ethnicity, abilities, and general social circumstances. Rawls explains that the purpose of such a negotiation was to arrive at legitimate principles of justice under fair conditions – hence "justice as fairness" (Rawls 2001, 3).

In *The Law of Peoples*, concerning justice and international law, Rawls extends his theories from liberal democratic states to "decent" peoples living in non-democratic international societies. Rawls envisions such "well-ordered hierarchical societies" to be

> non-liberal societies whose basic institutions meet specified conditions of political right and justice (including the right of citizens to play a substantial role, such as participating in associations and groups making political decisions) and lead their citizens to honor a reasonably just law for the Society of Peoples.
>
> (Rawls 2001, 106)

Well-ordered societies must satisfy a number of criteria: they must eschew aggressive aims as a means of achieving their objectives, honor basic human rights dealing with life, liberty, and freedom, and possess a system of law imposing bona fide moral duties and obligations, as distinct from human rights. Moreover, they must have law and judges to uphold common ideas of justice (Rawls 2001, 3).

Rawls demonstrated how the law of peoples may be developed out of liberal ideas of justice similar to, but more general than, the idea of "justice as fairness" presented in *A Theory of Justice* (Rawls 2001, 3). Just as in the original position, here the bargainers in the so-called second original position are representatives of peoples who are shorn of knowledge about their people's resources, wealth, power, and the like. Behind the veil of ignorance, the representatives of peoples

– not states, since states lack moral capacity – develop the principles of justice that will govern relations between them: *The Law of Peoples*.

It should be noted that there is a difference between John Rawls' theories of domestic and international justice. The principles of domestic distributive justice espoused by Rawls in *A Theory of Justice* did not apply to the international sphere. A pivotal reason for this is that the international community does not possess the basic institutions of a liberal democratic society necessary to institute and implement distributive justice. The machinery of government, consisting of a legislature that can make laws, an executive that implements such laws, and courts with compulsory jurisdiction that interpret and apply the laws of the state, does not exist on a global level. These factors were among the reasons that his book is titled *The Law of Peoples* rather than the law of nations or states.

Rawls emphasized the need for global order and stability over global distributive justice. Once the duty to assist burdened peoples is satisfied, there are no further requirements on economic distribution within Rawls' *The Law of Peoples*: inequalities across national borders are of no political concern as such. Individuals around the world may suffer greatly from bad luck, and may be haunted by spiritual emptiness. The practical goal of Rawls' *The Law of Peoples* is the elimination of the great evils of human history: unjust war and oppression, religious persecution and the denial of liberty of conscience, starvation and poverty, genocide and mass murder. The limits of this ambition mean that there will be much in the world to which Rawls' political philosophy offers no reconciliation (Wenar 2012).

Rawls seeks to determine the principles of cooperation for such "well-ordered peoples." Rawls posits that non-ideal conditions cannot adequately be addressed unless principles of justice are determined for ideal conditions. Otherwise, it is impossible to know what kind of just society to aim to establish and the necessary means to do so (Rawls 2001). A "realistic utopia," as Rawls prefers to call his theory, is an aspiration that does not reflect the existing reality of international law and relations.

Rawls emphasizes the crucial importance of peoples rather than states because of a people's capacity for "moral motives" that is lacking in the bureaucratic machinery of a state (Rawls 2001). Samuel Freeman correctly observes that a "people" for Rawls is a philosophical construct. It is an abstract conception needed to work out principles of justice for a particular subject – in this case, relations among different well-ordered liberal and "decent" societies (Feldman 2007, 1038). Rawls is not talking then about a people regarded as an ethnic or religious group (e.g. Slavs, Jews, Kurds) who are not members of the same society. Rather, a "people" consists of members of the same well-ordered society who are united under, and whose relations are governed by, a political constitution and basic structure. A people is envisioned as having effective political control over a territory that its members govern, and within which their basic social institutions take root. In contrast to a state, however, a people possesses a "moral nature" that stems from the effective sense of justice for its individual members. A people's members may have "common sympathies" for any number of non-requisite reasons, including shared language, ethnic roots, or religion. The most basic reason for members' common sympathies, however, lies in their shared history as members of the same society and consequent shared conception of justice and the common good.

The conclusion most pertinent to SD and the EP that Rawls elucidates is the duty of liberal democratic and decent hierarchical peoples to assist "burdened societies" to the point where burdened societies are enabled to join the "Society of Peoples." It is of particular pertinence that Rawls' duty of assistance does not absolve developing country governments of their obligation to take appropriate action. Rawls' concept of "peoples" has been criticized. Among his more cogent critics, Pogge (2004, 1743) and Nussbaum (2006, 236–244) question the validity of the distinction between peoples and states, and the difficulties of defining peoples. They claim their criticisms assume importance in any attempt to realize the "Society of Peoples" Rawls envisions as his realistic utopia. Such criticisms have actually been anticipated by Rawls, who pointed out that he eschewed the "state" as a polity because of its historical Hobbesian connotations in "realist" international political theory, which suggests that the power of states can be limited only by the states, and not by moral or legal constraints (Rawls 2001).

Paradoxically, the legal and political acceptance of SD by the community of nations may be seen as refuting Rawls' distrust of states at the theoretical level to the extent that the existing international legal framework of SD expressed for example, in the UNFCCC and CBD, lends itself to the Rawlsian ideal. Moreover, Rawls remains relevant at the practical and functional level, when it comes to the implementation of SD. As is more fully discussed in the next section, dealing with climate change and SD, the principle of SD has been invoked and erroneously applied to the NICs while the EP in the LDCs have been ignored.

Rawlsian sustainable development as it applies to the EP

A starting point for analyzing the international phenomena of the EP must begin with the fact that the EP should be identified primarily as "burdened societies" in the Rawlsian sense. Rawlsian principles will ensure that SD is applied to the EP. Furthermore, their special status as burdened societies must be highlighted rather than hidden. Additionally, it is important to draw attention to Rawls' suggestion on how the duty of assistance should be discharged, bearing in mind his particular conclusion that merely dispensing funds will not suffice to rectify basic and political injustice (Rawls 2001).

Rawls' warning that the mere distribution of funds will not rectify the targeted problems now becomes of special relevance. Many rulers, Rawls points out, have been callous about the well-being of their own peoples (Rawls 2001), and transferring resources to national governments does not ensure that they will be applied to the problems of the EP. For this reason, Rawls advocates that assistance be tied to the advancement of human rights. Tying assistance to human rights will also embrace the status of women who often are oppressed. It has, moreover, been shown that the removal of discrimination against women has resulted in major economic and social progress (Yunus and Weber 2007).

A realistic attempt to remedy energy poverty should be alive to the serious problems posed by sovereignty, and it should try to overcome them. While there are limited ways of bypassing states where they are impediments to energy justice, the irremovable fact is that sovereignty is the basis of international law. Aid, assistance or empowerment of the Energy Poor cannot ignore national sovereignty. Under our present system of international law and governance, SD requires that developed countries play a dominant part in alleviating the condition of the EP. It also invokes the need for action by national governments. Justice requires both that assistance be given and that such assistance be properly administered. The failure of foreign aid has been debated, and better ways of granting assistance must be found. Justice also requires that national governments take on the task of addressing the EP. It is not possible to lay the blame on avaricious rich countries alone.

Conclusion

Access to electricity as envisioned by the UN must remain the laudable final objective. But the daunting additional costs of electricity, which requires an estimated US$17 trillion (Bazilian and Pielke 2013, 77), and the time it will take to do so – realistically 30 years – will shunt the EP into limbo unless interim measures are also taken. Affordable Sustainable Energy Technologies (ASETs) of the kind referred to above for cooking, lighting, water, sanitation, and mechanical power seek to bridge the gap between the capital-intensive advanced technologies of the developed world, like electricity, and the traditional subsistence technologies of the EP. Beneficial energy, based on ASETs described above, are the intermediate rungs on the ladder of energy. The purpose of ASETs is to free the EP from the oppressive impacts of unhealthy and unreliable energy access, and to facilitate sustainable development in the LDCs.

Notes

1 For a full explanation of the criteria used see www.un.org/en/development/desa/policy/cdp/ldc/ldc_list.pdf.
2 New York, 9 May 1992, *United Nations Treaty Series* vol. 1771, No. 30822, p. 165.
3 Vienna, 23 May 1969, *United Nations Treaty Series* vol. 1155, No. 7310, p. 331.
4 Rio de Janeiro, 5 June 1992, *United Nations Treaty Series* vol. 1760, No. 30619, p. 79.

References

Barro, Robert J. 1998. "The East Asian Tigers have plenty to roar about." *Business Week*, April 27.

Bates, Liz, Steven Hunt, Smail Khennas, and Nararya Sastrawinata. 2009. *Expanding Energy Access in Developing Countries: The Role of Mechanical Power*. Warwickshire: Practical Action Publishing Ltd.

Bazilian, Morgan and Roger Pielke. 2013. "Making energy access meaningful." *Issues in Science and Technology* 29(4): 74–79.

Bruckner, Matthias. 2012. *Climate Change Vulnerability and the Identification of Least Developed Countries.* New York: United Nations Development Programme.

Feldman, Noah. 2007. "Cosmopolitan law?" *Yale Law Journal* 116(5): 1022–1070.

Global Alliance for Clean Cookstoves. 2012. *Clean Cookstoves can Save Lives and Empower Women.* Accessed January 11, 2014. https://cleancookstoves.org/binary-data/RESOURCE/file/000/000/278-1.pdf.

Hansen, James and Larissa Nazarenko. 2004. "Soot climate forcing via snow and ice albedos." *Proceedings of the Natural Academy of Sciences* 101(2): 423–428. doi: 10.1073/pnas.2237157100.

International Energy Agency. 2012. "Water for energy: is energy becoming a thirstier resource?" In *World Energy Outlook 2012*, 501–528. Paris: International Energy Agency.

Lam, N., K. Smith, A. Gautier, and M. Bates. 2012. "Kerosene: a review of household uses and their hazards in low and middle income countries." *Journal of Toxicology and Environmental Health* 15(6): 396–432. doi: 10.1080/10937404.2012.710134.

Legros, Gwénaëlle, Ines Havet, Nigel Bruce, and Sophie Bonjour. 2009. *The Energy Access Situation in Developing Countries: A Review Focusing on Least Developed Countries and Sub Saharan Africa.* New York: United Nations Development Programme: Environment and Energy Group, and World Health Organization.

Luckiesh, Matthew. 1920. *Artificial Light: Its Influence Upon Civilization*, 8th edn. New York: Library of Alexandria.

Makabenta, Yen. 2014. "No miracle, just a tiger cub economy." *The Manila Times*, May 26.

Nussbaum, Martha Craven. 2006. *Frontiers of Justice: Disability, Nationality, Species Membership.* Cambridge, Mass.: Belknap Press.

Peck, M. 2011. "Epidemiology of burns throughout the world, Part 1: distribution and risk factors." *Burns* 37(7): 1087–1100. doi: 10.1016/j.burns.2011.06.005.

Pogge, Thomas W. 2004. "The incoherence between Rawls' theories of justice." *Fordham Law Review* 72(5): 1739–1759.

Prüss-Üstün, Annette, Robert Bos, Fiona Gore, and Jamie Bartram. 2008. *Safer Water, Better Health: Costs, Benefits, and Sustainability of Interventions to Protect and Promote Health.* Geneva: WHO Library.

Ramanathan, V. and G. Carmichael. 2008. "Global and regional climate changes due to black carbon." *Nature Geoscience* 1: 221–227. doi: 10.1038/ngeo156.

Rawls, John. 2001. *The Law of Peoples.* Cambridge, Mass.: Harvard University Press.

Service, R. 2008. "Study fingers soot as major player in global warming." *Science* 319(5871): 1745. doi: 10.1126/science.319.5871.1745.

Shannon, Lisa. 2011. "The rape of Somalia's women is being ignored." *The Guardian*, October 12. www.theguardian.com/commentisfree/2011/oct/11/rape-somalia-women-famine. (accessed January 12, 2015).

Stewart, Ed. 2003. "How to select the proper human-powered pump for potable water." M.S. candidate, Michigan Technological University.

The Economist. 2012. "Solar lighting: lighting the way." *The Economist*, September 1. www.economist.com/node/21560983 (accessed January 12, 2015).

Thompson, Nicole A. 2014. "BRICS: industrialized countries with growing economic power." *Latin Post*, January 2. www.latinpost.com/articles/5436/20140102/brics-industrilized-countries-economic-power.htm (accessed January 12, 2015).

Trees, Water & People. 2015. *Dry Composting Latrines*. Accessed January 11. www.treeswaterpeople.org/programs/dry_composting_latrines/dry_composting_latrines.html.

UN General Assembly. 1992. "Rio Declaration on Environment and Development." In *Report of the United Nations Conference on Environment and Development*, June, 1992. www.un.org/documents/ga/conf151/aconf15126-1 (accessed January 12, 2015).

——. 2011. Resolution 65/151, *International Year of Sustainable Energy for All*. A/RES/65/151 (February 16). http://undocs.org/A/RES/65/151 (accessed January 12, 2015).

——. 2012. Resolution 66/288, *The Future We Want*. A/RES/66/288 (July 27). http://undocs.org/A/RES/66/288 (accessed January 12, 2015).

——. 2014. *Report of the Open Working Group of the General Assembly on Sustainable Development Goals*. A/68/970 (August 12). http://undocs.org/A/68/970 (accessed January 12, 2015).

United Nations. 2011. *Sustainable Energy for All: A Vision Statement by Ban Ki-moon, Secretary-General of the United Nations* (November). www.un.org/wcm/webdav/site/sustainableenergyforall/shared/Documents/SG_Sustainable_Energy_for_All_vision_final_clean.pdf (accessed January 12, 2015).

Visagie, E. and G. Prasad. 2006. *Renewable Energy Technologies for Poverty Alleviation South Africa: Biodiesel and Solar Water Heaters*. South Africa: Energy Research Centre.

Warwick, Hugh and Alison Doig. 2004. *Smoke – The Killer in the Kitchen*. London: ITDG Publishing.

Water Supply and Sanitation Collaborative Council (WSSCC). 2008. *A Guide to Investigating One of the Biggest Scandals of the Last 50 Years*. Geneva: WSSCC.

Watkins, Kevin. 2006. *Beyond Scarcity: Power, Poverty, and the Global Water Crisis*. Edited by United Nations Development Programme. New York: Palgrave MacMillan.

Wenar, Leif. 2012. "John Rawls." In *The Stanford Encyclopedia of Philosophy*, edited by Edward N. Zalta. http://plato.stanford.edu/archives/win2013/entries/rawls/ (accessed January 13, 2015).

WHO/UNICEF Joint Monitoring Programme for Water Supply and Sanitation. 2009. *Diarrhoea: Why Children Are Still Dying and What Can Be Done*. Geneva: WHO Library.

——. 2014. *Progress on Drinking Water and Sanitation: Joint Monitoring Programme Update 2014*. Geneva: WHO Library.

World Health Organization. 2006. *Fuel For Life: Household Energy and Health*. Geneva: WHO Press.

——. 2007. *Indoor Air Pollution Takes Heavy Toll on Health*. Media notes, April 30. www.who.int/mediacentre/news/notes/2007/np20/en/ (accessed January 13, 2015).

Yunus, Muhammad and Karl Weber. 2007. *Creating a World without Poverty: Social Business and the Future of Capitalism*. New York: Public Affairs.

Zabarenko, Deborah. 2011. "Water use rising faster than world population." *Reuters*, October 25. www.reuters.com/article/2011/10/25/us-population-water-idUSTRE79O3WO20111025 (accessed January 13, 2015).

5   Reflections on the moral foundations of a right to energy

E. Christian Brugger

This chapter argues that a *right to energy* is among the basic human rights that guarantee to all people access to goods necessary for living a dignified life.[1] More is necessary to living well than having one's material needs met. But no one whose minimal needs are not met is able to live well. The right to energy bears upon the meeting of these minimal needs.

To call something a right is to say that it is a requirement of justice. Justice aims to secure what is due to people. All people are due what is minimally necessary to living well. Therefore, the provision of necessary material goods such as energy should be organized around the prior aim of facilitating lives that can be lived well. Anyone involved in defending the right to energy must remember that simple access is not the end. The right to energy does not simply secure "stuff"; it secures an irreplaceable material foundation for the realization of more complete expressions of human fulfillment in individuals and communities.

This chapter is structured in three parts. The first part addresses the question: is there a right to energy? Here a working conception of the term "right" is formulated within the wider framework of an account of justice and the common good. It clarifies the meaning of the concept "a right to energy" with special emphasis on the object (or *res*) being rendered by the right. The second part asks: does a right to energy give rise to a claim of the Energy Poor upon the energy rich based upon a morally cognizable duty?

The argument attempts to identify who possesses the correlative duty to render the *res* (i.e., to make energy accessible to those who need it). Finally, if there is a right and a duty, how should this claim be satisfied by both the Energy Poor and the energy rich? This third part addresses some factors relevant to making sound judgments about rightful claims of energy deficient peoples.

It is hoped that the complex questions raised by this chapter will lead to more exhaustive scholarly inquiry and discussion, and even, if possible, to answers that may assist in ameliorating the tragic deprivation of energy suffered by so many today.

Part I: is there a "right" to energy?

"Right" and "rights"

To explore the nature and scope of the "right" to energy, one must begin by proposing at least an adequate definition of the concept of rights, a term much debated in the history of philosophy and notoriously slippery in its usage in public discourse. This chapter's discussion is conceptually rooted in classical philosophy. Until the end of the second century BC, the term "right" (in Latin: *ius*) possessed a principally legal connotation. At that century's close, however, it was united with the Stoic notion of the perfect and universal law, the *lex naturalis* (law of nature), and began to be understood as pertaining to something higher than human law; universal justice (Brugger 2004, 34–35). As a philosophical concept, this notion of *right* as *ius naturale* ("natural right") endured unmolested for over seventeen hundred years in the Western canon. The famous definition of the concept of justice by the Roman jurist Ulpian captures the sense: "justice is rendering to each his *ius* ("due") with a constant and firm will" (*iustitia est constans et perpetua voluntas ius suum cuique tribuens*).[2]

Perhaps no one in the Western rights tradition did more to systematize and clarify the meaning of *right* as *ius* than the thirteenth-century Dominican friar, Thomas Aquinas. He did so, however, entirely unacquainted with the subjective sense of the term right most familiar today, that is, right as a quality possessed by or inhering in a person ("my right," "her right") (Tierney 1997, 23). To Aquinas, right (ius) ensured justice between persons (*Summa Theologiae*). Following Aristotle's conception of justice, where individuals receive benefits according to their fair share of merits or virtue, Aquinas held that justice requires some measure of equality and consistency of one thing in reference to another (Aristotle, *Nicomachean Ethics*, V, 1134a 1–6; Thomas Aquinas, *Summa Theologiae*, II-II, q. 57, a.1c). To put it another way, *iustitia* was the condition of rightness that characterizes the proper measure of equality between parties.

It is important to see that the conceptual scope of the one term *ius* extends in two moral directions: to the one who bears a (moral and/or legal) duty and to the one who is the beneficiary of the object of that duty. From the perspective of one *doing* justice, *iustitia* asserts a requirement to render something – what is *due* – to another party; it asserts a duty. In fact, the principal emphasis of *ius* and *iustitia* till the seventeenth century was on duty. Nevertheless, the conception implicitly contains within itself a subjective meaning as well (Finnis 1980, 205). From the perspective of the one to whom an act of justice is rendered, we can say that his or her right/rights (*ius/iuris*) is/are at stake. In the classical conception, a right always correlates with a duty.

Hobbes' influential concept of natural right from *Leviathan* as paradigmatically a liberty (the "liberty each man hath, to use his own power, as he will himself, for the preservation of his own Nature") breaks with the classical correlative notion (Hobbes 1991, 91). Hobbes contrasts "right" (*ius*) to "law" (*lex*); and it is the latter (*lex*) and not the former (*ius*) that entails the notion of duty or obligation (ch. xiv). The ordinary modern idiom of rights does not follow Hobbes all the way down the path to a strict separation. There is, however, a uniquely modern tendency, going back to the eighteenth century, to assert rights as dogmatic claims, as political absolutes, demanding unimpeded application, without careful consideration of the correlative concept of duty.

This chapter does not attempt to resolve scholarly disagreements about the meaning of the term rights in philosophy, law and political science. However, an account of a "right to energy" must begin with an adequate conception of the term rights. The familiar Hobbesian rendering that disproportionately prioritizes the subjective pole of rights (right *as* "something beneficial which a person has … rather than 'that which is just in a given situation'") is not adequate (Finnis 1980, 208). This is because a right to energy, similar to postulated rights of water, food and housing, does no good if it lacks the understanding of the correlative duty to render the object of the right.

By contrast, Hohfeld's schema of the correlative relationship between rights and duties may be flexible enough to articulate a conception of rights in a discussion of the right to energy (1994, 495). This is in part because the assertion or ascription of a right in moral discourse always refers to one or more of four normative *entities* (which, following Finnis, are referred to as "benefits"): a *claim*, *liberty*, *power* or *immunity* (1980, 199–205). Right refers to some benefit enjoyed by a person – "party A" – in virtue of a basic principle or requirement of practical reasonableness (call this "human" or "moral right") or rule derived from more basic principles (call this "positive right"). The correlative benefit is either: (a) a *claim* that a different person – "party B" – should do or render something to party A; (b) a *liberty* relative to party B to do or not to do something; (c) a *power* relative to party B to do something; or (d) an *immunity* from having something done to party B or from the obligation of doing something. Each benefit correlates to a duty by a party other than the benefit-holder.

With respect to a right to energy, this may be defined as a *claim*, or the right of party A to reasonable access to energy. This implies party B's duty to ensure its accessibility. It may also mean a liberty, by which is meant party A's right to self-determination with respect to energy resources, e.g., in the selection and use of forms of energy technology. This means that party A is at liberty to choose to purchase, or not purchase, receive, or not receive, and the liberty to decide between forms of technology in accord with what party A judges to be most consistent with its welfare. In the realm of *liberty*, party B's duty is to avoid imperialistic and all otherwise unfair practices in the supply of technology. With regard to a right as *power*, party A has the right legally to defend itself against exploitative practices carried out by non-indigenous public or private entities in their supply and regulation of energy resources to party A. Party A also enjoys *immunity* not to be subject to unjust requirements (e.g., ruthless population policies) as conditions for access to energy technology. This is not meant to be a comprehensive examination of the four normative benefits of a right to energy (i.e., claims, liberties, powers and immunities), but rather an illustration of how a more comprehensive application should begin.

The right to energy pertains to justice among peoples

The right to energy falls under the broader framework of questions concerning justice in the distribution of resources. Problems of distributive justice principally bear upon the obligations of authorities in relation to members of a community. Globalization has to some degree relativized national boundaries. Consequently, distributive justice today inevitably concerns the distribution of resources not only within, but also between nations. In its broadest sense, we are treating questions of distributive justice between and among peoples. The right to energy constitutes a subset of norms within this broader framework.

Common goods and "the common good"

The subject matter of a "right to energy" is complex. Complications begin with the term energy itself, which may be referred to generally, and more accurately, as "energy resources." Insofar as energy resources are the subject matter of justice claims, they are, in different ways, incidents of communal enterprise (Finnis 1980, 166–167). They are *common* goods, *res*, over which no individual or group could ever rightly claim absolute possession, possession, that is, that excludes their being used for the benefit of others. To establish some *res* as a common good requires defending the proposition that sharing in that *res* is related to the realization of the social condition referred to as the "common good."

To elucidate an adequate understanding of the common good, one needs to avoid accounts of communal flourishing that rely on an overly strict notion of the subordination of a part (member) to the whole (community) (Aristotle, *Politics*, bk. 1, ch. 2, 1253a 18–29) as well as accounts that reduce human well-being to the maximization of pleasure-interests of the greatest number (Bentham, *Introduction to the Principles of Morals and Legislation*, ch. 1, nos. 2–6). The term as used in the social teaching of the Catholic Church avoids both excesses. The common good refers to a set of social "conditions" that allow groups and individual members reasonable access to possibilities to achieve their own fulfillment.[3] Finnis argues that these conditions facilitate the realization of values "for the sake of which [members of a community] have reason to collaborate with each other (positively and/or negatively) in a community" (1980, 155).

These conditions are established by and exist in the choices and commitments made by persons within the major domains of social life: the political, juridical, economic and cultural. Most forcefully they are instantiated and perpetuated by laws. But their most basic anthropological expression is in the habits of personal character (i.e., virtues and vices) and culture (e.g., attitudes, customs and conventions regarding concepts such as authority, family, community, money, sex, gender and religion). Whatever form they take and however they are instantiated, the "social conditions" act as principles of determination for practical reasoning and future choosing. As such they facilitate or militate against the realization of possibilities corresponding to human fulfillment.

Concept of human good?

The question of human good, within a pluralistic community, is certainly one of the most difficult in normative ethics. A substantive defense of a theory of value is far beyond the scope of this chapter. However, in arguing for a right to energy, the problem of what is meant by human fulfillment cannot be ignored. For if the concept of a human right refers to anything non-arbitrary, it singles out and secures something truly beneficial to individuals and communities. The resurgence of natural law reasoning in the past thirty years has corrected some of the deficiencies of earlier accounts by avoiding on the one hand overly prescriptivist theories without on the other conceding to ethical relativism. The following remarks on the concept of human good have been developed more extensively elsewhere.[4]

If seven people were asked, "what fulfills you?" seven different answers would likely result. If the question were asked of a hundred people, however, certain value categories would likely be repeated. People would be interested in realizing various forms of physical and psychological health, relational harmony, excellence in work and recreation, the acquisition of knowledge, aesthetic appreciation, harmony with God, inner peace, and marriage and family. They would also be interested in property, wealth and social status. The interest people take in these latter goods, however, is not for their own sakes, but for the sake of more basic forms of fulfillment that people believe these instrumental goods can help them realize (Aquinas, *Summa Theologiae*, pt. I, q. 5, a. 6). The more basic forms of fulfillment can also be referred to as goods, but not goods that exist apart from persons. These "basic human goods" – a term coined by the philosopher Germain Grisez – are aspects of individual and communal personal fulfillment (1983, 121–125). They are goods sought for their own sakes because they are judged in themselves to be choiceworthy.

Energy resources fall into the category of instrumental goods. These are external goods that may not be inherently good, but are useful for the achievement of human well-being (Aristotle, *Nicomachean Ethics*, bk. 1, no. 6). This is an important point. An account of justice and a right to energy must have reference to these goods. Jennifer Runyon, editor of *Renewable Energy World Magazine*, reminds us that the right to energy "is not really about the energy at all, but about the services that it provides" (2010). Said another way, access to energy resources is not – and hence must not be conceived of as – an end in itself. Saying this does not detract from its importance, any more than calling clothing, food and water, and housing instrumental goods detract from their importance. But the resources themselves do not constitute human fulfillment. Rather, they enable people to realize more basic forms of fulfillment. They are a means – often indispensable – to the promotion and protection of goods such as better health, stronger communities and families, and greater knowledge.

Looking at the negative aspects of the question, energy deficiency manifestly harms people. Examples are easy to find: lack of proper resources for cooking and heating means inefficient cookstoves and fires, which lead to respiratory illnesses, primarily for women and children, and exposure to disasters in the home; lack of resources for sanitation and water systems leads to infectious diseases and deficient health care; inordinate amounts of time needed to fetch water and firewood expose women and children to dangers; lack of motive energy impedes production processes, transportation and economic development; lack of lighting limits possibilities for study and blocks access to modern communication such as the internet, which limits productive participation in markets and culture; this leaves individuals and communities more vulnerable to economic and political forces.

If justice is our aim, and justice always seeks to secure the common good, and the common good is related to promoting and protecting basic human goods, then the pursuit of necessary instrumental goods such as energy should be ordered and limited by and assessed in relation to the prior aim of facilitating these more basic types of human fulfillment. Those involved in the promotion of rightful access to energy must keep their eye, as it were, on the ontological prize that access to energy makes possible: namely, the realization of a more complete expression of basic human fulfillment in individuals and communities.

What's in the right?

We can speak about a "right" to instrumental goods inasmuch as certain goods are necessary for the achievement of one or more of the basic forms of human fulfillment. Defending a right to energy means defending the thesis that certain energy resources are necessary today for living in a dignified and reasonably fulfilled manner. For purposes of speaking about the diversity of the resources, the following discussion divides the category of "energy resources" between four interrelated but distinct kinds of common goods. Each includes instrumental goods that are necessary for the achievement of a minimally acceptable expression of individual and communal well-being. That well-being cannot be consistently achieved by all members without the existence of political, juridical, economic and cultural conditions favorable to the full development of personality and the harmony of communities.

The goods are "common" inasmuch as they are *for* the benefit of the whole community, whatever their legal designation. No one is rightly excluded from a fair share in the benefits they supply, which is another way of saying all members of a community have a right to energy resources. Whatever the structure of legal ownership – i.e., ways of apportioning the resources under the legal category of "property" – they simultaneously exist as common goods. This is not meant to imply any strong conclusions regarding what kind of political system should be in place in order to realize the aim of fair access to energy resources. However, inasmuch as these resources are common goods, political authority rightly oversees their distribution.

Four types of energy resources

First, energy resources include *natural resources* not yet exploited or converted by human ingenuity, for example, solar energy, light, wind, water, hydrocarbons (oil, gas and coal) and arable land. Although these resources are yet to be the products of human initiative, they nevertheless characterize part of a community's native wealth; and communal self-determination requires that a community have access to its own natural resources to provide for the needs of its own members. The right to energy not only guarantees fair access to these resources, but immunity from their exploitation by foreign communities to the detriment of the indigenous community.

Second, raw materials need to be converted into useable forms of energy. The forms of energy need to be stored and transported. To do that, and to make use of the energy, people need machines and equipment to manipulate the energy for the carrying out of essential tasks. Consequently, energy resources include *hard technology, fuel and infrastructure* (e.g., electrical grids, photovoltaic systems, battery banks, generators, refined bio-fuels, radio transmission towers, appliances and electronics, home weatherization, roadways, airstrips, etc.). These resources only arise because of and through the exercise of human ingenuity. Since most communities today are not in a position to supply these resources exclusively from sources internal to themselves, cooperation between communities is a necessity. Designating hard technology, fuel and infrastructure as common goods does not necessarily imply common ownership, whether public or private (e.g., as in a cooperative). It does imply that the community as a whole understands and is committed to fair access by the whole community to the resources.

Third, to establish and maintain an environment in which fair access to energy can be guaranteed over time, certain social, economic and political benefits must be shared. These are *intangible social benefits*, and include innovative knowledge, technical education, social opportunities such as energy related jobs, economic incentives such as tax credits, rebates and grants, and support from political authority in the form of energy-friendly laws, especially laws that help minimize corruption, waste, pollution and cronyism. These are common goods in the sense that they are required for communities to achieve long-term stability in sharing in the goods discussed in the second category.

Finally, energy resources include *human resources*, for example, innovators, educators, managers, skilled workers (especially technicians) and investors. This category can only be considered "energy resources" in a qualified sense. People are never and hence should never be treated merely as resources to be employed for the benefit of others. But they rightly can be and often are viewed also as resources. Selective immigration policies can target skilled labor from the outside, talent willing to commit itself to the community's energy welfare. Educational and apprenticeship programs can be prioritized around the creation and management of energy resources in order to identify and nurture indigenous talent.

Part II: do the rights of the Energy Poor entail a cognizable moral duty on the energy rich?

Whose duty?

If access to energy is a right, then Energy Poor communities have a moral claim to it. Since no rightful claim can exist if there is not a correlative duty to render the object of the claim, then the question becomes whose duty is it to make energy accessible to those who need it? This is another complex question.

The duty belongs *in the first place* to those who need the energy. This follows from the "principle of autonomy" (Beauchamp and Childress 2009, 101–149). Autonomy is simply a technical term (derived from the Greek words for "self," *autos*, and "law," *nomos*) designating that people who are capable of self-direction have both a right and a responsibility to exercise it.[5] In virtue of one's status as a being of a rational nature – i.e., as a self, capable in kind of self-governance – one is in a primordial metaphysical sense, one's own; one is self-possessing. Or expressed another way, one is a *person* (Aquinas, *Summa Theologiae*, pt. I, q. 29, a. 3, reply to objection 2; Aquinas, *Commentary on the Sentences of Peter Lombard*, bk. I, d. 23, a. 1c, d. 26, q. 1, a. 1c.). One never belongs, in a strict sense, to anyone else. The proper form of governance (or determination) for a self, therefore, is self-governance paradigmatically expressed through the making and carrying out of free choices. So in order of priority, the duty to provide energy for oneself and one's dependents belongs to oneself.

The authority over any particular community has special responsibility to provide for the welfare of that community (i.e., for the community's good, or the "common good"). Because the distribution of energy resources bears upon fair access to common goods of the civil community, the duty to ensure that norms of fairness are upheld within the civil community belongs in a special way to civil authority.

What if local authorities are unable to ensure fair access to energy? On what grounds can it be argued that social duties to the welfare of others do not cease at the borders of sovereign states? Two general moral principles do most of the work answering these questions. The first, the *principle of solidarity*, elaborates a descriptive truth about the nature of civil society and the state. The principle does not function as a moral norm directive of action, but rather as a justifying ground for the application of other norms. It tells us that the concept of duty is not tendentious when speaking about people with whom I share little in common by noting that beyond race, language, national or economic status exists common humanity – that is, being human. The primordial human community is precisely the community of mankind. From the perspective of our shared humanity, all smaller communities, including nations, races and ethnic groups, are derivative. The localized interests of nations, races, cultures and political parties need to be qualified in light of this *principle of solidarity*. This is not to say that common humanity gives rise to the *strongest* duty. Family, religion and nationality all forge deeper bonds and give rise to weightier duties. Rather, common humanity is *a* ground for arguing that the energy welfare of persons, say, in Nepal or Tegucigalpa is not irrelevant to persons in the developed world: the needs of the developing world have some claim upon the developed. This does not yet settle the scope or strength of the duty. It does, however, provide reasons against a strongly isolationist position.

The interdependence of nations, that globalization makes particularly relevant today, has always been a reality. This, as mentioned above, is in part because the reasonable realization of goods necessary for living a dignified life can rarely be achieved within the limited bounds of one's community. Interdependence is, therefore, not an unfortunate state of affairs that developing nations must embarrassingly and developed nations begrudgingly endure. It is a fact of human existence. Donne's famous prose expresses the principle of solidarity more elegantly:

> If a clod be washed away by the sea, Europe is the less. As well as if a promontory were. As well as if a manor of thine own or of thine friend's were. Each man's death diminishes me, for I am involved in mankind. Therefore, send not to know for whom the bell tolls, it tolls for thee.
>
> (Donne [1624] 1990, 58)

The second principle is fairness, sometimes referred to as the *Golden Rule*. Fairness requires us to place ourselves in the position of others, especially those with perspectives we do not ordinarily identify with, and to consider from their perspectives what type of behavior we judge would be reasonable to expect from us. It would be unreasonable to render or fail to render to others what we would judge unreasonable for them to render or fail to render to us. The most famous formulation of the principle is by Jesus in his Sermon on the Mount (Matt. 7:24–27). But Christianity has no exclusive claim on the principle of fairness, which is found in different formulations in most every ethical code in history, as well as in prominent works of political philosophy of the last forty years.

Beginning from the principles of solidarity and fairness, there is sufficient ground for concluding that the compelling needs of persons and communities other than my own supply a reason for those outside the community to attempt to meet those needs. All can agree that some quantum and quality of energy is really an essential for survival today (abundant firewood is not going to suffice). And some communities do not possess the one or the other or both. So to whom does the duty fall to assist these communities?

Principle of subsidiarity

If care can be provided by "one's own," by members of one's own community, the shared sentiments generated by common language, race, history, religion and culture make it more likely that a higher quality of care will be delivered. An analogy might be drawn with nationalized health care. Without taking sides in the debate going on in the United States, few would disagree that if all the complex duties of distributing the best health care fairly could be met at a local level, then that would be best for patients and communities. Would anyone defend the proposition that in principle the administration of services critical to human well-being is best done by bureaus and departments staffed with officials who don't know my name, my people, my history and hence, very often, my real needs?

This requirement to keep care as local as possible is compatible with it being adequately delivered, and has sometimes been called the principle of subsidiarity and defended as a principle of justice. John Finnis formulates the principle as follows:

> In all those fields of activity, including economic activity, where individuals, or families, or other relatively small groups, can help themselves by their own private efforts and initiatives without thereby injuring (either by act or omission) the common good, they are entitled in justice to be allowed to do so, and it is unjust to require them to sacrifice their private initiative by demanding that they participate instead in a public enterprise.
>
> (Finnis 1980, 169)

It would be an injustice for a community of a higher order to interfere in the internal life of a community of a lower order, depriving the latter of the functions it can reasonably fulfill on its own (Pope John Paul II 1991).

But the principle of subsidiarity also prescribes that where needs cannot adequately be met by the efforts of those in one's local community, communities of a higher order rightly assist lower order communities to meet their needs, always with a view to the common good. If intra-national efforts are insufficient to remedy deficiencies, extra-national entities rightly offer assistance.

If there were such an entity as the "international community," with a recognized authority structure capable of exercising effective decision making capacity between and over national communities, then that authority, in the interests of the common good of nations, would bear an obligation to coordinate remedial measures for energy poorer nations.[6] But the term "international community" is still in many ways an abstraction. No world authority exists with effective power to coordinate assistance efforts on behalf of Energy Poor nations.[7]

So where do we turn when intra-national efforts are insufficient to remedy national deficiencies? Duties to aid Energy Poor nations fall to those communities whose resources are adequate to provide such aid – call them "energy rich" communities. Public authority – in the case of nations, national government – has the chief responsibility to assess and carry out a nation's international duties.[8] In the absence of an effective world authority, determining precisely who has the responsibility and the scope of the responsibilities is not simple. Whereas all nations have a certain obligation to meet the genuine basic needs of other nations, perhaps no one nation has an overriding moral duty to do so, such that it would be simply wrong for a nation which has surplus energy not to transfer some of it to some energy impoverished country.

Yet following from the principles of distributive justice and subsidiarity one may derive three prima facie conclusions about the assignment of duties. First, the more affluent and energy rich a nation is,[9] the greater the obligation it has to assist poorer nations. Second, culturally alike communities have a greater obligation to assist each other. If they share a common language, religion, racial constitution or history of struggle they share grounds for mutual understanding. This does not guarantee they will share positive sentiments or good will towards one another. But other things being equal, an English speaking country or a Muslim country is likely to understand the mindset, mores and needs of another English speaking or Muslim country better than a non-English speaking or non-Muslim country. Third, because sharing resources with neighbors – via pipelines, electrical grids or roadways – is likely to be simpler than exporting resources to far away communities, countries that are geographically proximate to one another have greater mutual duties than do countries that are very remote from one another.

These conclusions are prima facie. No one condition settles the question of the assignment of duty. But they can establish a strong presumption. If all three prevail in a given instance, then only very serious reasons would justify a nation in not coming to the assistance of its Energy Poor neighbor. But the first – availability of surplus resources – has an obvious preeminence in an assessment of duty. The extent of any community's duty can only be proportionate to what it reasonably is capable of performing. Cultural dissimilarity or geographical non-proximity does not exclude a more affluent country from international obligations. If it has surplus resources, it *should* put them at the service of energy impoverished nations, whatever the latter's culture or location. Moreover, both the gravity of the need of poor communities and the degree of surplus wealth of affluent ones will influence the presumptive duty of the latter to offer support.

The concept of *superflua* and the moral claims of Energy Poor communities

Establishing a duty to aid others in need requires to some degree defending the moral limits of private property, a task that is beyond the scope of this chapter. In drawing on the concept of "surplus wealth" (or "surplus energy") this account implicitly commits itself to certain premises concerning ownership. The following makes those implied premises explicit.

Going back to the early days of Christianity, a norm of justice has been repeated that prescribes that people have an obligation to place their *surplus* wealth at the disposal of those in need. Theologically the norm is grounded in the doctrine of creation: when God created the Earth, he created it for the sustenance of all human beings; no one therefore "owns" the Earth in an absolute sense; all are stewards. Philosophically the norm is grounded in the principles of equality, solidarity and justice. Our common humanity implies basic human equality and common responsibility. Common responsibility entails ensuring that the subsistence needs of all are met.

Aquinas' carefully articulated account of private property, useful for our purposes here, proposes a varying degree of common claim over all private possessions. He argues that owners should always use their property in a socially responsible way, in a way that supports the common good, especially the good of the poor. To set up his argument he makes several distinctions between levels of need in relation to resources (Finnis 1998, 191–196). He distinguishes between (a) resources necessary for survival (in cases of "extreme necessity"); (b) resources needed to meet one's responsibilities to family and household, especially the nurture and education of children, to business and wider professional vocation, and for repaying debts (i.e., needed to live "in a dignified way" – "*convenienter*"); and (c) the resources we possess after due provision is made for (a) and (b) (cf. Aquinas, *Summa Theologiae*). Aquinas refers to (c) as our "*superflua*" ("surplus resources").

Relying on these distinctions, Aquinas sets forth a two-fold norm: (1) *all* one's resources (i.e., everything from (a), (b) and (c) – what he refers to compendiously as "external things") should be held "as common" in the sense that one "is ready to communicate them" to others who are in "extreme necessity" (*extrema necessitate*), i.e., those who suffer from life threatening need (*Summa Theologiae*, pt. II-II, q. 66 a. 2c; q. 32 a. 5c). (2) One's *superflua* are to be held "as common" in the sense that they should be made available to those in "relative necessity" – "in need" – that is, people who, though not suffering from extreme necessity, lack the resources to live *convenienter* (in a dignified way) (Finnis 1998, 193).

We may add these insights to the prima facie conclusions on the assignment of duties noted above. The common claim over possessions as such yields different duties to owners based both upon the needs of others and the resources of owners. There is a strict duty of justice (not merely of charity) to come to the assistance of those in serious need (Aquinas, *Summa Theologiae*, pt. II-II q. 66 a. 7). The duty falls upon everyone (individuals and communities) aware of the other's needs and reasonably capable of relieving them. This applies to countries whose resources not only are in surplus, but merely sufficient to permit its member to live *convenienter*. But there is an even graver duty of justice to put one's surplus energy resources at the disposal of communities suffering from extreme necessity. The duty to share one's surplus resources, however, also extends, as a matter of justice, though not as grave, to those communities suffering from relative necessity.

Practically determining whether or to what extent a country has "surplus" energy and what it has a surplus *of* may sometimes be simple and straightforward. Saudi Arabia and Canada clearly have a surplus of crude petroleum and the United States has a surplus of certain intangible social benefits such as innovative knowledge and opportunities for technical education. The United States also has an abundance of natural gas. Refusing these resources to communities in need could be unjust, even seriously so.

But the question of surplus may not always be so simple. Does, for example, Mexico have a surplus of petroleum? It certainly has enormous oil reserves. Estimates as of 2013 placed them at 10.3 billion barrels (United States Energy Information Administration 2014). But the country's punishing tax burden on the state-owned oil producer is over 95 percent, which weakens the industry's ability to reinvest in infrastructure and exploration.

Part III: if there is a right and a duty, how should this claim be satisfied by both the Energy Poor and the energy rich?

Making sound judgments

Although developed and affluent nations should assist in facilitating the just distribution of energy resources to less developed nations, assessing the gravity of the duty and to whom precisely the duties are owed requires making sound judgments about rightful claims, legitimate duties and the rightful fulfillment of those duties. Sound judgments cannot be made without considering questions about the justice of wealthier peoples' overall treatment of poorer peoples, and the general structure of economic relationships between wealthier and poorer peoples. National interest always colors the motives of wealthier nations in their aid relations. Although the governing motive *should* be to ameliorate the problem of energy impoverishment, governments often give aid with strategic objectives in mind. Those involved with energy-aid to the developing world should ask what are those objectives and are they consistent with the morally prior aim of meeting the real needs of energy deficient peoples, viz., creating and sustaining conditions for long-term energy production and use consistent with the realization of basic human goods? The other side of this same coin is considering the capacity and the willingness of recipient regimes to distribute the energy income/resources fairly, for the common good, and not to use it as political weapons at home.

Second, sound judgments can only be made after all the claims of all the relevant persons upon whom issues of energy justice bear are taken into due consideration. The most pressing claims arise from those suffering from energy deprivation because they are most likely to be harmed by the status quo. But the common good of assisting communities must also be taken into consideration. There is no obligation to give assistance to other communities in grave need out of resources that are necessary to prevent oneself from experiencing similar need (Aquinas, *Summa Theologiae*, pt. I-II, q. 32, a. 6c). Moreover, an assisting country has no obligation to put resources that it needs for its members to live *convenienter* at the disposal of other communities who are not suffering grave need.

"For our children and our children's children" is rhetoric often heard on the lips of politicians, but rarely are the claims of future generations considered practically relevant to complex economic questions in the present. Suitable recognition is indeed due to the interests of children yet unborn who will be born and who will need to deal with the world left to them. This ought not to degenerate into a simplistic utilitarian calculus of counting potential heads. But we often can foresee future consequences of present action and to the extent that we foresee harms however unintentional to future generations we must factor them reasonably into our analysis.

Conclusion: the right to energy and the duty to provide it

Access to energy resources is a human right. It is a right inasmuch as energy resources today are necessary for the achievement of one or more of the basic forms of human fulfillment: physical and psychological health, relational harmony, excellence in work and play, acquisition of knowledge, aesthetic appreciation, harmony with God, inner peace, and marriage and family. The right to energy, although bearing upon instrumental goods (i.e., natural resources, hard technology and infrastructure, intangible social benefits and "human resources"), is itself basic insofar as it is grounded in the kinds of more basic human fulfillment that energy resources are a necessary means to realizing.

The common good entails a set of social conditions in which individuals and communities can pursue and realize ends corresponding to their genuine fulfillment (both *as* individuals and communities). The common good is only realized in those communities whose members are capable of securing sufficient food, water, shelter, education and communication, all of which today require access to energy resources. A "right" to energy therefore entails as its proper object everything *necessary* to securing that **access**.

The concept of right logically entails the concept of duty. Insofar therefore as access to energy resources is a right, there exists a corresponding duty to make provision for that access. The correlative relationship between the right (and right-holders) and duty (and duty-bearers) exists as follows:

The right: the right entails at least the following normative properties: (a) the *claim* to reasonable access to safe and efficient energy resources ("reasonable" defined as whatever is necessary for securing requisite food, water, etc., needed to live a dignified life); (b) the *liberty* to exercise self-determination in the securing of those resources; (c) the *power* to defend oneself and one's community effectively against the unscrupulous practices of presumed benefactors and providers of those resources; and (d) *immunity* against requirements imposed by outside communities as conditions for access to those resources when the conditions are unrelated to the basic purpose of securing those resources.

The duty: the correlative duty to the right to energy entails at least the following normative properties: (a) the duty to provide energy resources sufficient to live a dignified life. In regard to those communities that are unable from their own means to secure those resources, the duty falls to other communities to assist in their provision. Following the principle of subsidiarity – namely, that care is best exercised as locally as reasonably possible – neighboring and culturally alike communities capable of meeting their neighbors' needs should be first to offer assistance. The graver the need of energy impoverished communities, the graver the duty of other communities to assist in the provision of resources. Beyond neighboring and culturally similar communities, *all* communities not themselves suffering from extreme need have a moral duty to put resources at the disposal of communities in grave need. Those communities that have surplus resources have an especially grave duty to do so.

The duty also broadly entails (b) the duty to offer energy assistance with upright motives, which means, at a minimum, with the primary aim of ameliorating the needy community's energy deficiency. Whatever self-interest exists in the wider structure of motives in offering aid, benefactor communities should not be moved to attach any unjust conditions to their provision of resources. They should especially avoid imperialistic negotiations in which the recipient communities are not left free to exercise self-determination in securing the resources they judge to be most consistent with their energy welfare.[10]

Notes

1 I thank Jose Ambrozic for advising me on the topic and reading and commenting on several drafts of this chapter. I thank also Professors Gerald Bradley of Notre Dame and Germain Grisez of Mount Saint Mary's for valuable comments on an early draft.
2 The *Institutes of Justinian* opens its discussion of justice with Ulpian's definition (without attribution); J.B. Moyle translates *ius* as "due," as do most scholars of the twentieth century (1911).
3 See Vatican II, *Gaudium et Spes* (1965), no. 26; also Pope John XXIII, *Mater et Magistra* (1961), no. 65, *Pacem in Terris* (1963), no. 55–56 (see Tanner 1990).
4 See: Grisez 1983, ch. 5, pp. 115–138; Finnis 1983, ch. 2, pp. 26–53; Grisez et al. 1987, 106–108, 111–113.
5 Autonomy also implies that decisions for those who are unable to exercise self-direction, whether because of incomplete development or disability, should be made principally in accord with their own good.
6 Saying this begs the question of whether the establishment of a world authority capable of acting effectively on the juridical and political levels would be desirable. To be "effective" it would have to exercise coercive authority sufficient to ensure compliance with its mandates. This poses dangers of its own.
7 The UN has the power to publish documents (e.g., the Rio+20 document on sustainable development) and issue resolutions. But other than the resolutions of the Security Council, these are non-binding on member states.
8 This is qualified, of course, by the duty of civil authorities to provide first for the needs of their own communities.
9 By "energy rich" I include countries whose wealth is easily convertible to energy or that can easily grant access to energy resources.
10 We should add that benefactor communities have the right to know before committing resources that the resources they commit will be used efficiently to remedy the energy deficiency of the members of the recipient community, especially those in greatest need.

References

Beauchamp, Tom and James Childress. 2009. *Principles of Biomedical Ethics.* 7th edn. Oxford: Oxford University Press.
Bentham, J. 1982. *Introduction to the Principles of Morals and Legislation,* ch. 1, nos. 2–6. Edition by J.H. Burns and H.L.A. Hart. London: Methuen and Co.
Brugger, E. Christian. 2004. "Bioethical Controversies and the Language of Rights." *Global Virtue Ethics Review* 5, no. 1: 33–49.

Donne, John. 1990. "No Man Is An Island." In *Divine Poems, Sermons, Devotions, and Prayers* (Classics of Western Spirituality). Edited by John Booty. New Jersey: Paulist Press.

Finnis, John M. 1980. *Natural Law and Natural Rights*. Oxford: Clarendon Press.

——. 1983. *Fundamentals of Ethics*. Washington, DC: Georgetown University Press.

——. 1998. *Aquinas: Moral, Political, and Legal Theory*. Oxford: Oxford University Press.

Grisez, Germain. 1983. *The Way of the Lord Jesus*. Vol. 1, *Christian Moral Principles*. Chicago: Franciscan Herald Press.

Grisez, Germain, Joseph Boyle and John M. Finnis. 1987. "Practical Principles, Moral Truth and Ultimate Ends." *American Journal of Jurisprudence* 32: 99–151.

Hobbes, Thomas. 1991. *Leviathan*. Edited by Richard Tuck. Cambridge: Cambridge University Press.

Hohfeld, Wesley N. 1994. "Fundamental Legal Conceptions as Applied in Judicial Reasoning." In *Introduction to Jurisprudence*, edited by M.D.A. Freeman. 6th edn. London: Sweet & Maxwell.

Justinian. 1911. *Institutes*. Translated by J.B. Moyle. London: Oxford Clarendon Press.

Pope John Paul II, Encyclical Letter *Centesimus Annus* ("On the Hundredth Anniversary of *Rerum Novarum*"), 1991, no. 48.4–5.

Runyon, Jennifer. 2010. "Is Access to Energy a Human Right?" RenewableEnergyWorld. com, November 24. Accessed October 17, 2014. www.renewableenergyworld.com/rea/news/article/2010/11/is-access-to-energy-a-human-right.

Tanner, Norman P. (ed.). 1990. *Decrees of the Ecumenical Councils*, vol. 2. Washington 'DC: Georgetown University Press, p. 1084.

Tierney, Brian. 1997. *The Idea of Natural Rights: Studies on Natural Rights, Natural Law, and Church Law 1150–1625*. Grand Rapids, MI: Eerdmans.

U.S. Energy Information Administration. 2014. *International Energy Statistics*. Accessed October 17, 2014. www.eia.gov/cfapps/ipdbproject/IEDIndex3.cfm?tid=5&pid=57&aid=6.

6   Sustainable development

Ved P. Nanda

Introduction

Sustainable development (SD), widely recognized as a powerful principle which opened a new paradigm by integrating economic and social considerations into the development process, emerged onto the international agenda in the 1970s. It has gained universal attention by changing the traditional perspective that equated development with economic growth, to require linkage between economic viability, social development, and environmental aspects to ensure development that is sustainable. Thus, sustainable development bridged the initial North–South divide characterized by the developed states' focus primarily on environmental protection, and developing countries' main concern with developmental needs, by engendering a clear realization that both environmental and developmental concerns are equally valid and are not necessarily in conflict.

The evolution of the concept all began with the growing global concern over environmental degradation. In the 1960s Rachel Carson's book, *Silent Spring*, followed by Garrett Hardin's article, *Tragedy of the Commons*, and in 1972 by the Club of Rome's study, *The Limits to Growth* (Meadows et al. 1972), catalyzed public thinking about the fragility of the environment. These streams of thinking resulted in an epochal event: the UN Conference on the Human Environment held at Stockholm in June 1972. The Stockholm Declaration adopted at the conference included a broad statement emphasizing the importance of economic and social development but did not systematically address the critical relationship between environment and development (United Nations 1972, Preamble, para. 6). Because it did not satisfactorily formulate the importance of economic and social development, the conference, aimed at defending and improving the human environment for present and future generations, failed to satisfy the developing nations' concerns.

Eight years later, the International Union for the Conservation of Nature and Natural Resources (IUCN) published a study, *World Conservation Strategy – Living Resource Conservation for Sustainable Development*, stating as its goal "the integration of conservation and development to ensure that modifications to the planet do indeed secure the survival and wellbeing of all people" (International

Union for the Conservation of Nature and Natural Resources 1980, 1.12). It defined conservation as "the management of human use of the biosphere so that it may yield the greatest sustainable benefit to present generations while maintaining its potential to meet the needs and aspirations of future generations" (International Union for the Conservation of Nature and Natural Resources 1980, 1.14).

The IUCN's use of the term "sustainable development" and its definition of conservation presaged the formulation and popularization of sustainable development by the World Commission on Environment and Development, also known as the Brundtland Commission, after Gro Harlem Brundtland, the former Prime Minister of Norway, who chaired the Commission (United Nations 1987). The Report of the Commission, which was established by the Secretary-General in 1983 (UN 1983), defined sustainable development by explaining that "[h]umanity has the ability to make development sustainable to ensure that it meets the needs of the present without compromising the ability of future generations to meet their own needs" (United Nations 1987, Overview, sec. 3, para. 27), and recommended it as a perspective to address the relationship between economic development, the environment, and the North–South divide. The Commission emphasized the inexorable linkage between environment and development and the need to integrate economic and ecological considerations in decision-making. The object was to address the basic needs of all people and to protect natural resources.

Subsequently, the UN General Assembly convened the UN Conference on Environment and Development (UNCED or "Earth Summit") in Rio de Janeiro from June 3 through 14, 1992, to mark the twentieth anniversary of the Stockholm Conference and to address the North–South environment and development split, as well as to further develop international environmental law. The title of the Rio Declaration adopted at UNCED, *The Rio Declaration on Environment and Development*, clearly linked environment and development (United Nations 1992). The Declaration set forth principles on sustainable development, with Principle 1 setting the tone of a human-centered focus for the document, proclaiming that "[h]uman beings are at the centre of concerns for sustainable development. They are entitled to a healthy and productive life in harmony with nature."

For implementing a sustainable development regime, UNCED adopted a minutely detailed action plan entitled *Agenda 21* for managing the environment in the twenty-first century (United Nations 1992). The plan gave an in-depth meaning to sustainable development, placing high priority on the links between poverty reduction, economic efficiency, and environmental management. The General Assembly then established the Commission on Sustainable Development to assist in the implementation of the recommendations and decisions of the Earth Summit (United Nations 1997), which was replaced by the High-level Political Forum on Sustainable Development to monitor progress in implementing sustainable development commitments and to address new and emerging sustainable development challenges (United Nations 2014c).

Ten years later world leaders gathered in Johannesburg for the World Summit on Sustainable Development in August–September 2002, and adopted the Johannesburg Declaration on Sustainable Development, committing themselves "to build a humane, equitable and caring global society." They also adopted a "Plan of Implementation" strongly reaffirming their commitment to the Rio Principles and the full implementation of Agenda 21. The Conference emphasized the three reinforcing pillars of sustainable development: economic development, social development, and environmental protection (United Nations 2002).

Efforts at the United Nations to shape a sustainable development agenda designed to provide an integrated application of sustainable development include the adoption in 2000 of the Millennium Declaration and the Millennium Development Goals (MDGs), and in 2012 the outcome document of the United Nations Conference on Sustainable Development (Rio+20), entitled *The Future We Want*. Brisk activities are now under way to adopt the successor, Sustainable Development Goals (SDGs), at the conclusion of the MDGs in 2015. These efforts will be detailed in the next section. Here it will suffice to say that SD has been applauded as a universally accepted fundamental principle or *grundnorm* of international environmental law and policy (Guruswamy 2010, 233). There is indeed an emerging understanding that the principle of sustainable development has acquired the status of an organizing, higher order principle. In his separate opinion in the Gabčíkovo-Nagymaros Project (ICJ 1997), Judge Christopher Weeramantry, then Vice President of the International Court of Justice, considered sustainable development as "more than a mere concept" and "as a principle with normative value," which demands striking a balance between development and environmental protection.

The process of shaping a sustainable development agenda: from the Millennium Development Goals to the Sustainable Development Goals

In 2000, world leaders adopted the United Nations Millennium Declaration, committing to a global partnership for development and combating extreme poverty. They resolved to "spare no effort to free our fellow men, women and children from the abject and dehumanizing conditions of extreme poverty, to which more than a billion of them are currently subjected" (United Nations 2000, III, 11).

They also established the Millennium Development Goals which, along with the Millennium Declaration, placed people at the center of sustainable development. The MDGs set time-bound targets by which progress can be measured in reducing poverty, hunger, disease, and maternal and child mortality, and in promoting gender equality, health, education, environmental sustainability, human rights, and good governance. The eight MDGs form a blueprint with numerical benchmarks to be achieved by 2015. The goals range from halving extreme poverty to halting the spread of HIV/AIDS and providing universal primary education. These goals were: 1) eradicate extreme poverty and hunger; 2) achieve universal primary education; 3) promote gender equality and empower women; 4) reduce child mortality; 5) improve maternal health – reduce by three-quarters the maternal mortality ratio; 6) combat HIV/AIDS, malaria, and other diseases; 7) ensure environmental sustainability; and 8) create a global partnership for development (United Nations 2014b).

Notwithstanding the bold vision articulated by the Millennium Declaration and the ambitious agenda and concrete targets set by the MDGs, the Millennium Development Goals Report 2014 (United Nations 2014a) shows that the concerted efforts of national governments, the international community and civil society, as well as the private sector, have resulted in substantial progress in most areas. However, significant gaps and disparities remain and several goals will not be achieved. For example, one in four children under five years of age in the world suffers from inadequate height for her/his age (United Nations 2014a, 8, 14). The Report finds that "progress in reducing the number of children out of school has slackened considerably" (United Nations 2014a, 16) and that gender disparity in the labor market still exists (United Nations 2014a, 21). It also finds that the target diseases – HIV/AIDS, malaria and tuberculosis – still take a heavy toll, especially in developing countries (United Nations 2014a, 34–37). To illustrate, Wu Hongbo, Under-Secretary-General for Economic and Social Affairs, acknowledged in the 2014 Report Overview that:

- 162 million young children still suffer from chronic undernutrition;
- the mortality rate for children under age five stands at 48 deaths per thousand in 2012 which is caused by preventable diseases;
- in 2013 almost 300,000 women died from causes related to pregnancy and childbirth, although maternal death is mostly preventable;
- in 2012, 2.5 billion people were not using an improved sanitation facility and 1 billion still resorted to open defecation;
- 58 million children were out of school in 2012 and high dropout rates are a major cause for not achieving universal primary education; and
- the MDG agenda remains unfinished (United Nations 2014a, Overview).

This Report was followed in December 2014 by Secretary-General Ban Ki-moon's Synthesis Report on the post-2015 agenda to succeed the MDGs. In his Report, entitled *The Road to Dignity by 2030: Ending Poverty, Transforming all Lives, and Protecting the Planet* (United Nations 2014f), the Secretary-General found tangible results achieved by the global mobilization behind the MDGs and the resulting multilateral action. But, he said,

Amid great plenty for some, we witness pervasive poverty, gross inequalities, joblessness, disease and deprivation for billions ... The consequences of climate change have only just begun. These failings and shortcomings have done as much to define the modern era as has our progress in science, technology and the mobilization of global social movements.

(United Nations 2014f, 1.10)

Two decades after the Earth Summit, world leaders met at the UN Conference on Sustainable Development (CSD) at Rio de Janeiro, Brazil from June 20–22, 2012 (Rio+20), and endorsed the outcome document of the conference, entitled *The Future We Want* (United Nations 2012a). They renewed their commitment "to sustainable development and to ensuring the promotion of an economically, socially and environmentally sustainable future for our planet and for present and future generations" (United Nations 2012a, I.1). They recognized that the greatest global challenge is poverty eradication and that people are at the center of sustainable development (United Nations 2012a, 1.2, 1.6). They acknowledged that there had been insufficient progress and that setbacks had occurred since 1992 in the integration of sustainable development's three dimensions – economic development, social development, and environmental protection (United Nations 2012a, 1.20).

The world leaders resolved "to take urgent action to achieve sustainable development" and also renewed their commitment "to sustainable development, assessing the progress to date and the remaining gaps in the implementation of the outcomes of the major summits on sustainable development and addressing new and emerging challenges" (United Nations 2012a, 12). They also resolved to establish an intergovernmental process on the Sustainable Development Goals (SDGs) by constituting an open working group to propose SDGs to the General Assembly for consideration and appropriate action (United Nations 2012a, IV.B.248).

Following the Rio+20 CSD, the Open Working Group (OWG) held its first working session in March 2013 and met for 13 sessions before submitting its report in July 2014 (United Nations 2014d). In the meantime, a large number of studies, conferences, and colloquia were held under the auspices of the UN, businesses, civil society, and think-tanks to suggest to the OWG the Sustainable Development Goals for the post-2015 development agenda. The OWG enumerated 17 SDGs, accompanied by 169 targets which are to be further elaborated through indicators with measurable outcomes (United Nations 2014d, IV.18).

These goals are "action oriented, global in nature and universally applicable," build on the foundation laid by the MDGs, and are designed to respond to new challenges, and, according to the Report, the goals and targets "integrate economic, social and environmental aspects and recognize their interlinkages in achieving sustainable development in all its dimensions." These proposed SDGs emphasize poverty and hunger eradication, inclusive growth, access to affordable, reliable, sustainable, and modern energy for all, equality, and a people-centered agenda for sustainable development. They are:

Goal 1.   End poverty in all its forms everywhere.
Goal 2.   End hunger, achieve food security and improved nutrition and promote sustainable agriculture.
Goal 3.   Ensure healthy lives and promote well-being for all at all ages.
Goal 4.   Ensure inclusive and equitable quality education and promote lifelong learning opportunities for all.

Goal 5. Achieve gender equality and empower all women and girls.

Goal 6. Ensure availability and sustainable management of water and sanitation for all.

Goal 7. Ensure access to affordable, reliable, sustainable and modern energy for all.

Goal 8. Promote sustained, inclusive and sustainable economic growth, full and productive employment and decent work for all.

Goal 9. Build resilient infrastructure, promote inclusive and sustainable industrialization and foster innovation.

Goal 10. Reduce inequality within and among countries.

Goal 11. Make cities and human settlements inclusive, safe, resilient, and sustainable.

Goal 12. Ensure sustainable consumption and production patterns.

Goal 13. Take urgent action to combat climate change and its impacts.

Goal 14. Conserve and sustainably use the oceans, seas, and marine resources for sustainable development.

Goal 15. Protect, restore, and promote sustainable use of terrestrial ecosystems, sustainably manage forests, combat desertification, and halt and reverse land degradation and halt biodiversity loss.

Goal 16. Promote peaceful and inclusive societies for sustainable development, provide access to justice for all, and build effective, accountable and inclusive institutions at all levels.

Goal 17. Strengthen the means of implementation and revitalize the global partnership for sustainable development (United Nations 2014d, IV, 18).

The Synthesis Report by the Secretary-General endorsed the goals and targets proposed by the OWG. It provides six essential elements for delivering on the SDGs – dignity, people, prosperity, planet, justice, and partnership (United Nations 2014d, 3.3.66–86) – which explain the intent of the Agenda, but the Report does not indicate the explicit relationship between these elements and the proposed 17 goals.

The Report placed the broader international human rights framework at the core of sustainable development as an integrated agenda for economic, environmental, and social solutions, the framework to include "elements of economic, social, cultural, civil, and political rights, as well as the right to development" (United Nations 2014f, 3.4.82–83). It is worth noting that civil society groups have been critical of the lack of focus in the MDG framework. Consider, for instance, Amnesty International's warning: "World leaders risk deepening inequalities, discrimination, and injustice if human rights remain side-lined in the post-2015 development agenda" (Amnesty International 2013). The organization's Secretary-General, Salil Shetty, stated: "[Y]ou cannot have sustainable development without human rights" (Amnesty International 2014).

The Secretary-General expressed hope that the special UN Summit on Sustainable Development to be held at the UN Headquarters in September 2015 "will mark a paradigm shift for people and planet" (United Nations 2014f). That is when the post-2015 development agenda and a set of SDGs will be finalized. In sum, while the proposals in the Synthesis Report lack specificity, the Report presents a bold vision which should assist the intergovernmental negotiators as they prepare a new set of SDGs.

Energy as a goal of the SDGs

One of the major gaps in the MDGs was the absence of energy as one of the specified eight goals. Energy access is, however, a precondition for poverty eradication and indeed for human development, and the international community has long recognized the critical role of energy in all human endeavors. It was this recognition that led the General Assembly in 2010 to declare 2012 the International Year of Sustainable Energy for All. By making this declaration, members recognized that access to modern, affordable energy services is essential for developing countries in achieving the internationally agreed development goals, including MDGs (United Nations 2011a).

The General Assembly recognized that energy is indispensable for human well-being and development. It expressed concern that more than three billion people in developing countries rely on traditional biomass for cooking and heating and that 1.5 billion people do not have electricity, while millions of poor people are unable to pay for energy services even when they are available. Consequently, it reaffirmed support for

> the promotion of access to modern, reliable, affordable and sustainable energy services ... by the promotion of the development and dissemination of appropriate, affordable and sustainable energy technologies and the transfer of such technologies ... to developing countries.
>
> (United Nations 2011a, Preamble)

The General Assembly encouraged all concerned, including member states and the UN system,

> to increase awareness of the importance of addressing energy issues, including modern energy services for all, access to affordable energy, energy efficiency and the sustainability of energy sources and use, for the achievement of the international agreed development goals ... sustainable development and the protection of the global climate, and to promote action at the local, national, regional and international levels.
>
> (United Nations 2011a, op. para. 4)

Secretary-General's Sustainable Energy for All (SE4All) Initiative

The following year, the Secretary-General launched the Sustainable Energy for All (SE4All) initiative. He indicated the scale of the challenge – one out of every five people on Earth is without access to electricity, and nearly three billion people use wood, coal, charcoal, or animal waste to heat their homes and cook their meals, which exposes them and their families to smoke and fumes damaging their health and killing two million people each year (United Nations 2011b, preface).

The initiative seeks to ensure SE4All by 2030 through the achievement of three linked objectives: 1) ensuring universal access to modern energy services; 2) doubling the rate of improvement in energy efficiency; and 3) doubling the share of renewable energy in the global energy mix (United Nations 2011b, preface). After identifying the barriers that impede progress toward sustainable energy for all, including financial obstacles, pricing, and regulatory policies and practices, the Secretary-General formed a High-Level Group on Sustainable Energy for All, whose task was "to recommend an Action Agenda on the basis of which all stakeholders could make concrete commitments toward sustainable energy for all by 2030" (United Nations 2011b, 7, 9).

The Secretary-General's High-Level Group on Sustainable Energy for All

The Secretary-General's High-Level Group produced a Global Action Agenda in April 2012 (United Nations 2012b). The Agenda provides a concrete strategy for engagement by all stakeholders across different sectors of society, organized into 11 action areas. In September 2012, the Group's co-chairs submitted their report outlining their strategic, political, and financial accomplishments (United Nations 2012c). Their strategic accomplishment was in setting a framework for action and then defining a global action agenda (United Nations 2012b, 01). The political accomplishment was in securing endorsement of the Group's work from all over the world and attracting the voluntary participation of over 50 developing countries (United Nations 2012b, 01). Regarding the financial aspects, they attracted more than 100 commitments to action, which amounted to tens of billions of dollars which came from governments and businesses, showing robust public–private partnership. The Secretary-General detailed the commitments:

a More than 70 developing countries opted to work with the initiative, with many more following.
b More than $50 billion was pledged in support of the objectives of the initiative from the private sector and investors.
c Tens of billions of dollars were committed by multilateral development banks in Asia, Europe and Latin America.
d Hundreds of actions were catalyzed and commitments made in support of the three core objectives.

e   Commitments to support energy access will provide more than 1 billion people with access to modern energy during the lifespan of the initiative.
f   New public–private partnerships are being formed with regard to transport, energy efficiency, solar cooking, finance and energy access for the poor (United Nations 2014e, II.C.3.24).

The Secretary-General submitted to the General Assembly two reports on the United Nations Decade of Sustainable Energy for All – one in August 2013 (United Nations 2013) and the other in September 2014 (United Nations 2014e). He detailed in these reports the activities undertaken in support of the Decade and the outcome achieved. Included were the appointment of the Secretary-General's Special Representative for Sustainable Energy for All, the Decade launch, and the first annual SE4All Forum, all of which showed "strong support for including energy as part of the new development framework, including in its Sustainable Development Goals" (United Nations 2014e, para. 38).

The United Nations Conference on Sustainable Development

In the outcome document of the Rio+20 CSD, *The Future We Want*, world leaders recognized

> the critical role that energy plays in the development process, as access to sustainable modern energy services contributes to poverty eradication, saves lives, improves health and helps to provide for basic human needs.
> (United Nations 2012a, 125)

They stressed that "these services are essential to social inclusion and gender equality, and that energy is also a key input to production," committed to "facilitate support for access to these services by 1.4 billion people worldwide who are currently without them," and recognized that "access to these services is critical for achieving sustainable development" (United Nations 2012a, 125).

The world leaders further "recognized that improving energy efficiency, increasing the share of renewable energy, and cleaner energy-efficient technologies are important for sustainable development, including in addressing climate change" (United Nations 2012a, 128) and added:

> We are all determined to act to make sustainable energy for all a reality and, through this, help to eradicate poverty and lead to sustainable development and global prosperity. We recognize that the activities of countries in broader energy-related matters are of great importance and are prioritized according to their specific challenges, capacities and circumstances, including their energy mix.
> (United Nations 2012a, 129)

Proposal of the Open Working Group for SDGs – Goal 7

The proposed Sustainable Development Goals include a stand-alone goal on energy, Goal number 7, to ensure access to affordable, reliable, sustainable, and modern energy for all:

> 7.1 by 2030 ensure universal access to affordable, reliable, and modern energy services
>
> 7.2 increase substantially the share of renewable energy in the global energy mix by 2030
>
> 7.3 double the global rate of improvement in energy efficiency by 2030
>
> 7.a by 2030 enhance international cooperation to facilitate access to clean energy research and technologies, including renewable energy, energy efficiency, and advanced and cleaner fossil fuel technologies, and promote investment in energy infrastructure and clean energy technologies
>
> 7.b by 2030 expand infrastructure and upgrade technology for supplying modern and sustainable energy services for all in developing countries, particularly LDCs and SIDS.
>
> (United Nations 2014d, 15)

The integration of energy into the post-2015 development agenda by dedicating a separate Sustainable Energy Goal among the SDGs fills one of the major gaps in the MDG framework. Goal 7 covers the three objectives identified in the Secretary-General's Sustainable Energy for All initiative: 1) energy access; 2) energy efficiency; and 3) share of renewable energy (United Nations 2011b, Goal 7, 4). It seems appropriate to add a fourth objective: energy conservation through lifestyle change and thus reduced energy consumption in developed countries, as suggested by the Institute for Global Environmental Strategies (IGES) in Japan (Institute for Global Environmental Strategies 2014). The reason the institute offers is compelling:

> Neither energy efficiency nor renewable energy measures alone can cap global warming to within 2 degrees Celsius by 2030, according to Global Energy Assessment by the Institute for Applied Systems Analysis estimates ... However, the probability of limiting global warming to 2 degrees shoots up to 66–90% if the Sustainable Energy for All (SE4All) objectives for renewable energy and energy efficiency are simultaneously met ... This means that even if the world could achieve all SE4All goals ... it is still unlikely for the 2 degree target for climate change to be achieved.
>
> (Institute for Global Environmental Strategies 2014, 4.4)

Two other issues are worth considering. The first relates to Target 7.2, which calls for increasing substantially the share of renewable energy in the global energy mix by 2030. Admittedly, specific targets cannot be applied throughout the world, due to variations among countries related to renewable energy potential and the costs of raising the renewable proportion. Nevertheless, appropriate ambitious targets can and should be set based upon local and national variations, as suggested by IGES (Institute for Global Environmental Strategies 2014, 4.3).

The second issue relates to fossil fuel subsidies that, according to the International Energy Agency's report, *World Energy Outlook 2014*, totaled $550 billion in 2013, which is more than four times the subsidies paid to renewable energy and which are holding back investment in renewables and efficiency (International Energy Agency 2014). A target aimed at reducing fossil fuel subsidies is in order.

Conclusion

Recent developments related to sustainable development and sustainable energy are indeed promising. In the fall of 2015 the General Assembly will design SDGs to follow the expiring MDGs. The designation of sustainable energy as a dedicated SDG is indeed welcome. The challenge is to create the necessary infrastructure and to ensure effective implementation, which will require adequate funding and sharing of appropriate technology with the developing countries. Reporting, monitoring, and accountability, as well as policies and institutions designed to facilitate the achievement of these objectives are critical, to which intergovernmental negotiators must give priority.

References

Amnesty International. 2013. "UN Millennium Development Goals: Human rights must not be marginalized in post-2015 agenda." September 23. www.amnesty.org/en/articles/news/2013/09/un-millennium-development-goals-human-rights-must-not-be-marginalized-post-agenda/, accessed May 2, 2015.

———. 2014 "Post-2015 Agenda: human rights accountability key to progress Amnesty International tells UN." June 12. www.amnesty.org/en/articles/news/2014/06/post-agenda-human-rights-accountability-key-progress/, accessed May 2, 2015.

Carson, Rachel. 1962. *Silent Spring.* Boston: Houghton Mifflin.

Guruswamy, Lakshman. 2010. "Energy Justice and Sustainable Development." *Colorado Journal of International Environmental Law & Policy* 21: 231–275.

Hardin, Garrett. 1968. "The Tragedy of the Commons." *Science* 162: 1243–1248.

ICJ. 1997. *Case Concerning the Gabčíkovo-Nagymaros Project (Hung. v. Slov.)*, Judgment of 25 Sept. 1997. Separate Opinion of Vice President Weeramantry at 88. www.icj-cij.org/docket/files/92/7383.pdf, accessed May 2, 2015.

Institute for Global Environmental Strategies. 2014. "Policy Brief – Designing and Implementing an Energy Goal: Delivering Multi-benefits for Sustainable Development (No. 30)." November. http://pub.iges.or.jp/modules/envirolib/view.php?docid=5503, accessed May 2, 2015.

International Energy Agency. 2014. *World Energy Outlook 2014, Executive Summary 4 (2014)*. www.iea.org/publications/freepublications/publication/WEO_2014_ES_English_WEB.pdf, accessed May 2, 2015.

International Union for the Conservation of Nature and Natural Resources. 1980. *World Conservation Strategy: Living Resource Conservation for Sustainable Development*. IUCN: Gland, Switzerland.

Meadows, Donella H., Dennis L. Meadows, Jørgen Randers, and William W. Behrens III. 1972. *Limits to Growth: A Report for the Club of Rome's Project on the Predicament of Mankind*. New York: Universe Books.

United Nations. 1972. "Report of the United Nations Conference on the Human Environment." A/CONF.48/14/Rev.1 (June 5-16). www.un-documents.net/aconf48-14r1.pdf, accessed May 2, 2015.

——. 1983. General Assembly 38th Session, *Process of preparation of the Environmental Perspective to the Year 2000 and Beyond*. A/RES/38/161 (December 19). www.un.org/documents/ga/res/38/a38r161.htm, accessed May 2, 2015.

——. 1987. "Report of the World Commission on Environment and Development: Our Common Future." A/42/427. www.un-documents.net/our-common-future.pdf, accessed May 2, 2015

——. 1992. "Report of the United Nations Conference on Environment and Development." Rio de Janeiro, Brazil, June 3–14, 1992. (A/CONF/51/26) 1992.

——. 1997. General Assembly Resolution S-19/2, *Program for the Further Implementation of Agenda 21*. A/RES/S-19/2 (September 19). www.un.org/documents/ga/res/spec/aress19-2.htm, accessed May 2, 2015.

——. 2000. General Assembly Resolution 55/2, *Millennium Declaration*. (A/RES/55/2) (September 18). www.un.org/millennium/declaration/ares552e.pdf, accessed May 2015.

——. 2002. "Report of the World Summit on Sustainable Development." A/CONF.199/20 (September 4). www.un.org/jsummit/html/documents/summit_docs.html, accessed May 2, 2015.

——. 2011a. General Assembly Resolution 65/151, *International Year of Sustainable Energy for All*. A/RES/65/151 (February 16). http://daccess-dds-ny.un.org/doc/UNDOC/GEN/N10/521/60/IMG/N1052160.pdf?OpenElement, accessed May 2, 2015.

——. 2011b. "Sustainable Energy for All: A Vision Statement by Ban Ki-moon, Secretary-General of the United Nations." November. www.se4all.org/wp-content/uploads/2013/09/SG_Sustainable_Energy_for_All_vision_final_clean.pdf, accessed May 2, 2015.

——. 2012a. General Assembly Resolution 66/288, *The Future We Want*. A/RES/66/288 (July 27). www.uncsd2012.org/content/documents/727The%20Future%20We%20Want%2019%20June%201230pm.pdf, accessed May 2, 2015.

——. 2012b. "Sustainable Energy for All: a Global Action Agenda." A/67/175 (July 31). www.un.org/wcm/webdav/site/sustainableenergyforall/shared/Documents/SEFA-Action%20Agenda-Final.pdf, accessed May 2, 2015.

——. 2012c. Secretary-General's High-Level Group on Sustainable Energy for All, *Report of the Co-Chairs*. September. www.un.org/wcm/webdav/site/sustainableenergyforall/shared/Documents/09.2012%20-%20SE4ALL%20-%20Report%20of%20the%20Co-Chairs.pdf, accessed May 2, 2015.

——. 2013. "Report of the Secretary-General: United Nations Decade of Sustainable Energy for All" (A/68/309). August 6. www.se4all.org/wp-content/uploads/2013/10/a-68-309-SG-report-on-the-Decade.pdf, accessed May 2, 2015.

——. 2014a. "Millennium Development Goals Report 2014." www.un.org/millenniumgoals/2014%20MDG%20report/MDG%202014%20English%20web.pdf, accessed May 2, 2015.

——. 2014b. "Millennium Development Goals and Beyond 2015." www.un.org/millenniumgoals/index.shtml, accessed May 2, 2015.

——. 2014c. Economic and Social Council, "Adoption of the ministerial declaration of the high-level political forum." E/2014/L.22–E/HLPF/2014/L.3 (July 9). www.un.org/ga/search/view_doc.asp?symbol=E/2014/L.22&Lang=E, accessed May 2, 2015.

——. 2014d. "Report of the Open Working Group of the General Assembly on Sustainable Development Goals," A/68/970 (August 12). www.un.org/ga/search/view_doc.asp?symbol=A/68/970&referer=http://www.google.com/url?sa=t&Lang=E, accessed May 2, 2015.

——. 2014e. "Report of the Secretary-General: United Nations Decade of Sustainable Energy for All." A/69/395 (September 22). www.se4all.org/wp-content/uploads/2014/10/Decade-report.pdf, accessed May 2, 2015.

——. 2014f. "Synthesis Report of the Secretary-General On the Post-2015 Agenda: The Road to Dignity by 2030: Ending Poverty, Transforming All Lives, and Protecting the Planet" (advance unedited). December 4. www.un.org/ga/search/view_doc.asp?symbol=A/69/700&Lang=E, accessed May 2, 2015.

7 Energy security, poverty, and sovereignty

Complex interlinkages and compelling implications

Murodbek Laldjebaev, Benjamin K. Sovacool, and Karim-Aly S. Kassam

Introduction

Energy poverty is commonly defined in the energy and development studies literature as: (a) lack of access to electricity networks; or (b) dependence on burning solid biomass, such as wood, straw, and dung, in inefficient and polluting stoves to meet household energy needs. Energy is valued not so much for its own sake as for the services it enables to bring about. While energy can launch shuttles into space and power computers to work out complex mathematical problems, it is also used for basic services that are essential for human life such as lighting, cooking, heating, cooling, telecommunications, and earning a living (Practical Action 2010). As one study notes, in the developing world the energy for these basic services is frequently derived from wood, agricultural residues, animal dung, candles, kerosene, or by physical exertion (Sovacool et al. 2014).

However, the condition of energy poverty often extends well beyond the domain of households, or the discipline of economics, as shown in Table 7.1. It can touch upon nationwide energy security challenges and vulnerabilities, and also impinge on local sovereignty. In the first three sections of this chapter, we explore these three key overlapping concepts – energy poverty, energy security, and energy sovereignty – individually, and in the final section explain how they interact, and what this interaction means both for scholars interested in energy as well as for policymakers and planners seeking to address energy problems.

Energy poverty

International institutions, such as the International Energy Agency of the Organisation for Economic Co-operation and Development (OECD) have traditionally used a binary system to identify energy poverty: people either lack access to electricity networks or depend on solid fuels for cooking. However, recent work has shifted away from the binary approach. A tiered "energy results chain" (see Figure 7.1) has been identified and providing energy services requires a mix of energy sources (Practical Action 2014, 51). In other words, the tiered

Table 7.1 Overview of key concepts from the academic literature

Concept	Definition(s)	Topic/Theme	Discipline
Energy poverty	Lack of household access to electricity and energy services and dependence on solid biomass fuels for cooking	Access, affordability, quality	Development studies, public policy, welfare economics
Energy security	Reduced vulnerability of vital energy systems and sustained provision of energy services	Diversification, infrastructure security and reliability, security of supply	Energy policy, national security, public policy, security studies (political science)
Energy sovereignty	Local people determining their energy systems in ways that are culturally relevant and ecologically sustainable	Sociocultural, economic, ecological factors influencing energy decision making	Anthropology, behavioral economics, development sociology, human ecology, political ecology, psychology

framework demands that we first understand local energy needs, and then consider the options to address those needs.

In the first edition of the *Poor People's Energy Outlook* in 2010, Practical Action framed lack of access to energy services as a "form," an "outcome," and a "cause of poverty." It is a form of poverty because it restricts human capabilities to meet their needs and realize their full potential. It is an outcome of poverty because low-income individuals are limited in their financial abilities to afford goods and services that their better-off fellow citizens enjoy, even if those goods and services are ultimately unsuitable or unsustainable. And it is a cause of poverty because it "reinforces constraints in income generation potential, because many product and service-based enterprises and public services either rely on energy or are substantially improved in their productivity, profitability, or efficiency by the introduction of improved forms of energy access." Taken together, a "vicious circle" is created whereby "a lack of energy access leads to limited income-earning capability, which reduces purchasing power, which in turn limits the access to energy that could improve incomes" (Practical Action 2010, 28).

Breaking out of this vicious circle is not an easy task but not an impossible one either. Evidence from around the world indicates myriad benefits brought about by improving access to particular energy services. Energy services, particularly in the context of rural development, can be distinguished into two categories of use. First, the "residential use" or "consumptive use" of energy, for example, the provision of cooking, heating, and lighting services at home. Such energy use is "expected to positively impact the rural quality of life or improve rural living standards" (Cabraal et al. 2005, 118). Second, the "productive use" of energy, where energy is used to produce goods and/or services for consumption within as

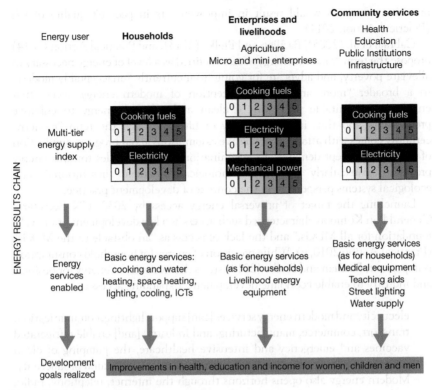

Figure 7.1 Conceptualizing energy services and energy poverty

Source: Adapted from Practical Action (2014, 51)

well as beyond village boundaries. This type of energy use is "expected to result in increased rural productivity, greater economic growth, and a rise in rural employment" and thus curbing rural out-migration (Cabraal et al. 2005, 188). Going beyond this traditional division of energy uses residential use can also be productive use due to the positive relationship, for instance, between provision of electricity and education and health improvements, which are in turn associated with higher income (Cabraal et al. 2005). In other words, educated and healthy humans with access to energy are more productive, and therefore better off than those who are not.

The *Poor People's Energy Outlook* since 2010 has emphasized that energy policies in developing countries fall short of catering to energy needs of the poor. However noble a goal of rural electrification may be, such policy is essentially misguided when it does not meet households' cooking needs in the home and mechanical power needs at work. The *Poor People's Energy Outlook 2014* divides energy services into three broad areas: *energy for households, energy for earning a living,* and *energy for community services.* As illustrated in Figure 7.1, these services encompass the full spectrum of energy needs (except for mobility), the adequate provision of which would result in improvements in people's quality of life (Practical Action 2014).

Cabraal et al. (2005), Bazilian and Pielke (2013), and Practical Action (2014) propose the term "modern energy access" defined as a level of energy necessary to alleviate poverty, and advocate for going from currently "unacceptably modest" to a broader "more ambitious" conception of modern energy access that encompasses equitable provision of clean and efficient energy to enhance productivity and thus improve quality of life. Although the term "modern" certainly comes with attached normative assumptions about progress, application of this new concept demands a reexamination of our attitudes towards energy provision, particularly from a technological, financial, institutional, and ecological systems perspective in the context of development practice.

Launching the target of universal energy access by 2030, UN Secretary-General Ban Ki-moon characterized such access as a key development priority, "a foundation for all MDGs," and the lack of access as "an obstacle to the MDGs" (Practical Action 2010, v). While provision of energy for household consumption is important, Bazilian and Pielke (2013) stress the necessity of energy for business and industry to enable economic development. Expanding access to

> electricity and modern energy services [can] support lighting, communication, transport, commerce, manufacturing, and industry, [and] enable refrigerated vaccines and emergency and intensive healthcare, the pumping of clean groundwater for drinking and irrigation to increase agricultural productivity. Modern energy also opens horizons through the internet, telephony, radio, and television.
>
> (Sovacool et al. 2014, 42)

Energy security

The concept of energy security is ubiquitous in the literature. Many analysts and experts have dealt with the challenge of addressing energy security issues (Hughes 2009; Löschel et al. 2010; Vivoda 2010; Sovacool and Brown 2010; Sovacool and Mukherjee 2011; Sovacool 2011), and these efforts contributed to the evolution of the concept. As a result, an approach emerged in the past decade that aims to parcel out the energy security challenges into different "aspects" or "dimensions" (Cherp and Jewell 2011). To illustrate this approach several examples are in order. The widely known 4 A's of energy security are: "availability" (elements relating to *geological* existence), "accessibility" (*geopolitical* elements), "affordability" (*economical* elements), and "acceptability" (*environmental* and societal elements) (Kruyt et al. 2009, emphasis in original). Similar to this classification, Sovacool and Brown (2010) suggest "availability" (independence and diversification), "affordability" (low and stable price, high quality fuel/service), "efficiency" (technical and economic efficiency of energy technologies/services, and conservation), and "environmental stewardship" (sustainable use of resources). An alternative classification developed by Von Hippel et al. (2011) clusters the energy security challenges around six dimensions, namely, "energy supply, economic, technological, environmental, social/cultural, and military/security." In a similar vein, Alhajji (2010) classifies the challenges into six dimensions, with slight variation, but takes a further step to demonstrate the interrelationship among the dimensions in terms of "competition" and "interaction," discussed below.

Comparing such attempts at comprehensive conceptions of energy security highlights the significant differences in relevance of different policy issues. However, the rationale and methods for selecting and grouping certain aspects, but not others, are not always clear or systematic (Cherp and Jewell 2011). Furthermore, over-generalization can result in oversight of contextual importance (Cherp 2012). A survey of the literature contended that energy security is

> commonly found embedded in discussion framed around a handful of notions which denote unimpeded access or no planned interruptions to sources of energy, not relying on a limited number of energy sources, not being tied to a particular geographic region for energy sources, abundant energy resources, an energy supply which can withstand external shocks, and/or some form of energy self-sufficiency.
>
> (Chester 2010, 885)

Recognizing the variety of interpretations, Chester suggests that the term is not well understood in the literature because energy security is "polysemic in nature, capable of holding multiple dimensions and taking on different specificities depending on the country (or continent), timeframe or energy source to which it is applied" (Chester 2010, 886). Therefore, Chester discourages against formulating a common standard definition or metric; rather, she emphasizes that the underlying assumptions be made explicit through providing definitions.

Considering the multiplicity of dimensions to energy security, Cherp and Jewell, in their extensive review of literature, integrate various energy security concerns into three perspectives: "robustness," "geopolitics" (which they refer to as "sovereignty"), and "resilience" (see Table 7.2) (Cherp and Jewell 2011). Each perspective has emerged in the analysis of energy security from different academic disciplines, ranging from security studies to engineering to economics. The underlying concerns dealt with in the literature converge on the risks of disruptions to energy systems, particularly four risk factors: "natural (e.g., resource scarcity, extreme natural events), technical (e.g., aging of infrastructure, technological accidents), political (e.g., intentional restriction of supplies or technologies, sabotage and terrorism), and economic (e.g., high or volatile prices)" (Cherp et al. 2012, 330). Consequently, Cherp et al. define "a nation's energy security as protection from disruptions of energy systems that can jeopardize nationally vital energy services" (Cherp et al. 2012, 329). The outcome of such "protection from risks" is "independence, reliability, resilience, availability, accessibility, affordability, or sustainability of energy systems" which constitute the key "dimensions" in the classification of energy security challenges as discussed above (Cherp et al. 2012, 330).

Recently Cherp and Jewell succinctly defined energy security as *low vulnerability of energy systems*, acknowledging flexibility and contextual adaptation. Based on this definition, we conceptualize energy security as minimizing the vulnerability of vital energy systems and enabling the provision of energy services. The issue of energy poverty can easily be overshadowed by the geopolitical, technical, and economic considerations (see Table 7.2). Furthermore, Cherp and Jewell (2014) assume the state is the main actor to ensure energy security. This assumption overlooks the agency of local communities in directly addressing their energy security needs.

Energy sovereignty

Energy sovereignty emphasizes the role of local people and their institutions in determining their energy systems in ways that are culturally relevant and ecologically sustainable. This concept was articulated by the indigenous peoples from the Americas and by the social movements in the Global South (Friends of the Earth International 2006; Moreno and Mittal 2008; Paradis et al. 2009). It draws on the clarion call by the rural poor for *food sovereignty* which advocates for local people's right to determine their food systems, make their own food choices, possess the capacity (knowledge, money, technology) to exercise their rights, and control the means of production based on ecological possibilities (Via Campesina 1996; Indigenous Peoples' Consultation on the Right to Food 2002; Forum for Food Sovereignty 2007; Patel 2009; Kassam 2009; Kassam 2010; Kassam et al. 2010; Ruelle et al. 2011).

Table 7.2 Three perspectives on energy security

Perspective	Geopolitics	Robustness	Resilience
Historic roots	War-time oil supplies and the 1970s oil crises	Large accidents, electricity blackouts, concerns about resource scarcity	Liberalization of energy systems
Key risks for energy systems	Intentional actions by malevolent agents	Predictable natural and technical factors	Diverse and partially unpredictable factors
Primary protection mechanisms	Control over energy systems. Institutional arrangements preventing disruptive actions	Upgrading infrastructure and switching to more abundant resources	Increasing the ability to withstand and recover from various disruptions
Parent discipline	Security studies, international relations, political science	Engineering, natural science	Economics, complex system analysis

Source: Modified from Cherp and Jewell (2011, 206)*

* We have changed the title of "Sovereignty" to "Geopolitics" for the sake of clarity and to avoid confusion when we introduce our own notion of "Energy Sovereignty" below.

Specifically, energy sovereignty is a framework that recognizes the individual, community, or nation's rights, and strengthens their abilities to exercise choice within all components of energy systems, including sources, means of harnessing, and uses, in order to satisfy their needs for energy. The problem of lack of energy in rural communities is illustrative. Proponents of the conventional energy security approach view the problem in terms of energy deficit that is a function of chronic shortage of energy supply due to low generation capacity (i.e., lack of energy resources) and/or affordability for most households. To eliminate the energy deficit, they may advocate policy measures to: (a) increase generation capacity; and/or (b) reduce cost. Local communities play little or no role in such policy discussions because the measures are devised at the national (sometimes international) level. In contrast, the proponents of energy sovereignty at the sub-national level would view the problem through the prism of local people's needs and preferences. They would underscore people's rights, knowledge, and technological capacities as well as local ecological possibilities to determine which potential energy resources need to be harnessed, for what purpose, by whom, and how.

We maintain that energy sovereignty can be better understood by exploring the decisions that people make at the community level to meet their energy needs. Thus, the literature on household energy decision making is very relevant. Understanding the factors that enable or prevent certain energy uses provides insight into the motivations behind certain decisions, which can then be used to design and deploy targeted measures to eliminate energy poverty and achieve energy security.

Household energy decision making is a very complex process, and the literature reviewed explains various determinants of energy choice. The "energy ladder" model with income as its primary determining variable provides a compelling explanation (Hosier and Dowd 1987; Gregory and Stern 2012; van der Kroon et al. 2013). However, an alternative model of "fuel stacking" is challenging this perspective. Empirical evidence indicates that households use a variety of fuels for different purposes at the same time, rather than transitioning completely from lower to higher efficiency fuels with increase in their income (Masera et al. 2000; Heltberg 2005; Hiemstra-van der Horst and Hovorka 2008). Moreover, there are many other variables that influence household energy choices, such as age, gender, culture, taste preferences, and cooking habits.

Many studies have found that household income is the most common factor influencing energy decision making. More income, particularly for urban households, is associated with a shift away from firewood to commercial fuels, such as charcoal, kerosene, liquefied petroleum gas (LPG), and electricity (Fitzgerald et al. 1990; Heltberg 2005; Mensah and Adu 2013). In rural areas, better-off households tend to use more kerosene (Nnaji et al. 2012). Households in the lowest-income quintiles use more crop residue (Mensah and Adu 2012). Regardless of income levels, however, rural households continue to rely on firewood for their thermal needs (Heltberg 2005; Mensah and Adu 2013). As for lighting needs, with increasing income levels, households use less kerosene and more electricity, where electricity is accessible (Fitzgerald et al. 1990).

Fuel price is another economic indicator of fuel choice. Higher prices of LPG confine households into using more wood; yet, higher wood price leads to using less wood (Fitzgerald et al. 1990; Heltberg 2005). Similarly, higher kerosene price is negatively related to its use for cooking (Fitzgerald et al. 1990). However, the reverse is true for price and use of kerosene for lighting. This is explained partially by additional costs of transporting kerosene to remote areas (i.e., areas with poor electricity access), and partially by the habits of purchasing kerosene frequently and in small quantities (Fitzgerald et al. 1990).

Reliability also determines energy choices. Households with reliable access to LPG are more likely to adopt LPG and less likely to use crop residue and firewood. Conversely, with erratic or no access to LPG, but reliable access to firewood, households tend to use less LPG and more firewood (Fitzgerald et al. 1990; Mensah and Adu 2013).

Demographic characteristics also determine household energy use to some extent. Larger households use more fuel, reflecting higher energy demand as well as the availability of additional labor to procure firewood, and affordability of cooking for many people (Heltberg 2005; Nnaji et al. 2012). Furthermore, larger households are more likely to use firewood and less likely to use LPG as "the associated economic burden of increasing family size affects households' ability to switch to cleaner fuels" (Mensah and Adu 2013).

Age and gender are also important indicators of household energy choice. Older heads-of-household are found less likely to use more efficient fuels like LPG (Mensah and Adu 2013). Similarly, male-headed households are more likely to use firewood and crop residue (Mensah and Adu 2013). Households with more female members are found to use more wood, which is explained by women's responsibility for firewood collection and cooking (Heltberg 2005). However, contrary to the expectation that loyalty is developed over time to using firewood, in Enugu State, Nigeria, older women used more charcoal (Nnaji et al. 2012). The elderly may lack the strength to collect firewood.

Educational attainment of household members is associated with less use of firewood and more of LPG. Thus, education is considered a strong determinant of fuel switching (Heltberg 2005; Mensah and Adu 2013). Education provides opportunities for better income; therefore, households devote less time to procuring biomass and more time to earning income, a part of which they use to purchase commercial fuels. Women with secondary education or higher are found to use more charcoal as they engage in other income-generating activities and lack time for wood collection (Nnaji et al., 2012). However, the contrary was found in another study, that an increase in the level of education of the wife is negatively correlated with the use of charcoal. The study offers two explanations: (a) alternative fuels are not accessible, therefore, everyone uses firewood; (b) female servants may collect wood for cooking. Such services are rare in rural areas (Pundo and Fraser 2006).

Dwelling characteristics of households can be indicative of energy use patterns. More rooms in a dwelling unit means less wood and more LPG use, which is paradoxical, but can be due to wealth affect, i.e., larger dwelling units usually belong to more affluent households who can afford commercial fuels (Heltberg 2005). The assumption that households living in modern-type dwelling units are likely to use firewood alternatives proved unsubstantiated in the case of Kisumu district in Kenya (Pundo and Fraser 2006). Richer households may prefer cleaner houses, but continue to use firewood because extra money is spent on priority needs, or there is a separate designated place for cooking (Pundo and Fraser 2006). Presence of internal cooking facilities was found to be associated with more charcoal and kerosene use in Enugu State, Nigeria (Nnaji et al. 2012). These energy carriers emit less smoke and, thus, are better suited for use inside the house. Furthermore, households renting the dwelling unit are likely to use charcoal or kerosene in order to avoid staining the walls and roofs (Pundo and Fraser 2006). Alternatively, households living in a shared dwelling unit are more likely to use LPG because of space constraints for storing firewood (Mensah and Asu 2013).

Cultural factors influence household energy choice. Taste preferences and cooking habits are difficult to capture theoretically and assess quantitatively (Heltberg 2005). Nonetheless, some proxy indicators can be useful in revealing the effect of culture on energy use. Cooking practices determine fuel choice. Urban households in Java, Indonesia consuming more steamed rice are found to use more energy (specifically, kerosene) compared to those boiling their rice (Fitzgerald et al. 1990). Cooking time is also an important indicator of fuel choice as meals taking a longer time to cook are prepared using firewood whereas those taking a shorter time use either charcoal or kerosene. This may be motivated by higher prices of the latter fuels that households cannot afford for longer durations of cooking time (Pundo and Fraser 2006). Even in relatively well-off households "cultural beliefs may keep working women to a common culture and societal life style of using firewood" (Pundo and Fraser 2006).

Synthetic conceptual framework

A plethora of economic and sociocultural factors influence energy poverty, energy security, and household energy decision making in developing countries. While some factors may be within control of local people, some are clearly out of their reach. Successful programs and projects aimed at eradicating energy poverty and improving energy security need to address these factors. The concepts of *energy security*, *energy poverty*, and *energy sovereignty* can be adapted into a synthetic conceptual framework to meet this task. *Energy security* is context-dependent as is the concept of *energy poverty*. *Energy sovereignty* is a relatively new term that places household and community decision making at the core to eliminate energy poverty and improve energy security. Table 7.3 indicates how the three concepts interact and are interconnected.

As our synthetic conceptual framework suggests, energy poverty reflects the current condition of access to energy services at the level of the community and household – this constitutes the *problem*. Rural communities continue to rely on solid biomass (wood, shrubs, animal dung) to meet their thermal energy needs. Although many communities are connected to the grid, access to electricity is

Table 7.3 Synthesis into a common conceptual framework

Concept	Definition	Scale	Technology	Mutual interactions
Energy poverty	Lack of household access to electricity and energy services and dependence on solid biomass fuels for cooking	Household	Cookstoves and off-grid/ mini-grid systems	Energy poverty lowers overall resilience of households to cope with energy threats and, in extreme situations, lead to civil unrest; it can also shape the historical trajectory of community decisions which influence future options.
Energy security	Reduced vulnerability of vital energy systems and sustained provision of energy services	National, geopolitical	Larger electricity networks, oil and natural gas markets	Energy vulnerabilities and disruptions in supply can heighten energy poverty when fuels are not available or supply networks are not reliable, in turn diminishing the ability of households to achieve sovereignty by constraining their decisions and options.
Energy sovereignty	Local people determining their energy systems in ways that are culturally relevant and ecologically sustainable	Household, Community	Appropriate technology (c.f. Schumacher 1973)	Household and community participation is a key part of national energy security planning strategies that are accountable and legitimate; household decision makers are, of course, the prime actors involved in perpetuating or escaping energy poverty.

not reliable. In the cold season, when energy needs are particularly acute, households experience daily blackouts. To assess the level of energy poverty is to take account of energy needs, such as cooking, heating, and lighting, and the extent to which they are met. In other words, the fundamental need of a household is expressed through its specific energy need. Thus, energy poverty must be assessed at the level of the household and community.

Within our conceptual framework, energy security is treated as a *goal* – a state of being, in which the vulnerabilities of the energy systems are reduced and energy services are provided to a satisfactory level. For example, in the electricity sector, dams are physically safe, the grid is renovated, and small-scale technologies are installed to service the remote communities. At the local level, this chapter articulates energy poverty as a key vulnerability. Elimination of energy poverty leads to achievement of energy security whereby energy needs of households in a community are met to their satisfaction.

Energy sovereignty is a *process* to reach the goal of energy security. The key question is: how are energy needs met? This is a process of complex decision making that is influenced by many factors including cultural values, financial wherewithal, technological capability, and ecological foundation of households. An interplay of these factors leads to decisions and choices about use of certain energy resources and pathways. Figure 7.2 illustrates the complex linkages between energy poverty, energy security, and energy sovereignty.

Conclusions and implications

Our conceptual synthesis of energy poverty, security, and sovereignty results in at least three contributions for energy scholars, national policymakers, and development practitioners.

First, the integrated nature of energy poverty–security–sovereignty strongly suggests that energy needs must be understood appropriately and that communities be engaged in the process so that they may express their particular energy needs. This means that there is no "one-size-fits-all" solution to rural energy poverty. To guide this analytically intensive process, the energy services approach advocated by Practical Action may be used as an effective instrument. It takes a wide range of energy services into account in identification of needs as well as the means to meet those needs (Practical Action 2014). Cultural significance, ecological sustainability, and suitability of technology for intended interventions should be given priority in addition to technical reliability, fuel costs, and pricing schemes. Community engagement and decision making is central to sovereignty, and therefore to eradicating poverty and achieving security.

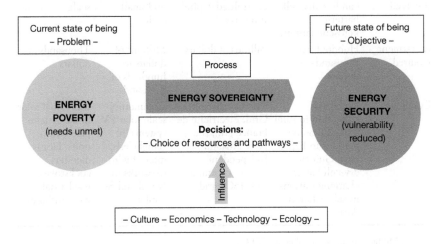

Figure 7.2 Conceptual interlinkages between energy poverty, security, and sovereignty

Second, for policymakers, the inclusion of energy sovereignty into our framework provides yet another justification for devolution of decision making to the local level. When communities are engaged in their problem solving, the national government can assist with technical expertise and financial support. As Table 7.4 illustrates, possibilities for energy access are differentiated by scale and scope of coverage as well as required investment for each option. Policymakers and practitioners should recognize that there are infinite number of ways an energy access program can result in failure, but only a few where they can result in success. Failure is more common than success (Sovacool et al. 2014, 80). We further add that community participation and decision making (sovereignty) plays a key role in the success of development projects. In short, our framework suggests that energy development planners not only ask "energy security by which technology," but "energy security for whom?"

Table 7.4 Summary of technological options that expand energy access

	Conventional options	Grid electrification	Micro-grids	Off-grid technology
Scale	Community and household	National, regional, and even international	Community	Household
Geographic radius	< 30 km^2	More than 50 km^2	1 to 49 km^2	< 1 km^2
Number of customers	Dozens to thousands	Thousands to millions	Dozen to hundreds	Usually a dozen or less
Installed capacity	Various	More than 10 MW	20 kW to 10 MW	< 20 kW
Technologies involved	Woody biomass, candles, dry cell batteries, kerosene lanterns	Large-scale, centralized capital intensive	Medium-scale and small-scale	Very small-scale
Investment required	Hundreds to thousands of dollars	Billions of dollars	Millions of dollars to hundreds of thousands	Thousands of dollars
Examples	Fuelwood collection in rural areas, kerosene markets in Papua New Guinea, dry-cell battery charging stations in sub-Saharan Africa	The North China Grid, Electricité de France grid, the New England Independent System Operator (NE-ISO) grid	Community-scale solar PV systems in Bangladesh, micro-hydro networks in Nepal and Sri Lanka	Individual solar home systems, pico-hydro units, biogas digesters, cookstoves, residential wind turbines

Source: Modified from Sovacool et al. (2014, 7)

Third, and lastly, for development practitioners our framework provides a compelling rejection of the "fuel switching" or "energy ladder" approach. Energy sources or forms are not necessarily mutually substitutable to deliver a certain energy service. As a case in point, much effort has been expanded to provide more efficient cookstoves; however, the rates of adoption and use seldom approach the level of expectations. One of the major reasons for low adoption of technically improved devices is that they do not deliver the desired kind of service. For example, certain staple foods require a different way of cooking, such as open fire, that the new devices are intentionally designed to contain – because the goal is to reduce smoke exposure and maximize combustion. This design is incompatible with the desired objective of householders for the staple food that cannot be prepared properly using the new device. Hence, such inappropriate technologies are usually discarded. Therefore, close attention must be paid to the kind of energy service desired by the people and only after that a suitable technology may be developed to provide such service.

In short, development organizations should adopt the energy services approach to their energy provision projects and strive to meet the energy requirements for household activities, earning a living, and community services. Consistent effort is necessary to involve local communities in the projects to better provide for their desired services. Furthermore, the projects should make use of locally available energy sources that are linked with people's livelihoods. In this manner, energy projects provide appropriate technology that suits people's needs – ensuring that energy security does not come at the cost or expense of poverty and sovereignty, and vice versa.

References

Alhajji, Anas. 2010. "Dimensions of energy security: competition, interaction and maximization." In *Energy Security in the Gulf: Challenges and Prospects*. Abu Dhabi, United Arab Emirates: The Emirates Center for Strategic Studies and Research.

Bazilian, Morgan, and Roger Pielke. 2013. "Making energy access meaningful." *Issues in Science and Technology* 29(4):74–78.

Cabraal, R. Anil, Douglas Barnes, and Sachin Agarwal. 2005. "Productive uses of energy for rural development." *Annual Review of Environment and Resources*, 30(1): 117–144. doi:10.1146/annurev.energy.30.050504.144228

Cherp, Aleh. 2012. "Defining energy security takes more than asking around." *Energy Policy* 48: 841–842. doi:10.1016/j.enpol.2012.02.016.

———. 2014. "The concept of energy security: Beyond the four As." *Energy Policy* 75: 415–421. doi:10.1016/j.enpol.2014.09.005.

Cherp, Aleh and Jessica Jewell. 2011. "The three perspectives on energy security: intellectual history, disciplinary roots and the potential for integration." *Current Opinion in Environmental Sustainability* 3(4): 202–212. doi:10.1016/j.cosust.2011. 07.001.

Cherp, Aleh., A. Adenikinju, A. Goldthau, F. Hernandez, L. Hughes, J. Jansen, J. Jewell, M. Olshanskaya, R. Soares de Oliveira, B. Sovacool and S. Vakulenko. 2012. "Chapter 5 – Energy and security." In *Global Energy Assessment – Toward a Sustainable Future*, 325–384. Cambridge, UK: Cambridge University Press.

Chester, Lynne. 2010. "Conceptualising energy security and making explicit its polysemic nature." *Energy Policy* 38(2): 887–895. doi:10.1016/j.enpol.2009.10.039.

Fitzgerald, Kevin, Douglas Barnes, and Gordon McGranahan. 1990. "Interfuel substitution and changes in the way households use energy: the case of cooking and lighting behavior in urban Java." Industry and Energy Department working paper. Energy series paper; no. 29. Washington, DC: World Bank. Accessed December 16, 2013. http://documents.worldbank.org/curated/en/1990/10/441847/interfuel-substitution-changes-way-households-use-energy-case-cooking-lighting-behavior-urban-java.

Forum for Food Sovereignty. 2007. "Declaration of Nyéléni." Declaration of the Forum for Food Sovereignty, Sélingué, Mali, February 27. Accessed January 19, 2015. www.nyeleni.org/spip.php?article290.

Friends of the Earth International. 2006. "The Abuja Declaration." Abuja declaration resolution of FoFI International Conference on Climate Change. Abuja, Nigeria, September 28–29. Accessed January 19, 2015. http://members.foei.org/en/what-we-do/climate-and-energy/latest-news/the-abuja-declaration.

Gregory, Jack, and David Ian Stern. 2012. "Fuel choices in rural Maharashtra." CCEP Working Papers, Centre for Climate Economics & Policy, Crawford School of Public Policy, The Australian National University. Accessed December 16, 2013. http://econpapers.repec.org/RePEc:een:ccepwp:1207.

Heltberg, Rasmus. 2005. "Factors determining household fuel choice in Guatemala." *Environment and Development Economics* 10(03): 337–361. doi:10.1017/S1355770X04001858.

Hiemstra-van der Horst, Greg, and Alice J. Hovorka. 2008. "Reassessing the 'energy ladder': household energy use in Maun, Botswana." *Energy Policy* 36(9): 3333–3344. doi:10.1016/j.enpol.2008.05.006.

Hosier, Richard H., and Jeffrey Dowd. 1987. "Household fuel choice in Zimbabwe: an empirical test of the energy ladder hypothesis." *Resources and Energy* 9(4): 347–361. doi:10.1016/0165-0572(87)90003-X.

Hughes, Larry. 2009. "The four 'R's of energy security." *Energy Policy* 37(6): 2459–2461. doi:10.1016/j.enpol.2009.02.038.

Indigenous Peoples' Consultation on the Right to Food. 2002. *Declaration of Atitlán, Guatemala. Indigenous Peoples' Consultation on the Right to Food: A Global Consultation.* Atitlán, Sololá, Guatemala, April 17–19. Accessed January 19, 2015. http://cdn5.iitc.org/wp-content/uploads/2013/07/FINAL_Atitlan-Declaration-Food-Security_Apr25_ENGL.pdf.

Kassam, Karim-Aly. 2009. "Viewing change through the prism of indigenous human ecology: findings from the Afghan and Tajik Pamirs." *Human Ecology* 37(6): 377–390. doi:10.1007/s10745-009-9284-8.

——. 2010. "Pluralism, resilience, and the ecology of survival: case studies from the Pamir Mountains of Afghanistan." *Ecology and Society* 15(2): 8. Accessed December 16, 2013. http://www.ecologyandsociety.org/vol15/iss2/art8/.

Kassam, Karim-Aly, Munira Karamkhudoeva, Morgan Ruelle, and Michelle Baumflek. 2010. "Medicinal plant use and health sovereignty: findings from the Tajik and Afghan Pamirs." *Human Ecology* 38(6): 817–829. doi:10.1007/s10745-010-9356-9.

Kruyt, Bert, D. P. van Vuuren, H. J. M. de Vries, and H. Groenenberg. 2009. "Indicators for energy security." *Energy Policy* 37(6): 2166–2181. doi:10.1016/j.enpol.2009.02.006.

Löschel, Andreas, Ulf Moslener, and Dirk T. G. Rübbelke. 2010. "Energy security – concepts and indicators." *Energy Policy* 38(4): 1607–1608. doi:10.1016/j.enpol.2009.03.019.

Masera, Omar R., Barbara D. Saatkamp, and Daniel M. Kammen. 2000. "From linear fuel switching to multiple cooking strategies: a critique and alternative to the energy ladder model." *World Development* 28(12):2083–2103. doi:10.1016/S0305-750X(00)00076-0.

Mensah, Justice Tei, and George Adu. 2013. "An empirical analysis of household energy choice in Ghana." No 2013:6, Working Paper Series, Department of Economics, Swedish University of Agricultural Sciences. Accessed December 16, 2013. http://EconPapers.repec.org/RePEc:hhs:slueko:2013_006.

Moreno, Camila, and Anuradha Mittal. 2008. *Food and Energy Sovereignty Now: Brazilian Grassroots Position on Agroenergy*. Oakland: The Oakland Institute and Brazilian Terra de Direitos (TDD). Accessed December 16, 2013. http://www.oaklandinstitute.org/sites/oaklandinstitute.org/files/biofuels_report.pdf.

Nnaji, C. E., E. R. Ukwueze, and J. O. Chukwu. 2012. "Determinants of household energy choices for cooking in rural areas: evidence from Enugu State, Nigeria." *Continental Journal of Social Sciences* 5(2): 1–11.

Paradis, Gina, James Yockey, and Tracey LeBeau. 2009. *Seneca Nation of Indians Energy Organizational Planning*. Santa Fe: Red Mountain Energy Partners. doi:10.2172/951271.

Patel, Raj. 2009. "Food sovereignty." *Journal of Peasant Studies* 36(3): 663–706. doi:10.1080/03066150903143079

Practical Action. 2010. *Poor People's Energy Outlook, 2010*. Rugby, UK: Practical Action Publishing.

Practical Action. 2014. *Poor People's Energy Outlook, 2014: Key Messages on Energy for Poverty Alleviation*. Rugby, UK: Practical Action Publishing.

Pundo, Moses O., and Gavin C. Fraser. 2006. "Multinomial logit analysis of household cooking fuel choice in rural Kenya: the case of Kisumu district." *Agrekon* 45(1): 24–37. Accessed December 16, 2013. http://purl.umn.edu/31730.

Ruelle, Morgan L., Stephen J. Morreale, and Karim-Aly S. Kassam. 2011. "Practicing food sovereignty: spatial analysis of an emergent food system for the Standing Rock Nation." *Journal of Agriculture, Food Systems, and Community Development* 2(1): 163–179. doi:10.5304/jafscd.2011.021.005.

Schumacher, E. F. 1973. *Small is Beautiful: Economics as if People Mattered*. New York: Harper & Row.

Sovacool, Benjamin. K. 2011. "Evaluating energy security in the Asia pacific: towards a more comprehensive approach." *Energy Policy* 39(11): 7472–7479. doi:10.1016/j.enpol.2010.10.008.

Sovacool, Benjamin. K., and Marilyn A. Brown. 2010. "Competing dimensions of energy security: an international perspective." *Annual Review of Environment and Resources* 35(1): 77–108. doi:10.1146/annurev-environ-042509-143035.

Sovacool, Benjamin. K., and Ishani Mukherjee. 2011. "Conceptualizing and measuring energy security: a synthesized approach." *Energy* 36(8): 5343–5355. doi:10.1016/j.energy.2011.06.043.

Sovacool, Benjamin. K., M. Kryman, and T. C. Smith. 2014. "Energy, poverty, and development: a global review." In *Energy, Poverty, and Development*, 1–126. London: Routledge Critical Concepts in Development Studies Series.

van der Kroon, Bianca, Roy Brouwer, and Peter J. H. van Beukering. 2013. "The energy ladder: theoretical myth or empirical truth? Results from a meta-analysis." *Renewable and Sustainable Energy Reviews* 20: 504–513. doi:10.1016/j.rser.2012.11.045.

Via Campesina. 1996. "Food sovereignty: a future without hunger." Declaration of Via Campesina, Rome, Italy, November 11-17. Accessed January 19, 2015. http://www.voiceoftheturtle.org/library/1996%20Declaration%20of%20Food%20Sovereignty.pdf.

Vivoda, Vlado. 2010. "Evaluating energy security in the Asia-Pacific region: a novel methodological approach." *Energy Policy* 38(9): 5258–5263. doi:10.1016/j.enpol. 2010.05.028.

Von Hippel, David, Tatsujiro Suzuki, James H. Williams, Timothy Savage, and Peter Hayes. 2011. "Energy security and sustainability in Northeast Asia." *Energy Policy* 39(11): 6719–6730. doi:10.1016/j.enpol.2009.07.001.

8   Energy poverty and the environment

Carmen G. Gonzalez

Introduction

Public debates over energy policy are increasingly dominated by the specter of climate change. According to the Intergovernmental Panel on Climate Change (IPCC), greenhouse gas emissions increased at a faster rate from 2000 to 2010 than over the three preceding decades, reaching the highest levels recorded in human history. In order to avoid irreversible climate disruption, greenhouse gas emissions in the year 2050 must be 40 to 70 percent lower than they were in 2010, and must decline to zero by the end of the century (IPCC 2014). Unless drastic measures are taken to curb our dangerous dependence on fossil fuels, severe disruption of the planet's climate is inevitable.

Caused overwhelmingly by high-consuming people in the world's most affluent countries (the global North), climate change will have a disproportionate impact on the people in poor and middle-income countries (the global South) who contributed least to the problem (Birol 2015; Gordon 2007). The near three billion people in Asia, Africa, and Latin America who face daily hardships due to lack of modern energy for cooking, heating, sanitation, lighting, transportation, and basic mechanical power (the Energy Poor) will be disparately burdened by the adverse environmental consequences of global climate disruption. Floods, droughts, rising sea levels, and more frequent and severe storms will exacerbate food and water insecurity and inflict disease, death, and dislocation (Birol 2015; Srinivasan et al. 2008).

Will efforts to reduce greenhouse gas emissions consign the Energy Poor to perpetual deprivation? Or can energy poverty be addressed in ways that mitigate climate change, fulfill the human rights of the world's Energy Poor, and promote the transition to sustainable energy?

In a world of striking economic inequality and looming ecological collapse, the prospects for collective action to address energy poverty appear dim. However, this chapter argues that tackling energy poverty presents a rare win–win solution to the challenges posed by climate change that can bridge the North–South divide and lay the groundwork for the eradication of energy poverty.

This chapter proceeds in four parts. First, it examines the colonial and post-colonial roots of North–South inequality. Second, it frames the North–South divide over climate change through the concepts of climate debt and climate justice. Third, it argues that North–South collaboration to reduce black carbon emissions can effectively and inexpensively mitigate climate change, foster climate justice, and combat energy poverty. Finally, the chapter discusses several elements of a justice-based approach to climate change and energy poverty.

Colonial and post-colonial roots of North–South inequality

European colonization of Asia, Africa, and the Americas paved the way for contemporary economic and social inequality by dispossessing indigenous peoples, enslaving millions of Africans, and importing indentured workers to toil for their colonial overlords in far-flung destinations. The colonial encounter also devastated the ecosystems of the colonized territories through logging, mineral extraction, and plantation agriculture (Ponting 1993; Gordon 1997).

Colonialism transformed subsistence economies into economic appendages of Europe that supplied raw materials for industrialization and purchased European manufactured products. The achievement of political independence by much of the global South in the nineteenth and twentieth centuries did not significantly alter its subordinate role in the international division of labor. Through its control over a significant portion of the planet's natural resources, the North was able to live beyond the constraints of its own resource base and achieve an unprecedented material standard of living. However, "[m]uch of the price of that achievement was paid by the population of the Third World in the form of exploitation, poverty, and human suffering" (Ponting 1993, 223).

In the aftermath of World War II, the United States assumed the leadership of the global North, and proceeded to reconstruct war-torn Europe and Japan and to establish the legal architecture for contemporary globalization (Sachs, 2010). Most of the global South was under colonial domination when the legal institutions that would govern the post-war economic order were created, and the South's role in the development of these institutions was negligible. The World Bank, the International Monetary Fund (IMF), and the 1947 General Agreement on Tariffs and Trade (GATT 1947) facilitated the North's ongoing exploitation of the South's natural resources by promoting the free flow of goods, services, and capital across national borders (Ponting 1993).

In the decades following World War II, decolonization movements in the global South succeeded in liberating most of Asia and Africa from colonial rule. Southern nations mobilized to create a more equitable international economic order by using their numerical superiority in the United Nations General Assembly to pass resolutions favorable to the global South (Rajamani 2006). Recognizing that Southern poverty was caused by Northern economic domination, they demanded enhanced participation in global governance, technology transfer, special trade preferences, the right to subsidize infant industries, debt forgiveness, the stabilization of export prices for Southern commodities, and the right to nationalize the foreign companies exploiting their natural resources (Gordon 2009; Gordon and Sylvester 2004). In short, Southern nations sought to redress long-standing North–South economic inequality through special and differential treatment in international economic law (Ismail 2008).

The debt crisis of the 1980s brought these efforts to a grinding halt and enabled the Bretton Woods Institutions (the IMF and the World Bank) to impose on Southern nations the free market economic model known as the Washington Consensus. In exchange for debt repayment assistance from the IMF and the World Bank, debtor nations in the global South were compelled to adopt a one-size-fits-all economic model consisting of trade liberalization, deregulation, privatization of publicly owned enterprises, elimination of social safety nets, and the intensification of primary commodity exports to service the foreign debt (Gordon 2009). The lifting of Southern agricultural tariffs and abolition of agricultural support rendered small farmers destitute by placing them in direct competition with highly subsidized Northern farmers. The opening of Southern markets to Northern manufactured products jeopardized nascent industries. The result was massive impoverishment in the global South and an eruption of "IMF riots" in numerous Southern countries (Gonzalez 2004).

The export-driven economic reforms mandated by the IMF and the World Bank reinforced the South's economically disadvantageous dependence on the export of primary commodities. This economic specialization is detrimental to the global South due to the declining terms of trade for primary products relative to manufactured goods – a phenomenon first described by economists Raul Prebisch and Hans Singer and confirmed by subsequent empirical studies (Cypher 2009). Indeed, these free market economic reforms facilitated the North's over-consumption of the planet's natural resources by increasing the supply and lowering the price of timber, minerals, and agricultural products (Martinez-Alier 2002).

The North's economic policies exacted an enormous environmental toll. Much of the environmental degradation in the global South can be traced to export-oriented production rather than domestic consumption (Rees and Westra 2003). Impoverished and desperate for foreign capital, many Southern nations have become dumping grounds for hazardous wastes from the global North, havens for polluting industries (including the environmentally devastating petroleum industry that supplies the North's voracious appetite for fossil fuels), and targets for large-scale acquisitions of agricultural lands (the so-called "land grabs") by investors from Northern and middle-income Southern states (Pellow 2007; Black 2010; Cotula 2013). The North's economic policies also produced global environmental problems that will affect present as well as future generations, such as climate change and ozone depletion.

The World Trade Organization (WTO) agreements, which succeeded the 1947 GATT, exacerbated Southern poverty by systematically favoring Northern states. First, the WTO failed to remove the Northern agricultural subsidies that impoverished Southern farmers (Gonzalez 2002). Second, the WTO impeded the efforts of Southern states to industrialize and diversify their economies (Gordon 2009). The WTO restricted the ability of Southern countries to use tariffs and subsidies to promote potentially dynamic new industries; required

Southern countries to dismantle the import barriers that protected nascent Southern industries from technologically superior Northern competitors; and imposed onerous new obligations in the areas of intellectual property, investment, and services (Garcia 2004; Lee 2006). Economic historians have long recognized that the United States, Japan, Germany, the United Kingdom, South Korea, and Taiwan prospered on the basis of protectionism and only preached free trade after their industries were powerful enough to compete on global markets. International economic law constrains the ability of Southern states to deploy the very policies that contributed to Northern prosperity (Amsden 2009; Chang 2008; Reinert 2007; Chang 2002).

Scholars, activists, and Southern governments have argued that the global North owes an ecological debt to the global South for widespread poverty and environmental degradation resulting from centuries of economic exploitation (McLaren 2003). Climate change and other environmental ills must be understood through the prism of North–South inequality. The plight of the Energy Poor is likewise a product of an international economic order that systematically marginalizes vast segments of humanity. The following section examines the concepts that have been developed in the context of climate change to address environmental inequities between the global North and the global South as well as within nations.

Climate debt, climate justice, and the North–South divide

The North–South conflicts over climate change have frequently been articulated in the language of climate debt and climate justice. This section examines these two distinct, but interrelated concepts, and the ethical and legal duties that they impose.

Climate debt

Climate debt is a term coined in the global South to describe the imbalance between those who suffer and die from climate change and those who bear primary responsibility for the problem. Climate debt theory posits that the costs of climate change mitigation and adaptation should be borne by those who contributed most to the climate crisis. In other words, climate debt is an example of the polluter pays principle, requiring the global North to internalize the consequences of its own emissions (Paredis et al. 2008).

The global North industrialized rapidly and cheaply by exploiting the South's natural resources and by utilizing more than its fair share of the atmosphere to deposit its greenhouse gas emissions. Between 1880 and 1990, the global North generated 84 percent of the planet's fossil fuel-based carbon dioxide emissions and 75 percent of deforestation-related carbon dioxide emissions (Mickleson 2005). While China recently surpassed the United States as the world's top *current* carbon dioxide emitter, the per capita emissions of the global North continue to dwarf those of the South (Worldwatch Institute 2009). According to the World Bank, the average US citizen consumes 3.5 times more energy than a typical person in China and over ten times more than a resident of India. Even major oil-producing nations, such as Nigeria, Iran, and Venezuela, maintain levels of energy consumption far below US averages (World Bank 2011).

In short, the North has incurred a climate debt to the South for its historic and current contribution to climate change and for its prodigious carbon footprint (Mickelson 2005; McLaren 2003; Simms 2009). Indeed, the preamble to the United Nations Framework Convention on Climate Change (UNFCCC) implicitly recognizes this climate debt by observing

> that the largest share of historical and current global emissions has originated in developed countries, that per capita emissions in developing countries are still relatively low and that the share of global emissions originating in developing countries will grow to meet their social and developmental needs.
>
> (UNFCCC 1992, preamble)

Article 3(1) of the UNFCCC requires the global North to take the lead on efforts to combat climate change (UNFCCC 1992). The Kyoto Protocol institutionalizes this approach by imposing binding emission reduction obligations only on Northern countries (Kyoto Protocol 1997). In so doing, the UNFCCC and the Kyoto Protocol adopt the principle of common but differentiated responsibility, which imposes asymmetrical obligations on the North and the South in light of their relative contribution to environmental problems, their financial and technical resources, and their economic and ecological vulnerability (Stone 2004). This principle is discussed more fully in later in this chapter.

Climate justice

The demand for climate justice has its origins in the theory and practice of the environmental justice movement, which arose in the United States in the 1980s as a grassroots response to the concentration of polluting industry and abandoned hazardous waste sites in low-income communities and communities of color (Cole and Foster 2001; Mickelson 2009). Environmental justice scholars and activists underscored four distinct but interrelated dimensions of environmental injustice. They alleged distributive injustice in the form of inadequate access to environmental amenities (such as parks and open space) and disparate exposure to environmental hazards (such as toxic wastes); procedural unfairness due to the exclusion of socially and economically marginalized communities from governmental decision-making; corrective injustice in the form of inadequate enforcement of the environmental laws; and social injustice because environmental degradation is inextricably intertwined with broader social ills, such as poverty and racism (Kuehn 2000).

The discourse of environmental justice has been adopted by a variety of environmental social justice movements in both the global North and the global South, and has spawned transnational environmental justice networks dedicated to specific issues, including food justice, water justice, energy justice, and climate justice. The language of environmental justice is morally compelling, and has enhanced the visibility of marginalized communities by giving voice to their struggles and facilitating transnational alliances (Walker 2012; Schlosberg 2013).

Environmental justice also has an important North–South dimension. The primary cause of global environmental degradation is the over-consumption of the planet's finite resources by a transnational global elite located in the global North and in the urban centers of the global South (Sachs and Santarius 2007; Rees and Westra 2003). However, the consequences of unsustainable economic activity are borne disproportionately by the planet's most vulnerable communities, including racial and ethnic minorities, indigenous peoples, and the poor (Rees and Westra 2003).

Drawing upon the four dimensions of environmental injustice discussed above, this chapter adopts a four-part definition of climate justice consisting of distributive justice, procedural justice, corrective justice, and social justice. Climate change raises issues of distributive justice because the global North is responsible for the vast majority of historic greenhouse gas emissions, maintains an average per capita carbon footprint far above that of Southern nations, and reaps the benefits of a consumption-driven, fossil fuel-based development model while externalizing the social and environmental costs (Mickelson 2005). By contrast, Southern states and marginalized communities in both the North and the South bear a disproportionate share of the consequences of climate change due to their vulnerable geographic locations and limited resources for adaptation and disaster response (Anand 2004; United Nations 2012). Climate change raises issues of procedural justice because the North dominates the institutions of global economic and environmental governance, including the IMF, the World Bank, the WTO, and multilateral environmental treaty negotiations. Southern perspectives and priorities are frequently marginalized (Anand 2004; Hossay 2006; Peet 2009). Climate change also raises issues of corrective justice. From the indigenous communities devastated by climate change to the small island states facing imminent extinction, the nations and communities most burdened by climate change have been unable to obtain compensation for climate change-induced harms or cessation of the harmful conduct (Burkett 2009; Tsosie 2007). Finally, climate change raises issues of broader social injustice because it is intimately connected with the North–South power imbalances that perpetuate economic inequality and enable the North to consume a disproportionate share of the planet's resources (Roberts and Parks 2008).

The climate change negotiations are difficult, complex, and multi-faceted. However, they will likely flounder unless the North is willing to seriously grapple with climate debt and climate justice. Southern nations have frequently voiced frustration with Northern intransigence, describing the climate change negotiations as "rich nations telling the South what is and is not going to happen" (Gordon 2007, 1622). The growing clout of BASIC nations (Brazil, South

Africa, India, and China) has only complicated the negotiations by revealing the tensions between the economic and environmental priorities of countries like China and India and those of more ecologically vulnerable countries, such as the small island states (Happaerts and Bruyninckx 2013).

One way to bridge the divisions and foster collaboration is to offer an inexpensive and effective method of mitigating climate change that also hastens the transition to renewable energy in the South and provides energy to the world's nearly three billion Energy Poor. The following section discusses energy poverty as the missing link in the climate change negotiations.

Energy poverty and climate change: the missing link

Energy poverty is concentrated in the Least Developed Countries (LDCs), the nations singled out by the United Nations (UN) for their low income, high vulnerability to economic and environmental shocks, and small and geographically remote economies. The Energy Poor also reside in middle-income Southern nations, such as China, Brazil, and India, where their plight is often obscured by the rapidly increasing consumption levels of the middle class and the elite. Indeed, Guruswamy persuasively argues that it is a mistake to identify the Energy Poor with the state in which they reside because the Energy Poor are not stakeholders in the political process and are generally ignored by their own governments and by the international community (Guruswamy 2010).

Energy poverty is a form of transnational environmental injustice that exhibits the four distinct aspects of environmental injustice discussed above. First, the Energy Poor experience distributional injustice because they are denied equitable access to the clean and affordable energy necessary for a dignified existence. Ironically, many of the Energy Poor reside in energy-rich countries whose lucrative petroleum exports line the pockets of transnational corporations and kleptocratic national elites (Soares 2007). For example, 80 percent of Africa's petroleum is exported (much of it to service the foreign debt) while the Energy Poor make do with dried animal dung, wood, and other locally available fuels (Nelson 2004). Second, the Energy Poor experience procedural injustice because they are politically marginalized and do not have the opportunity to participate in governmental decision-making regarding energy policy (Guruswamy 2010). Third, the Energy Poor are subject to corrective injustice because they generally have no remedy in domestic or international tribunals to secure access to clean and affordable energy. Indeed, conflicts between transnational oil corporations and local communities have occasionally turned violent because the Energy Poor often bear the human health and environmental costs of oil drilling with limited or no access to its economic benefits (Soares 2007). Finally, energy poverty is inextricably intertwined with a host of other social ills, including economic inequality, gender bias, child labor, and lack of access to health care and education.

The climate change negotiations represent a unique opportunity for Northern countries to repay the climate debt and foster climate and energy justice by financing the provision of clean, renewable energy to the world's Energy Poor. Regrettably, the climate change negotiations have given short shrift to energy poverty because the Energy Poor emit minimal greenhouse gases. For example, the Copenhagen Accord acknowledges the importance of ensuring that low emitting countries "continue to develop on a low emission pathway" (United Nations Climate Change Conference 2009, Art.7), but fails to allocate funding to fulfill this objective. This omission is regrettable because the UNFCCC's preamble explicitly recognizes the need to increase energy consumption in the global South "for the achievement of sustained economic growth and the eradication of poverty" (UNFCCC 1992, preamble).

The lack of attention to energy poverty in the climate change negotiations is puzzling for at least four reasons. First, energy poverty poses an enormous threat to human health. According to the World Health Organization, reliance on biomass for cooking and heating results in over four million premature deaths per year from respiratory, cardiovascular, and other ailments caused by exposure to indoor air pollution. Most of the victims are women and children (WHO 2014).

Second, the black carbon emitted by the combustion of biomass constitutes the second most significant contributor to climate change after carbon dioxide. Black carbon, when it is airborne, warms the planet by absorbing solar radiation more effectively than other greenhouse gases, such as tropospheric ozone and methane (Ramanathan and Carmichael 2008; Bond et al. 2013). When black carbon is deposited on snow and ice in the Arctic and Antarctic regions, it lowers their ability to reflect solar radiation and thereby accelerates melting and consequent sea level rise (Jacobson and Streets 2009).

Third, dependence on biomass for energy is a significant contributor to deforestation. Deforestation produces soil erosion and deprives local communities of other valuable ecosystem services, including flood control, drought resistance, regulation of rainfall, habitat for biodiversity, and enhancement of water quality. Deforestation also destroys valuable carbon sinks, and the burning of biomass emits greenhouse gases (Myers 1997).

Finally, the lack of attention to black carbon in the climate negotiations is perplexing because the cost of reducing black carbon emissions is minimal relative to other greenhouse gases and because the benefits are potentially enormous (Guruswamy 2010). Whereas carbon dioxide can reside in the atmosphere for 50 to 200 years, black carbon dissipates in as little as one week if existing emissions cease (Ramanathan and Carmichael 2008). In other words, "helping to move one-third of the global population away from biomass burning will have the effect of reducing global warming more efficiently than merely reducing carbon dioxide emissions" (Guruswamy 2010, 246).

In short, addressing energy poverty represents a win–win proposition in the climate change negotiations – an inexpensive mitigation strategy that enhances the well-being of the Energy Poor while avoiding environmental "tipping points" by producing immediate emissions reductions. Although providing modern electrical energy to the Energy Poor would be an expensive decades-long undertaking, numerous appropriate sustainable energy technologies (ASETs) are presently available. These include decentralized electricity generating systems based on solar, wind, and local biodiesel; efficient cook-stoves; and solar thermal heating. Decentralized electricity generation is particularly appropriate because the majority of the world's Energy Poor reside in sparsely populated rural areas of the global South, where extension of the existing electric grid would be cost-prohibitive (Guruswamy 2011). Decentralized renewable energy-based systems can provide the Energy Poor with electrical power without tying them to existing fossil fuel-based energy systems that are cumbersome, expensive, polluting, and vulnerable to capture by corrupt national elites. ASETs thereby promote democracy, self-determination, and local control in addition to mitigating climate change, providing energy to the nearly three billion Energy Poor, and hastening the global South's transition to sustainable energy.

A justice-centered approach to climate change and energy poverty

A justice-centered approach to climate change and energy poverty entails respect for environmental human rights, the re-invigoration of common but differentiated responsibility in international environmental law, and greater attention to corporate accountability. It also calls for a bold and visionary reconceptualization of the dominant economic paradigm to reduce material disparities while respecting the planet's biophysical limits. The remainder of this chapter discusses these guiding principles and their relation to climate and energy justice.

Environmental human rights

Climate justice, like environmental justice more broadly, is grounded in human rights, including the rights to life, health, and cultural integrity, the right to a safe and healthy environment, the right to be free from race and sex discrimination, and the right to information, participation, and access to justice (Gonzalez 2013). In January 2009, the United Nations Human Rights Council published a report detailing the human rights implications of climate change. The report concluded that climate change poses direct and indirect threats to the rights to life, food, water, health, housing, and self-determination, and that its effects "will be felt more acutely by those segments of the population who are already in vulnerable situations due to factors such as gender, poverty, age, minority status, and disability" (United Nations High Commissioner for Human Rights 2009).

Chapter 5 of this volume raises the question of whether there is a right to energy, and the present chapter argues that there is such a right. Although most human rights treaties do not contain explicit environmental provisions, global and regional human rights tribunals have allowed individuals and communities affected by environmental degradation to bring claims against their governments based on human rights violations caused by inadequate environmental protection (Knox 2009). These tribunals have concluded that failure to protect the environment may violate the rights to life, health, property, privacy and family life, an adequate standard of living, and the collective rights of indigenous peoples to their ancestral lands and resources (Boyle 2007; Shelton 2009). For example, in *López Ostra v. Spain* (1994) and *Guerra v. Italy* (1998), the European Court of Human Rights found that failure to regulate industrial air pollution violated local residents' right to respect for privacy, family life, and home guaranteed by the European Convention on Human Rights. In *Yanomani v. Brazil* (1985), the Inter-American Commission on Human Rights determined that the government's decision to construct a highway through Yanomani territory and to authorize the exploitation of the territory's resources constituted a violation of the Yanomani's rights to life, health, liberty, personal security, and residence and movement under the American Declaration of the Rights and Duties of Man. In *Mayagna (Sumo) Awas Tingni Community v. Nicaragua* (2001), the Inter-American Court of Human Rights held that the government violated the collective property rights of indigenous peoples under the American Convention on Human Rights when it granted a logging concession on their ancestral lands to a private company. Human rights tribunals have emphasized that states have an obligation to refrain from directly violating human rights as well as a duty to protect these rights by regulating the conduct of private parties such as corporations (Knox 2009). In *Öneryildiz v. Turkey* (2004), for example, the European Court of Human Rights determined that the government's inadequate regulation of a waste disposal operation in an urban area violated the right to life and property under the European Convention on Human Rights.

While no human rights tribunal has yet concluded that failure to provide access to energy constitutes a human rights violation, energy is essential for cooking, lighting, heating, refrigeration, sanitation, health care, and the pumping of clean water for drinking, bathing, and crop irrigation. The environmental precedents referenced above can be used to argue that access to energy is implicit in a variety of existing human rights obligations, including the rights to life, health, food, water, and an adequate standard of living (Bradbrook et al. 2008). In addition, the Convention on the Elimination of All Forms of Discrimination Against Women (CEDAW) explicitly obligates states parties to ensure that rural women "enjoy adequate living conditions, particularly in relation to housing, sanitation, electricity, and water supply, transport and communication" (CEDAW 1979, Art. 14[2][h]).

Grounding demands for energy justice in the language of human rights creates legal rather than simply moral obligations to address energy poverty. It also provides the opportunity to exert pressure on states through the UN human rights institutions. For example, the appointment of a Special Rapporteur on the right to energy as well as the development of guidelines by the UN Commission on Economic, Social and Cultural Rights to implement this right could elevate the profile of energy poverty in both domestic and international fora – including the climate change negotiations. Recognition of the human right to energy could also encourage funding agencies (such as the World Bank) to prioritize renewable energy projects designed to benefit the Energy Poor (Bradbrook et al. 2008). An additional benefit of a human rights approach is its potential to trump other norms of international law (Anton and Shelton 2011). For example, in order to combat energy poverty and facilitate the South's transition to renewable energy, it is essential that conflicts between the North's intellectual property rights and the human rights of the Energy Poor be resolved in favor of the latter. If the clean energy technologies of Northern countries (and of Southern clean energy leaders like China) are unaffordable due to patent protection, then efforts to address climate change and eradicate energy poverty may be jeopardized (Kapur 2011). Finally, the ability of aggrieved individuals and communities to bring human rights claims in domestic or international tribunals can shine a spotlight on corrupt and unresponsive governments (and their corporate collaborators) and create political mobilization for change.

Re-invigoration of common but differentiated responsibility

A justice-centered approach to energy poverty requires recognition and redress of North–South economic and political inequality arising from the colonial and post-colonial practices described in the first part of this chapter. International environmental law has developed an important principle designed to mitigate North–South inequality – the principle of common but differentiated responsibility. Principle 7 of the Rio Declaration on Environment and Development articulates this principle as follows:

> In view of the different contributions to global environmental degradation, States have common but differentiated responsibilities. The developed countries acknowledge the responsibility that they bear in the international pursuit of sustainable development in view of the pressures their societies place on the global environment and of the technologies and financial resources they command.
>
> (UN Conference on Environment and Development 1992)

The UNFCCC explicitly adopts this principle in Article 3 (1), which provides that the "Parties should protect the climate system for the benefit of present and future generations of humankind, on the basis of equity and in accordance with their common but differentiated responsibilities and respective capabilities" (UNFCCC 1992, Art. 3[1]). The principle of common but differentiated responsibility has been included in several additional environmental treaties, including the Vienna Convention for the Protection of the Ozone Layer, the Montreal Protocol on Substances that Deplete the Ozone Layer, the Convention on Biological Diversity, the United Nations Convention on the Law of the Sea, and the Kyoto Protocol (Gonzalez 2007).

Regrettably, the principle of common but differentiated responsibility remains controversial. The United States, in particular, has refused to accept moral or legal responsibility for its historic contribution to climate change and other environmental problems. In addition to rejecting the Kyoto Protocol, the United States went so far as to submit an interpretive statement on Principle 7 of the Rio

Declaration disclaiming any legal responsibility for historic acts of environmental degradation (Kovar 1993).

One of the primary reasons for the impasse in the climate change negotiations is the North's refusal to take responsibility for the colonial and post-colonial practices that enabled Northern states to industrialize and prosper at the expense of the planet's most vulnerable human beings. As Rajamani (2006) points out, this refusal to be held accountable

> seeks to wipe the colonial past from our collective memories and start afresh, as if past patterns of exploitation have little bearing on current inequities, and the efforts of developing countries to raise them time and again are no more than special pleading.

The realization of climate justice and energy justice through the negotiation of a successor to the Kyoto Protocol requires accountability for past wrongs and re-invigoration of the principle of common but differentiated responsibility. The world's high-consuming societies must radically reduce their greenhouse gas emissions in order to create the environmental space necessary for Southern nations to eliminate energy poverty. These high-consuming Northern countries must also finance climate change mitigation and adaptation in the global South. However, middle-income Southern countries (like China and India) do bear responsibility for their contributions to climate change and must contribute their fair share to collective solutions. The successor to the Kyoto Protocol should impose differential responsibilities on nations rather than exempting Southern countries from binding greenhouse gas reduction obligations. Criteria for such differentiation should include past, current, and projected future greenhouse gas emissions – as well as vulnerability and capacity to contribute to collaborative efforts to combat climate change. Above all, North–South and South–South conflicts in the climate change negotiations must not obscure the environmental and human rights benefits of rapid action to mitigate climate change by providing ASETs to the Energy Poor. One important vehicle for incorporating energy access into the climate regime is the Green Climate Fund discussed in Chapter 13 of this volume.

Corporate accountability

From the oil drilling operation of Chevron/Texaco in Ecuador to those of Royal Dutch Shell in the Niger Delta, transnational corporations engaged in extractive industries are notorious for their human rights abuses and their destruction of local environments – including those of the Energy Poor (Soares 2007; Stephens 2002). Far from protecting their citizens, post-colonial states, eager to secure foreign investment, often strive to create a friendly environment for these corporations by entering into one-sided trade and investment agreements that protect the property rights of the foreign investor and restrict the ability of Southern states to regulate in the public interest (Simons 2012; Sornarajah

2006). In addition to the local harm inflicted by these corporations, recent reports indicate that 50 corporations (primarily oil companies) and 40 government-controlled enterprises are responsible for 63 percent of anthropogenic greenhouse gas emissions from the Industrial Revolution through 2010 (Goldenberg 2013).

A justice-based approach to energy poverty requires creative use of international and domestic law to regulate the conduct of the fossil fuel industry both at home and abroad. Currently, the geographic separation between the country of incorporation (the home state) and the country where extractive activities take place (the host state) may allow corporations to escape moral condemnation from shareholders and the public in the home state for human rights and environmental abuses in their overseas operations. Furthermore, if these operations are conducted in the host state through a local subsidiary, then the legal distinction between the parent company in the home state and the subsidiary in the host state may make it difficult for the legal system to impose liability for the acts of the subsidiary on the parent company and its shareholders despite the profits that they derive from this conduct. Under well-settled corporate law principles, the subsidiary is deemed a separate legal person, and the parent company is not generally liable for the actions of its subsidiaries. In addition, the doctrine of state responsibility generally does not attribute the conduct of private corporations to the states in which they are incorporated or the state in which they conduct their operations (De Jonge 2011).

While a discussion of the legal strategies to achieve corporate accountability (and the limitations of these strategies) is beyond the scope of this chapter, the relevant insight is that international and domestic law have been deployed in a variety ways from the colonial era to the present to limit the ability of states to regulate corporate misconduct – particularly corporate misconduct that takes place abroad (Simons 2012; Simons and Macklin 2014). There are a variety of strategies that might be pursued to achieve corporate accountability, including strengthening the environmental enforcement capacity of Southern countries, holding Northern countries liable for failure to regulate the extraterritorial conduct of their corporations, allowing victims of human rights and environmental abuses to sue in the home country of these corporations, and developing treaties requiring the imposition of standards of conduct on these corporations. In June 2014, the United Nations Human Rights Council (2014) voted to convene a working group to develop a legally binding instrument to impose human rights obligations on corporations. While the feasibility of this approach is questionable given the opposition of Northern countries, it is important to recognize and address the role of corporate actors in the perpetuation of the fossil fuel economy, including human rights and environmental abuses during the extraction process.

Re-conceptualizing development

Climate change is merely one symptom of a deeper structural problem: an economic development model premised on the myth of unlimited economic growth. From the post-World War II era to the present, Northern aid, trade, and financial institutions have promoted the growth-at-any-cost economic model as the solution to global poverty and inequality (Sachs and Santarius 2007). By externalizing the environmental and social costs of economic activity, this model has destroyed ecosystems, depleted natural resources, and inflicted unspeakable violence on poor communities in both the North and the South (Rees and Westra 2003). The world's most affluent countries (the US, the European Union, and Japan) and its rising economic powers (Brazil, Russia, India, and China) currently account for nearly 70 percent of global greenhouse gas emissions, and these emissions are rising (Gonzalez 2013). If all countries of the world pursue the growth-at-any-cost economic model, the result will be catastrophic.

If we are to enhance the living standards of the Energy Poor without exceeding ecological limits, it is essential to develop a different paradigm of economic development that places human well-being and the health and resilience of the planet's ecosystems at its center rather than relying on gross domestic product (GDP) as a proxy for human flourishing. This will require coordination with finance, energy, land use, public health, trade, investment, and other areas of law and policy to facilitate the transition to a low carbon, climate resilient, equitable model of development. A powerful justice narrative, coupled with scientific, technical, and legal arguments, can help generate the political will necessary to make this transition a reality.

Closing

Climate change and energy poverty present daunting moral challenges at the intersection of human rights and the environment. A justice-centered approach to energy poverty and climate change must recognize the historic roots of these challenges and seize opportunities to bridge the North–South divide. The burning of biomass for cooking and heating produces black carbon, the second largest contributor to climate change after carbon dioxide. Energy poverty destroys forests, ravages local ecosystems, and denies billions of people the right to life, health, food, water, and an adequate standard of living. The modest sums required to provide ASETs to the Energy Poor can foster North–South collaboration, achieve immediate reductions in greenhouse gas emissions, fulfill the human rights of the Energy Poor, and promote the transition to sustainable energy. The world's high-consuming societies must ultimately reduce their greenhouse gas emissions in order to enable Southern countries to elevate the living standards of the poor and marginalized. They must also finance climate change mitigation and adaptation in the global South and transfer renewable energy technology. However, taking action to mitigate black carbon emissions by providing ASETs to the Energy Poor would produce an immediate decline in one highly potent but short-lived greenhouse gas (black carbon), thereby providing a short reprieve from climate catastrophe and an opportunity to hammer out and implement long-term solutions to the problems of climate change and energy poverty.

References

Amsden, Alice. 2009. *The Developing World's Journey through Heaven and Hell*. Cambridge: MIT Press.

Anand, Ruchi. 2004. *International Environmental Justice: A North-South Dimension*. Burlington: Ashgate.

Anton, Donald and Dinah Shelton. 2011. *Environmental Protection and Human Rights*. Cambridge: Cambridge University Press.

Birol, Fatih. 2015. "Achieving Energy for All Will Not Cost the Earth." In *Energy Poverty: Global Challenges and Local Solutions*, ed. Antoine Halff, Benjamin Sovacool, and Jon Rozhon, 11–20. Oxford: Oxford University Press.

Black, Brian C. 2010. *Crude Reality: Petroleum in World History*. Lanham: Rowman & Littlefield.

Bond, Tammy C., et al. 2013. "Bounding the Role of Black Carbon in the Climate System: A Scientific Assessment." *Journal of Geophysical Research: Atmosphere*, 118 (11): 5380–5552.

Boyle, Alan. 2007. "Human Rights or Environmental Rights? A Reassessment." *Fordham Environmental Law Review* 18: 471–511.

Bradbrook, Adrian J., Judith G. Gardam, and Monique Cormier 2008. "A Human Dimension to the Energy Debate: Access to Modern Energy Services." *Journal of Energy and Natural Resources* 26(4): 526–551.

Burkett, Maxine. 2009. "Climate Reparations." *Melbourne Journal of International Law* 29 (10): 516–535.

Chang, Ha-Joon. 2002. *Kicking Away the Ladder: Development Strategy in Historical Perspective*. London: Anthem Press.

Chang, Ha-Joon. 2008. *Good Samaritans: The Myth of Free Trade and the Secret History of Capitalism*. New York: Bloomsbury Press.

Cole, Luke and Sheila Foster. 2001. *From the Ground Up: Environmental Racism and the Rise of the Environmental Justice Movement*. New York: New York University Press.

Convention on the Elimination of All Forms of Discrimination Against Women (CEDAW). 1979. UNGA Res. 34/180, 34 U.N. GAOR Supp. (No. 46) at 193, U.N. Doc. A/34/46.

Cotula, Lorenzo. 2013. *The Great African Land Grab? Agricultural Investments and the Global Food System*. London: Zed Books.

Cypher, James M. 2009. *The Process of Economic Development*. New York: Routledge.

De Jonge, Alice. 2011. *Transnational Corporations and International Law: Accountability in the Global Business Environment*. Cheltenham: Edward Elgar.

Garcia, Frank J. 2004. "Beyond Special and Differential Treatment." *Boston College International and Comparative Law Review* 27: 291–317.

Goldenberg, Suzanne. 2013. "Just 90 Companies Caused Two Thirds of Man-made Global Warming Emissions." *The Guardian*, November 20. www.academia.edu/6448836/TNCs_and_Environmental_Pollution. Accessed December 15, 2014.

Gonzalez, Carmen G. 2002. "Institutionalizing Inequality: The WTO, Agriculture, and Developing Countries." *Columbia Journal of Environmental Law* 27: 433–490.

Gonzalez, Carmen G. 2004. "Trade Liberalization, Food Security, and the Environment: The Neoliberal Threat to Sustainable Rural Development." *Transnational Law & Contemporary Problems* 14: 419–498.

Gonzalez, Carmen. 2007. "Genetically Modified Organisms and Justice: The International Environmental Justice Implications of Biotechnology." *Georgetown International Environmental Law Review* 19: 584–608.

Gonzalez, Carmen. 2013. "Environmental Justice and International Environmental Law." In *Routledge Handbook of International Environmental Law*, ed. Shawkat Alam, Md Jahid Hossain Bhuiyan, Tareq M.R. Chowdhury, and Erika J. Techera, 77–97. Abingdon: Routledge.

Gordon, Ruth. 1997. "Saving Failed States: Sometimes a Neocolonialist Notion." *American University Journal of International Law and Policy* 12 (6): 904–971.

Gordon, Ruth. 2007. "Climate Change and the Poorest Nations: Further Reflections on Global Inequality." *University of Colorado Law Review* 78: 1559–1623.

Gordon, Ruth. 2009. "The Dawn of a New, New International Economic Order?" *Law and Contemporary Problems*. 72: 131–162.

Gordon, Ruth E. and Jon Sylvester. 2004. "Deconstructing Development." *Wisconsin International Law Journal*. 22 (1): 1–86.

Guerra v. Italy, European Court of Human Rights, Application No. 14967/89, Reports of Judgments and Decisions 1998-I (February 19, 1998).

Guruswamy, Lakshman. 2010. "Energy Justice and Sustainable Development." *Colorado Journal of International Environmental Law* 21: 231–275.

Guruswamy, Lakshman. 2011. "Energy Poverty." *Annual Review of Environmental Resources* 36: 139–161.

Happaerts, Sanders and Hans Bruyninckx. 2013. "Rising Powers in Global Climate Governance: Negotiating in the New World Order." Leuven Centre for Global Governance Studies Working Paper No. 124.

Hossay, Patrick. 2006. *Unsustainable: A Primer for Global Environmental and Social Justice*. New York: Zed Books.

Intergovernmental Panel on Climate Change (IPCC). 2014. *Climate Change 2014: Mitigation of Climate Change* (Working Group III Contribution to the Fifth Assessment Report of the Intergovernmental Panel on Climate Change). Cambridge: Cambridge University Press.

Ismail, Faizel. 2008. "Rediscovering the Role of Developing Countries in GATT before the Doha Round." *Law and Development Review* 1: 49–72.

Jacobson, Mark Z. and David G. Streets. 2009. "Influence of Future Anthropogenic Emissions on Climate, Natural Emissions, and Air Quality." *Journal of Geophysical Research: Atmospheres (1984–2012)*. 114: 1–21.

Kapur, Kavita. 2011. "Climate Change, Intellectual Property, and the Scope of Human Rights Obligations." *Sustainable Development Law and Policy* 11: 58–97.

Knox, John H. 2009. "Climate Change and Human Rights Law." *Virginia Journal of International Law*. 50 (1): 163–218.

Kovar, Jeffrey D. 1993. "A Short Guide to the Rio Declaration." *University of Colorado Journal of International Environmental Law and Policy* 4 (1): 119–140.

Kuehn, Robert R. 2000. "A Taxonomy of Environmental Justice." *Environmental Law Reporter* 30: 10681–10703.

Kyoto Protocol to the United Nations Framework Convention on Climate Change. 1997. 2303 UNTS 148; reprinted in 37 ILM 32 (1998).

Lee, Yong Shik. 2006. *Reclaiming Development in the New World Trading System*. Cambridge: Cambridge University Press.

López Ostra v. Spain, European Court of Human Rights, Application No. 16798/90 Series A no. 303-C (December 9, 1994).

Martinez-Alier, Juan. 2002. *The Environmentalism of the Poor: A Study of Ecological Conflicts and Valuation*. Cheltenham: Edward Elgar.

Mayagna (Sumo) Awas Tingni Community v Nicaragua, Inter-American Court of Human Rights, (ser.C) No. 79 (August 31, 2001).

McLaren, Duncan. 2003. "Environmental Space, Equity and the Ecological Debt." In *Just Sustainabilities: Development in an Unequal World*, ed. Julian Agyeman, Robert D. Bullard, and Bob Evans, 19–37. Cambridge: MIT Press.

Mickelson, Karin. 2005. "Leading Towards a Level Playing Field, Repaying Ecological Debt, or Making Environmental Space: Three Stories about International Environmental Cooperation." *Osgoode Hall Law Journal* 43 (1–2): 137–170.

Mickelson, Karin. 2009. "Beyond a Politics of the Possible? South-North Relations and Climate Change." *Melbourne Journal of International Law* 10 (2): 1–13.

Myers, Norman. 1997. "The World's Forests and Their Ecosystem Services." In *Nature's Services: Societal Dependence on Natural Ecosystems*, ed. Gretchen C. Daily, 215–235. Washington, DC: Island Press.

Nelson, Patricia. 2004. "An African Dimension to the Clean Development Mechanism: Finding a Path to Sustainable Development in the Energy Sector." *Denver Journal of International Law and Policy* 32: 615–652.

Öneryildiz v. Turkey, European Court of Human Rights, Application No. 48389/99, ECHR 2004-XII (November 30, 2004).

Paredis, Erik, Gert Goeminne, Wouter Vanhove, Frank Maes, and Jesse Lambrecht. 2008. *The Concept of Ecological Debt: Its Meaning and Applicability in International Policy*. Rosemead: Academia Scientific.

Peet, Richard. 2009. *Unholy Trinity: the IMF, World Bank and WTO*. London: Zed Books.

Pellow, David Naguib. 2007. *Resisting Global Toxics: Transnational Movements for Environmental Justice*. Cambridge: MIT Press.

Ponting, Clive. 1993. *A Green History of the World: The Environment and the Collapse of Great Civilizations*. New York: Penguin Books.

Rajamani, Lavanya. 2006. *Differential Treatment in International Environmental Law*. New York: Oxford University Press.

Ramanathan, V. and G. Carmichael. 2008. "Global and Regional Climate Changes Due to Black Carbon." *Nature Geoscience* 1: 221–227.

Rees, William E. and Laura Westra. 2003. "When Consumption Does Violence: Can There be Sustainability and Environmental Justice in a Resource-Limited World?" In *Just Sustainabilities: Development in an Unequal World*, ed. Julian Agyeman, Robert D. Bullard, and Bob Evans, 99–124. Cambridge: MIT Press.

Reinert, Eric. 2007. *How Rich Countries Got Rich ... and Why Poor Countries Stay Poor*. New York: Caroll and Graf.

Roberts, J. Timmons and Bradley Parks. 2008. *A Climate of Injustice: Global Inequality, North South Politics, and Climate Policy*. Cambridge: MIT Press.

Sachs, Wolfgang. 2010. "Environment." In *The Development Dictionary: A Guide to Knowledge as Power*, ed. Wolfgang Sachs, 24–37. New York: Zed Books.

Sachs, Wolfgang and Tilman Santarius. 2007. *Fair Future: Resource Conflicts, Security and Global Justice*. London: Zed Books.

Schlosberg, David. 2013. "Theorizing Environmental Justice: The Expanding Sphere of Discourse." *Environmental Politics* 22 (1): 37–55.

Shelton, Dinah. 2009. "Environmental Rights and Brazil's Obligations in the Inter-American Human Rights System." *George Washington International Law Review* 40 (3): 733–777.

Simms, Andrew. 2009. *Ecological Debt, Second Edition: Global Warming and the Wealth of Nations*. London: Pluto Press.

Simons, Penelope C. 2012. "International Law's Invisible Hand and the Future of Corporate Accountability for Violations of Human Rights." *Journal of Human Rights and the Environment* 3 (1): 5–43.

Simons, Penelope and Audrey Macklin. 2014. *The Governance Gap: Extractive Industries, Human Rights, and the Home State Advantage*. Abingdon: Routledge.

Soares, Ricardo de Oliveira. 2007. *Oil and Politics in the Gulf of Guinea*. New York: Columbia University Press.

Sornarajah, M. 2006. "Power and Justice: Third World Resistance in International Law." *Singapore Year Book of International Law* 10: 19–57.

Srinivasan, U. Thara, Susan P. Carey, Eric Hallstein, Paul A.T. Higgins, Amber C. Kerr, Laura E. Koteen, Adam B. Smith, Reg Watson, John Harte, and Richard B. Norgaard. 2008. "The Debt of Nations and the Distribution of Ecological Impacts from Human Activities." *Proceedings of the National Academy of Science* 105 (5): 1768–1773.

Stephens, Beth. 2002. "The Amorality of Profit: Transnational Corporations and Human Rights." *Berkeley Journal of International Law* 20 (1): 45–90.

Stone, Christopher D. 2004. "Common but Differentiated Responsibilities in International Law." *American Journal of International Law* 98 (2): 276–301.

Tsosie, Rebecca. 2007. "Indigenous Peoples and Environmental Justice: The Impact of Climate Change." *University of Colorado Law Review* 78 (4): 1625–1677.

United Nations. 2012. *Resilient People, Resilient Planet: A Future Worth Choosing*. http://uscib.org/docs/GSPReportOverview_A4%20size.pdf. Accessed December 15, 2014.

United Nations Climate Change Conference, Dec. 7–18, 2009, Copenhagen Accord, UN Doc. FCCC/CP/2009/L.7 (Dec. 18, 2009) (Copenhagen Accord).

United Nations Conference on Environment and Development. 1992. Rio Declaration on Environment and Development, UN Doc. A/CONF.152/26 (vol. I) reprinted in 31 ILM 874, Principle 7.

United Nations Framework Convention on Climate Change (UNFCCC). 1992. Concluded at Rio de Janeiro, 9 May 1992. 1771 UNTS 107, reprinted in 31 ILM 849 (1992).

United Nations General Assembly, Human Rights Council. 2014. *Elaboration of an International Legally Binding Instrument on Transnational Corporations and Other Business Enterprises with respect to Human Rights*, UN Doc. A/HRC/26/L.22/Rev.1 (June 25). Accessed March 4, 2015. http://undocs.org/A/HRC/26/L.22/Rev.1.

United Nations High Commissioner for Human Rights. UN Doc. A/HRC/10/61. 2009. *Report on the Relationship between Climate Change and Human Rights*. www.ohchr.org/Documents/Press/AnalyticalStudy.pdf. Accessed December 15, 2014.

Walker, Gordon. 2012. *Environmental Justice: Concepts, Evidence, and Politics*. Abingdon: Routledge.

World Bank. 2011. *Energy Use* (kg of oil equivalent per capita). http://data.worldbank.org/indicator/EG.USE.PCAP.KG.OE. Accessed December 15, 2014.

World Health Organization (WHO). 2014. *Household Air Pollution and Health*, Factsheet No. 292. www.who.int/mediacentre/factsheets/fs292/en/. Accessed December 15, 2014.

Worldwatch Institute. 2009. *State of the World: Into a Warming World*. New York: W.W. Norton & Company.

Yanomani v. Brazil, Case 7615 (Brazil), 1984–1985 Annual Report of the Inter-American Commission on Human Rights 24, OEA.

Part 3

Assessing the various challenges

9   Assessing challenges to development

Mark Safty

Introduction

The identification and analysis of barriers to development of energy infrastructure and to achieving "energy access" in the poorest regions of the world should occur within a framework that provides a system for understanding, prioritizing, classifying and mitigating the effects of the barriers. Numerous papers, books and articles discuss barriers to development, but the literature often identifies development barriers and their perceived severity without meaningful prioritization or classification.[1] The purpose of this chapter is to steer away from generalized thought and comment about barriers, and to evaluate barriers in a structured process based on the assessment of specific project profiles and issues.

This chapter begins by considering what it means to provide "energy access for the poor." Next is a summary of the commonly identified categories of challenges to providing energy access to the poor and a description of some of the specific barriers that populate each category. This very highly generalized set of barriers is far too broad, and such barriers are not often analyzed under consistent or critically evaluated frameworks. Because the availability of and access to project funding is a primary and universally recognized barrier to development (International Energy Agency 2014, 107–109; International Renewable Energy Agency 2012, 16; United Nations Environment Programme 2012, 17), the third part of this chapter focuses on a risk assessment framework to analyze and discuss the barriers in the context of project financing. Finally, the concluding section of this chapter focuses briefly on the need for and desirability of well-designed and maintained information-sharing mechanisms that will facilitate the replication of creative risk mitigation strategies.

Understanding the objective

It is helpful to begin by defining the phrase "energy access for the poor" to effectively articulate the goals underpinning current development activities and thereby identify relevant barriers to energy access in poor regions.

The approximately 1.3 billion people in the world who lack access to electricity are divided roughly equally between developing Asia and sub-Saharan

Africa (International Renewable Energy Agency 2012, 533). These are the people who need energy access.[2] For these people, "energy access" has been defined by the International Energy Agency (IEA) as "a household having reliable and affordable access to clean cooking facilities and a first electricity supply connection, with a minimum level of consumption ... that increases over time to reach the regional average" (International Energy Agency 2011, 12).[3]

What it will take to provide such access is the subject of some debate. According to Secretary-General Ban Ki-moon's 2011 Vision Statement, achieving this level of electricity access for these 1.3 billion people will require an estimated investment of $50 billion per year over the 2010–2030 time frame (Ki-moon 2011, 8). IEA's 2014 estimate of the required investment through 2030 is $30 billion per year (International Renewable Energy Agency 2012, 539).

The required investment, regardless of the amount, will be provided by a combination of funders: governments, multi-lateral lenders, traditional commercial lenders to the infrastructure sector, non-profits, NGOs, and private investors, among others. Across the spectrum of these funding sources, the acceptability of risk varies depending on the nature and objectives of the funder. However, regardless of the funding source, project risks will, and should be, identified and assessed in the context of a framework that has evolved as the infrastructure finance model used by global lenders. Substantially all of the barriers to achieving these goals can be identified and evaluated with this model, and it can in turn be determined whether specific energy projects are financeable.

Generic or macro barriers

The traditional word used to describe the challenges that stand between the need for electric service in the poorest parts of the world and the development, completion, and operation of the infrastructure necessary to provide that service is "barriers." The notion of a "barrier" to development creates a dualistic mindset: "there is a barrier, it must be removed." There is a difference, and not just a semantic one, between thinking about the removal of a "barrier" and thinking about how to mitigate, work around, or address a risk factor associated with the funding of a project. A barrier begs to be removed and only removed; addressing a risk factor invites a host of approaches.

The analysis of Watson et al. includes a thoughtful discussion and categorization of macro barriers. It classifies barriers into four main categories: Economic, Technical, Political/Institutional, and Cultural/Social/Environmental (2012). A partial list of specific barriers identified in the literature surveyed in Watson et al. includes those listed under each category in Table 9.1.

Watson et al. acknowledge that "classification of barriers is not straightforward" and "point[s] to the importance of understanding barriers and interventions in integrated ways" (2012). The perspective of one providing funds for a project is one such integrated way to understand barriers, as this involves defining and considering exactly what types of risks the barriers present or reflect, analyzing whether funding is available, and identifying the available mitigation measures

Table 9.1 Categorization of macro barriers

Economic	Lack of access to finance
	High technology and infrastructure costs
	Low capacity for cost recovery (poor customers unable to pay)
Technical	Quality and performance of equipment
	Capability to support operations and maintenance
Political/Institutional	Resistance of vested interests
	Lack of political power of the unserved and underserved
	Weak regulatory mechanisms
Cultural/Social/Environmental	Misalignment of design and needs
	Negative views of technology
	Climate change impacts

or devices that can be applied. Even a very general review of these barriers clearly shows that few of them can be effectively evaluated outside the context of a specific project. Consider the technical development barrier, for example, arising out of a lack of local capacity to train and employ workers to operate and maintain power sector assets; this is a location-specific barrier. Recognizing that the barrier is, or may be, widespread (but not universal) has some value. But evaluating ways in which the barrier is or can be addressed in the context of the risk it poses to lenders on a specific project has real value, and this insight can be extrapolated to a higher level.

A critical review of certain of the generic or macro barriers reinforces the desirability of thinking about barriers in a project-specific context. Two examples are the general "lack of financing" barrier and the "climate change" barrier. Existing literature consistently identifies a lack of financing or funding as a key barrier to development of energy access for the poorest. Numerous studies attempt to quantify the amount of investment needed to achieve energy access at Millennium Development Goal (MDG) levels (see note 3), and while there is considerable variance in the estimates, most agree that the total investment needed in the impoverished world is a very small fraction of the total global investment in energy infrastructure that is needed and expected in the coming years.

The articulated macro financing barrier is that adequate capital and financing are not available to achieve energy access for the poor. IEA estimated in 2014 that $9.6 trillion of global power sector investment is required until 2035 in order to maintain current supply and meet growing demand (International Energy Agency 2014, 26). Comparing IEA's 2014 estimate of the cost of energy access for the poorest as being $30 billion/year until 2030 means that only approximately 5 percent of the total to be spent in the world for energy infrastructure in the next 20 years is needed to make significant energy access advances in the poor world.

The problem does not seem to be with the availability of funding. The problem seems to be that 95 percent or more of what is needed for energy infrastructure will flow to the developed world and not to the poorest and underserved regions (International Energy Agency 2014, 105). This will happen naturally and without conscious policy directive because money avoids risk and seeks safe and secure returns. The higher the demand for money in the developed world, the less will flow to the poorest parts of the world. The funding barrier should be rearticulated to say that financing is not limited or precluded by a lack of funding or funding sources, but by the need to address certain financing risks in the least developed world so that more money from the global pool flows there.

Concern about the climate change impact of providing electricity access to 1.3 billion people is another example of a barrier that can be evaluated in macro terms. Unless this electricity is provided using renewable and non-fossil technologies, it will certainly result in an increase of greenhouse gas emissions. However, lack or limited acceptance of knowledge about the negligibility of the amount of energy needed to achieve the MDG targets is the real barrier. The Global Network on Energy for Sustainable Development (GNESD) notes "the amount of commercial energy that would be needed to overcome the energy poverty situation globally is negligible compared to the world's energy production" (2004, 6).[4] An increase of 1 percent in the emission of greenhouse gases is worth addressing, but it is not a barrier to development.

Aggressive efforts to promote the use of renewable energy sources as a means to create energy access, while environmentally sound, can give rise to other challenges. Because achieving the MDG is expected to result in negligible increased greenhouse gas emissions, development should proceed aggressively on the assumption that renewable power is the preferred approach, but not to the extent that conventional fossil fuel options are disregarded if they offer satisfactory ways to mitigate financing risks, improve local economics, promote and ensure energy reliability, enhance education and health care advances, and provide an infrastructure framework that will promote future service expansion through more widespread adoption of renewable technologies.

As this part demonstrates, at the macro level, general or universal barriers to development can be overstated, misstated, and are quite often anxiety producing. It is important to distinguish between risk factors or barriers that are project-level or project-specific and the generic or macro barriers described in much of the existing literature, because at the project level, it is possible to categorize, evaluate, and mitigate specific risks. The identification, assessment, and mitigation of risk using the infrastructure finance model provides such a project-specific approach.

Financing and risk: project-specific analysis

Project finance (PF), classically defined as "nonrecourse financing predicated on the merits of a project rather than the credit of the project sponsor," is based on "predictable regulatory and political environments and stable markets, which combine to produce dependable cash flow" (Hoffman 1989, 181).[5]

In the developing world, the pure nonrecourse PF model will rarely work well because the regulatory, political, and market environments are not often highly enough evolved to serve as a basis for nonrecourse debt (supported only by project revenue streams and not other outside forms of security). Credit enhancement in the form of guarantees of third parties covering project risks are often necessary to protect lenders in developing-world projects. More critically, the uncertainty caused by local instability or immaturity of policies and regulation leads to unallocated or even unknown risks.

Infrastructure financing (IF) is meant to include traditional PF structures but also includes partial recourse, guaranteed or third-party supported obligations and structures, modified and creative repayment schedules, insurance products, and other risk mitigation devices not always seen or required in developed-market PF structures.[6]

Echoing Hoffman's statement that PF is based (in part) on "predictable regulatory and political environments," the International Renewable Energy Agency (IRENA) says that the first focus in achieving energy access should be on mobilizing finance through regulation (International Renewable Energy Agency 2012, 9).[7] True, perhaps, but numerous and repeated efforts at structuring regulatory systems have not been as effective as hoped. Until these frameworks can overcome their challenges, a more effective approach is to assess and evaluate risks associated with development, completion, and operation of specific projects and create options for addressing the risks. If local conditions allow, the use of agreements or memoranda among governmental actors, communities, and specific project developers may be an effective alternative to a regulatory scheme that is imported from another part of the world. Moreover, the dark side of a regulatory system is the burden of compliance. An imported regulatory scheme may be more difficult to comply with than a series of well-developed agreements embedded with creative and effective enforcement provisions.

IRENA's 2012 Report also suggests that the most effective financing programmes must amount to a "flexible package of funding mechanisms," and that "financing mechanisms must be flexible and adaptable" (57). This is a lot to ask for. It seems inconsistent with the rule articulated by the author Thomas Hardy in his 1874 novel *Far from the Madding Crowd* which, paraphrased, is that it is far safer to evaluate an opportunity that presents itself and extemporize a procedure to fit it than to get a good plan matured and wait for a chance of using it.

Money (and the parties that make it available for infrastructure) rarely exhibits great flexibility. The burden is not typically placed on the money to be flexible; the burden is on the developer to be flexible in the planning, design, construction, and operation of the project in a way that will allow the developer to address known and potential risks. It is a shared burden, but not an equally shared burden. The point of using the IF model to identify and evaluate risks is that the model places a premium on the ability of the developer to find satisfying solutions to the problem that money does not like risk.

Grants and equity investments are not the same as debt, and it might seem that the money from these sources cares less about risks. In a way, it does, if only because debt instruments like promissory notes and bonds carry no promise of a future where the investment returns more to its owners than expected. Lenders, if all goes well, earn a rate of interest, some fees, and the return of their investment. It is natural that those who stand to benefit if things go well would accept more risk, but only a bit more, depending on the project. IF model of analysis of project risks and barriers is relevant to equity investors in that it informs those investors in a way that helps them to evaluate the potential upside in a project and decide what are the acceptable risks.

This is not to say that the goal of creative, flexible, and adaptable funding mechanisms is not worthwhile. Rather, it is unlikely that the goal will be achieved in a vacuum. Experts should focus on flexible and adaptable solutions to financing risk within the context of existing and historic credit risk analysis. As will be seen in evaluating several specific examples of risk mitigation below, a theme that becomes apparent is that the greatest possible integration of projects into the economic, social, and environmental characteristics of the community served by the project often results in ways to address risks.

In the IF context, the identification and assessment of risk by lenders or equity investors proceeds along a particular, recognizable path. The analysis begins with identification and categorization by the phase(s) of the project that will be affected by the risk. Project phases are uniformly identified as "development," "completion," and "operational" (Hoffman 1989, 181).[8]

Development risks are identified as those that relate to the ability of the project sponsors or proponents to identify, secure access to, and maintain control over a site adequate for the project, and to identify and obtain all necessary permits and approvals for the development, completion, and operation of the project. Some commonly observed development risks include non-existent or inadequate land ownership and use laws, environmental rules, or regulatory systems applicable to a particular development activity.

Completion risks include any factor or force that will adversely impact the physical construction and installation of the project. Examples include the threatening of site control permits and approvals, the competence and experience of the contractor and suppliers, the adequacy of construction agreements, testing and proof of technology and designs, and the availability, scope, and enforceability of remedies associated with third-party defaults during the process. The availability and sufficiency of funding to complete construction and the available insurance, bonding, or guarantees to cover potential losses or costs are some risks to be managed and mitigated. Other completion risks include force majeure events and political instability.

Operational risks include some of the foregoing, such as force majeure, political risk, continuing site access, and others that relate to post-construction performance of the project. Analysis of operational risks requires an assessment of management and operator qualifications and the availability of necessary resources (feed stocks like coal, gas, petroleum, and other materials in the case of conventional energy technologies and water flow, wind flow or solar insolation in the case of renewable power generation). Revenue or market risk – the risk that the project will not have adequate cash flow for operating costs, debt service, and a return on investment – is a key operational risk.

The IF model of risk identification, assessment, and mitigation extends sequentially through a project to inquire how things can go wrong. Because it has a holistic framework (all identified risks must be addressed in conjunction with all others), it allows for the resolution or mitigation of risks with comprehensive, integrated structuring. Analysis based on the IF model of risk assessment establishes a high bar for specific projects to clear, but it produces an analysis that is comprehensive and coherently organized.

The IF analysis may make it compellingly clear that a particular project cannot achieve the standards required for IF, but it has the advantage of identifying all project issues so that it can be ascertained what risks a non-traditional, non-IF based provider of funds must accept. Barriers that may not apply to a non-traditional investor will be identified, and risk assessment using the IF model may be over-inclusive, but if the objective is to address, accept, or dismiss a risk to overcome a barrier, after-the-fact appearance or identification of risks and barriers are avoided. The over-inclusiveness of the model is therefore helpful.

Having identified a project risk, it can be placed in its proper context in the IF model to consider specific solutions to the problem. Here are a few extended examples that evaluate selected political/institutional, economic, and technical barriers.

Example 1: inadequate or non-existent land ownership and use laws

To say that the development, completion, and operation of power generation projects in Country X is hampered by a non-existent or inadequate legal structure for the ownership and use of land creates a presumption of non-financeability. To say instead that a particular project in a specific location requires a reasonable demonstration of the ability to create a lasting set of land control and use rights creates a different and less daunting presumption.

It is a simple matter of perspective – to say that the absence of coherent land use rules is a barrier precluding the development of the project because financing rules require site control by the developer is not the same as saying that in order for a specific project to proceed some kind of structure must be established that will confer necessary land rights to the developer, and that once created, that structure must endure circumstances that might arise in the future.

To create a structure which can successfully pass stress-testing solves the problem of lenders. If site control during the development, construction, and long-term operation phases of the project can be reasonably assured and attendant risks properly mitigated, financing may be available.

For example, in the development phase, if land use rights sufficient to pass a baseline test of site control can be arranged contractually with a local community or parties who can control or protect the use of a site, financing might be available if the future completion and operation risks associated with site control can also be identified and assessed. Specifically, a community contract-based structure for the use of land might provide a baseline, especially if a broad base of stakeholders and community members are parties to the arrangement. If typical developed-world methods of land use regulation supported by enforcement are unavailable, contractual or quasi-contractual engagement of many stakeholders may provide an acceptable alternative.

Consider the hypothetical example of a small hydro project in East Africa. The project would involve the reconstruction and repowering of a facility, built 20 years or more ago, which has been abandoned. Analysis of the project site under the IF model would disclose that many development risks are negligible or manageable, that the project is accessible, and that construction activities would not be hampered by issues like a lack of roads for transport of equipment. Other development and completion barriers are capable of resolution.

The most significant development, construction, and operational barrier is the fact that the country has no coherent land rights structure. Ghana and Sierra Leone are examples of nations where there is a lack of clarity about land rights.[9] The concern of lenders extends to the ways in which the lack of formally established rights can impact development, completion, and operation. Engaging all stakeholders in a process of articulating a shared goal and intention to support the project, and the expression of those shared goals in writing and oral narrative, could help to prevent future rules, policies, or other actions that threaten the project's site control. A well-designed collaborative/community structure of this type is not a perfect substitute for a well-ordered, legislatively created, and judicially enforceable system of land control, but it could be adequate to assess and mitigate a significant risk to a specific project to a degree that financing might be available, or at least available with a minimum level of credit support in the form of guarantees or reserve accounts.

Lender acceptance of site control risk is never, and can never be, based on an expectation that land control is not absolutely free from the threat of diminution or loss. Even in well-established land rights systems there is always a risk of change in property rights through the exercise of eminent domain powers, or through land use, zoning, environmental, or other regulatory changes that can adversely affect site control and use. Lenders are offered significant protection if there exists a broad-based coalition of stakeholders who have committed themselves to a project and will work together to resist rule changes or other actions that would threaten the project. Possibilities emerge when the focus is on the nature of the risks and how to mitigate them as opposed to rigidly declaring that national, enforceable land rights laws are a mandatory prerequisite to the availability of financing.

Example 2: lack of market demand and payment capacity are barriers to development

As noted, the IF analytical model closely evaluates the risk that a project's ability to produce adequate revenue to operate the project and service debt may not be available. One of the most frequently noted barriers to energy development in poorer countries is the operational or revenue risk embedded in the absence of sufficient income levels to pay for demanded and used energy. This risk, among the most intuitive and important in infrastructure finance, is not an "on/off" risk. Specifically, unless the risk is that very little or no revenue will be produced, the issue is more appropriately articulated as the amount (sizing) of the debt. The management and mitigation of the revenue risk created by poverty requires deliberate thought and action around the prioritization, scaling, and phasing of projects, and identification of clear markers of progress and milestones for expansion of debt and projects – consumer poverty is a matter of degree.

Consumer demand is also a matter of degree. It should be remembered that energy access itself is not the end goal – the end goals are reduced poverty and improved economic and educational opportunities, all of which could be positively impacted by energy access. Lack of progress on these goals can itself be a barrier. While challenging, a process of identifying sectors or communities with relatively better ability to pay (and, importantly, identifying sectors or communities that will economically benefit the most), and designing projects to serve these customers will mitigate revenue risk and enhance financing options and possibilities.[10]

Working with lenders to establish financial measures to support the expansion of infrastructure to serve more people will promote future expansion as opposed to the development of a project to serve a few people which is then left behind to develop more, similar projects. If the financing structure of a project serving small business or commercial enterprises includes specific milestones (for example, the achievement of stated debt service coverage ratios) which will trigger the advance of additional funds for equity takeout (thereby facilitating the flow of equity to the project) or project expansion, the revenue risk concerns of lenders are minimized and the potential for increasing energy access is enhanced. If the lenders' goals are mitigation of revenue risk, the reward for capably managing the risk should be additional funding. Structuring credit and prioritizing projects in a way designed to secure commitments for future funding will result in diminishing revenue risk. Community-based development, carefully prioritized and backed by creative lending structures, offers hope for resolution of revenue-adequacy barriers.

Example 3: the lack of local capacity to support ongoing project operations is a barrier

This barrier to development finds support in generations of anecdotes about developed-world efforts to install infrastructure in poor regions. The central theme of these anecdotes is that governments or NGOs from the developed world appear on the scene and develop water, energy, or other infrastructure projects. Returning years later, they are asked by local communities if they have returned to repair a facility that has been broken for a period of time.[11] It is in the immediate best interest of both developers and lenders to evaluate whether local capacity exists for project operations and management (O&M).

The risk assessment model for infrastructure finance demands that the operational risks associated with long-term project maintenance be addressed by establishing credible and sustainable risk mitigation, usually through extended-term contracts with equipment suppliers or independent service providers on fair and reasonable terms. The existence of this barrier is not, by itself, a bad thing, but the world is changing dramatically, and for the better in this regard. As project development has taken hold in the developing world, companies that manufacture or install electricity generation equipment have recognized the enormous potential opportunity for their businesses. Financiers require developers to demonstrate long-term maintenance capacity. The suppliers of equipment have responded and developed innovative ways to provide operational stability.[12] As noted by Watson et al. (2012) it is important to "understand barriers and interventions in an integrated way." The importance of the O&M barrier should not be understated, much less dismissed, but it is a barrier to which there are plausible market-based solutions that already exist and continue to advance. Addressing and integrating other front-end risks like those discussed in the previous two examples will facilitate growth in levels of project development. As more projects are installed, the market for O&M services will increase and multiple service providers will emerge to further mitigate project-operation risks.[13]

Information collection and sharing

Since 2004, the International Energy Agency (IEA) has published an index (the Energy Development Index, or EDI) which "is designed as a composite measure of a country's progress in making the transition to modern fuels and modern energy services" (International Renewable Energy Association 2012, 541). Just as it is important to define goals like "energy access" as was done earlier in this chapter, it is important to have tools for tracking progress towards the stated goals. The EDI, according to IEA, is a "multi-dimensional index that tracks energy development country-by-country" and is "intended to help understanding of the role that energy can play in human development" (International Renewable Energy Association 2012, 541).

However, this approach is incomplete. Stating and tracking goals involves aspirational thinking and outcome reporting that may not always be reliable or complete. It does not help us understand (or even be informed) about what works. It would be an infinitely more useful exercise to collect, publish, and update a database of specific mitigation measures employed in the context of projects throughout the developing world. A collection of summaries of ways to structure around risks, with adequate context provided, maintained in a searchable format, could be an immensely valuable tool. Certainly the global financial community has a sufficient commitment to energy development, and desire to avoid or mitigate risk, that it could support the creation and maintenance of a widely accessible information service.

Conclusion

Broad-based and generalized discussion of barriers is useful to a degree, but it ignores the reality that development of projects is an inescapably local process, dependent on local conditions, that needs to focus on specific steps that are achievable within a local context. When general or categorical barriers and their attendant or associated financing risks are analyzed at the project level, it is possible to imagine and implement mitigation schemes. Establishing and preserving a broad-based network of local stakeholders and partners becomes the most effective way to address some of the most pronounced barriers.

Discussion of barriers to development which do not take place in a specific and well-defined context are often unhelpful and even misleading. Project-specific analysis of challenges and barriers, using widely used and relatively straightforward risk assessment methods from the IF model, can produce creative solutions. However, risk assessment under this model must incorporate thoughtful and diligent assessment of unintended consequences if investment failure is to be avoided. If progress is to be made, the global investment community must create and use methods of widely sharing information about innovative financing structures and solutions.

Notes

1 "Despite the large body of work analyzing barriers to, and interventions for, using modern energy services, there is a highly uneven spread of coverage and a significant lack of high quality research" (Watson et al. 2012, 2).

2 Ten countries (four in Asia and six in Africa) represent two-thirds of the total. The ten countries with the largest populations lacking access to electricity are India, Bangladesh, Nigeria, Ethiopia, Indonesia, Democratic Republic of the Congo, Pakistan, Tanzania, Kenya, and Uganda (International Energy Association 2012, 533).

3 The "minimum levels of consumption," defined as 250kwh/yr. for rural households and 500kwh/yr for urban households, can be more tangibly expressed as the use of ten small (25w) light bulbs for approximately 12 percent of the hours in a year (International Energy Agency 2011, 12). A Standard "Energy Star" home refrigerator requires approximately 500kwh/yr. for continuous operation. The three objectives of the Millennium Development Goal are: (1) ensuring universal access to modern energy services; (2) doubling the rate of improvement in energy efficiency; and (3) doubling the share of renewable energy in the global energy mix (Ki-moon 2011, 4).

4 "According to UNDP, providing the poor with modern energy services as in the MDG Energy Vision would increase global energy demand by only about 1 percent of its current level" (Global Network on Energy for Sustainable Development 2004, 6).

5 Hoffman's article is one of a small number of works that discuss the basics of project finance in a comprehensive way. Hoffman's organizational approach to understanding

PF informs much of the discussion of specific risk assessment and mitigation tools in this chapter, but the framework set forth herein also draws heavily on the author's nearly 30 years' experience in the field.

6 The importance of exploring and utilizing these mitigation devices was underscored by the October 2014 Business Council of the United Nations Review in its discussion of the Catalytic Finance Initiative discussed at the Summit. The Review discusses the intended use by the Initiative of "first loss and mezzanine tranches, risk guarantees and new insurance products" (United Nations Environment Programme 2014, 5–6).

7 IRENA's report states that "governments should seek to mobilize [energy] finance in two comprehensive ways: first, by setting overarching regulatory and incentive framework … and second by using targeted public to fill or overcome specific financing gaps and barriers" (International Renewable Energy Agency 2012, 19).

8 These generic risk categories are overlapping – specific risks can potentially impact one or more of the project phases, but using the categories is helpful in considering mitigation strategies.

9 Difficulty in securing land for business in Ghana is addressed in *Guide to Electric Power in Ghana* (Resource Center for Energy Economics and Regulation 2005). For a discussion of Sierra Leone in this context see *2013 Investment Climate Statement – Sierra Leone* (United States Department of State 2013, 1).

10 Planning projects to take advantage of targeted subsidies to support the affordability of electricity is an important consideration as well, although the success of these programmes has been "mixed" according to GNESD (Global Network on Energy for Sustainable Development 2004, 13 n. 11).

11 An example of these anecdotes is the one related by Rory Stewart in his 2006 book *The Prince of the Marshes*. Stewart, a Scottish infantry officer and diplomat was assigned the governorship of two remote Iraqi provinces for the Coalition Provisional Authority in 2003. Upon his arrival in the marshy southern Iraqi province of Amara, the first locals to greet him asked if he had come to repair a water system built and then abandoned by the British government decades earlier.

12 Examples of global companies with O&M activities in the developing world include the Irish firm ESB International and Martifer Solar of Portugal.

13 This point is discussed in *Climbing the Renewables O&M Learning Curve.* (PricewaterhouseCoopers 2013) The PwC report expresses optimism about the future of developing O&M solutions in the renewable energy sector on the basis of the experience of the mobile telecom sector.

References

Global Network on Energy for Sustainable Development. 2004. *Making Power Sector Reform Work for the Poor: Summary for Policymakers*. Accessed April 27, 2015. www.gnesd.org/publications/energy-access-theme

Hoffman, Scott. 1989. "A Practical Guide to Transactional Project Finance: Basic Concepts, Risk Identification, and Contractual Considerations." *The Business Lawyer* 45, no. 1 (November): 181–232.

International Energy Agency. 2011. *World Energy Outlook 2011: Energy for All: Financing access for the poor*. Excerpt of the World Energy Outlook 2011 presented at the Energy for All conference, Oslo, Norway, October 2011. Accessed January 26, 2015. www.worldenergyoutlook.org/media/weowebsite/energydevelopment/weo2011_energy_for_all.pdf.

International Energy Agency. 2014. *World Energy Investment Outlook*. Accessed January 26, 2015. www.iea.org/publications/freepublications/publication/WEIO2014.pdf.

International Energy Association, 2012. *Measuring Progress towards Energy for All.* Accessed January 26, 2015. www.worldenergyoutlook.org/media/weowebsite/energy development/2012updates/Measuringprogresstowardsenergyforall_WEO2012.pdf.

International Renewable Energy Agency. 2012. *Financial Mechanisms and Investment Frameworks for Renewables in Developing Countries.* Abu Dhabi: International Renewable Energy Agency. Accessed January 26, 2015. www.irena.org/Document Downloads/Publications/IRENA%20report%20-%20Financial%20Mechanisms%20 for%20Developing%20Countries.pdf.

Ki-moon, Ban. 2011. *Sustainable Energy for All, A Vision Statement.* United Nations. Accessed January 26, 2015. www.un.org/wcm/webdav/site/sustainableenergyforall/ shared/Documents/SG_Sustainable_Energy_for_All_vision_final_clean.pdf.

Lamott, Anne. 1994. *Bird by Bird.* New York: Pantheon Books.

PricewaterhouseCoopers. 2013. *Climbing the Renewables O&M Learning Curve.* Accessed January 26, 2015. www.pwc.com/us/en/technology/publications/cleantech-perspectives/ pdfs/pwc-cleantech-renewables-o-and-m-learning-curve.pdf.

Resource Center for Energy Economics and Regulation. 2005. *Guide to Electric Power in Ghana.* Accra: University of Ghana. Accessed January 26, 2015. www.beg.utexas.edu/ energyecon/IDA/USAID/RC/Guide_to_Electric%20Power_in_Ghana.pdf.

Stewart, Rory. 2006. *The Prince of the Marshes.* Orlando Fl: Harcourt Books.

United Nations Environment Programme. 2012. *Financing Renewable Energy in Developing Countries.* Geneva: United Nations. Accessed January 26, 2015. www.unepfi.org/ fileadmin/documents/Financing_Renewable_Energy_in_subSaharan_Africa.pdf.

United Nations Environment Programme. 2014. "Bank of America Announces $10 Billion Catalytic Finance Initiative to Accelerate Clean Energy Investments that Reduce Carbon Emissions." September 23. Accessed January 26, 2015. www.unep.org/ Documents.Multilingual/Default.asp?DocumentID=2796&ArticleID=11000&l=en.

United States Department of State. 2013. "2013 Investment Climate Statement – Sierra Leone." Accessed January 26, 2015. www.state.gov/e/eb/rls/othr/ics/2013/204729.htm.

Watson, J., R. Byrne, S. Castle-Clarke, C. Fry, M. Morgan Jones, J. Opazo, and F. Tsang. 2012. "What are the major barriers to increased use of modern energy services among the world's poorest people and are interventions to overcome these effective?" *Collaboration for Environmental Evidence,* CEE Review 11-004. Accessed January 26, 2015. www.environmentalevidence.org/wp-content/uploads/2014/07/CEE11-004.pdf.

10 Behavioral challenges and the adoption of appropriate sustainable energy technologies

Margaret Njirambo Matinga, Joy S. Clancy, Vincent Doyle, and Harold Annegarn

Introduction

About two billion people – 40 percent of humanity – lack access to modern energy services such as electric lighting, modern biomass, and liquefied petroleum gas (LPG) (IEA 2011, 52), using instead kerosene (paraffin)[1] for lighting and traditional biomass (firewood, charcoal, and dung) or coal for cooking and heating. This exacerbates, and, arguably, causes poverty, since those without such services are deprived of opportunities. These people – the Energy Poor – must perform activities such as food processing manually. Irrigation is limited to hand watering with buckets, limiting the area of land that can be irrigated. Capacity to study and socialize is limited due to poor and expensive lighting, while access to electronic media is limited due to the high costs of batteries. Collecting firewood takes up time that could be used for other productive activities and exposes collectors to hazards, including snake bites, injuries, assaults, and chronic musculoskeletal injuries (Echarri and Forriol 2005; Matinga 2010; Parikh 2011). Firewood collection is metabolic energy-intensive, which may have adverse health effects where caloric intake is limited. Cooking with traditional fuels exposes cooks to particulate matter, carbon monoxide, poly-aromatic hydrocarbons, and other polluting compounds. Estimates show that household air pollution – largely from cooking – was responsible for 4.3 million deaths, representing 7.7 percent of global mortality (WHO 2014, 17).

Since the late 1990s, understanding has increased regarding the adverse developmental impacts of lack of access to modern energy services, leading to increased international efforts to address the situation. In 2012, the United Nations (UN) launched the *Sustainable Energy for All* (SE4ALL) initiative, with three main goals to achieve by 2030: a) provide universal access to modern energy services; b) double the global rate of improvement in energy efficiency; and c) double the share of renewable energy in the global energy mix (SE4ALL n.d.). This and other global energy initiatives have catalyzed a flow of financial resources to the energy sector. Among pathways for achieving the SE4ALL goals is a focus on promoting *Appropriate Sustainable Energy Technologies* (ASETs), including decentralized energy technologies. While this concerted international energy initiative is the first of its kind, efforts to improve energy access among the poor are nothing new. However, evidence suggests failures are rife, with multiple ASET projects in Africa, Asia, and Latin America that were abandoned after being lauded initially as the ultimate solutions. Reasons for failure or limited adoption of "improved" energy technologies include: high costs; inadequate communication of the benefits; unreliable supply chains of technologies or fuels; poor performance of ASETs, absent community engagement; mismatch between technology design and user needs; differences between priorities of decision makers and users; and behavioral challenges posed by intended beneficiaries.

Aware of the reasons for failure of previous energy projects, the current thrust in the promotion of ASETs adopts multi-faceted approaches, which include addressing energy and tax policies related to ASETs, strengthening supply systems including involving male and female users as sales agents, improving financing, and increasing awareness of benefits. Experience has shown that, even when target groups are presented with good information, affordable energy technologies, and other support services, some among the Energy Poor continue to use traditional energy forms. Despite such evidence, there has been little focus on behaviors of adopters and abandoners of ASETs, or general energy-related behaviors in developing countries. Where behaviors have been discussed, the discussions have been superficial, conceptualizing these behaviors as barriers rather than attempting a deeper understanding of such behaviors, their logic of practice, meanings, and interactions between technology and user behaviors. This chapter examines these "behavioral challenges" and their logic, within the limited available literature.

Scope of the chapter

Although ASETs comprise several categories, this chapter refers largely to cooking because firstly there is limited literature on other ASETs with respect to behavioral challenges; and secondly, cooking technologies are among the few ASETs requiring several behavioral changes for their adoption and use. Although the scope of this book excludes grid electricity, this chapter makes a digression into electricity for three reasons. There is a paucity of energy behavioral studies in developing countries, and grid electricity studies form a substantial part of the available literature. Also by drawing parallels between ASET and electricity use, the chapter shows some commonality of behavioral challenges towards adoption, thereby debunking the myth that adoption problems associated with ASETs exist simply because users prefer "superior energy sources" such as electricity. The third reason is to highlight how ASETs might be better suited to address some of the behavioral challenges associated with adoption of modern energy technologies in general – whether electricity, LPG, improved cookstoves, or solar lanterns.

Method

This chapter is based on a literature study of energy technology adoption and use. It assumes a gender perspective in analyzing behavioral challenges related to

ASETs. Gender is a concept that refers to a system of socially defined roles, privileges, attributes, and relationships between men and women, which are learned and not biologically determined. The concept of gender as used here is about the relational position of women and men, rather than discussing them as discrete entities. However, it does not deny the mediation that comes about from socio-economic factors (Clancy et al. 2012).

The choice and use of energy is intimately linked to the gender related roles and responsibilities that society assigns. For example, in most of the developing world, women are responsible for collecting firewood and cooking. The behavior of women and men is regulated by the gendered responsibilities and attributes that society assigns to them. Engaging in actions within expected gender boundaries can attract cultural capital[2] and rewards, while acting outside these boundaries can provoke sanctions.[3] If the benefits of adopting new technologies are perceived as congruent with gendered behaviors, such technologies might be adopted. Contrariwise, if the adoption of the technology involves actions that are seen to be outside the boundaries of preferred gender behaviors, social sanctions might be imposed on adopters. If such sanctions are seen as too costly, the ASETs or new behaviors might be rejected.

Behaviors and factors that affect ASET adoption

Purchasing behaviors

Purchasing behaviors can determine whether Energy Poor individuals get the opportunity to test or adopt ASETs. Despite the sparse evidence on how purchasing decisions regarding ASETs are made, and the factors affecting these decisions, purchasing decisions are dependent on factors including economic situation, class, gender, power relations (between sellers, buyers, and users), and fashions. The limited research that is available in the energy sector has focused on economic determinants and information as factors affecting purchasing and consequently adoption and use of ASETs; however, purchasing is about much more than money and information.

Within gender and energy studies, the suggestion is often made that, in many developing countries, men have more economic power than women and are unwilling to buy, or may not consider buying, technologies such as improved cookstoves (Clancy et al. 2012); however, empirical studies are too few to test this hypothesis. Buying decisions are affected by product availability, moderated by knowledge and mobility, among other factors (Cecelski and Matinga 2014). Thus, one reason why men may be reluctant to buy improved cookstoves may not be their "uncaring" attitude towards women's hardships in firewood collection and cooking, but in their lack of knowledge regarding improved cookstoves. Improved cookstoves are typically promoted to women and rarely to men – sending the message that these are women's technologies – thereby depriving men of knowledge to support purchasing decisions. In contrast, solar lights are targeted at both women and men, although there appears some bias towards targeting men because they are seen as (and often are) the key decision makers regarding cash expenditure.

Taste and flavor

Food, flavor, and taste are inherently linked to geographies and cultures. According to Bourdieu (1984), taste is an expression of cultural capital, so cultures are distinguished by, and connected to, the flavor and taste of foods among other tastes. Preferences for food cooked on traditional fireplaces contributes to resistance to ASETs such as improved cookstoves, solar cookers, and even LPG (Saptyani 2011; Atteridge et al. 2013, 44; Matinga 2004). Thus:

> [M]ost people agree that food cooked on charcoal tastes better than food cooked on hotplates. Especially beans, which you can cook in an earthen pot on the traditional fire but on the hotplate, you use metal pots and the beans taste of metal. You do not get the nice flavor.
>
> Female respondent in Mbayani (Matinga 2004)

However, ASETs are not always seen as incongruent with "traditional" tastes and flavor preferences. In Malawi, in a survey of five villages, respondents did not perceive improved biomass cookstoves to negatively influence the taste of food (Concern Universal 2012). The respondents qualified such sentiments with statements that both the stoves and the three-stone fire produce smoke and use firewood, implying they were conscious or apprehensive that no-smoke stoves or stoves using fuels other than firewood might change the flavor of food.

Taste and cooking technologies are not a developing country-specific issue, as sometimes portrayed. Rather, they exemplify the human need to maintain cultural identities. While the transition to improved technical performance of ASETs is relatively new in the developing world, similar transitions have occurred in the developed world, with comparable focus by promoters on technical parameters. Examination of countries that transitioned from cooking with traditional fuels shows that attitudes do change but over a long time. Brewer (2000) highlights the anxieties of consumers when gas stoves were being introduced in the United States of America from the 1850s onwards. She noted how the gas stove was lauded:

> A fire can be made ... in a single minute. The heat is intense and the flame clean, there is no ashes, no smoke and the amount [of gas] burned according to the degree of heat desired ... can be regulated with the utmost nicety.
>
> (Brewer 2000, 221)

Brewer comments that such

> laudatory media reviews such as this one failed to tell the readers what they most wanted to know. How did gas stoves perform in people's homes?

What did they cost to buy and operate? Did they alter the taste of food?
Were they safe?

(Brewer 2000, 222)

In other words, while the promoters of the gas cookstove were focused on
answering technical questions, the targeted users had different questions, linked
to their interactions with the technology: How would the technology "behave"
in their homes? How would it change and affect their daily practices? Experience
shows that little has changed in how producers and consumers evaluate the
appropriateness of new technologies.

Convenience of use and the "hassle factor"

ASETs must fit the users' way of life. Humans have acquired expertise on how
to start and manage open fires for specific cuisines, making use of locally
available biomass. In many countries in Africa, cooking the staple food (*n'shima*,
nsima, *ugali*, *pap*, *posho*, *sadza*, in eastern and southern Africa, or *banku*, *tuozaafi*,
and *omotuo* in Ghana) requires stirring a stiff porridge-like dish that requires a
robust stove that can take stirring and pounding stresses. In Ghana, *banku*,
tuozaafi, and *omotuo* are often cooked using round-bottomed pots, requiring
sturdy stoves. Improved cookstoves that meet these criteria are currently not
widely available (GACC 2013). In Latin America, tortillas are often cooked on
a *comal* (smooth, flat griddle, made of clay or cast iron). While LPG is a clean
fuel, users find LPG stoves unsuitable for cooking tortillas for family meals since
only two tortillas can be cooked at a time (Masera et al. 2000). In comparison,
a *comal* placed on a traditional cookstove cooks up to eight tortillas
simultaneously (Clancy et al. 2012). In Ethiopia and Eritrea, stoves such as the
Kenyan Ceramic Jiko, popular in southern and eastern Africa, were unsuited to
cooking the staple food, *injera* – a spongy, pancake-like flatbread. The Mirte
stove, an adaptation of the traditional Magogo stove that fits the cooking
peculiarities of *injera*, is proving to be popular.

In addition to cooking methods, adopting new technologies often requires
changed practices of fuel preparation and handling. Open fires are flexible and
can adapt to diverse fuel types (firewood, dung, and post-harvest waste), and
varying quality and sizes of biomass. In contrast, many improved cookstove
designs specify restrictions on type and size of solid fuel to achieve optimal
performance. Others even require change of pot types and utensils, adding to the
trouble and expense – the "hassle factor" – that a household must endure to
effectively use the new ASET.

Although householders are aware that dry firewood produces less smoke and
burns more efficiently compared to wet firewood, for a number of reasons,
including scarcity of dry wood and rains, their choice is often limited and they
use wet wood (Concern Universal 2012). This study found that households
sometimes revert to using open fires because improved cookstoves are less
tolerant of wet, gnarled, or knotted wood, and do not tolerate maize stalks, cobs,

or trash, burning poorly if any of these are used. Yet, these are important fuels used by many households, especially in times of firewood shortages.

In an evaluation of factory-manufactured wood-burning stoves in Dadaab refugee camp in Kenya, it was reported that Philips, Vesto, and Save80 stoves, although highly efficient, require firewood be split into small pieces before use, imposing an extra fuel preparation task on users (USAID 2010, 82). While users correctly recognized Save80 as the most efficient of the three stove types tested, it was the least popular stove because it required frequent fire tending. Other stoves presented challenges in heat control that required the pot to be removed and replaced during the cooking process. A number of candidate gasifier stoves display similar characteristics. Such inconvenience leads to resistance in changing cooking practices, and may result in undercooked or improperly cooked food, or increasing risks of burns, which can further deter change.

On the Esperanza tea estate in Malawi, inconvenience of use linked to poor heat control (and other cultural factors discussed below) led to abandonment of the Esperanza improved biomass stove because the stove burnt food easily and burnt holes through pots within 6 to 12 months (Concern Universal 2012). Given that the ability to cook well is often seen as an important attribute of a woman, improper heat control that results in burnt, improperly cooked, or inedible food can have serious consequences. A study in 41 countries shows an average 21 percent of women reported that wife beating is justified if the wife burns food (World Bank 2012). Consequently, convenient heat management is likely to be a higher priority than fuel efficiency for many users.

Solar cookers require that cooking be done outdoors, which might be inconvenient for women with young infants and no care support, as the child then has to be exposed to the sun. It presents difficulties when it rains, is overcast, in late evenings, or is too sunny (for foods that require constant tending), or be considered inappropriate in locations where neighbors may not have food to cook for the day.

The behavioral challenges that limit the adoption of ASETs for cooking present a contrast to the relative ease with which ASETs for lighting are adopted. The adoption of lighting ASETs, such as portable solar lanterns, has recently risen, due to their convenience and ease of use. Unlike cookstoves, lighting products seldom require culturally important changes. The newer low-powered LED portable solar lanterns require little management in contrast to traditional solar photovoltaic (PV) installations, for which users had to learn to manage the battery and panels. The high convenience and low hassle factor of solar lanterns have contributed to a willingness to use and maintain them, aided in some cases by capabilities to charge mobile phones. Meanwhile, the sustainability of PV installations, especially owner-managed ones, continues to be problematic.

Costs and behaviors of users and promoters

Costs of ASETs are not a type of behavior, but costs do affect economic decisions and behaviors in the adoption of ASETs. High costs can deprive target beneficiaries of opportunities to transition from traditional energy use. In addition, costs of technology govern how users behave, including when they use ASETs and their fuels. High costs of LPG, for example, mean that most poor users – if they have access to it – can afford to use it only for quick-cooking foods, and will practice fuel-stacking behaviors in order to reduce energy costs.[4]

On the supply side, the costs of technologies determine who participates in the value chain of ASET distribution and, consequently, the target markets. This effectively determines to whom the opportunities for adopting ASET are available. In the stove sector, NGOs and other agents intensely promote simple mud stoves to rural women, as stoves become "international objects of development." In general, men are marginally involved, and if they are, often as promoter agents from NGOs who train women in manufacture of the stoves. They act as intermediaries, distributing to markets outside the immediate location of the producers or producer groups (Concern Universal 2012). On the other hand, the increase in factory-manufactured stoves and the increasing monetization and internationalization of stoves has seen an increase in men's inclusion in stove value chains. Often these are middle class, urban men, although there are efforts to include women in these modern stove value chains.

Various behavioral patterns of both development agents and the cultures in which these technologies are being transferred explain this pattern. Despite many of the NGOs and development agents promoting gender with equity in mind, their approaches often presume that women are a homogenous group and are universally poor. As such, women are offered little choice except for the lowest-cost (and often lowest-performance) technologies. The assumption appears to be that the lower cost and lower-tech the technologies are, the more likely that women will be successfully involved. In other words, gender approaches to ASETs remain integrative and not transformative.

In addition, new governance mechanisms aimed at improving quality of products, promoting their adoption, and improving the perception of the poor towards ASETs have brought about layers of bureaucracy that likely exclude women or at least allocate them to certain parts of the value chains. This occurs because women often require permission of male partners to sign what are perceived as major contracts, or to travel to distant urban locations, where much engagement with formal institutions occurs.

Development agents are not the only factor to affect this cost–gender nexus. The cultures in which ASETs are introduced offer different opportunities for women and men. Technologies (including ASETs), products, and services that are seen as major purchases, and acquisition of durable assets is often regarded as the responsibility of men. Women, in turn, are responsible for what are perceived as minor (low-cost) purchases and consumables. The limited mobility of most women in developing countries also means that high-value ASETs, often sold in urban centers, are not as accessible to women. Limited access to (adequate) finance among women, and among the urban and rural poor, further restricts purchase of high-value ASETs. Low technical competency, resulting from historical exclusions of women from technical education, further alienates women's access to technologically advanced ASETs. This is showcased by the GVEP's DEEP Project[5] in East Africa that supported energy entrepreneurs with a range of financial and non-financial services, and set out to involve equal numbers of female and male entrepreneurs. Despite DEEP offering their support services to both female and male entrepreneurs, women tended to engage in improved cookstoves and briquette production, while men engaged more in solar, biogas, and battery charging businesses, which are seen as more high-tech, requiring techno-engineering skills, and are perceived as more modern than improved cookstoves (Kariuki and Balla 2012, 9).

Over time, people perceive different ASETs as being gender- and class-specific. Mud stoves are perceived as rural, poor, and female, while high-performance, factory-produced, and/or imported stoves become urban, low-to-middle income, and male. In between are stoves that are considered low-income and urban, often produced and promoted by young urban males with links to international development agencies. The perception of technologies has implications beyond the simple attachment of generalizations to ASETs used for cooking or the end use of ASETs; it also indicates the underlying skills that women and men are socialized to acquire. In developing countries, women are more likely to promote technologies or products to other women (in their social networks). Thus, if female entrepreneurs are mostly selling low-tech ASETs or cooking ASETs, female users will also have access to these, but are less likely to have access to other higher technology ASETs.

There are several entities working to increase the number of female participants in ASET entrepreneurship, thus comprising exceptions to the above generalizations. Greenway Grameen in India, co-owned by female industrial engineer Neha Juneja, exemplifies this movement. Social entrepreneurship projects such as Solar Sister, Barefoot Engineers, the Alternative Energy Promotion Centre (AEPC) in Nepal, and the African Biogas project also work to increase the number of women in these traditionally male-dominated areas. NORAD supports technical training for women to participate in ASET value chains as micro-hydro operators, bio-digester masons, and solar technicians (NORAD 2011).

Research suggests that men seem to be more willing to become involved with household chores after electrification, and this has been found in a variety of settings, including Sri Lanka (Massé 2003), South Africa (Annecke 2005, 51; Matinga 2010), China and Laos (Kelkar and Nathan 2005), and in Zanzibar (Winther 2008). This implies that the gendering of technologies, the focus on cooking technologies for women, and specifically efforts to improve cookstoves for women may present a missed opportunity for transforming gender roles, although these technologies might be serving women's welfare needs.

Fear of change and the meanings of technology

Energy use is a practice of culture, not just a matter of technological mastery. To make the decision to transition from traditional fuels to ASETs, potential adopters of ASETs must compare benefits that are often unknown and uncertain at the initial stages of adoption, with known benefits and (often hidden) costs of their current technologies and practices. Such changes can provoke fears of these uncertain costs, whether monetary or non-monetary, including costs related to cultural capital.

A techno-centric view towards adoption of energy technologies has dominated the energy sector; this view assumes that because provision of modern energy is a conduit for imparting modernity, it is not only universally desired but also inherently and wholly a positive process. Even in ASET circles, appropriateness of technology has often been determined by external agents and assumed to mean that small, locally produced, low-cost technologies are appropriate, without understanding the culture, traditions, politics, and energy justice issues that surround energy supply, access, and use, and the inherent fears that accompany change.

Practices such as cooking or use of fire are deeply embedded in traditional cultures. For many tribes in Africa, Asia, and Latin America (as was the case in pre-industrial Europe), life without a hearth is unimaginable. Thus, "Even if there is no food, but there is fire, I am still happy, because the stove brings the family together" (a mother from Kagiso, South Africa, quoted in Van Niekerk 1998, 3). "The Pedi expression for 'my children' is *'bana beso'* – children of my fireplace" (Mönnig 1978, 237, quoted in Van Niekerk 1998, 3).

Thus, changing from what is known and practiced for generations to something that is new may invoke fears, whether related to the technology itself or to practices and cultural connections. Transitions to LPG are often hindered by fears that the gas will explode (Kojima 2011, 97; Saptyani 2011). New electricity connections in South Africa have been resisted for fear of disturbing or chasing ancestors (Van Niekerk 1998, 3; Matinga 2010).

As with any technology, these fears are not universal, even within a small group of homogenous people. In the Tsilitwa and Cutwini villages in South Africa, while the older generations were fearful of how they would communicate to ancestors if they did not use open fires, others, especially the younger generation, were keen on the modernity embedded in and delivered by electric power (Matinga and Annegarn 2013). A study in Malawi found that 38 percent of Esperanza improved stove users were fearful of feeding guests food that had been cooked while the cook was standing,[6] the remaining 62 percent found the ability to cook while standing to be a welcome change. It was more comfortable than and reduced back pain associated with cooking in a seated, cramped position (Concern Universal 2012).

The meanings of practices often change over time and so even in transition from traditional energy technologies ASETs can take on powerful new and positive meanings. In South Africa, although coal stoves are an alien technology that diffused extensively to the people of the Highveld in the late nineteenth century, the stove over the years has become extremely meaningful to the user communities. In an account of coal stove usage on the Highveld (Hoets 1995, quoted in Van Niekerk 2006), a woman householder responded, "My coal stove is my life, without it my life will be meaningless."

Access to electricity and gas have been ascribed values of freedom or modernity (Matinga 2010; Winther 2008; Matinga and Annegarn 2013), positive associations which aid in overcoming hurdles associated with adopting these technologies.

Meanings and politics of technology and the behaviors of those who promote it

Energy use can attain political meanings, and this is especially notable among decision makers. In the past, policy makers in developing countries have preferred central grid electricity (Victor and Heller 2009; Eberhard 2005) and have been reluctant to create supportive policies for ASETs. ASETs were seen as "hippie" solutions or inferior to grid electricity. In some quarters, promotion of ASETs was seen as a barrier to progress towards full electrification, and hence politically unacceptable. Secondly, early ASET projects in developing countries were often of poor quality. When combined with poor management capacity, this factor resulted in ASETs either under-performing, or failing within a short period. ASETs obtained a poor reputation that cemented the view that they were inferior technologies. This view was exacerbated by the developed world's increasing consumption of fossil fuels simultaneously with their promotion of ASETs in the developing world. Policy makers therefore perceived the promotion of ASETs as an appeasement and part of a patronizing agenda and large-scale grid electricity gained political significance among them. In other countries such as South Africa, where electricity was provided along racial lines, provision of electricity in the immediate post-apartheid period signified a break from racial oppression, so that little attention was paid to ASETs (Matinga et al. 2014).

Thus, the diffusion, adoption, and use of ASETs have been affected not only by user behaviors but also by behaviors of powerful agents that formulate policies on a global scale.

Addressing behavioral challenges associated with ASETs

Addressing behavioral challenges associated with ASETs is one of the most important steps if the goals of Sustainable Energy for All (by 2030) are to be achieved. Without addressing behaviors that inhibit adoption and sustained use of ASETs, many of the push-strategies, such as regulatory interventions and technological innovations, are unlikely to translate into success. To begin with, there is a need to increase understanding of these behavioral challenges, and the logic of practices that underpin the behaviors.

Despite knowledge that behaviors affect adoption and use of ASETs, there is scant research to inform interventions. Instead, most attention is paid to raising awareness among potential users of the benefits of adopting ASETs. While awareness campaigns are a necessary component of implementation strategies, they are unlikely to succeed if the perceptions and beliefs underlying specific behaviors are unknown or not understood. Understanding behaviors and incorporating them into solutions will require utilizing a wider variety of research approaches and methods than the currently preferred quantitative methods and rapid appraisals. In-depth methods, such as ethnography, will allow deeper understanding of the logic behind user behaviors. It is difficult to uncover deeply embedded cultural issues with predesigned questions, uninformed by the setting and practice therein, as is the case in many surveys. Rapid appraisals may not be illuminating because the time spent with respondents is often too short to discover deeply rooted beliefs that inform actions, as respondents themselves may not see these beliefs as connected to energy use.

Research and development is slowly moving from focus on technical issues such as efficiencies and emissions reductions, to usability and convenience, but more needs to be done. Such research and development should include the opinions and expertise of the targeted users on the features they would desire or aspire to in a technology. Including user opinions proved important in the case of the ceramic Jiko in Kenya where women suggested a change to the design, in order to make it more stable (Kammen 1995). The Kenyan Ceramic Jiko is now one of the most adopted improved cookstoves in eastern and southern Africa. Balance must be struck between technical achievements and non-technical user needs.

Research has repeatedly shown how gender shapes everyday life, and the energy sector is no exception, as this chapter and Chapter 4 illustrate. The energy sector continues to build on programmed gender experiences, especially since the formation of the International Network on Gender and Sustainable Energy, following the 1995 Fourth World Conference on Women in Beijing (UN Women n.d.). Moving forward, the energy sector needs to regard gender as a relational concept as opposed to current focus on women and men as separate entities. Questions must be asked how femininity and masculinity concepts shape and are shaped by ASETs, and how gender risks and benefits associated with specific ASETs are perceived by potential users. Only when such factors are understood can approaches for promoting ASETs include a transformative agenda, something that is thus far lacking. Information on costs and benefits of ASETs, as well as traditional fireplaces and technologies, must be framed in terms of men's and not just women's interests. In this way, men can acquire adequate information on ASETs (especially those related to women's roles, such as improved cookstoves) and on why they should invest in them.

There is a need for open dialogue between policy makers and users on the opportunities and benefits presented by ASETs. Certain ASETs must be acknowledged as transitional options, while policies and finances are mobilized for improved ASETs and other options. The politics underlying different ASETs must be acknowledged and addressed. Target groups must be presented with a range of options across ASET categories (different lighting systems, different stove types) to enable users to choose ASETs that best fit their budgets and inclinations.

In promoting widespread adoption of ASETs, having community champions, such as local political, social, cultural, and/or religious leaders, supporting such technologies and leading by example, has been shown to be useful in encouraging people to purchase and use ASETs. Government institutions close to communities using ASETs are a way of improving adoption through demonstration, and by debunking myths about the inferiority of ASETs. Finally, the intended users of ASETs need to be engaged fully in the conception, specification, and implementation of such technologies – the solution of energy poverty is inextricably linked to the solution of gender and poverty in the developing world.

Notes

1 Although kerosene is a modern fuel, it has a range of adverse influences, and is considered a transition fuel (Swart 2012).
2 Cultural capital – a concept drawn from Bourdieu – can be considered as a currency, both tangible and intangible, that one acquires by being, and in order to be part of a particular social class. It can include taste (figuratively or otherwise), accents, mannerisms, knowledge, qualifications (formal and informal), titles, brands of products that one uses, etc. Because cultural capital defines groups to which one belongs, it (along with income) defines access and control of resources and confers status and power (Bourdieu 1984).
3 For example, a woman who is seen as submissive may be perceived as more womanly and desirable as a wife in a society where being a wife increases the status of a woman. This can be seen as a reward for conforming to gender roles and attributes especially because in certain communities, being a wife is often the only livelihood option available to the majority of the women.
4 Fuel stacking is the practice of using more than one fuel for the same application. For example instead of cooking with LPG at all times, a household might use fuels such as LPG for boiling water for tea, and use charcoal for cooking beans or other main meals.
5 Global Village Energy Partnership (GVEP) is a partnership that supports local businesses in developing countries to increase access to modern energy. The Developing Energy Enterprises Project (DEEP), which ran from 2008 to 2013, aimed to develop sustainable micro and small energy enterprises by providing supportive financial and non-financial services, including capacity building.
6 The reason for this fear is rooted in the culture of respect.

References

Annecke, W. 2005. *Whose Turn is it to Cook Tonight? Changing Gender Relations in a South African Township.* Case Study Report, United Kingdom: Department for International Development, Research for Development. Accessed February 22, 2015. http://r4d.dfid.gov.uk/PDF/Outputs/Energy/R8346_finrep_annecke.pdf.
Atteridge, A., M. Heneen, and J. Senyagwa. 2013. *Transforming Household Energy Practices among Charcoal Users in Lusaka, Zambia: A User-centered Approach.* SEI Working Paper No. 2013-04. Stockholm: Stockholm Environmental Institute.
Bourdieu, P. 1984. *Distinction: A Social Critique of the Judgement of Taste.* Translated by R. Nice. Cambridge, Massachusetts: Harvard University Press.
Brewer, P.J. 2000. *From Fireplace to Cookstove: Technology and the Domestic Ideal in America.* New York: Syracuse University Press.
Cecelski, E. and Matinga, M.N. 2014. *Cooking with Gas: Why Women in Developing Countries Want LPG and How They Can Get It.* Report developed for the World LP

Gas Association by ENERGIA International Network on Gender and Sustainable Energy October 2014

Clancy, J.S., M.N. Matinga, S. Oparaocha, and T. Winther. 2012. *Gender Equity in Access to and Benefits from Modern Energy and Improved Energy Technologies*. World Development Report 2012 Background Paper. Leusden, Netherlands: ETC Foundation, ENERGIA. Accessed February 22, 2015. http://doc.utwente.nl/79143/1/WDR_Norad_ENERGIA_Main_Paper.pdf.

Concern Universal. 2012. *Socio-cultural Acceptability of Improved Cook Stoves in Balaka, Dedza and Mulanje 2012*. Herefordshire, UK and Blantyre, Malawi: Concern Universal. Accessed January 14, 2015. http://concern-universal.org/what-we-do/reports/ (select Improved Cookstoves Full Report 2012).

Eberhard, A. 2005. "From state to market and back again: South Africa's power sector reforms." *Economic and Political Weekly*, December 10, 5309–5317.

Echarri, J.J. and F. Forriol. 2005. "Influence of the type of load on the cervical spine: a study on Congolese bearers." *Spine Journal* 5(3): 191–196.

GACC. 2013. *Global Alliance for Clean Cookstoves*. Accessed February 22, 2015. www.cleancookstoves.org/.

Hoets, Penny. 1995. "'My coal stove is my life, without it my life will be meaningless': electrification of townships exploring some myths." *Household Energy for Developing Communities: Conference, Exhibition and Workshop*. Midrand, 18–21.

IEA. 2011. *Energy for All: Financing Access for the Poor. Special Excerpt from the World Energy Outlook 2011*. Paris: International Energy Agency. Accessed February 22, 2015. www.worldenergyoutlook.org/media/weowebsite/energydevelopment/weo2011_energy_for_all.pdf.

Kammen, D. 1995. "Cookstoves for the developing world." *Scientific American* 273: 72–75.

Kariuki, P. and P. Balla. 2012. *GVEP's Experience with Working with Women Entrepreneurs in East Africa*. Nairobi: Global Village Energy Partnership (GVEP).

Kelkar, G. and D. Nathan. 2005. "Gender relations and the energy transition in rural Asia." *ENERGIA News* 8(2): 22–23.

Kojima, M. 2011. *The Role of Liquefied Petroleum Gas in Reducing Energy Poverty*. Washington D.C.: World Bank.

Masera, O.R., B.D. Saatkamp, and D.M. Kammen. 2000. "From linear fuel switching to multiple cooking strategies: a critique and alternative to the energy ladder model." *World Development* 28(12): 2083–2103.

Massé, R. 2003. *Impacts of Rural Electrification on Poverty and Gender in Sri Lanka*. Labastide-Murat: MARGE. Accessed February 22, 2015. www.worldlibrary.org/wplbn0000025818.aspx.

Matinga, M.N. 2004. *Supply and Demand Side Benefits and Costs of Low Cost Electrification in Malawi: A case of Mbayani Township*. Unpublished MSc thesis. Cape Town: University of Cape Town.

Matinga, M.N. 2010. *We Grow up with It: An Ethnographic Study of the Experiences, Perceptions and Responses to the Health Impacts of Energy Acquisition and Use in Rural South Africa*. Unpublished PhD Thesis. Enschede: University of Twente.

Matinga, M.N. and H. Annegarn. 2013. "Paradoxical impacts of electricity on life in a rural South African village." *Energy Policy* 58: 295–302.

Matinga, M.N., J.S. Clancy, and H.J. Annegarn. 2014. "Explaining the non-implementation of health-improving policies related to solid fuels use in South Africa." *Energy Policy* 68: 53–59.

Mönnig, H.O. 1978. *The Pedi*. Pretoria: J.L. van Schaik.

NORAD. 2011. *Gender Equality in Financing Energy for All.* Norad Report 20/2011. Oslo: NORAD.

Parikh, J. 2011. "Hardships and health impacts on women due to traditional cooking fuels: a case study of Himachal Pradesh, India." *Energy Policy* 39(12): 7587–7594.

Saptyani, G. 2011. *Kerosene to LPG Conversion Program in Indonesia. A Case Study of Yorgyakarta on the Effects on Women's Livelihoods.* Unpublished Masters Thesis. Enschede: University of Enschede.

SE4ALL. n.d. *Sustainable Energy for All Initiative,* United Nations, Vienna. Accessed February 22, 2015. www.se4all.org/our-vision/our-objectives/.

Swart, D. 2012. "Busting household energy myths in SA." Press briefing from PASASA – Paraffin Safety Association of South Africa. Accessed January 14, 2015. www.paraffinsafety.org/busting-household-energy-myths-in-south-africa/.

UN Women. n.d. *Fourth World Conference on Women, Beijing, 1995.* New York: UN Commission on the Status of Women. Accessed February 22, 2015. www.un.org/womenwatch/daw/beijing/.

USAID. 2010. *Evaluation of Manufactured Wood-burning Stoves in Dadaab Refugee Camps, Kenya.* A report compiled by Berkeley Air Monitoring Group. Washington D.C.: USAID.

Van Niekerk, A.S. 1998. "A place to feel at home: a social perspective on the family hearth in Africa." *Boiling Point* (Intermediate Technology Development Group) (41): 3–5.

Van Niekerk, W. 2006. "From technology transfer to participative design: a case study of pollution prevention in South African townships." *Journal of Energy in Southern Africa* 17(3): 58–64.

Victor, D.G. and T.C. Heller (eds). 2009. *The Political Economy of Power Sector Reform: The Experiences of Five Major Developing Countries.* Cambridge: Cambridge University Press.

WHO. 2014. *Burden of Disease from Household Air Pollution for 2012.* Geneva: World Health Organization.

Winther, T. 2008. *The Impact of Electricity. Development, Desires and Dilemmas.* Oxford: Berghahn Books.

World Bank. 2012. *World Development Report 2012: Gender Equality and Development.* Washington D.C.: World Bank.

11 Measuring access for different needs

Simon Trace

Introduction

There is currently no universally recognized definition of what energy access actually means, no accepted minimum standard of service that constitutes the threshold between someone being in or out of energy poverty. The absence of a minimum standard is a major impediment to poor people's rights to access a basic service that underpins economic and social development. It is difficult to understand how progress towards the United Nations Sustainable Energy for All (UNSE4All) Initiative's goal of universal access by 2030 can be assessed, for example, when it is not clear whether "access" is defined as a single solar lamp, a light in every room, or having sufficient energy for productive purposes and motive power.

Measuring energy access in a more accurate and appropriate way, informed by what really matters to poor people, throws new light on the problem of energy access. It also points us to better solutions. So having the right definitions and ways of measuring energy access as key tools for setting targets and guiding policies and investments is critical.

What data does exist at the moment on energy access at national levels is very poor. There are no accurate figures, for example, of the capacity and output of decentralized electricity systems (off-grid and mini-grid) compared to the grid. Access is traditionally measured in terms of household connections to grid electricity and the use of a modern fuel for cooking. This fails to recognize the use of energy for productive ends or community services, neglects the role of mechanical power and intermediate technologies, and does not consider how people use and ultimately benefit from energy. The result is that there is currently no clear overview of the status of energy access at national levels.

This chapter draws heavily on the NGO Practical Action's 2014 *Poor People's Energy Outlook* report and looks at potential definitions of energy access and ways of measuring across three important domains: energy for households, enterprises, and community services. It also proposes measurement standards to assess progress and discusses the challenges such approaches pose.

Energy for households

Energy poverty denies millions of people the basic standard of living that people want, need, and have a right to. Without access to energy to cook, heat the home, earn a living, and fully benefit from health, education, and cultural opportunities, whole communities are trapped in lives of drudgery and subsistence.

From the perspective of poor people, the energy service (sufficient light, warmth, etc.) is more important than the source. Although different supplies and appliances can be used for multiple services (a stove for both cooking and heating rooms in cold climates), there are five service categories that comprise the key dimensions of energy access for households:

- lighting
- cooking and water heating
- space heating
- cooling
- information and communications.

In the following section, for each energy service, there is a short discussion of why such service is important, and what might constitute a minimum standard. This is, to some extent, controversial and country specific. However, it is an important step in quantifying what universal access to energy by 2030 (one of the aims of the UN's SE4All), entails in reality.

Lighting

Lighting is a fundamental human need. People who cannot simply flick a switch to light their homes lose many productive hours as soon as the sun sets. It's estimated that in 2010, 1.2 billion people (17 percent of the global population) did not have access to electricity (Banerjee et al. 2013). As a result, people resort to lighting such as candles, kerosene lamps, or even simply flaming brands that are polluting, dangerous, and provide low-quality light.

The impact of adequate lighting

Studies suggest that having access to lighting is hugely valued by poor families. A study in Rwanda found that once grid electricity was available, 80 percent of households switched completely from traditional lighting sources (GTZ and SenterNovem 2009). SolarAid's impact report found that rural African families were saving around $70 per year with the money commonly spent on better food, education, and farming. Children were spending an average of an extra hour studying per night. There were more qualitative impacts, with lighting bringing people together and helping them feel safe and secure after dark (SolarAid 2013).

Minimum standard for adequate lighting

In its Energizing Development programme (EnDev), GIZ proposes that a minimum acceptable level of light in a household is 300 lumens (comparable to a 30W incandescent bulb). In workplace settings it has been found that this is a threshold below which there is a rapid increase in accidents (Reiche et al. 2010). It is sufficient for reading and other household tasks. This report argues that 300 lumens should be available for a minimum of four hours per night.

Cooking and water heating

Cooking is a daily need, with around 80 percent of the foods humans consume needing to be cooked, and yet this is a relatively neglected area of intervention. In 2009 a study found that only 2 percent of energy strategies in the least developed countries addressed cooking (Havet et al. 2009).

Two in every five people (2.8 billion in 2010) rely on wood, charcoal, or animal waste to cook their food (Banerjee et al. 2013). Only 27 percent of those who rely on solid fuels (biomass or coal) are estimated to use improved cookstoves. Access to these stoves is even more limited in least developed countries and sub-Saharan Africa, where only 6 percent of those who use traditional biomass are taking advantage of such options (Legros et al. 2009).

Minimum standards for cooking energy

The minimum standard for access to clean cooking solutions should cover fuel use, time, stove efficiency, and pollution. As with lighting, the standards proposed by the GIZ EnDev programme are appropriate (GTZ-HERA 2009), combined with WHO's indoor air quality guidelines (WHO 2006) and a time-limit for the collection of fuels:

- 1 kg woodfuel or 0.3 kg charcoal or 0.04 kg LPG or 0.2 litres of kerosene or biofuel per person per day, taking less than 30 minutes per household per day to obtain.
- Minimum efficiency of improved solid fuel stoves to be 40 percent greater than a three-stone fire in terms of fuel use.
- Ambient air quality measured as annual mean concentrations of indoor particulate matter ($PM_{2.5}$) <10 µg/m³ in households, with interim goals of 15 µg/m³, 25 µg/m³ and 35 µg/m³.

Space heating

Space heating is an important function of household stoves and heating appliances, particularly at higher altitudes and during cold seasons (see Table 11.1). Despite this, it is often overlooked by policy-makers and designers of stoves programmes. Depending on customs and traditions, people either want to

Table 11.1 Health effects of various temperatures

Temperature	Health effects
24°C	Top range of comfort
21°C	Recommended living room temperature
<20°C	Mortality rate begins to rise
18°C	Recommended bedroom temperature
16°C	Resistance to respiratory diseases becomes weakened
12°C	More than two hours at this temperature raises blood pressure and increases heart attack and stroke risk
5°C	Significant risk of hypothermia

Source: Keatinge (2006)

use their cooking stove to also provide warmth, or they have a separate stove for heating their home. It is estimated that half a billion people in South and South-East Asia alone use stoves for space heating during the cooler seasons or at night (Hulscher, 1997).

In the mountainous areas of Asia, households generally use 70–80 percent of primary energy directly for cooking and 20–25 percent directly for space heating. Improved stoves focus much more of this escaped heat on the pot, funnelling smoke and hot gases out through a flue or chimney. The unfortunate trade-off of this efficiency is that householders might need to have a separate fire to keep warm.

Minimum standards for space heating

Considering the health impacts of lower temperatures, a minimum standard for daytime indoor air temperature of 18°C has merit. This should be achieved by means that do not entail indoor smoke, are affordable, and do not require excessive time in collecting fuel.

Cooling

Cooling is a critical energy service for the preservation of food and medicines and for keeping spaces at habitable temperatures in hot countries. The majority of developing countries are located in the hottest regions of the planet; nearly four billion people live in areas with annual average ambient temperatures above 22.5°C. For more than one billion people living in South Asia and sub-Saharan Africa, the average temperature for the hottest month of the year exceeds 30°C.

Energy for cooling contributes to poverty reduction in various ways, notably prolonging the life of food and reducing waste, but its contribution is not often recognized. Even passive cooling systems that use no electricity can be very effective (Practical Action 2006).

Minimum standards for cooling

As with space heating, cooling is not a widely recognized energy service, and yet it can be critical for poverty reduction. We propose the following two dimensions of a minimum standard for cooling for households:

- Ability of households to extend the life of perishable products by a minimum of 50 percent over that allowed by ambient storage.
- Keep maximum apparent indoor air temperature of 30°C.

Information and communications

Information and communication technologies (ICTs), defined as technologies that can process and transmit information and facilitate communication via electronic means (Marker et al. 2002), are now established as key tools for alleviating poverty. The link between energy and ICT is more fully explored in Chapter 19 in this volume.

ICTs (such as radio, televisions, computers) are by their nature heavily dependent on energy and those without it lack access to information that could make a real difference in their lives: information about the composition and delivery of services from public institutions, about political activities and their human rights, about the market value of their goods and produce, and about education and livelihoods options.

By mid-2012, there were 2.4 billion internet users worldwide (34 percent of the global population) (Internet World Stats 2012), and 3.2 billion mobile phone subscribers. The growth in access has been rapid. However, there is still a risk that inequitable access to ICTs may exacerbate growing inequalities in income, knowledge, and power between men and women, income or ethnic groups, or urban and rural populations. For example, a woman is 23 percent less likely than a man to own a mobile phone if she lives in sub-Saharan Africa and 37 percent less likely if she lives in South Asia (GSMA 2010).

Access to energy has enabled the uptake of ICTs, even in remote rural areas of developing countries, through grid extension or the ability to charge batteries. Most people rely on batteries as their energy source for ICTs charged by solar panels or diesel generators.

Minimum standards for energy for ICTs

As with other energy services, a minimum standard needs to focus on the service provided by ICTs rather than simply access to the technology. In order to achieve sufficient development benefits, and focusing on the household level, the following is proposed:

- Ability of people to communicate electronic information from their household.

- Ability of people to access electronic media relevant to their lives and livelihoods in their household.

Energy for earning a living

For billions of the world's poorest people, the ability to earn a living depends on access to energy. Having lighting after dark to keep a shop open longer, or fuel for an engine to mill grain or a pump to irrigate land, can be the difference between earning a decent livelihood and remaining at or below the subsistence level and in poverty. It is this direct connection between energy and poverty reduction that is most cited in the discussion over energy poverty, but is least well understood in practice.

Energy and earning off the land

Agriculture contributes significantly to the economic and social foundations of most developing countries. Some 2.5 billion people, 45 percent of the developing world's population, live in households depending primarily on agriculture and an agri-based economy for their livelihoods. In the developing world, the agricultural sector generates on average 29 percent of GDP whilst it provides work to 65 percent of the labour force, with a disproportionate number being income and energy poor (GIZ 2011). Hence, increased agricultural productivity is a primary driver for food security, income generation, development of rural areas, and therefore global poverty reduction. Better access to energy will be required to meet the 70 percent increase in productivity that will be necessary to feed the nine billion global population expected by 2050 (FAO 2009).

Increasing productivity

For poor farmers, agricultural production activities are still based to a large extent on human and animal energy, as there is often insufficient mechanical, electrical, and chemical (fuels) energy available. Energy use and draft power in South Asian food grain production is illuminatingly dealt with in Chapter 18 of this volume. Mechanical power is a particularly important input in any farming system, used in *land preparation, planting, cultivation, irrigation,* and *harvesting.* Three distinct types of farm-power systems can be identified according to the relative contribution of humans, draft animals, and machinery (GIZ 2011):

1 *Human work* for tilling, harvesting and processing.
2 *Animal work* to provide various energy inputs.
3 *Energy technologies* including *renewable energy* (e.g. solar or wind pumps, solar dryers, water wheels, biomass conversion technologies), **fossil fuel-based technologies** (e.g. diesel engines and pumps), and *hybrid systems* (a combination of fossil and renewable energies for motive and stationary power applications and processing agricultural products).

The type of farm-power system available to farmers is a significant factor in determining the area of land they can cultivate; human-powered farms typically cultivate 1–2 hectares (ha) per year, draft animal hirers cultivate 2 ha, farmers owning draft animals cultivate 3–4 ha, tractor hirers cultivate about 8 ha, and farmers owning tractors cultivate more than 20 ha (FAO 2009).

Improved agro-processing and marketing

For many poor rural households who rely on their own farm produce for the basic staple of their diet, processing crops by hand at home is the only option. This role is typically performed by women and is extremely labour intensive. Households may also need to carry or transport heavy produce long distances to be processed by powered machinery, often at great expense.

Agro-processing extends markets in which goods can be sold and permits sales at higher prices and in larger quantities (FAO 2009). Furthermore it transforms agricultural produce into both food and non-food commodities through processes ranging from simple preservation (e.g. sun drying) or transformation (e.g. milling) to the production of goods by more capital and energy-intensive methods (e.g. food industry, textiles, paper). Agro-processing often depends on resources and expertise of small enterprises, co-operative millers, or other specialists who provide important energy services to farmers.

Modern energy services can significantly reduce the time and heavy work involved in traditional agro-processing while improving incomes for smallholder farmers with higher prices from finished products. For example, the multifunctional platform project in Mali that is widely used for agro-processing saved women customers on average 2–6 hours per day (UNDP 2012).

Energy and micro and small-scale enterprises (MSEs)

Many poor people in the developing world earn their living running businesses such as street-side stalls, food stalls, or workshops. These micro and small-scale enterprises (MSEs) have specific energy needs, in addition to those of households. In order to better understand the ways energy access contributes to earning a living through small enterprise activity, this section considers the range of energy services used in MSEs and the steps needed to realize increased incomes from those services.

Energy activities in MSEs – service, manufacture, and processing sectors

The manufacture, service, and processing sectors have different energy needs. In service enterprises, appliances are typically limited to lighting and other appliances for comfort (e.g. fans, TV) and communication (e.g. computers and telephones). Manufacturing enterprises require particular kinds of appliances that demand high amounts of energy for mechanical power, heat for processing, or electricity for welding or other activities. Food and other processing enterprises share energy needs with both the service and manufacturing sectors.

Common energy services in enterprises

MSEs require many of the same energy services as households. Lighting for work after dark can improve productivity and incomes, particularly in areas where customers have a demand for evening services. Other energy services provide a better environment for customers, entrepreneurs, and workers, such as cooling from electric fans, heating, and ICT applications including TV and radio. Cooking and water heating also serves customers and employees alike.

Energy services – what matters for enterprises

As described above, enterprises require multiple energy services at different stages of production and processing. Tea production, for example, uses a series of energy services including withering, shredding, fermenting, and drying, and typically uses electricity, fuels, and mechanical power at different stages. The amount of energy required is also variable, based on the scale of the enterprise. Four aspects of energy access are especially important to enterprises and entrepreneurs (see Table 11.2).

Energy for community services

Energy is crucial to community services, which are themselves fundamental to improving the lives of poor people, and achieving the Millennium Development Goals and the objectives of the nascent post-2015 sustainable development agenda. This chapter focuses on the role of, obstacles to, and opportunities for, energy provision in four key community service areas:

- *Health care:* hospitals, clinics and health posts
- *Education:* schools, universities, and training centres
- *Public institutions:* government offices, police stations, religious buildings, etc.
- *Infrastructure services:* water and street lighting.

These categories provide a useful way of analysing community services, and defining and measuring access to energy. Health is examined below as an example.

Health care

Health-care systems are a cornerstone of development and central to improving people's lives. The health sector includes a broad range of institutions from rural health posts to specialist hospitals in large cities, administered through a variety of public, private, and faith-based service providers.

Table 11.2 Enterprise energy access matrix

| | Energy supply | | | |
	Electricity	Fuels	Mechanical power	Appliance
Reliability	Availability (hours per day) Predictability (timetabled or intermittent)	Availability (days per year)	Availability (days per year)	Downtime (%), linked to ease of maintenance and availability of spare parts
Quality	Voltage and frequency fluctuation (+/– 10%)	Moisture content (%)	Controllability	Convenience, health and safety, and cleanliness of operation
Affordability	Proportion of operating costs (%) – including capital cost payback if financed	Proportion of operating costs (%) Time to gather as proportion of working day (%)	Proportion of operating costs (%) Time spent (if human powered) as proportion of working day (%)	Proportion of operating costs (%) – including capital cost payback if financed
Adequacy	Peak power availability (kW)	Energy density/ calorific value (MJ/Kg)	Peak power availability (kW)	Capacity compared with available resource and market (% capacity)

Source: Practical Action (2012)

A critical component of an effective health-care facility is access to energy. People have little chance of receiving adequate care where health-care facilities lack electric lighting, refrigerators, or sterilization equipment. Yet an estimated one billion people in the world are served by health facilities that are completely without electricity (Practical Action 2014). Problems due to a lack of access to energy in health facilities include (EC 2006):

- inability to provide clinical services after sunset;
- poor lighting conditions for performing operations;
- poor storage facilities for vaccines and medicines requiring refrigeration;
- poor facilities for sterilization of medical tools;
- inability to power laboratory equipment to diagnose patients' diseases;
- poor ability to communicate with medical specialists or to call for transport to a health facility with a higher degree of specialization;
- limitation to traditional cooking facilities, resulting in inefficiencies, poor air quality, and possible inadequate food intake by patients;
- difficulty in deploying health officers in remote rural areas.

While the relationship between health facilities' energy access and people's health is subject to many factors, energy is vital for improving health services.

Measuring access to energy for health

There is a glaring lack of data about energy supplies or services in health facilities. The planned expansion of the SE4All initiative's Global Tracking Framework should address this, although it will take time to be rolled out. It will need to build on existing national data collection initiatives such as the Service Provision Assessment (SPA) survey and the Service Ability and Readiness Assessment (SARA).

Defining and measuring energy access

Existing figures fail to give an accurate picture of the extent to which people are or are not able to access the energy services that matter to them. Current definitions do this by:

- *Over-counting:* Counting those with a grid connection to electricity as having energy irrespective of affordability or reliability of the supply. In many developing countries, load-shedding and break-downs mean electricity is often unavailable at certain times of day and that unplanned outages regularly occur. This means although someone has a connection, they may not have access to minimum levels of evening lighting, cooling, space heating, or for productive uses.
- *Under-counting:* Using grid connectedness fails to count people who have a reasonable level of energy services (lighting, ICTs, a fan for cooling) supplied from sources beyond the grid. It also fails to count those with good quality biomass cookstoves.

A second problem with the binary system of measuring access is its insufficient ability to analyse inequalities (between those with the best access and those with the worst), or the setting of national or sub-national targets to try to address those inequalities. It also does not recognize progress that might have been made through improving access to decentralized electricity, or improved biomass cookstoves.

In an effort to address these weaknesses, the NGO Practical Action, in its series of publications under the title of the *Poor People's Energy Outlook* (PPEO), developed and tested a set of criteria that provide a more accurate picture of access to energy supplies and services. The PPEO 2010 and 2012 proposed and refined an *Energy Supply Index* and a set of *Minimum Standards for Household Energy Services* (see Tables 11.3 and 11.4), which illustrate a flow of impacts from the right kind of *energy supply*, leading to a minimum level of *energy services*, to enable the realization of *development goals*.

Table 11.3 Energy supply index

Energy supply	Level	Quality of supply
Household fuels	0	Using non-standard solid fuels such as plastics
	1	Using solid fuel in an open/three-stone fire
	2	Using solid fuel in an improved stove
	3	Using solid fuel in an improved stove with smoke extraction/chimney
	4	Mainly using a liquid or gas fuel or electricity, and associated stove
	5	Using only a liquid or gas fuel or electricity, and associated stove
Electricity	0	No access to electricity at all
	1	Access to third party battery charging only
	2	Access to stand-alone electrical appliance (e.g. solar lantern, solar phone charger)
	3	Own limited power access for multiple home applications (e.g. solar home systems or power-limited off-grid)
	4	Poor quality and/or intermittent AC connection
	5	Reliable AC connection available for all uses
Mechanical power	0	No household access to tools or mechanical advantages
	1	Hand tools available for household tasks
	2	Mechanical advantage devices available to magnify human/animal effort for most household tasks
	3	Powered mechanical devices available for some household tasks
	4	Powered mechanical devices available for most household tasks
	5	Mainly purchasing mechanically processed goods and services

Source: Practical Action (2012)

Table 11.4 Minimum standards for household energy access

Energy service		Minimum standard
Lighting	1.1	300 lm for a minimum of 4 hours per night at household level
Cooking and water heating	2.1	1 kg woodfuel or 0.3 kg charcoal or 0.04 kg LPG or 0.2 litres of kerosene biofuel per person per day, taking less than 30 minutes per household per day to obtain
	2.2	Minimum efficiency of improved solid fuel stoves to be 40% greater than a three-stone fire in terms of fuel use
	2.3	Annual mean concentrations of particulate matter ($PM_{2.5}$) < 10 $\mu g/m^3$ in households, with interim goals of 15 $\mu g/m^3$, 25 $\mu g/m^3$ and 35 $\mu g/m^3$
Space heating	3.1	Minimum daytime indoor air temperature of 180C
Cooling	4.1	Households can extend life of perishable products by a minimum of 50% over that allowed by ambient storage
	4.2	Maximum apparent indoor air temperature of 30°C
Information and communications	5.1	People can communicate electronic information from their household
	5.2	People can access electronic media relevant to their lives and livelihoods in their household

Source: Practical Action (2012)

In addition, the enterprise energy access matrix looks at attributes of energy supply that are particularly important for enterprises: reliability, quality, affordability, and adequacy across the energy supply types of electricity, fuels, and mechanical power. It also highlights the energy services that are particularly important through the proxy of various basic appliances.

The PPEO 2012 applied these measures to six communities in Kenya, Nepal and Peru (Figure 11.1). In each country, one community was mostly

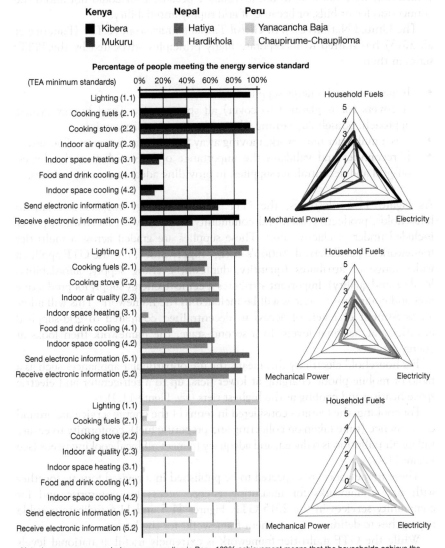

Note: In some cases, e.g. Indoor space cooling in Peru, 100% achievement means that the households achieve the minimum standard in normal ambient conditions, without an energy service being needed.

Figure 11.1 TEA and ESI scores in six communities in Kenya, Nepal and Peru

Source: Practical Action (2012)

grid-connected, and the other was beyond the grid. The two communities in Kenya were urban slums, whilst the others were rural villages. The results highlighted how, despite grid connections, there were significant gaps in people's levels of energy access. In all the rural examples, the lack of access to mechanical power was particularly striking. In line with the global norm, lower proportions of households had access to a minimum acceptable level of cooking fuels and stoves than had access to electricity. It was further found that those with a grid connection were not able to use it regularly because they could not afford the connection fee or bills, or because of grid supply unreliability.

The United Nations SE4All *Global Tracking Framework (GTF)* (Banerjee et al. 2013) has started to incorporate many principles advocated by the PPEO series in that:

- It measures both energy supplies and services.
- It covers (or is planned to cover) all spheres of a Total Energy Access approach: household, earning a living, and community services.
- It is a multi-tier framework, moving away from binary measures of access.
- It recognizes and validates the importance of intermediate technologies, off-grid and decentralized supplies, in providing adequate energy services.

As Figure 11.2 illustrates, the GTF identifies *energy supplies* relevant to households, productive uses, and community services, with mechanical power included under productive uses. These supplies are graded across a multi-tier framework as per Practical Action's energy supply index, but the GTF applies a wider range of attributes (quantity, duration, evening supply, affordability, legality, and quality). Important attributes specific to energy supply for productive uses and community services will be included in the framework. This will allow an assessment of levels of access to decentralized compared to grid-supplied electricity at national levels. In a second stage, the framework then looks at energy services.

For household electricity this means the use of particular appliances such as a radio or mobile phone charging at lower tiers, up to a refrigerator and electric space heating and cooling at the highest tiers (see Figure 11.3).

For cooking, the features considered in terms of the energy service are around convenience (time taken on collecting and preparing fuel), conformity to ensure indoor air pollution is reduced, and adequacy to meet all local cooking needs (see Figure 11.4).

These frameworks are expected to be published in a revised format, together with new frameworks for measuring energy access for enterprise and for community services in the 2015 GTF. Figures 11.5 and 11.6 indicate possible approaches to defining measurement frameworks for the latter.

While the GTF multi-tier framework is extremely useful at national levels and in highlighting inequalities, there is still a need for a global cut-off point below which people cannot be considered to "have access" to energy. One suggestion, made by Practical Action and based on a comparison of its Minimum

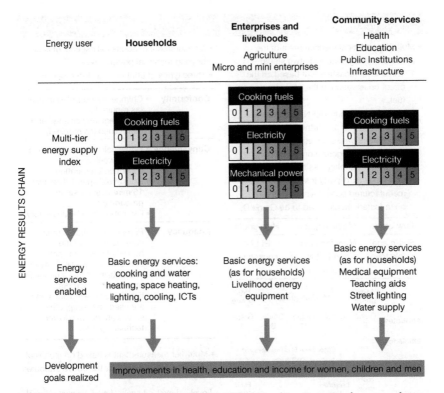

Figure 11.2 Components of the UNSE4All Global Tracking Framework proposed access measurement system

Source: Practical Action (2013)

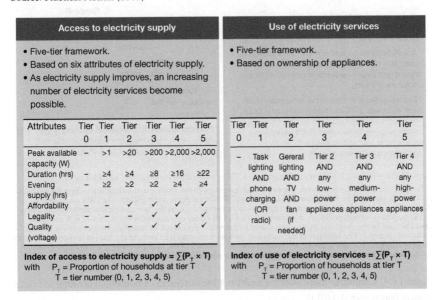

Figure 11.3 Candidate framework for multi-tier measurement of household electricity access

Source: Banerjee et al. (2013)

Step 1: Technical performance	Step 2: Actual use

Step 1: Technical performance

- Multi-tier technical measurement of the primary cooking solution in two steps:
  1. Three-level measurement based on the direct observation of the cookstove and fuel.
  2. Manufactured non-BLEN cookstoves (medium grade) are further categorized into four grades based on technical attributes. This grade categorization would only be possible for cookstoves that have undergone third-party testing. Non-BLEN manufactured cookstoves that have not been tested are assumed to be Grade D.

Low grade	Medium grade	High grade
Self-made[1] cookstove	Manufactured[2] non-BLEN cookstove	BLEN[3] cookstove

	Low grade	Medium grade			High grade
Attributes	Grade E	Grade D	Grade C	Grade B	Grade A
Efficiency		Certified Non-BLEN manufactured cookstoves			
Indoor pollution	Self-made cook-stoves or equivalent	Uncertified Non-BLEN manu-factured cook-stoves			BLEN cook-stoves or equivalent
Overall pollution					
Safety					

[1] A self-made cookstove refers to a three-stone fire or equivalent, typically made by an untrained person without the use of premanufactured parts.

[2] A manufactured cookstove refers to any cookstove available in the market (including cookstoves from artisans and small local producers trained under a cookstove program).

[3] BLEN cookstove refers to stove independent fuels (such as biogas, LPG, electricity, natural gas). BLEN equivalence of more fuels (such as ethanol) would be examined going forward. Non-BLEN cookstoves include most solid and liquid fuels for which performance is stove dependent.

Step 2: Actual use

- Measurement of additional aspects of access beyond technical performance.
- Three types of attributes, as listed below:

Conformity	• Chimney/hood/pot-skirt used (as required). • Stove regularly cleaned and maintained (as required).
Convenience	• Household spends less than 12 hrs/week on fuel collection/preparation. • Household spends less than 15 min/meal for stove preparation. • Ease of cooking is satisfactory.
Adequacy	• Primary stove fulfills most cooking needs of the household, and it is not constrained by availability or affordability of fuel, cultural fit, or number of burners. • If multiple cooking solutions are used (stacking), other stoves are not of a lower technical grade.

- Multi-tier measurement is based on technical performance adjusted for the above attributes.

Level 0	Level 1	Level 2	Level 3	Level 4	Level 5
					Grade-A w/o CCA w/CCA
				Grade-B w/o CCA w/CCA	
			Grade-C w/o CCA w/CCA		
		Grade-D w/o CCA w/CCA			
	Grade-E w/o CCA w/CCA				

Index of access to household cooking = $\sum (P_T \times T)$

with P_T = Proportion of households at level T

  T = level number (0, 1, 2, 3, 4, 5)

Note: BLEN = biogas-LPG-electricity-natural gas; CCA = conformity, convenience, and adequacy.

* The proposed multi-tier framework (above) is complementary to the multi-tiered technical standards for cookstove performance proposed by the Alliance led International Workshop Agreement (IWA). The IWA multi-tier standards provide the basis for measurement of cookstove performance on the four technical attributes—efficiency, indoor pollution, overall pollution, and safety (annex 4). Laboratory measurements based on the IWA standards would be used by the multi-tier framework (above) to determine the overall technical performance of the primary cookstove in step-1. The objective of the multi-tier framework (above) is to measure the level of household access to cooking solutions. It builds upon the technical performance of each of the multiple cooking solutions being used in the household (including the use of non-solid fuels), while also taking into account CCA attributes.

Figure 11.4 Candidate framework for multi-tier measurement of household cooking solutions

Source: Banerjee et al. (2013)

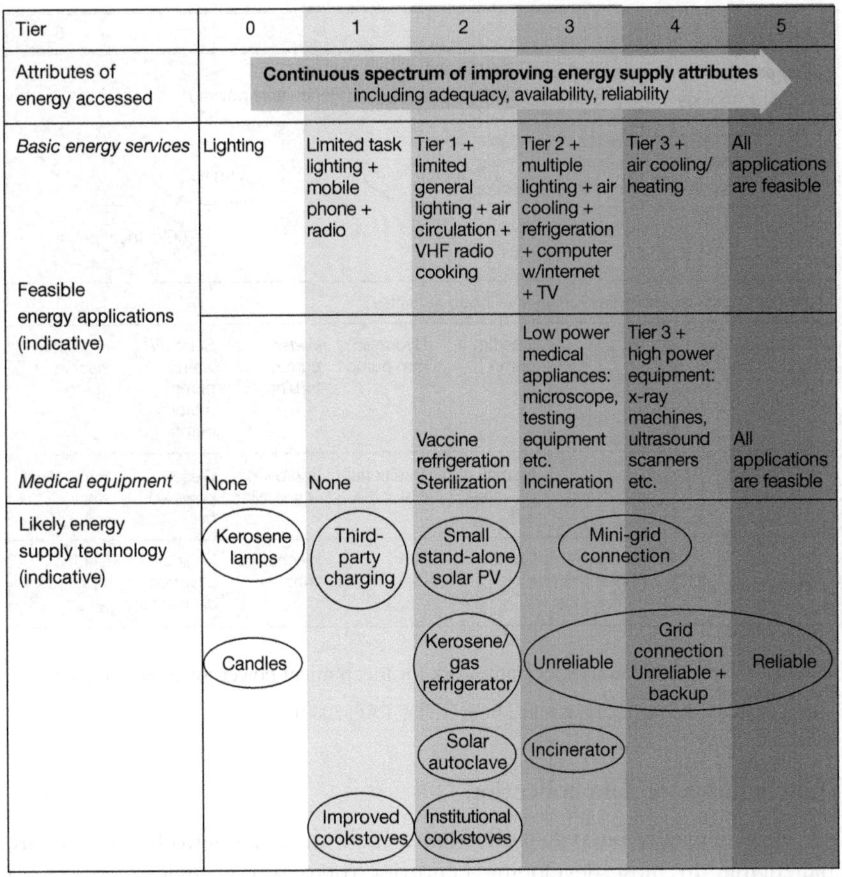

Tier	0	1	2	3	4	5
Attributes of energy accessed	**Continuous spectrum of improving energy supply attributes** including adequacy, availability, reliability →					
Basic energy services	Lighting	Limited task lighting + mobile phone + radio	Tier 1 + limited general lighting + air circulation + VHF radio cooking	Tier 2 + multiple lighting + air cooling + refrigeration + computer w/internet + TV	Tier 3 + air cooling/ heating	All applications are feasible
Feasible energy applications (indicative)				Low power medical appliances: microscope, testing equipment etc.	Tier 3 + high power equipment: x-ray machines, ultrasound scanners etc.	
Medical equipment	None	None	Vaccine refrigeration Sterilization	Incineration		All applications are feasible
Likely energy supply technology (indicative)	Kerosene lamps / Candles	Third-party charging / Improved cookstoves	Small stand-alone solar PV / Kerosene/ gas refrigerator / Solar autoclave / Institutional cookstoves	Mini-grid connection / Unreliable / Incinerator	Grid connection Unreliable + backup	Reliable

Figure 11.5 An indicative framework for defining and measuring access to energy for health centres

Source: Practical Action (2013)

Standards and the Energy Supply Index with the GTF framework, is that Tier 3 represents a level of energy access which begins to be truly enabling and at which could therefore be considered an international standard, above which, people should be counted as having adequate "energy access."

Tier	0	1	2	3	4	5
Likely energy supply technology resource	Human power			Renewable power		
			Animal power		Engine	
						Electrical power
Possible energy technologies for key livelihood activities						
Water pumping	Bucket	Treadle pump	Hydraulic ram pump	Water-current turbine	Solar PV water pump, motorised pump	High power electric pump
Agro-processing	Hand pounding	Animal powered mill	Traditional water mill	Improved water mill	Diesel-powered mill	High power electric mill
Small-scale manufacturing	Hand tools	Treadle tools	N/A	Mechanical lathe	Engine-powered circular saw	Electric saw

Figure 11.6 Indicative multi-tier framework for mechanical power for productive use
Source: Practical Action (2013; adapted from UNDP/PAC 2009)

The challenge of data collection

The new demands on data collection which these frameworks present are challenging. In most developing countries there is no single agency with responsibility for delivering comprehensive energy services that cover both grid and off-grid energy supplies and which cross the three domains of household, enterprise, and community services. Consequently there is no single agency responsible for providing an overall view of progress towards universal access. The situation is further complicated by the level of data required to paint an accurate picture of access levels. As has been argued above, this goes beyond simple binary distinctions of connection/no connection.

The most likely solution to these problems is to use a household survey approach to data collection. The most obvious route would be to include appropriate questions in existing national surveys carried out on a regular basis at the moment in many countries (such as national censuses or donor funded surveys such as the United States Agency for International Development's [USAID's] demographic and health surveys [DHS] and living standards measurement surveys [LSMS], etc.). However, as the amount of questions required is significant, expansion of these surveys to more comprehensively cover energy access is not practical. Instead specifically commissioned national energy access surveys, based on statistically significant sampling of the population, is the most promising way forward and the one that has been adopted by the UN SE4All GTF for 2015 and beyond.

Finally, in addition to data collection challenges there are also technical issues to be overcome related to the implementation of the measurement frameworks. For example, in terms of household cooking solutions, there is a wide range of stoves whose performance can be highly context-specific, meaning allocating a particular stove to a particular tier is not straightforward. The SE4All tracking framework proposes a network of designated certification agencies and testing laboratories for country-level certification and labelling. Data collection is being supported for SE4All opt-in countries, but may need to be rolled out globally if this framework is adopted for post-2015 goals on energy access.

Collecting meaningful data is a fundamental stepping stone in the SE4All ambition to deliver universal energy access by 2030. Having the right definition and measures will be critical to ensuring an energy access target in the post-2015 development framework is set at a level which will drive positive change. The value for poor people will come not in the application of the Global Tracking Framework itself, but the use of its findings as a tool to highlight gaps, inequalities, and to guide investment and policy focus to the places it is needed most.

References

Banerjee, S. G., Bhatia, M., et al. (2013) *Global tracking framework. Vol. 3 of Global tracking framework.* Sustainable energy for all. Washington D.C.; The World Bank. http://documents.worldbank.org/curated/en/2013/05/17765643/global-tracking-framework-vol-3-3-main-report (Accessed 08 April 2014).

EC (2006) *The role of energy services in the health, education and water sectors and cross-sectoral linkages.* Brussels: European Commission.

FAO (2009) *How to feed the world in 2050,* background paper for the high-level forum on how to feed the world in 2050. Rome: FAO.

GIZ (2011) *Modern energy services for modern agriculture: a review for smallholder farming in developing countries.* Bonn and Eschbor, Germany: GIZ – HERA – Poverty-orientated Basic Energy Services. Available from: http://poweringag.org/sites/default/files/giz2011-en-energy-services-for-modern-agriculture.pdf (Accessed 08 April 2014).

GSMA (2010) *Women & mobile: a global opportunity. A study on the mobile phone gender gap in low and middle-income countries.* London: GSMA, Cherie Blair Foundation for Women and Vital Wave Consulting.

GTZ-HERA (2009) Intervention A: market introduction of efficient woodfuel stoves, in *Cooking energy compendium.* Available from: https://energypedia.info/index.php/GIZ_HERA_Cooking_Energy_Compendium (Accessed 08 April 2014).

GTZ and SenterNovem (2009) *Energising development: report on impacts.* Eschborn, Germany: GTZ. Available from: www.government.nl/files/documents-and-publications/reports/2009/06/01/energising-development-report-on-impacts/energising-development.pdf (Accessed 08 April 2014).

Havet, I., Chowdhury, S., Takada, M. and Cantano, A. (2009) *Energy in national decentralization policies.* New York: UNDP.

Hulscher, W. (1997) *Stoves for space heating and cooking at different altitudes and/by ethnic groups.* Regional Wood Energy Development Programme in Asia (RWEDP) Report, No.

28. Bangkok: FAO. Available from: www.fao.org/DOCREP/006/AD589E/AD589E00. HTM (Accessed 08 April 2014).

Internet World Statistics. (2012) *Usage and populations statistics*. Available from: www. internetworldstats.com/stats.htm (Accessed 08 April 2014).

Keatinge, W. (2006) Interviewed in *Why more people die in the winter*. BBC News. Available from: http://news.bbc.co.uk/1/hi/health/5372296.stm (Accessed 08 April 2014).

Legros, G., Havet, I., Bruce, N., Bonjour, S. (2009) *The energy access situation in developing countries. A review focusing on the least developed countries and Sub-Saharan Africa*. New York: UNDP and WHO.

Marker, P., McNamara, K. and Wallace, L. (2002) *The significance of information and communication technologies for reducing poverty*. London: Department for International Development (DFID).

Practical Action (2006) *Refrigeration for developing countries*, Practical Action Technical Brief. Available from: http://answers.practicalaction.org/our-resources/item/refrigeration-in-developing-countries (Accessed 08 April 2014).

Practical Action (2010) *Poor people's energy outlook 2010*. Rugby, UK: Practical Action Publishing.

Practical Action (2012) *Poor people's energy outlook 2012*. Rugby, UK: Practical Action Publishing.

Practical Action (2013) *Poor people's energy outlook 2013*. Rugby, UK: Practical Action Publishing.

Practical Action (2014) *Poor people's energy outlook 2014: key messages on energy for poverty alleviation*. Rugby, UK: Practical Action Publishing.

Reiche, K., Grüner, R., Attigah, B., Hellpap, C. and Brüderle, A. (2010) *What difference can a PicoPV system make?* Eschborn, Germany: GTZ, Energizing Development.

SolarAid (2013) *Impact report*. Solar Aid. Available from: www.solar-aid.org/assets/ Uploads/Publications/Impact-report-web-updated.pdf (Accessed 08 April 2014).

UNDP (2012) *Integrating energy access and employment creation to accelerate progress on the Millennium Development Goals in sub-Saharan Africa*. United Nations Development Program and Practical Action Consulting.

UNDP/PAC (2009) *Expanding energy access in developing countries: the role of mechanical power*. Rugby, UK: Practical Action Publishing.

WHO (2006) *Air quality guidelines for particulate matter, ozone, nitrogen dioxide, and sulfur dioxide. Global update 2005. Summary of risk assessment*. WHO/SDE/PHE/OEH/06.02. Geneva: World Health Organization.

Part 4
The way forward

12 Decentralized power in countries of ECOWAS region

A case study

Pradeep Monga, Alois P. Mhlanga, and Martin Lugmayr

Introduction

With an expanding population of over 335 million in mid-2014, the Economic Community of West African States (ECOWAS) and its 15 Member States represent approximately one-third of sub-Saharan Africa's total population.[1] The region encompasses a diverse set of demographic, socio-economic, and social contexts.

Population size ranges from Cape Verde (539,000) to Nigeria (177,156,000), while gross domestic product (GDP) per capita ranges from USD 800 in Niger to USD 4,400 in Cape Verde. Overall, most ECOWAS Member States continue to face major development challenges, with 13 Member States classified as "Least Developed Countries (LDCs)" by the United Nations (Auth and Musolino 2014).

These factors, along with demographic trends including urbanization and accelerating economic development, contribute to and are influenced by the region's severe energy crisis. The current status of the energy systems hampers the social, economic, and industrial development of the entire region. The countries concurrently face the interrelated challenges of energy poverty, energy security, and climate change.

For most of the countries, major power grids provide power only to major cities leaving the majority living in rural and peri-urban areas without access to electricity. Unless and until special efforts are made, the region may not be able to meet the SE4ALL target of universal energy access for all by 2030. It is therefore critical that, along with extension of the national grid, decentralized energy systems facilitate provision of clean energy services to rural and peri-urban areas in the ECOWAS region for the foreseeable future. Experience from across the region shows that communities that do not have access to grid electricity do pay more for the same energy services compared to those with access to the grid. As such, decentralized energy solutions are effective solutions to providing energy services at comparable prices. In addition, properly designed decentralized energy solutions do bring about multiple socio-economic benefits that include youth employment, empowerment of women and girl children. Furthermore, improved and better cooking facilities reduce mortality due to exposure to indoor air pollution associated with traditional biomass energy-based cooking.

Energy poverty and affordability in West Africa

The increasing power shortages in urban areas and the lack of access to modern, affordable, and reliable energy services in rural areas are interwoven with a variety of economic, social, environmental, and political problems. In most ECOWAS countries the electricity networks are of limited scope and reliability, and serve mainly urban centres and suburbs.

In 2010 it was estimated that nearly 175 million people had no access at all to electricity services in the ECOWAS region. Amongst them, 25 percent are living in urban and 75 percent in rural areas. In some ECOWAS countries, less than 10 percent of the rural population has access to electricity services (see Figure 12.1). Only Cape Verde and Ghana were able to raise the rates close to universal access. Traditional biomass represents the bulk of the final energy consumption, reaching up to 70–85 percent in some of the ECOWAS countries (Saho 2012, 196).

Due to the significance of diesel and heavy fuel-based electricity generation, the consumer tariffs are very high in most of the ECOWAS countries. The average tariff rate is around 13.6 c€/kWh, but in some countries it is much higher.

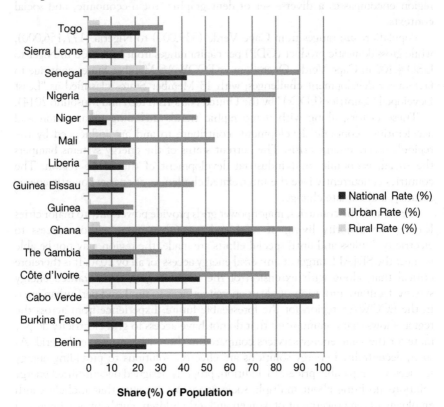

Figure 12.1 Electricity access rates in urban and rural areas in the Economic Community of West African States

Source: ECREEE (2012)

In Liberia and Mauritania the consumer tariffs are higher than 21 EUR/cents per kWh (for a monthly consumption of more than 200 kWh). In Cape Verde the consumer tariff peaks at around 25 EUR/cents per kWh for a monthly consumption below 60 kWh and 30 EUR/cents per kWh for higher consumption. The general ability and willingness to pay the monthly electricity bill are very low (ECREEE 2012).

There are significant energy pricing inequalities between urban and rural areas and among different social groups. The urban and rural poor in West Africa spend proportionately more of their income on poor quality energy services than the better-off do on better quality services. Whereas urban areas tend to use energy higher up the energy ladder (e.g. electricity, charcoal, kerosene, etc.), rural areas continue to rely on traditional biomass for meeting their energy requirements for cooking and lighting.

In rural areas served mainly by diesel powered mini-grids, consumers often pay higher tariffs than in cities where the electricity tends to be subsidized (see Figure 12.2). The operating average cost of centralized diesel generation units in West Africa is estimated at 20.4 €/kWh. Very often tariffs do not cover these

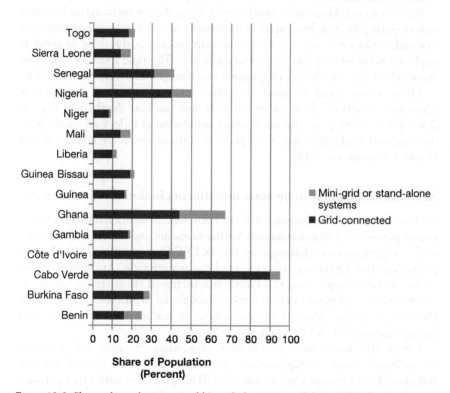

Figure 12.2 Share of population served by grid-electricity and decentralized systems (mainly diesel generators) in the ECOWAS region in 2012

Source: ECREEE (2012)

costs. The operating costs of small-scale diesel-based rural mini-grids can reach up to 2 €/kWh due to the higher fuel and transport costs (Rolland 2012, 280). The escalating price levels have led to the shutdown of many rural diesel generation units in past years.

This unfolding scenario has obvious implications for efforts geared towards boosting socio-economic activities, attracting much needed investments for poverty eradication, the provision of basic social services, and the attainment of the Millennium Development Goals (MDGs). The lack of access to modern, affordable, and reliable energy services is a major obstacle for development and is interrelated with a variety of economic, social, environmental, and political problems in West Africa.

Public services like education, health care, and public safety cannot be delivered with desired efficiency and effectiveness. Schools and universities cannot provide Information and Communication Technology (ICT) services. The absence of lighting makes it impossible to study or work at home in the evening, and the lack of street lighting in public places is a safety hazard. Due to the absence of reliable energy supply small and medium-sized enterprises (SMEs) and agro-industries are not productive and competitive.

Women and children often spend hours a day gathering fuelwood and carrying water to satisfy the daily basic needs of the household. Often the same women have to spend considerable amounts of time manually processing, threshing, or grinding staple foods before they can be cooked and eaten. The time spent for collecting fuelwood reduces considerably the proportion of daylight hours otherwise available.

These hours could be used for other income-generating activities or education at school. It is estimated that four million deaths per year in developing countries are the result of the inhalation of indoor air smoke from the combustion of solid fuels. Sixty percent of these deaths are female (World Health Organization 2014).

Regional cooperation to up-scale investments in decentralized energy

In "business as usual" scenarios – without considerable additional investments – energy poverty and its consequences for the economy and society will continue to be a predominant challenge in the ECOWAS region in 2030. This is particularly true for the population in rural and remote areas. At the background of the severe energy crisis, ECOWAS has increased its efforts to create an integrated regional power and gas market through the West African Power Pool (WAPP). It is also taking a leadership role in up-scaling renewable energy and energy efficiency (RE&EE) investments.

Given the importance of creating economies of scale and reducing transactional costs of implementing power projects, the United Nations Industrial Development Organization (UNIDO), together with other partners namely the ECOWAS Commission, the Austrian Development Agency, and Government of Spain, have established a regional centre for promoting Renewable Energy and Energy Efficiency (ECREEE) in 2010. As part of its mandate, the Centre has been leading the process of developing and executing the ECOWAS Renewable Energy Policy (EREP), which among others, also focuses on decentralized power.

The policy document was adopted by the ECOWAS Energy Ministers in October 2012. It foresees that by 2020 the share of grid-connected RE (including large hydro) in the overall regional electricity mix will increase to 35 percent by 2020 and 48 percent by 2030. The share of "new renewable energy" such as wind, solar, small hydro, and bioelectricity (excluding large hydro) is projected to increase to around 10 percent by 2020 and 19 percent by 2030. These targets translate to an additional 2.425 MW of renewable electricity capacity by 2020 and 7.606 MW by 2030 (ECREEE 2012).

The policy also includes ambitious targets for the up-scaling of decentralized RE solutions in rural areas. To provide universal access to electricity services by 2030 it is envisaged that around 75 percent of the rural population will be served through grid extensions and around 25 percent by RE powered (hybrid) mini-grid and stand-alone systems. The installation of 60,000 mini-grid systems by 2020 and 68,000 between 2020 and 2030 is envisaged. Moreover, the policy foresees the installation of 210,000 stand-alone systems by 2020 and 262,000 units by 2030 (ECREEE 2012) – see Figures 12.3 and 12.4. The ECOWAS Renewable Energy Policy (EREP) estimates an overall investment need of roughly 32.3 billion Euro to reach the decentralized renewable energy targets.

Besides just the policy framework, ECREEE has been working on developing capacity of market players and enablers in developing decentralized renewable energy systems. This includes dedicated training to project developers and financiers on the business of decentralized RE systems on one side, and then training of regulators and policy makers on the regulation of decentralized RE systems on the other. Through these capacity-building activities, a critical mass of market actors and enablers will be established that will promote investments in decentralized RE systems. In sum, ECREEE's activities seek to create uniform market environments conducive to investments in RE and EE,

Rural RE Electricity Targets	2020	2030
Share of rural population supplied by mini-grids and stand-alone systems in %	22%	25%
Mini-grids to be installed	60,000 3,600 MW	128,000 7,680 MW
Stand-alone systems	210,000	262,000
Investment (b€)		32.3

Figure 12.3 The rural renewable energy electricity targets in the ECOWAS Renewable Energy Policy (EREP)

Source: ECOWAS (2012)

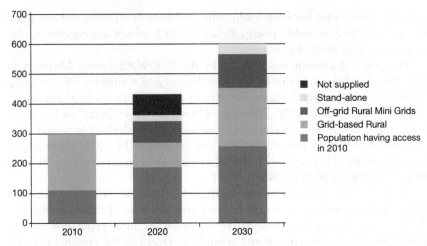

Figure 12.4 The potential contribution of decentralized renewable energy mini-grid and stand-alone systems to universal access to electricity by 2030

Source: ECOWAS Renewable Energy Policy (2012)

including decentralized RE systems. Through this regional approach, it is envisaged that investments in decentralized RE systems will attain economies of scale that will result in cost reduction and increased service delivery.

Decentralized renewable energy solutions and opportunities

During the last decades, a broad range of proven decentralized and centralized RE&EE technologies and solutions, ready to meet the various energy service demands in urban or rural areas, have been developed. Decentralized power solutions, when based on RE systems, are particularly effective if they are combined with energy efficiency (EE) measures. If planned carefully and in accordance with quality principles, such investments are associated with multiple benefits and opportunities for West African countries.

There is a significant technically and economic feasible potential for RE development of decentralized power systems in countries of West Africa because "these resources are generous and well distributed among the countries" (Elayo et al. 2012, 86):

- Wind potential is concentrated in the coastal zones (Cape Verde, Senegal, The Gambia, and possibly Ghana, Mali, and Nigeria). The overall wind assessments provide only general information on the potential. Site-specific surveys and measurements are required to verify the seasonal variation of wind regimes and determine the financial viability of the potential.
- Small hydro potential is located particularly but not exclusively in the southern part of the region (Côte d'Ivoire, Ghana, Guinea, Guinea-Bissau, Liberia,

Togo and Sierra Leone) while solar power is abundant in the northern regions (Niger, Burkina Faso, Niger, and the northern part of Ghana and Nigeria).

- Except for Cape Verde and the Sahelean areas of Mali, Burkina Faso, and Niger, biomass resources are well distributed across the region, with a propitious potential in the southern region.

- Finally, solar power is especially favourable in the northern desert areas of the ECOWAS region in Mali and Niger and in the north-eastern part of Nigeria with a potential of 1,700 kWh/installed kWp/year. The coastal areas of Liberia, Côte d'Ivoire, Ghana, and Nigeria do not benefit to the same extent from this resource with an average potential of 1,200 kWh/installed kWp/year. For the remaining areas, the average potential is about1,500 kWh/ kWp/year.

As decentralized energy systems, stand-alone RE systems and RE-based (including hybrid) mini- and micro-grids are well prepared to improve access to modern, reliable, and affordable energy services particularly in rural and remote areas of West Africa which are located in far-flung areas away from the grid. There are plenty of proven technical applications available to meet the energy requirements of rural settlements and industries without building up expensive central grid or logistic systems. The extension of the grid to very scarce populated rural areas is often not the least cost option. The dispersed character of rural settlements in many ECOWAS countries is a good setting for RE solutions.

In addition, there is huge potential of integrating renewable energy systems into already existing fossil fuels based decentralized systems and mini-grids. As part of efforts to increase rural electrification, most countries in the region have over the years installed fossil fuels powered mini-grids that in most cases operate for specific hours during the day. As in the case study in The Gambia (Table 12.1), the integration of a solar system to the mini-grid is bringing multiple benefits that include savings in fuel consumption and reduces the difficulty and costs associated with transporting fuel to this remote area. In addition, the region installed multifunctional platforms programs where small diesel power engines were installed and a variety of end use equipment was attached (mills, alternators, oil presses, etc.) in rural areas. In such cases renewable energy system will build on already existing management structures and business models.

Several household surveys undertaken in the ECOWAS region have revealed that RE-based decentralized systems can meet the priority needs of the rural poor, boost local development, contribute to poverty reduction and help to create wealth, improve health care, create jobs, and enhance water supply and sanitation + productive uses. They can be useful for processing and conserving agricultural products (e.g. solar drying and/or refrigeration of fish) and the improvement of access to essential services (e.g. solar cooling of vaccinations in health posts, basic lighting in rural schools, water pumping, and desalination).

RE-based (hybrid) mini-grids can decrease the costs of the many installed diesel generators throughout the ECOWAS region. The simple injection of RE

Table 12.1 Case studies

---

60 kWp PV system operating (hybrid) with a 200kW (3 engines) diesel mini-grid system at Kaur, The Gambia.

The 200kW diesel system supplies power to villages and households in Kaur area in The Gambia and operates for 11 hours as follows 0900–1300hrs and 1800–0100hrs. The project has brought about several benefits that include a net annual diesel savings of about US$ 30,000. In addition, other savings in terms of replacement cost of diesel gensets, regular O&M, insurance and repairs. This project was installed under an ongoing UNIDO/GEF project and based on the success of the project, the country now plans to install over 500kWp system in the area and an additional 5MW in mini-grids in the near future.

Source: UNIDO/GEF project – Promoting renewable energy based mini for productive uses in rural areas.-www.thegef.org/gef/project_detail?projID=3922

312 kWp PV hybrid system for Bambadinca St Claro, Guinea-Bissau

The project is co-funded by the European Union, UNIDO, ECREEE and the Government of Portugal and is supplying around 650 households and 6,500 inhabitants with sustainable electricity services. The project boosts also the productivity and income of agricultural groups in the village area. The system comprises of more than 1,200 photovoltaic panels, 216 batteries and three diesel generators.

---

power in existing diesel-based mini-grids can significantly reduce the diesel bills of many local communities. Mini-grids can be developed around a number of business models and power generation options, and are increasingly incorporating renewable generators – mainly solar PV, wind, and small hydro into their design.

Status of decentralized energy markets

Most ECOWAS countries have started to mainstream RE solutions into national development programs and policies (e.g. education, health, agriculture). However, so far the market for decentralized energy solutions has not reached economies of scale. The region is far from attaining the rural electrification targets of the ECOWAS Renewable Energy Policy (EREP). Major efforts are needed to create an enabling environment for private sector investments.

Throughout ECOWAS countries, renewables have long played a significant role in supplying power for activities like pumping for drinking water and agricultural irrigation (e.g. Cape Verde, The Gambia). Estimates of total installed decentralized RE capacity are unreliable, as few Member States collect data on self-generation or off-grid projects. However, data on distributed PV capacity in The Gambia, Guinea-Bissau, Niger, Nigeria, Mali, Burkina Faso, Cape Verde, and Sierra Leone indicate increasing use of the technology.

It is reported that Mali has a total of 13 installed off-grid solar PV projects, ranging in size from 2 kW to 24 kW. The Malian Agency for the Development of Household Energy and Rural Electrification has been particularly active in developing mini-grids, including 21 hybrid PV–diesel projects adding up to 2.1 MW (Auth and Musolino 2014).

Gam-Solar has installed solar pumping systems in nearly 80 villages of The Gambia, providing potable water to more than 200,000 people. Guinea-Bissau has installed a considerable number of off-grid PV systems for health posts and schools. A 312 kW PV–diesel hybrid mini-grid system is currently under installation in the Bafata region with support of the European Commission and UNIDO.

In Liberia, solar PV has been installed in 205 public health facilities through the Rural and Renewable Energy Agency's Renewable Energy for Health Care Facilities project. The Senegalese Agency for Rural Electrification is implementing Rural Electrification Projects (ERILs) using solar systems to electrify more than 650 community centres and more than 120 rural localities.

In Ghana, the Ghana Energy Development and Access Project (GEDAP), implemented by the Ministry of Energy and Petroleum with national and international partners, aims to deploy approximately some 7,500 solar PV systems in schools, hospitals, and off-grid communities. Solar technology is also being used throughout the region to supply lighting, either through PV lighting systems or solar lanterns.

Barriers facing decentralized energy markets

The introduction and usage of RE technologies for decentralized power systems in the ECOWAS region face various policy, regulatory, capacity, knowledge, awareness, and financial barriers which need to be addressed as priorities. Due to these constraints the private sector engagement has remained very limited. Most of the implemented rural RE projects in West Africa were highly subsidized and were not based on sustainable business models.

Rural electrification in the region has over the years adopted a two-tier approach, namely, the extension of the grid, and the deployment of decentralized systems. Whereas the policy landscape for grid-based electrification has significantly developed over the years, the same does not apply for decentralized power systems. Decentralized power-based rural electrification policies, regulations, and legal frameworks have often remained unclear and underfinanced. In fact most countries in the region do not have a policy and regulatory framework for private sector engagement in the decentralized power systems. The national utility still has the mandate to supply power to rural areas, yet most of the utilities do not have the capital to invest in such new projects. However, particularly in the rural electrification sector long-term stability and planning are key factors to attract the private sector. There is a demand for publicly available long-term rural electrification strategies, flexible and standardized regulation to encourage project development, and harmonized quality standards that will ensure confidence in technologies. There is also need for a local manufacturing and service industry.

There is a widespread lack of knowledge on business models for decentralized power systems based on microfinance and microleasing. Microfinance includes two different approaches described by Simon Rolland as the One-Hand model (Bangladesh/Grameen Shakti model) and the Two-Hand model (Sri Lanka/SEEDS model). Microleasing models, such as the fee-for-service and the lease/hire, are usually led by service providers and, in this case the energy provider owns the system and provides only a service, including maintenance and quality insurance. This differs from the microfinance approach, where the customer gains the ownership over the system after the payback period.

(Rolland 2012, 285)

Management of decentralized power systems such as mini-grids remains a challenge. Community owned systems faces challenges in determining and setting up viable tariffs. The collection of fees can be problematic. Management models where a private entity is tasked with the overall management of the mini-grid systems have been more successful. In some cases, this tends to be compromised when making decisions that may be socially difficult such as raising tariffs.

Also for RE-based (hybrid) mini-grids, there are a number of other business models that have been successfully utilized. If a mini-grid in an isolated area does not attract the interest of the private sector or utility, the community-based model can be used. In such cases the community becomes the owner and operator of the system, providing maintenance, collecting tariffs and being responsible for management services.

Beyond microfinance, entrepreneurial finance (debt or equity) still remains the most important – and the most difficult – financing segment in promoting market development. Access to affordable finance, along with sound and replicable business models to ensure project sustainability, are the key economic triggers of rural electrification.

Given the development nature of the use of renewable energy decentralized systems in rural areas of the region, private sector funding for these projects has tended to be led by public sector financing schemes.

There is a lack of technical capacities and information on decentralized power systems, key technologies and issues at all levels. National and local governments often still do not believe in renewable technologies, and commercial banks very often do not completely understand the financial structures and technical basics of RE technologies. Capacity building in the banking sector is key.

Most governments have set up Rural Electrification Agencies (REAs) and/or Rural Electrification Funds (REFs) to promote decentralized rural electrification. However, due to inadequate financial and technical RE expertise, they have been unable to make much impact so far.

Conclusion

There is need for a paradigm shift in promoting decentralized energy systems for productive uses from the current focus on electrification to energization. The earlier approach is premised on energy provision as an end or business in itself, while the latter focuses on providing energy services which create an important role for decentralized energy systems among others. In line with this latter approach, decentralized energy systems that focus on productive uses have been more successful and viable and will become increasingly important as the population of the region grows. As such, decentralized energy systems, especially those that are based on RE systems, need to be integrated in sectors like small and medium scale enterprises, agriculture production, and agro-processing, to ensure sustainability and replicability. In addition, RE decentralized systems that are imbedded in other ongoing sectors like housing development, health, etc. have tended to be more sustainable in the long term. In terms of policy and regulation, the region already includes countries that have actively enacted policies and regulations that create a conducive environment for private sector investments in decentralized energy systems. Other countries in the region would need support from institutions like ECREEE, UNIDO, etc. in developing policies and regulations that are in line with the strategic interest of each of the countries, and are also in accord with the regional momentum.

Note

1   ECOWAS Members States are namely Benin, Burkina Faso, Cape Verde, Côte d'Ivoire, The Gambia, Ghana, Guinea, Guinea-Bissau, Liberia, Mali, Niger, Nigeria, Senegal, Sierra Leone, and Togo.

References

Auth, Katie and Evan Musolino. 2014. *ECOWAS Renewable Energy and Energy Efficiency Status Report 2014*. Paris, France: REN21 Secretariat.
ECREEE. 2012. *ECOWAS Renewable Energy Policy (EREP)*. Praia, Cape Verde: ECREEE Secretariat.
Elayo, Hyacinth, Martin Lugmayr, David Vilar, and Mahama Kappiah. 2012. "ECOWAS Renewable Energy Policy (EREP)." In *Renewable Energy in Western Africa: Situation, Experiences and Trends*, edited by David Vilar, 196–200. Canary Islands: Casa África.
Rolland, Simon. 2012. "Renewable Energy Markets for Rural Electrification." In *Renewable Energy in Western Africa: Situation, Experiences and Trends*, edited by David Vilar, 277–288. Canary Islands: Casa África.
Saho, Bah F. M. 2012. "Bioenergy Potentials in West Africa." In *Renewable Energy in Western Africa: Situation, Experiences and Trends*, edited by David Vilar, 196–200. Canary Islands: Casa África.
World Health Organization. 2014. "Household air pollution and health." Accessed March 5, 2015. www.who.int/mediacentre/factsheets/fs292/en/.

13 Green Climate Fund, Sustainable Development Goals, and energy access

A new opportunity for climate change and development

Martin Hiller, Andreas Zahner, Katrin Harvey, and Amy Meyer

Introduction

The agendas of climate change and development have a huge potential for supporting each other, leading to a stepwise transformation to low carbon practices while enhancing development results in a variety of areas. Energy services play a pivotal role in this context, especially for stimulating other development priorities; at the same time, providing low carbon solutions for these new development demands delivers modern and effective technologies as well as business and financing models.

This chapter proposes combining elements of two major United Nations efforts addressing climate change and development, the Framework Convention on Climate Change (UNFCCC) and the Sustainable Development Goals (SDGs). An examination of the current status of the Green Climate Fund (GCF), established through the UNFCCC, and the encouraging progress of the UN Open Working Group of the SDGs reveals that a fresh approach to mitigation and adaptation measures in coordination and combination with development assistance techniques is possible. On the example of the new strategy of the Renewable Energy and Energy Efficiency Partnership (REEEP) and its project portfolio, the chapter illustrates the attractiveness of a combined approach especially for fostering small and medium enterprises.

The UNFCCC, climate finance, and the Green Climate Fund

At the fifteenth UNFCCC Conference of the Parties (COP) in December 2009 in Copenhagen, Parties failed to establish a coherent and global climate policy regime, missing out on what had been so far the world's best opportunity to integrate external environmental cost into the global economy. Instead, during late hours, governments decided to address climate finance as a key lever to generate more effective climate action, proposing an investment initiative into climate change of US$ 100 billion per annum from 2020, referring to a – so far non-specified – combination of public and private finance under the new Green Climate Fund (GCF). Separate "Fast-Start Finance" of US$ 30 billion was deployed by industrial countries in the first three years after the Copenhagen declaration (UNFCCC 2010). This major financing signal replaced the binding legal agreement that had been the original aim of COP15 – though at the time no one knew how to fill in the detail.

Climate finance

The Copenhagen outcome was by no means the start for generic climate finance, as a plethora of other funds and initiatives at multi- and bilateral level had been invested earlier. These include the Global Environment Facility, a funding arm of the UNFCCC, which also acts for a number of other international agreements; the Adaptation Fund under the UNFCCC; the Climate Investment Funds of the World Bank; and bilateral funding arms such as Norway's Energy Plus, the UK's International Climate Fund (ICF), and Germany's International Climate Initiative (ICI). Last but not least, the UNFCCC's own market-based mechanisms, first and foremost the Clean Development Mechanism, were set up to channel private financing into low carbon and development economic activities, accounting for "over 1.4 billion certified emission reductions being issued and over USD 215 billion being invested" (UNFCCC 2013).

By the time the GCF was conceived, these and other climate financing bodies had already prepared the landscape of public finance for climate action considerably. The challenge that became more prominent at the time of the Copenhagen COP was the question of how public funding could leverage appropriate (and much greater) private investment. The Green Climate Fund is set up to provide at least part of the answer.

The Green Climate Fund (GCF)

The GCF aims at allocating US$ 100 billion annually from public and private sources to mitigation and adaptation projects in the developing world. Agreed upon at the sixteenth COP in Cancun, Mexico, in November 2010, and enacted a year later in Durban, South Africa, the GCF entered its first active period in late 2014, having reached a level of over US$ 10 billion at the twentieth UNFCCC Conference of the Parties in Lima, Peru, in December 2014 (GCF 2015). Earlier in 2014, the GCF agreed its administrative policies (GCF 2014) which triggered the start of its implementation.

In the course of 2015, the GCF will accredit a number of implementing agencies, ranging from multi- and bilateral donors to civil society and business actors, and to refine further the exact ways in which finance from the Fund can be used and disbursed. In principle, the GCF will be able to use a range of financial deployments such as concessional loans, grants, and loan guarantees. At a side event at COP20 in Lima, Peru, business representatives voiced strong support for designing the financing role of the GCF in a way that allows private investors to offset early risk.

The Sustainable Development Goals and energy access

The Sustainable Development Goals (SDGs) originated at the United Nations Rio+20 conference in Rio de Janeiro in 2012, setting out a post-2015 development agenda while building on the experience and architecture of the Millennium Development Goals (MDGs). These come to a close in 2015, and reactions to their achievements have been mixed, with some actors finding inspiration and increased focus in the program while others see over-ambition and lack of accountability (Hulme 2009). Internalizing this feedback and seeking improvement, the UN is now finalizing the creation of a new set of targets under the Sustainable Development Goals or SDGs (UN 2013).

The proposed SDGs which are currently undergoing final adjustments include seventeen individual goals, more than doubling the number of goals compared to the MDGs. In his summary conclusions in December 2014, the UN Secretary-General defined a layer of six essential elements for delivering the SDGs: Planet, People, Dignity, Prosperity, Justice, and Partnership (cited here in no hierarchal order). In the context of this chapter, the SDGs show two other remarkable features: first, the Goals are valid for all UN nations, in contrast to the MDGs that aimed at developing nations only; the SDGs are intended to set "a truly universal transformation of sustainable development" (UN 2014). Second, specific goals were set for both energy and climate change: Goal 7 – Ensure access to affordable, reliable, sustainable and modern energy for all, and Goal 13 – Take urgent action to combat climate change and its impacts (the UNFCCC remains the central UN body to create this action) (UN 2014).

The SDGs therefore present a strong basis for global development planning; they need to be used as a basis for action on energy access as much as on climate change, both on emission reductions and on adaptation.

Climate change, development, and MSMEs

In something akin to a knee-jerk reaction, development has often been squared off against protection of the climate, resulting in a game of "either/or" when it should be one of mutual progress (Baer et al. 2008). Expenditure so far on development initiatives to achieve the MDGs, both private and public, has been rising yet all of the progress that has been achieved could be undone by climate change (UN 2007; World Bank 2010). As UN Secretary-General Ban Ki-moon stated in a general address to the press: "This is our opportunity to advance sustainable development; encourage new kinds of cleaner technologies, industries and jobs; and integrate climate change risks into national policies and practices" (UN 2007).

The importance of micro, small and medium-sized enterprises

Of special importance to economic development, and therefore to changing fundamental economic paradigms such as energy supply, are Micro, Small and Medium Enterprises or MSMEs. Research by the International Finance Corporation (IFC) shows that one-third of global GDP is produced by MSMEs. In this research, MSMEs are defined by number of employees – less than 10 employees, between 10 to 50 employees, and from 50 to 300 employees – though other factors can be taken into account and definitions vary greatly between different countries (Kushnir et al. 2010). The IFC says there are 200 to 245 million formal and informal enterprises without loan or overdraft but would need access to such finance, and over 90 percent of these are formal or informal MSMEs (Stein et al. 2013).

At the same time, MSMEs are extremely relevant to reducing carbon emissions: Parker et al. (2009) quote estimates showing that 60 percent of carbon emissions originate from SMEs. While working with this layer of the economy is certainly more arduous than focusing on large corporations only, it is critical for low carbon development and for prosperity creation.

SE4All – Sustainable Energy for All

The fact that sustainable energy access is now that high on the agenda of international development is a direct result of a unique UN initiative called Sustainable Energy for All (SE4All). The initiative is under the guidance of the UN Secretary-General (UN 2012). By focusing on energy access as well as on low carbon, clean energy targets, SE4All provides the intellectual basis for bringing mitigation activities together with the development paradigm of energy access. Centering around a global action agenda with seven "sectoral" areas, SE4All facilitates a process in which low carbon energy solutions are taken forward with the ambitious goal to also solve the problem of lacking access to modern energy services.

Sustainable energy as enabler for SDGs

Most parts of modern life are in some way or other influenced by the use and availability of services linked to energy: the provision of light, cooling or heating, cooking, equipment, productive energy for businesses are needed for the majority of SDGs. Looking at the SDGs from an energy perspective helps clarify what kind of energy services people require to cover a specific development need. Focusing on energy services rather than production opens the space to new and creative solutions, such as off-grid, distributed power approaches, or creative combinations with existing grid solutions.

One way to boost clean energy services is to focus on specific sectors. In a recent investigation for the Food and Agriculture Organization of the United Nations (FAO), the *Renewable Energy and Energy Efficiency Partnership (REEEP)* investigated four business models within the Water–Food–Energy Nexus (Zahner 2014). Since its ninth Project Call (REEEP 2012), the organization has put priority to energy solutions within agrifood value chains. This sectorial investigation allows REEEP to select and support specific small or medium enterprises which provide energy solutions for irrigation, cooling, heating, drying, or processing. The regular REEEP Calls for Proposals are deliberately kept open to cover a variety of commodities since similar energy solutions may be applicable to a variety of agricultural product chains.

An outline of a case study shall exemplify this methodology.

Case study: energy efficiency and biogas production in the tofu and tempeh MSMEs in Indonesia

The case study is drawing from experiences of two projects from the REEEP portfolio, implemented by Mercy Corps[1] and the Environmental Technology Center[2] in Indonesia.

The tofu and tempeh sector in Indonesia, essential for the provision of these staple products, consists of approximately 85,000 Micro, Small and Medium Enterprises (MSMEs), which collectively employ 285,000 workers and generate around US$ 78 million per year (World LP Gas Association 2014). These are hampered by a variety of factors such as inefficient energy sources, inadequate wastewater disposal, indoor air pollution, lack of hygiene, insufficient access to finance, low awareness of new technologies, and low-paid employees. Clean energy technologies (in this case a fuel switch from firewood to biogas or LPG) can provide suitable, scalable and sustainable solutions to improve access to clean energy and water while mitigating environmental damage and reducing poverty.

Albeit government authorities recognize the problem, current relevant regulations only target larger enterprises and the lack of government regulation has led to poor sanitation, safety and health conditions, and high detrimental environmental impacts:

- High water consumption: tofu and tempeh production are water-intensive processes. About 60 kg of soybeans and 2,700 liters of water are required to produce 80 kg of tofu.
- Water pollution: one kg of soybean processed in the tofu industry generates about 10 liters of liquid waste and 250gr of solid waste, most of which is released into rivers and fields without treatment, producing greenhouse gas emissions and pollution.
- Air pollution: smoke from wood burning stoves leads to unhealthy labor conditions.
- High emissions from untreated waste: Based on Intergovernmental Panel on Climate Change (IPCC) calculation methodologies the emissions from untreated wastewater alone from the entire Indonesian tofu and tempeh industry amount to 0.9 million tons CO_2 equivalents per year.[3]

- Businesses use firewood which results in a per-factory emissions average of 450 tons CO_2/year and sector-wide emissions of 30 million tons.
- The potential reduction of GHG emissions in the whole tofu and tempeh sector is estimated at 80 percent, e.g. by the use of biogas technologies (BPPT 2013).
- Unsafe food: soybeans are often boiled in repurposed oil drums, which contain harmful chemical residues, and producers may add other harmful chemicals, including formaldehyde, to extend shelf-life. Consumers need access to tofu and tempeh products that are safe and hygienic, although willingness to pay for healthier products seems to be limited, particularly for low income consumers.

Case study: the business case for MSMEs in the tofu and tempeh sector[4]

Technology options

Traditional production using firewood: soybeans are traditionally cooked using direct heat or in a steam boiler. The firewood is typically gathered in parks, forests around town, from secondary sources such as furniture factories and construction sites, or purchased. In many locations firewood has become increasingly scarce resulting in rising costs (money and time expenditure).

Fuel switch to Liquefied Petroleum Gas (LPG): the fuel switch from firewood to LPG substantially reduces air pollution and improves hygiene of the tofu and tempeh products, but producers switching to LPG have to invest in new cooking equipment (stainless steel vats, energy efficient steam boilers). Business cases for such investments are difficult to calculate due to large price fluctuations for both LPG and firewood. LPG prices for 3 kg LPG tubes increased from US$ 1.09 to US$ 1.64 between 2013 and early 2014.

Biogas to substitute LPG: using biogas reduces producers' dependence on LPG and firewood, improves wastewater treatment, and reduces air pollution and greenhouse gas emissions. The biogas reactors convert the liquid and solid waste of tofu and tempeh production into methane gas (CH_4) and are able to substitute the LPG usage in the production process by up to 30 percent. Additionally, the effluent (waste) produced by the biogas reactor can be used as fertilizer or fish feed without any treatment. This means that there is a potential income opportunity for selling the waste products to the farming sector.

The REEEP/Mercy Corps project is promoting small scale fixed dome biogas reactors mainly for peri-urban areas, a technology provided by a local company.[5]

Tofu industry: comparing pre- and post-switch production costs and benefits

In 2014, Mercy Corps conducted a participatory cost–benefit analysis workshop in Jakarta, Bogor and Bekasi attended by over 170 tofu and tempeh producers.

The analysis in Table 13.1 is focusing on tofu industries at a size of 300 kg soybean input per day; conversion rate (as of April 2014): 1 US$–11,000 IDR.

The switch to LPG and energy efficient steam boilers saves average production costs of US$ 1,827 per year (US$ 152 per month, US$ 5 per day) compared to the traditional production using old equipment and firewood (even at current high LPG prices). But it takes more than one and a half years for MSMEs to pay off the initial investment (US$ 3,182) based on the annual cost savings (US$ 1,827). These calculations are based on the current LPG price of IDR 16,000 per 3 kg canister (April 2014), whereas the economics were much better a year earlier, when the LPG price was IDR 12,000 per canister and this same producer would have had annual savings of US$ 3,680.

There are a number of very important positive co-benefits:

- Time savings of 1.5 to 2 hours per day. Producers may choose to use this opportunity to rest or engage in other activities that may be important to the family.
- Reputational and marketing benefits based on the cleaner kitchen and end-products, e.g. by obtaining a government certification, which opens markets to restaurants and supermarkets.
- Avoided risk of firewood scarcity: cheap firewood is increasingly difficult to obtain in many locations. Many tofu producers assume that this will become a much bigger problem in the future.
- Better health conditions in production facilities: no more smoke from wood burning stoves.

Business case for biogas digester in the tofu industry

In its 2014 analysis, Mercy Corps developed the cost–benefit analysis shown in Table 13.2 for the case of tofu producers with a production of about 300 kg soybeans per day, energy needs of 45 kg LPG per day and a production of 25m³ biogas per day (equivalent to 12 kg LPG per day):

Table 13.1 Costs by energy source

Pre-switch using old oil drums and firewood		*Post-switch using new steam boiler and LPG*	
Costs of wood per year[1]	9,818 USD	Cost of LPG per year[2]	7,855 USD
Cost of old steam boiler per year[3]	182 USD	Cost of energy efficient steam boiler per year[4]	318 USD
TOTAL per year	10,000 USD	TOTAL per year	8,173 USD

1 About 0.9 USD for firewood to cook 10 kg soybeans
2 45 kg LPG per day needed to cook 300 kg soybeans, 1.45 USD per 3 kg LPG tube
3 One old steam boiler costs about USD 727 and lasts about four years
4 One energy efficient steam boiler costs about USD 3,182 and lasts about ten years

Table 13.2 Fuel, capital, and maintenance costs

Capital and maintenance costs	
Capital costs	6,171 USD
Design live time	10 years (~3,600 days)
Capital costs per day	1.7 USD (6,171 USD / 3,600 days)
Maintenance costs per day (estimate)	0.05 USD
Fuel cost saving	
Fuel cost saving per day[1]	5.8 USD
Fuel cost saving less maintenance costs (per day)	5.75 USD
Pay-back period based on cost savings	
Fuel cost savings after 3 years	6,210 USD (equivalent to initial capital costs)

1 12 kg LPG per day replaced by biogas, costs for 3 kg LPG tubes at 1.45 USD

Note: a payback period of three years is considered very long for most tofu producers and therefore needs relevant support schemes to become feasible (see Table 13.3).

Opportunities for the Green Climate Fund

The case study above exemplifies how much sectoral insight can be provided through analyzing a limited number of MSME companies that actively introduce changes to their operations, if one focuses on specific sectors or sub-sectors of the economy and thereby creates comparability. By investing into detailed observation of these processes one can obtain critical information that helps kick-start markets for access to clean energy. Only based on detailed analysis and understanding can obstacles for company growth be removed and effective opportunities be created or made accessible. This recognition is the result of a year-long analysis of REEEP's own project portfolio and experiences which led to a new strategic approach that was launched in 2014 with a first set of new projects under the new REEEP call (REEEP internal analysis 2012, unpublished).

REEEP's Theory of Change is based on the recognition that there is a large capacity for low carbon businesses and initiatives that also create wealth, especially at the SME level. In fact, low carbon development MUST go hand in hand with the creation of prosperity, encompassing environmental, human, and economic benefits; this is true everywhere but deserves most attention in lower income countries. This combination is one form of practical enactment of the SDGs, it is congruent with SE4All, and it is the best way for bodies related and in the service of the UNFCCC to drive low carbon development.

Table 13.3 Barriers and potential solutions for biogas use in the tofu industry

Barrier	Potential solution
Financial risks	
• High investment costs and relatively long payback periods (more than 1 year for the fuel switch from firewood to LPG gas and new cooking equipment, and about 3 years for the use of biogas). • Low financial capacity of the sector – specifically for small scale family enterprises. • Lack of lending facilities, particularly for small-scale projects. Limited access to loans due to lack of collaterals such as land titles or houses. Also biogas digesters are in most cases not accepted as collateral by banks. • Lack of government incentives: while conventional energy (e.g. LPG) is subsidized (consumers pay below marginal costs) and negative externalities (water pollution, GHG emissions) are not considered in the energy pricing and taxation the positive impacts of biogas energy are not valued with incentives. • Price fluctuations for both fuel types, firewood and LPG, as well as for soybeans have a negative impact on biogas business models with a timeframe of 10 years.	• Government regulations to improve environmental, sanitation, safety and health conditions in the MSME tofu and tempeh industry. • Government policies – incentives, taxation schemes – to help reduce capital costs for biogas digesters. • Government policies to support MSMEs in the sector to access finance for fuel switch from firewood and LPG to biogas.
Technology and usability risks	

• MSMEs in the tofu and tempeh sector have to take the risk of biogas technology that has not been proven on a large scale. The technology is supplied by relatively new companies in the market, leaving clients vulnerable if companies cease to operate and cannot provide maintenance and repair.
• More complex technologies require training for the users. Most tofu and tempeh producers have low educational backgrounds and lack the knowledge of technologies and environmental considerations.
• Scattered location of micro, small and medium businesses hamper efficient roll out and maintenance service for biogas digesters.
	• Producers, technology providers, and governmental and non-governmental organizations promoting modernization of the tofu and tempeh sector need to:
	  – Reliably evaluate technology options in this rapidly evolving, data-limited context (targeted R&D tailored to needs of MSME).
	  – Establish demonstration sites to increase awareness and reduce risk perception amongst the tofu and tempeh producers
	  – Provide adequate information and training for service providers and tofu and tempeh producers.
	• Government institutions to provide support through certification of viable technologies and establishment of PPPs and distribution schemes.

An SME focus for the Green Climate Fund

Complementary to its important focus on low carbon businesses and ventures, the GCF could increase its likelihood of success by embracing the SDGs and specifically SE4All as an essential component of its strategic equipment. By developing specific programs for the development of SMEs, structured along sectoral and sub-sectoral lines as in the REEEP model, the GCF could thereby create a triple benefit:

1   Identify and stimulate promising low carbon enterprises and support them in attracting private capital.
2   Through monitoring such hands-on experiences in great detail, realize a bottom-up, deep insight and understanding of the sector in a particular country and/or region.
3   Create long extensive records on specific pivotal sectors such as agrifood value chains, in order to establish long-term data sets that allow comparison between countries or regions, sectors, and specific finance and policy conditions.

The key in this work lies in putting sufficient emphasis on monitoring and evaluation (M&E). Based on REEEP's own work it became apparent that anxious concern about "transaction cost" acts as a barrier to detailed M&E especially where smaller business ventures are concerned; in fact, the fear of such cost often prevents systematic support of Smaller and Medium Enterprises at all. The notion of "cost" should therefore be radically changed, as the insights and understanding achieved are in fact a "transformational gain," an essential way to get real market information that proves its worth by helping us understand how to develop whole industrial and business sectors.

Conclusion

The Green Climate Fund – and other multilateral public donors – should pay heed to stimulating the SME level of economies in developing countries. This chapter recommends an approach which has been developed by REEEP over the last two years and which REEEP is currently implementing; this approach is based on both the low carbon priorities of the international climate treaty and the priorities of the Sustainable Development Goals and specifically the UN initiative SE4All. Combining these priorities means striving for low carbon solutions that – at the same time – help achieve prosperity. This approach will have to identify sectors that are ready for low carbon technologies at the SME level and that are relevant in terms of development potential; one example for such a sector that REEEP selected are agrifood value chains. With a strong M&E system as investigative backbone, REEEP is convinced that the sectoral approach allows using individual experiences and insights gained from individual companies to understand the whole sector. The result eventually allows economies to actively de-risk entire business sectors and ensure access to new technologies as well as to private finance.

Notes

1 REEEP webpage: www.reeep.org/projects/scaling-energy-efficiency-tofu-and-tempe-smes-indonesia
2 REEEP webpage: www.reeep.org/projects/planning-and-policy-support-producing-re-biogas-indonesian-tofu-industry
3 Note that these 0.9 mt CO_2e only stem from untreated water in the tofu sector. However, production practices are extremely energy inefficient and environmentally damaging. Businesses use firewood which results in a per-factory emissions average of 450 tons CO_2/year and sector-wide emissions of 30 million tons.
4 All of the figures quoted subsequently are derived from research conducted by BPPT, Mercy Corps, and REEEP, mostly quoted from internal project documents.
5 Digesters made of fiberglass to be used for individual tofu and tempeh producers or groups up to four producer units, price at about USD 1,500–8,000 depending on the size of digesters; waste input requirements are 90 percent liquid waste plus 10 percent solid waste or kitchen garbage.

References

Baer, P., T. Athanasiou, S. Kartha, and E. Kemp-Benedict. 2008. *The Greenhouse Development Rights Framework: The Right to Development in a Climate Constrained World*, revised second edition. Berlin: Heinrich Böll Foundation, Christian Aid, EcoEquity and the Stockholm Environment Institute.
BPPT. 2013. "Environmental Technology Centre at the Agency for the Assessment and Application of Technology: Development of Planning and Policy Support for Improving the Potential Production of Biogas as Renewable Energy in Indonesia's Tofu Industries." REEEP project document (internal).
Green Climate Fund. 2014. "Administrative Policies of the Fund." GCF/BM-2014/01. Accessed March 7, 2015. http://gcfund.net/fileadmin/00_customer/documents/pdf/GCF_B_BM_Administrative_Policies_fin_20140205.pdf.
——. 2015. "Green Climate Fund Initial Resource Mobilisation (IRM)." Accessed March 7, 2015. http://news.gcfund.org/wp-content/uploads/2015/02/pledges_GCF_dec14.pdf.
Hulme, David. 2009. "The Millennium Development Goals (MDGs): A Short History of the World's Biggest Promise." BWPI Working Paper No. 100. Accessed March 7, 2015. http://dx.doi.org/10.2139/ssrn.1544271.
Kushnir, Khrystyna, Melina Laura Mirmulstein, and Rita Ramalho. 2010. "Micro, Small, and Medium Enterprises Around the World: How Many Are There, and What Affects the Count?" In *MSME Country Indicators 2010*. Washington, DC: International Finance Corporation.
Parker, Craig, Janice Redmond, and Mike Simpson. 2009. "Review of Interventions to Encourage SMEs to Make Environmental Improvements." *Environment and Planning C: Government and Policy* 27(2): 279–301.
REEEP. 2012. "REEEP 9th Project Call." Accessed March 7, 2015. www.reeep.org/news/reeep-calls-project-proposals-new-%E2%82%AC41-million-funding-cycle.
Stein, Peer, Oya Pinar Ardic, and Martin Hommes. 2013. *Closing the Credit Gap for Formal and Informal Micro, Small, and Medium Enterprises*. Washington, DC: International Finance Corporation.

United Nations. 2007. *Secretary-General Address to High-Level Event: SG/SM/11175, GA/10619, ENV/DEV/950*. Department of Public Information, News and Media Division, New York. Accessed March 7, 2015. www.un.org/News/Press/docs/2007/sgsm11175.doc.htm.

——. 2012. "UN Secretary-General: Sustainable Energy for All – A Global Action Agenda, April 2012." Accessed March 7, 2015. www.se4all.org/wp-content/uploads/2014/01/SEFA-Action-Agenda-Final.pdf

——. 2013. UN Secretary-General, "A Life of Dignity for All: Accelerating Progress towards the Millennium Development Goals and Advancing the United Nations Development Agenda beyond 2015." New York, 26 July. Accessed March 7, 2015. http://sustainabledevelopment.un.org/content/documents/5527SR_advance%20unedited_final.pdf.

——. 2014. Secretary-General MDG Synthesis Report: "The Road to Dignity by 2030: Ending Poverty, Transforming All Lives and Protecting the Planet." Accessed March 7, 2015. www.un.org/ga/search/view_doc.asp?symbol=A/69/700&Lang=E.

UNFCCC. 2010. "Decision 1/CP.16, COP 16, IV.A Finance." Accessed March 7, 2015. http://unfccc.int/resource/docs/2010/cop16/eng/07a01.pdf#page=17.

——. 2013. Decision 3/CMP.9; "Guidance Relating to the Clean Development Mechanism." Accessed March 7, 2015. http://unfccc.int/resource/docs/2013/cmp9/eng/09a01.pdf#page=8

World Bank. 2010. *Overview: Changing the Climate for Development*. World Development Report 2010. Accessed March 7, 2015. http://web.worldbank.org/WBSITE/EXTERNAL/EXTDEC/EXTRESEARCH/EXTWDRS/0,,contentMDK:23062354~pagePK:478093~piPK:477627~theSitePK:477624,00.html.

World LP Gas Association. 2014. "The Role of LP Gas in Food Production; Tofu and Tempeh Production in Indonesia." A WLPGA Case Study. Accessed March 7, 2015. www.exceptionalenergy.com/uploads/Modules/Ressources/The%20Role%20of%20LP%20Gas%20in%20Food%20Production%20-%20Case%20Study.pdf.

Zahner, Andreas. 2014. "Making the Case: How Agrifood Firms are Building New Business Cases in the Water-Energy-Food Nexus." REEEP. Accessed March 7, 2015. www.reeep.org/nexus.

14 The role of appropriate sustainable energy technologies (ASETs) as a means for promoting access to energy for all

Jason B. Aamodt and Blake M. Feamster

Growth for the sake of growth is the ideology of a cancer cell.

(Abbey 1977)

Introduction

There is *hope* that the Millennium Development Goals (the MDGs) and their successors, the Sustainable Development Goals (the SDGs), will address the issues of equitable development confronting our world today (UN 2012). As the world reaches the MDGs' measuring point in 2015, the energy dimensions of Sustainable Development have crystallized (Clark 2010). The world now recognizes the importance of energy to development, and the problems caused by a lack of access to energy *for all* (UN General Assembly 2011; UN Secretary-General 2011; UN Sustainable Development 2014).

Approximately 2.6 billion people have little or no access to energy they need for heat, light and cooking (IEA 2014). The lack of "adequate, affordable, reliable, high quality, safe and environmentally benign energy services to support economic and human development" is "energy poverty" (Reddy 2000, 59). Historically, "[w]omen [and children] living in poverty are particularly badly served by the energy forms they are using at present … they increase vulnerability and threaten wellbeing" (Clancy et al. 2002, 20).

The SDGs, which seek to eliminate energy poverty by 2030, use a new term: "modern energy services" (UN Sustainable Development 2014). Modern energy services does not mean energy, but instead the work that is often done or the benefits that are obtained from devices in the more developed portions of the world's societies.

Unfortunately, "modern energy services" is becoming a euphemism for access to electricity. Equating a *fuel* (electricity) to an energy *service* (heat, light, cooking) is not intellectually consistent. First, many fuel sources, of which electricity is one, can supply needed services. Second, equating electricity to needed energy services ignores decades of literature that rejected the concept (Woroniuk and Schalkwyk 1998). More than a decade ago the move away from a fuel source solution to analyzing energy service needs "enable[d] better access by the poor" (Clancy et al. 2002, 10).

There is another, practical argument against a fuel based solution, while acknowledging the politics of universal electric service (UN General Assembly 2011). The costs of universal electric service are enormous and the time needed will span at least to the next generation. Electricity ironically – and wrongfully – condemns those who are today without needed energy services to a lifetime of inequality and energy poverty; such a result cannot be intended as intergenerational equity requires providing energy services to those living now. A nimbler response is needed – one that relies upon simpler solutions that can be implemented in ways that make a real difference in real people's lives – now.

Such solutions already exist and are based upon common sense and efficient technologies that fit within the social, economic and technological capacities of those in need – they are "Appropriate and Sustainable Energy Technologies" or "ASETs" (Guruswamy 2010, 257). They reduce costs, time delays and the continued suffering that accompanies an electricity-focused approach.

While ASETs encompass the notion of technology, they do not suggest that any *particular* technology may be better suited to an energy service need than another. Rather, in various ways, ASETs meet energy service needs for cooking, lighting, sanitation, clean drinking water and motive power. ASETs *include* improved cookstoves and more efficient cooking fuels that do not create indoor air pollution. An open three-stone fire, or something similar to it, is the cooking technology used by approximately 2.6 billion people today (UN Sustainable Development 2014). Lighting – often from an open, smoky kerosene lamp – can better be provided by a range of solar bulbs and other lighting devices, including biogas. Clean drinking water can be created by efficient and inexpensive water filters, and the motive power needed for water pumping can be provided by biogas or alcohol powered engines. Mechanical power can also be delivered with treadle pumps, hand operated machines, better yolks and harnesses for draft cattle, windmills and solar panels. All of these things are ASETs, which can be defined as technologies that work with locally available technology, are climate emission neutral (or better), and can be built, operated and maintained with local knowledge. Most importantly, they are technologies that are valued by the communities where they are used.

There are interlocking theoretical and conceptual frameworks of physics and socioeconomics providing a theoretical foundation for the practicality of ASETs. To illustrate that framework, this chapter is structured in five parts: Part I explores the relationship between the SDGs, energy services for all, and Sustainable Development showing how ASETs are an important part of the next steps in equitable development.

Part II briefly outlines the "World Energy Dynamic" as it exists today and is predicted to occur in the future, utilizing the standard metrics, while acknowledging uncertainties and ranges of opinion. The World Energy Dynamic is contrasted with the "Poor Energy Dynamic," examining the changing modes of access to energy services among the world's poor.

Part III briefly sketches the relationship between energy efficiency and transformation, major ecological concerns and the lack of access to energy services by the world's poor. Energy services deficits aggravate ecological concerns today, and may make them worse in the future. Part III also reviews the ASETs currently being used to meet the SDGs, and concludes with observations on how ASETs might be more widely applied to meet the SDGs.

Part IV examines some of the conceptual and theoretical justifications for using ASETs to meet the MDGs, including physics and economics. These perspectives strongly support broadly deploying ASETs to ensure access to energy services to all. Part V summarizes the conclusions reached in this chapter.

Part I. Energy for all, the SDGs, and Sustainable Development

The technological dimension

In many cases, a lack of access to energy services is really a lack of access to practical *technology* that will improve lives and promote equitable development (Farina 2011). The poorest often live in nations controlling vast energy resources. For instance, Nigeria ships oil offshore to the developed world, while flaring massive quantities of natural gas. Millions in the Niger Delta lack access to clean water, cooking and basic lighting (Yumkella 2012). Simple technologies could harness the flared gas, making it available at little cost. While there are social, governmental and other needs, part of the solution is ASETs focused on the energy needs in local communities.

Another example of an ASET might be found with a family in remote Indonesia. Discarded agricultural and household wastes – rice husks, food waste, etc. – decompose in the environment emitting methane and polluting water resources. These bio-wastes contain huge stores of energy. While the compost sits in the field, no useful work is available. Much of that energy, however, *could* be captured. There are already many technologies – alcohol or biogas digesters – that power modern stoves, heaters, lights and water pumps. Capturing the agricultural wastes will also reduce local water pollution and mitigate climate change by reducing methane emissions.

The historical dimension

The question of energy access has long been considered. The question of energy access was an important part of the Brundtland Commission's report in 1987 (UN General Assembly 1987). The Brundtland Commission's report led, at least in part, to Agenda 21, which set out, *inter alia*, to "Promote Sustainable Energy and Transport Systems in Human Settlements" (UN Conference 1992, para. 7.5). In direct response to Agenda 21, the United Nations in the "Millennium Declaration" created a framework of action meant to eradicate extreme poverty, gender inequality, and major diseases, while promoting sustainable development and good governance (UN General Assembly 2000). The MDGs were created in response to the Millennium Declaration, and contain eight broad goals and numerous subsidiary targets (Hulme 2009).

Though energy is a necessary ingredient for *all* eight of the Goals, no MDG focused on energy (Birol 2007).

The United Nations General Assembly declared 2012 as the "International Year of Sustainable Energy for All" (UN General Assembly 2011), and in 2012, declared this the "International Decade of Sustainable Energy for All" (UN General Assembly 2012). United Nations Secretary-General Ban Ki-moon previously issued his vision statement, "Sustainable Energy for All." In it, he established certain energy access goals for 2030, setting the stage for the SDGs (UN Secretary-General 2011).

With the heightened attention brought to energy justice by the General Assembly's Resolutions, and Secretary-General Ban Ki-moon's White Paper, energy access for all has become a sustainable development mission obtaining independent recognition.

Part II. The world energy *dynamic* – and the role of ASETs

Throughout the world, the energy resources used to meet growing needs are changing. In 2010, worldwide, energy use was 12,132 Mtoe or "million tons of oil equivalent." Oil is the largest source of energy supply, at nearly 4,000 Mtoe. A little more than 1,200 Mtoe of biomass was used to make useful energy in 2010 – which accounts for about 10 percent of useful energy. Renewables accounted for just less than 100 Mtoe in 2010. Renewable energy use is expected to increase, as is natural gas, while the mix of other energy resources is expected to marginally fluctuate over the next 20–25 years (IEA 2011).

China is perhaps the world's bellwether concerning the changing energy dynamic. China's growth as an energy consumer is startling: in less than a decade, energy consumption in the country doubled. By 2035 the IEA predicts that China's energy consumption will be nearly equal to the total energy use in all of North America *and* Europe, *combined* (IEA 2011).

Just 20 years ago China might have been considered a developing country. Today China's Gross Domestic Product is second only to the United States. Recently China surpassed the United States as the largest emitter of greenhouse gasses – emissions spurred largely by the use of energy (Aamodt and Wequin 2014).

In 2013 China's energy use per person was much lower, for instance, than that of the United States. When GDP increases, it has been observed that the per person energy use rate increases as well. Accordingly, as GDP increases in China – and in the developing world generally – worldwide rates of energy consumption will grow (Fridley et al. 2010).

Approximately 20 percent of the world's Energy Poor live in China. In response, China instituted a nationwide biogas program that provides energy to 120,000,000 people (Qu et al. 2013). Indeed, by the end of 2010, biogas supplied 22.5 percent of China's rural population with some of their energy needs (Gosens et al. 2013).

In many least developed regions, access to energy stands in sharp contrast to China's biogas efforts, or the situation in developed countries. On the continent of Africa, for instance, 58 percent of the population has no access to electricity. Sixty-five percent rely on traditional methods of biomass burning to cook (UN Economic and Social Council 2014, 473).

Predictions for the future energy dynamic in the Least Developed Countries are bleak. The International Energy Agency (the IEA), in its World Energy Outlook, points to the "New Policy Scenario," as a cause. The "New Policy Scenario" is in fact the group of existing policies from today carried forward to 2030. The IEA predicts that the number of persons who lack access to energy services will in 20–25 years be about the same as it is today (IEA 2011). At the same time, the number of those who are expected to die from exposure to smoke from cooking with three-stone fires and other ancient technologies would likely stay the same or increase over the next 20–25 years (IEA 2011, 469, 489, 505). Meaning in 2030, the number of deaths from smoke inhalation as a result of cooking fires will likely be essentially the same as the number of deaths caused by malaria, tuberculosis, and AIDS – *combined* – in that same year (IEA 2011, 489, figure 13.10). Such policies do not meet the goal of energy access for all (IEA 2011).

The IEA imagined an alternate scenario that cuts into those dire predictions. To do so, the IEA calls on the world to invest about $1 trillion over 20 years (in 2010 dollars) to provide electricity to those who do not have it (IEA 2011). The IEA estimates that this $1 trillion price tag is about 3 percent of the total spending for energy infrastructure. Despite its *relatively* small size, the cost is huge, and it is not clear where the needed money is obtained, or whether those newly connected to the electric grid could pay for the electricity (IEA 2011). Paying customers are the economic engine that supports modern electric services today (US Department of Energy 2003). It is therefore not clear how an electrified scenario helps.

Despite these criticisms of the electrified scenario, the IEA's figures show that ASETs like clean cookstoves are viable. Under the IEA's Trillion Dollar Scenario, $74 billion is needed to completely solve the clean cooking dilemma, providing modern energy cooking services to nearly two billion people, saving nearly 2,000,000 lives *per year* from the effects of soot resulting from the use of three-stone fires (IEA 2011).

Assuming the IEA is right, that a $1 trillion budget is *ultimately* needed, and that it represents about 3 percent of the world's energy spending in the next 20 years, the $74 billion which solves the cookstove problem is a little more than 0.22 percent of the overall energy infrastructure budget. Therefore, spending about 0.22 percent of the world's energy infrastructure budget on improved cookstoves would, applying the IEA's figures, save more than 40,000,000 lives over the next 20 years. That is a bargain.

Part III. The environmental and practical dynamic

This section explores two ASETs: cookstoves and biodigesters, demonstrating the practical and environmental benefits that can be brought to bear by their widespread use.

Cookstoves, black carbon and climate change

Cookstoves range from fabricated devices that utilize only commercial, modern elements to improved indigenous designs. By reducing the smoke emitted, cookstoves can reduce black carbon. Black carbon is known to contribute to global warming. According to some estimates, black carbon is the number two contributor to climate change after carbon dioxide (*The Economist* 2013). Inefficient burning in cookstoves contributes to the black carbon problem (Bond et al. 2013). The impacts of carbon dioxide on the atmosphere last for decades, but soot's effects are short lived (Bond et al. 2013; Shindell et al. 2012; Service 2008). Unlike carbon dioxide, which remains in the atmosphere for centuries and even millennia (Archer et al. 2009), black carbon attenuates in the atmosphere quickly when the source is removed. As a result, reducing black carbon production would have a substantial impact on climate change – and it could have that impact quickly (Carmichael et al. 2013).

Cookstoves hold a significant, though not immediately apparent, economic advantage. According to the IEA, it will cost more than $15 trillion to reduce carbon dioxide emissions so as to place the world on a trajectory for *only* a two-degree *increase* in worldwide temperature by 2035 (IEA 2011, 205). If black carbon is responsible for 18 percent of the climate change potential relating to human emissions, then some fraction of the $15 trillion price tag for climate change modifications might be saved by instead spending $74 billion on ASET cookstoves.

If, for the sake of assumption, and to make the assumption conservatively, black carbon from the two billion cooking fires accounts for only 5 percent of all the black carbon emitted in the world (Bond et al. 2013), then eliminating stone age cooking fires and replacing them with efficient cookstoves could reduce the human caused impacts of climate change by as much as 1 percent. The total cost to eliminate black carbon from cookstoves ($74 billion) is equal to approximately 0.5 percent of the climate change budget ($15 trillion). Accordingly, cookstoves could be twice as effective at fighting climate change as other methods.

However, better stoves are not the end of the story. The stove must be used and maintained. Unfortunately, some studies show the stoves sometimes are unused, or are not properly maintained, and as a result, do not have a positive benefit (Duflo et al. 2012; J-PAL 2012). Nonetheless, questions concerning the efficacy of cookstove programs indicate systems of evaluation can be applied in order to help the programs achieve success (Smith et al. 2007).

Biodigesters, land-based pollution and "found" energy resources

Energy for illumination and cooking needs can be met using biodigesters. In its most simplified form, "[t]he dung from two to four cows (or five to ten pigs) can produce enough gas for all cooking, and sometimes lighting too" (Ashden 2007). Like natural gas, biogas can be used to cook, heat homes, light rooms, power cars and other machines, and generate electricity (Ashden 2007). Leftovers from biogas can be a high-quality fertilizer which may be valuable in a rural setting (Sovacool and Drupady 2012). Because biogas is produced from agricultural wastes that otherwise are discarded, harnessing biogas can not only reduce water and air pollution, but the energy source is also inherently "renewable." Moreover, biogas digesters treat pathogens, reducing suffering from infectious diseases (Aamodt and Wequin 2014).

Using biogas for lighting and cooking can replace many, if not all the energy services in a home. In Nepal, 208,000 biogas plants were installed as of 2010, serving 1.25 million people, reducing black carbon and eliminating 630,000 tons of carbon dioxide emissions (Ashden 2007). As mentioned above, millions of biogas units are supplying household energy to about 120,000,000 people in China. Large-scale biogas units can also be used to generate electricity utilizing standard engine technologies.

Some say the costs of biogas are high (Akinbami et al. 2011). However, high construction costs are associated with industrial-type materials of concrete and steel. More indigenous materials of clay or brick can be used, reducing costs substantially (Lin 2007). In India, extraordinarily low-cost solutions have been engineered and deployed successfully (Ashden 2007). A study of inexpensive Peruvian biodigesters indicates that cost should no longer be a barrier even in harsh climates where more industrial level materials might once have been needed (Ferrera et al. 2011). Perhaps more convincingly than any other argument, the facts of biogas deployment indicate its economic strength. There are 50,000,000 household-sized biogas plants and more than 10,000 biogas-electric plants in operation worldwide (Ashden 2007).

Part IV. The theoretical dynamic

With these facts in mind, the perspectives of physics and economics, in light of the practical issues already addressed, independently demonstrate that ASETs must be a part of the *energy for all* solution. This interlocking review of physics and economics is relevant and important to the current debate because these disciplines focus on efficiency. Enhancing energy efficiency is one of the new SDGs (UN Sustainable Development 2014).

Physics perspectives

The laws of thermodynamics are immutable. They are a set of rules within which our world exists without reference to our consent or governance. While they are rules of a different order, the laws of energy must be understood and considered in policy with the same diligence that the laws of governance are addressed.

The first law of thermodynamics provides that the total quantity of energy in the universe is constant – it can neither be created nor destroyed. Were that the end of the story, the problem with energy access could be quickly solved. But, the second law of thermodynamics provides that *upon use*, the quality of energy is degraded, irreversibly. This second law, also known as "Carnot's Law" is often called "entropy." Entropy is at once the bedrock for the science of understanding chemical reactions, and a method to calculate the statistical likelihood of the transfer of energy from one state to another when work is performed (Hiebert 1981).

Entropy is what we *perceive* as "inefficiency" because that "degraded" energy is converted into forms that we cannot use, like waste heat that is radiated away from a light bulb. For instance, entropy requires that when natural gas is burned to produce electricity, the quantity of the energy in the electricity thus produced must be less than the quantity of the energy that was originally in the natural gas. To put it another way, the useful work after an energy transformation is always less than the starting point. The difference in potential has, in this example, become heat, which is usually "lost" to the atmosphere. While the heat is energy, it is a degraded form of energy that is difficult or impossible to capture and re-concentrate for useful work. The more efficient the technology is at transforming energy into useful work, the less energy is lost to entropy.

These scientific laws apply directly to the question of what technologies ought to be employed to extract useful work because maximizing efficiency could increase the available energy. ASETs, it turns out, are highly efficient. For instance, compare the use of: 1) natural gas generated electricity to run a cookstove in a modern home; to 2) the use of biogas to run a similar cookstove. A properly operating power plant in the modern world is likely to convert about 40 percent of the energy in the natural gas into electricity, though some of the newest and most advanced electric power plants can approach 60 percent (US Energy Information Administration 2010). For the electricity to be useful, it must be transmitted to its end user. Transmission results in a variety of losses. In the United States in 2010, electricity transmission and distribution losses average about 7 percent (US Energy Information Administration 2014). Then, when the electricity is used, the appliances that use it have efficiency losses – caused by the inescapable law of entropy. An electric cookstove commonly found in a home in the United States or Europe has a thermal efficiency of 13 percent. A gas cooking stove that may be found in a modern home has a 23 percent efficiency – which happens to be the efficiency of a well-tended three-stone fire (Kemna and Peteri 2010). Conversely, an improved wood burning cookstove, like those made available by the Global Cookstove Alliance, are 40 percent efficient or more. Figure 14.1 sets out the relative efficiencies of cooking appliances.

Moreover, the "modern" and *inefficient* use of energy ignores the significant energy costs associated with the exploration for, development of, extraction and transmission of the natural gas, oil or coal to a centralized power station, which are significant (Coughlin 2012). Those costs ought to be accounted for in the efficiency of the stove top, but they are not. Those extraction costs do not exist with biogas recovery, for instance.

Biogas provides another example of contrasting efficiencies: biogas is largely methane, and is practically very similar to natural gas. Therefore, a comparison can be made in proportional terms between the energy in natural gas and the energy in biogas – used for lighting. While it may be argued that gas lighting is

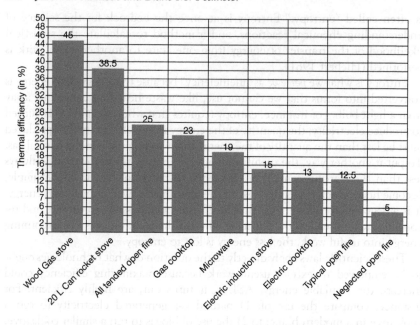

Figure 14.1 Thermal efficiencies of cooking appliances in poor and rich countries
Source: (Decker 2014)

"antiquated," the fact of the matter is that it is currently in use in many *modern* cities around the world. Moreover, biogas is having an ever increasing role as feedstock for energy supply in modern industry in the United States (Herringshaw 2009), and as we have seen, in China, Nepal and India.

The efficiency of biogas starts with its source: matter that would otherwise be discarded, eliminating the significant costs of extracting and developing the fuel, as well as the costs associated with disposal. Biogas is also usually generated close to the place where it is used, eliminating the losses involved in transmission. Therefore, biogas is inherently more efficient because transportation losses are likely to be less, or non-existent (Herringshaw 2009). Therefore, a biogas stove top, which is already significantly more efficient than an electric stove top, has the additional benefit of eliminating transmission loss resulting in an exponentially more efficient energy source.

The benefits of this built-in efficiency are multiple. In developing countries that do not have significant carbon based energy sources, using ASETs like biogas for cooking and lighting can help maintain the nation's sovereignty by eliminating a developing country's dependence on foreign sources of energy. Additionally, assuming the use of traditional fossil fuels, which has been the case in China and India, using ASETs has the potential to reduce climate emissions. Moreover, the use of bio-waste to create biogas has other significant benefits: improving the sanitation of the wastes by digesting them, reducing the potential for land-based pollution of rivers, lakes and oceans, reducing odors that would normally be produced by the wastes, and producing high-quality fertilizer (Herringshaw 2009).

Finally, and perhaps most closely related to the goal of sustainably and equitably providing energy to all, increased efficiency should make the end user's *cost* for energy lower. The cost benefits of ASETs can be significant. Looking at the overall picture of potential climate change benefits, local pollution reduction, and the opportunities for local entrepreneurship and the resulting development of economic opportunities, ASETs like biogas deserve increased attention.

Economic perspectives

Economics is an increasingly important part of rational decision making. While many of these issues of economics and energy access are comprehensively covered in Chapter 1, by David Stern, this chapter briefly considers a way that a particular offshoot of economic theory – one proposed by Robert Ayres – might be applied to ASETs.

A major problem with classical economic theory is that it minimizes the place of energy in economic growth. Specifically, mainstream neoclassical economists do not accept the idea that there is a strong causal link between growth and energy consumption (Ayres 2008). In calculating the value of an economy – what economists and news anchors call the "gross domestic product," or GDP – inputs are classically divided into accounts for "capital" and for "labor." Energy is often not even accounted for in an individuated way (Ayres and Ayres 2009).

Addressing the energy blind spot in economic theory, Robert Ayres pioneered an argument that any economic system depends on energy inputs in addition to physical materials and capital. He demonstrates how and why energy is critical to economic growth. Ayres asserts that access to energy is vital for the development within LDCs. Ayres demonstrates how the world, including LDCs, can use existing energy resources without relying on fossil fuels (Ayres and Warr 2009).

Ayres points out that "to get to the post-fossil fuel economy without sinking into Third World decay in the meantime, we need to use old technology in new ways" (Ayres and Ayres 2009, 87). Perhaps one might call ASETs "old technology." No matter, they should be considered a bridge to a sustainable energy future.

Ayres sets out eight policy prescriptions for such a sustainable energy future – he calls them "components" (Ayres and Ayres 2009, 98). A number of Ayres' components are of particular relevance. He asserts that our focus should be on ways to better utilize existing technologies so that future development can be maximized. This assumption applies equally to the Energy Poor, and offers a prescription for ways to dynamically grow sustainably in the future through the adoption and application of ASETs.

Another of Ayres' components is to recycle waste energy streams. Harnessing biogas involves the recycling of waste energy streams – and more – by reducing localized pollution, while easing climate change concerns. Ayres' fifth component for the United States' energy future is to decentralize electric power by creating

ASETs are already a decentralized micropower revolution. For instance, biogas is easily and cheaply adapted to electric generation. Rooftop solar is the definition of decentralized power. Therefore, ASETs may already be an efficient solution for the goal of electric energy access through energy decentralization.

Ayres' sixth component is to substitute energy services for products. The point of Ayres' substitution is that while one could substitute the three-stone fire with a (less efficient) electric stove, the person who is hungry for dinner wants a properly cooked meal, not fire or electricity. Therefore, ASETs, which carefully address the substantial social issues related to energy use in the home and traditional methods of food preparation, and do so more efficiently, are an answer that meets an energy service need.

Part IV. Conclusion

A review of the practicalities of ASETs, the harsh boundaries of the laws of energy and the predictions of energy economists, like Ayres, demonstrate that ASETs are an important part of energy for all. While there is a felt political need to extend electricity to the world's poor, energy justice should not stop there. Rather, the focus needs to be on the energy needs and wants of the developing world. Focusing on needs then allows for the use of ASETs as part of a bridge to an equitable future – for all.

References

Aamodt, Jason and Chen Wequin. 2014. "Can the Chinese biogas experience shed light on the future of sustainable energy development?" Denver Journal of International Law and Policy. 42 (Summer): 427.
Abbey, Edward. 1977. The Journey Home: Some Words in Defense of the American West. New York: Dutton.
Akinbami, J.-F.K., M.O. Ilori, T.O. Oyebisi, I.O. Akinwumi and O. Adeoti. 2011. "Biogas energy use in Nigeria: current status, future prospects and policy implications." Renewable and Sustainable Energy Reviews 5 (1): 97–112. doi:10.1016/S1364-0321(00)00005-8.
Archer, David, Miachael Eby, Victor Brovkin, Andy Ridgwell, Long Cao, Uwe Mikolawjewicz, Ken Caldeira, Katsumi Matsumoto, Guy Munhoven, Alvaro Montenegro and Kathy Tokos. 2009. "Atmospheric lifetime of fossil fuel carbon dioxide." Annual Review of Earth and Planetary Sciences 37 (1): 117–134. doi:10.1146/annurev.earth.031208.100206.
Ashden. 2007. "BIOTECH, India: turning food waste into cooking gas." Ashden Awards Case Study. Accessed February 27, 2015. www.ashden.org/files/BIOTECH%20full_0.pdf.
Ayres, Robert U. 2008. "Sustainability economics: where do we stand?" Ecological Economics 67 (2): 281–310. doi:10.1016/j.ecolecon.2007.12.009.
Ayres, Robert U. and Edward Ayres. 2009. Crossing The Energy Divide: Moving from Fossil Fuel Dependence to a Clean-Energy Future. Upper Saddle River, NJ: Pearson Prentice Hall.

Ayres, Robert U., and Benjamin Warr. 2009. *The Economic Growth Engine: How Energy and Work Drive Material Prosperity.* Cheltenham, UK: Edward Elgar.

Birol, Fatih. 2007. "Energy economics: a place for energy poverty in the agenda?" *The Energy Journal* 28 (3): 1–6.

Bond, Tami, Sarah Doherty, David Fahey and Piers Forster. 2013. "Bounding the role of black carbon in the climate system: a scientific assessment." *Journal of Geophysicial Research: Atmospheres* 118 (11): 5380–5552. doi:10.1002/jgrd.50171.

Carmichael, Gregory R., Sarika Kulkarni, Yafang Chen, V. (Ram) Ramanathan and Scott Spak. 2013. "Short-lived climate forcing agents and their roles in climate change." *Procedia – Social and Behavioral Sciences* 77: 227–236. doi:10.1016/j.sbspro.2013.03.082.

Clancy, Joy S., Margaret Skutsch and Simon Batchelor. 2002. "The gender-energy-poverty nexus: finding the energy to address gender concerns in development." UK Department of International Development Project. CNTR998521. Accessed February 27, 2015. www.riaed.net/IMG/pdf/DFID_Doc_Energy_Gender.pdf.

Clark, Helen. 2010. Foreward to *Beyond the Midpoint: Achieving the Millennium Development Goals.* New York: UNDP. Accessed February 27, 2015. http://uncdf.org/gfld/docs/midpoint-mdg.pdf.

Coughlin, Katie. 2012. "A mathematical analysis of full fuel cycle energy use." *Energy* 37 (1): 698–708. doi:10.1016/j.energy.2011.10.021.

Decker, Kris De. 2014. "Well-tended fires outperform modern cooking stoves." *Low Tech Magazine.* Accessed February 27, 2015. www.lowtechmagazine.com/2014/06/thermal-efficiency-cooking-stoves.html.

Duflo, Esther, Michael Greenstone, Rema Hanna and Radha Muthiah. 2012. Posted by Brian Clark Howard. "Clean cookstoves must be rethought so they actually get used in developing world." *Voice* (blog). *National Geographic.* Accessed February 27, 2015. http://newswatch.nationalgeographic.com/2012/06/18/clean-cookstoves-must-be-rethought-so-they-actually-get-used-in-developing-world/.

Farina, Michael F. 2011. "Flare gas reduction: recent global trends and policy considerations." General Electric Company. Accessed February 27, 2015. www.ge-spark.com/spark/resources/whitepapers/Flare_Gas_Reduction.pdf

Ferrera, Ivet, Marianna Garfí, Enrica Uggetti, Laia Ferrer-Martí, Arcadio Calderon and Enric Velo. 2011. "Biogas production in low-cost household digesters at the Peruvian Andes." *Biomass and Bioenergy* 35 (5): 1668–1674. doi:10.1016/j.biombioe.2010.12.036.

Fridley, David G., Nina Zheng and Nathaniel T. Aden. 2010. "What can China do? China's best alternative outcome for energy efficiency and CO_2 emissions." doi:10.2172/1000056. Accessed February 27, 2015. www.osti.gov/scitech/servlets/purl/1000056.

Gosens, Jorrit, Yonglong Lu, Guizhen He, Bettina Bluemling and Theo A.M. Beckers. 2013. "Sustainability effects of household-scale biogas in rural China." *Energy Policy* 54: 273–287. doi:10.1016/j.enpol.2012.11.032.

Guruswamy, Lakshman. 2010. "Energy justice and sustainable development." *Colorado Journal of International Environmental Law and Policy* 21 (2): 231–276.

Herringshaw, Brian. 2009. "A study of biogas utilization efficiency highlighting internal combustion electrical generator units." Honors Thesis, Ohio State University.

Hiebert, Erwin. 1981. *Historical Roots of the Principle of Conservation of Energy.* New York: Arno Press.

Hulme, David. 2009. "The Millennium Development Goals (MDGs): a short history of the world's biggest promise." (Working Paper 100.) Brooks World Poverty Institute.

Accessed February 27, 2015. www.bwpi.manchester.ac.uk/medialibrary/publications/working_papers/bwpi-wp-10009.pdf.

International Energy Agency (IEA). 2011. *World Energy Outlook 2011*. Accessed February 27, 2015. www.iea.org/publications/freepublications/publication/weo2011_web.pdf.

——2014. *Energy Poverty*. Accessed February 27, 2015. www.iea.org/topics/energypoverty/.

J-PAL Policy Briefcase. 2012. *Up In Smoke*. Cambridge, MA: Abdul Latif Jameel Poverty Action Lab. Accessed February 27, 2015. www.povertyactionlab.org/publication/up-in-smoke.

Kemna, R. and P. Peteri. 2010. "Quooker energy analysis." Van Holsteijn en Kemna B.V. Accessed February 27, 2015. www.vhk.nl/downloads/Energy%20analysis%20Quooker%20main %20final%20april%202010.pdf.

Lin, Dai. 2007. "The development and prospective of bioenergy technology in China." *Biomass and Bioenergy* 15(2): 181–186. doi:10.1016/S0961-9534(98)00007-5.

Qu, Wei, Qin Tu and Bettina Bluemling. 2013. "Which factors are effective for farmers' biogas use? – Evidence from a large-scale survey in China." *Energy Policy* 63: 26–33. doi:10.1016/j.enpol.2013.07.019.

Reddy, Amulya. 2000. "Energy and social issues" in *World Energy Assessment*, 39–60. New York: United States Development Programme. Accessed February 27, 2015. www.undp.org/content /dam/aplaws/publication/en/publications/environment-energy/www-ee-library/sustainable-energy/world-energy-assessment-energy-and-the-challenge-of-sustainability/World%20Energy%20Assessment-2000.pdf.

Service, Robert F. 2008. "Climate change. Study fingers soot as a major player in global warming." *Science*. 319 (5871): 1745. doi:10.1126/science.319.5871.1745.

Shindell, Drew, Johan C. I. Kuylenstierna, Elisabetta Vignati, Rita van Dingenen, Markus Amann, Zbigniew Klimont et al. 2012. "Simultaneously mitigating near-term climate change and improving human health and food security." *Science* 335 (6065): 183–189. doi:10.1126/science.1210026.

Smith, Kirk R., Karabi Dutta, Chaya Chengappa, P.P.S. Gusain, Omar Masera, Victor Berrueta et al. 2007. "Monitoring and evaluation of improved biomass cookstove programs for indoor air quality and stove performance: conclusions from the household energy and health project." *Energy for Sustainable Development* 11 (2): 5–18. doi:10.1016/S0973-0826(08)60396-8.

Sovacool, Benjamin K. and Ira Martina Drupady. 2012. *Energy Access, Poverty, and Development: the Governance of Small-Scale Renewable Energy in Developing Asia*. Burlington, VT: Ashgate Pub Co.

The Economist. 2013. "Global warming: the new black." January 19. Accessed February 27, 2015. www.economist.com/news/science-and-technology/21569686-soot-even-worse-climate-was-previously-thought-new-black.

UN. 2012. *Millennium Development Goals Report*. Accessed February 27, 2015. www.un.org/millenniumgoals/pdf/MDG%20Report%202012.pdf.

UN Conference on Environment and Development. 1992. "Agenda 21." Accessed February 27, 2015. https://sustainabledevelopment.un.org/content/documents/Agenda 21.pdf.

UN Economic and Social Council. 2014. *Committee for Development Policy Report on the Sixth Session*. E/2004/33. Accessed February 27, 2015. www.un.org/special-rep/ohrlls/ldc/E-2004-33.pdf.

UN General Assembly. 1987. *Report of the World Commission on Environment and Development: Our Common Future*. Accessed February 27, 2015. www.un-documents.net/our-common-future.pdf.

———. 2000. *United Nations Millennium Declaration*. Resolution 55/2. Accessed February 27, 2015. www.un.org/millennium/declaration/ares552e.htm.

———. 2011. *International Year of Sustainable Energy for All*. Resolution 65/151. Accessed February 27, 2015. www.un.org/ga/search/view_doc.asp?symbol=A/RES/65/151.

———. 2012. *Promotion of New and Renewable Sources of Energy*. Resolution 67/215. www.un.org/en/ga/search/view_doc.asp?symbol =A/RES/67/215.

UN Secretary-General. 2011. *Sustainable Energy for All*. Accessed May 29, 2015. www.se4all.org/wp-content/uploads/2013/09/SG_Sustainable_Energy_for_All_vision_final_clean.pdf.

UN Sustainable Development Knowledge Platform. 2014. *Sustainable Development Goals*. Accessed February 27, 2015. https://sustainabledevelopment.un.org/sdgsproposal.

US Department of Energy. 2003. *Grid 2030: A National Vision For Electricity's Second 100 Years*. Accessed February 27, 2015. http://energy.gov/sites/prod/files/oeprod/DocumentsandMedia/Electric_Vision_Document.pdf.

US Energy Information Administration. 2010. "Electricity." Accessed February 27, 2015. www.eia.gov/electricity/annual/pdf/table5.3.pdf.

———. 2014. *How Much Electricity is Lost in Transmission and Distribution in the United States?* Accessed February 27, 2015. www.eia.gov/tools/faqs/faq.cfm?id=105&t=3.

Woroniuk, B. and J. Schalkwyk. 1998. "Energy policy and equality between women and men." *The Swedish International Development Cooperation Agency*. Accessed February 27, 2015. www.oecd.org/dac/gender-development/1849338.pdf.

Yumkella, Kandeh. 2012. *Partner for Prosperity* (speech). PowerPoint from the Energy Justice Conference in Boulder, CO, September 17. Accessed February 27, 2015. www.colorado.edu/theotherthird/sites/default/files/Yumkella%20Colorado_energy_justice_sept_2012_final%20%282%29.pptx.

15 Globalization of markets for ASETs

Stephen Katsaros and Elizabeth Neville

Introduction

Appropriate Sustainable Energy Technologies (ASETs) define a class of products designed specifically for, and used by, the Energy Poor, or the 1.3 billion people in the world without access to electricity (International Energy Agency 2014). ASETs must be affordable, portable, and easy to distribute at a price point that the market can bear. Whether these products relate to energy, access to water, agricultural methods, transportation, or other life-enhancing technologies, the enterprise approach is the only way to reach the billions of people who need these products most. Accordingly, this chapter delineates Nokero's use of the enterprise approach in delivering one class of ASETs: sustainable energy products.

International law has institutionalized the principle that the world's poor have a right to sustainable development (United Nations 1992). Sustainable development encompasses the idea that global environmental protection must be pursued in tandem with the right of all people to advance economically and technologically to meet their basic human needs (United Nations 1987). The word "sustainable" begs further explanation in this context. Sustainability defines a system that requires limited inputs for maximum outputs. Thus, sustainable development refers to progress in people's quality of life in a manner that maintains the balance between inputs and outputs. Historically, human development has occurred unsustainably, whether through overutilization of natural resources, polluting practices, and human fatigue (the cause of shortened lifespans through intense labor). The unsustainable nature of these practices can be mitigated through the use of technology. Whereas development has historically occurred unsustainably, ASETs present the opportunity to rewrite history by lifting the Energy Poor out of poverty in a sustainable manner.

The term "enterprise approach" also begs further explanation. The enterprise approach is a development approach that utilizes market forces to bring ASETs and other development materials to the Energy Poor in all corners of the world. The enterprise approach presents a contrast to the "aid approach," which consists of giving away or heavily subsidizing development materials to the Energy Poor. In the enterprise model, inventors innovate new products, inventions are patented, patented products go into production, and these products are sold through a supply chain in which every person involved makes a profit. Enterprise models have been at the center of nearly all development and technological advancement throughout human history; for example, the enterprise approach propelled global exploration, as explorers purchased ships, canned goods, and sails made by entrepreneurs and craftspeople. As described in further detail later in this chapter, Nokero has found that the enterprise ("paid") and aid approaches can work effectively in conjunction to promote sustainable development, but that the enterprise approach is the most sustainable model to lift countries, villages, families, and individuals out of poverty and into a modern quality of life.

Nokero represents the belief that the world can be improved by challenging antiquated practices in creating light. From a technical perspective, Nokero has seen tremendous success. Nokero's experience has demonstrated that replacing a kerosene lamp with a solar light bulb improves the economics, environment, and health of a community. Nokero has also proven that it is possible to sell products to the very poorest people in the world by challenging the price point at which technology can be sold. Aid is not required to lift 1.3 billion people out of energy poverty; rather, energy poverty alleviation will occur through entrepreneurship, innovation, and the sale of goods invented specifically for the needs of these customers.

This chapter begins by explaining the problem Nokero's products seek to solve: the dangers of fuel-based (kerosene) lighting. Then, this chapter describes Nokero's individual story. This chapter then explores Nokero's success and the reasons therefor. Then, this chapter discusses specific and general challenges to the business of distributing ASETs and how Nokero addresses these challenges. Finally, this chapter presents lessons learned from Nokero's experiences and delineates insights for moving forward with sustainable development through ASETs.

The dangers of fuel-based lighting

Among the global Energy Poor, an estimated 500 million households utilize fuel for lighting, particularly kerosene (Lam, Smith, et al. 2012, 396). The use of kerosene for lighting is connected to several dangers suffered by the Energy Poor, including problems of health, safety, environmental pollution, and economic policy. Nokero and other sustainable lighting companies strive to eliminate these dangers by replacing kerosene lamps with solar lights.

Kerosene burned through indoor appliances, including lamps, emits a number of pollutants, including particulate matter, elemental carbon, carbon monoxide, formaldehyde, polycyclic aromatic hydrocarbons, sulfur dioxide, and nitrogen oxide (Lam, Smith, et al. 2012, 400–401, 408). Studies have linked this indoor air pollution to several health issues: lung disease, respiratory infections, asthma, cancer, cataracts, and possibly tuberculosis (Lam, Smith, et al. 2012, 415–426). The health risks associated with the use of kerosene lamps are especially problematic given that the Energy Poor typically do not have access to modern health care, as unelectrified health facilities lack power to store medicines and sterilize medical supplies (Provost 2013).

Kerosene lamps also present bodily safety hazards to the Energy Poor, particularly poisonings, fires, and explosions (Lam, Smith, et al. 2012, 396). Kerosene ingestion has been linked to several health symptoms, including abdominal distension, breathlessness, fever, convulsions, unconsciousness, cough, and, in some cases, death (Gupta et al. 1992, 980). Children among the Energy Poor are especially prone to ingesting kerosene oil; one study indicated that accidental kerosene oil ingestion comprised nearly half of all hospital admissions due to accidental child poisonings in India. Kerosene oil is often stored in soft drink bottles or plastic jars within reach of children, which may exacerbate the frequency with which children accidentally consume it.

Kerosene lamps are highly volatile and prone to explosion, a major cause of household fires and burns in the developing world. The tendency of kerosene lamps to tip over and spill oil while burning also presents a major fire and burn hazard (Shepherd and Perez 2007). The World Health Organization estimates that burns cause 265,000 deaths each year, primarily in poor countries (2014). In one children-focused study, conducted in Benin City, Nigeria, kerosene explosions caused over half of the total hospital admittances for burns (Oludiran and Umebese 2009).

In addition to the aforementioned risks of indoor air pollution, the use of kerosene for lighting pollutes the natural environment. Kerosene is a product of the distillation of crude oil, and, accordingly, a non-renewable "fossil fuel" (Shepherd and Perez 2007, 4). When burned, 7 to 9 percent of the kerosene in wick lamps is converted to black carbon, also known as "soot" (Lam, Chen, et al. 2012). This is of great global consequence, given the widespread use of kerosene for lighting, and the fact that black carbon is the second greatest man-made contributor to climate change (Bond et al. 2013). Kerosene also emits carbon dioxide, the greatest man-made contributor to global climate change (Tedsen 2013).

Finally, kerosene presents a great economic danger to the Energy Poor, on global, national, and household levels. Globally, $38 billion per year is spent – and burned – on kerosene (Webster 2012). In Kenya, alone, it is estimated that $896 million of kerosene is burned per year (United Nations Environment Programme 2013); this is especially problematic given that kerosene is imported. This figure demonstrates that close to one billion dollars are leaving the country every year. With an inherent break-even point, this money could be more productive in local circulation, rather than going to a foreign, oil-producing country. Additionally, the Energy Poor have limited financial means, yet kerosene lamps are expensive to operate. In parts of Africa, kerosene costs comprise 10–25 percent of household monthly budgets (Lighting Africa 2013). This money could be more productively used on the household level, as well, by allowing family members to spend on educational, entrepreneurial, or health care costs, rather than continuously burning their money on unhealthy, dangerous, polluting kerosene.

Nokero's story

On the morning of January 23, 2010, a Colorado inventor and US Patent Agent named Steve Katsaros sketched the world's first solar light bulb. Mr. Katsaros planned to launch a single-purpose company to sell this one product online with virtual staff. At that time, Mr. Katsaros did not know about energy poverty, and he did not know that 1.3 billion people currently lack access to electricity; he simply knew that he was creating a light bulb that would be useful on construction sites or around the home as a modern convenience. Four days later, he filed a patent application, quit his job at a law firm, and struck out to create a company called Nokero. While the "solution" – a solar light bulb – was conceived, the "problem" was not apparent at first. Mr. Katsaros assumed this product would be sold to big box retailers in the developed world to light the patios and walkways in the United States. However, within days of conceiving the product, the Nokero team realized the problem of energy poverty, and the global company was formed to tackle the expensive and dangerous use of kerosene-based lighting. Derived from the phrase "No Kerosene," Nokero envisions a world without kerosene lamps. In naming the company as such, the Nokero team pulled the mission of the company to the highest level of importance in the brand: the name.

In June 2010, Mr. Katsaros and the Nokero team launched the company. They saw online sales of $50,000 within the first month of launching Nokero's original solar light bulb product, the N100. Six months after that, Nokero launched their iconic solar light bulb, the N200. Based on the real-world failures of the original product, the N200 utilizes a pivoting solar panel. From that point forward, performance increased tremendously.

Nokero creates and sells solar-powered products created specifically for people without access to electricity. Nokero began by specializing in solar-powered light bulbs; however, as the company has worked in this sector, Nokero has also created other technologies tailored to the needs of the Energy Poor. Nokero's products generally contain a solar panel, and solar panels can be applied to an exhaustive list of products for the market, such as solar phone chargers. As of the date of this publication, Nokero has begun growing into industrial applications, which use higher levels of kerosene than do personal uses. While hundreds of millions of kerosene lamps are used in homes nightly, there are other high-usage applications of kerosene lamps, such as their use by artisanal fishermen. For example, in Tanzania alone it is estimated that 100,000 kerosene lamps each burn $600 of kereosene per year to attract fish that are then caught in nets (Gengnagel et al. 2013).

Nokero's products are ASETs, Affordable Sustainable Energy Technologies, because they are specifically designed to support the Energy Poor in bridging the gap between energy poverty and electrification. The most important features of an ASET are durability, affordability, intuitive design, and function recognition. While the features of durability and affordability are self-explanatory, intuitive design and function recognition beg further explanation. Intuitive design refers to the principle that the function of technology must be clear from the design of the product; this is why Nokero's solar bulbs are shaped like light bulbs. Generally, people know what a light bulb is and what it can do, but the Energy Poor lack the grid electricity to light a light bulb. Thus, function recognition must also be clear. This refers to the idea that, for an end user to trust and successfully adopt technology, the ASET must be designed so that a salesperson can easily convey proper use to the end user. This has been especially clear in optimizing the training of end users to aim a solar panel fully to the sun.

The end users of Nokero's products are varied, and they span all demographics within the Energy Poor. Nokero's end users range from five-year-old schoolchildren learning how to read to the members of various countries' armed services. This variety in demographics has prompted the need to develop a line of products; it is simply impossible to provide appropriate function across that range of users without having a line of products. In the four years that Nokero has been developing and commercializing products, at the time of this writing, they have created and put twelve different products into manufacture; each of these products is targeted at a particular demographic of end user. Nokero has learned that if a company attempts to integrate too many functions into one product to address different customer needs, a company runs the danger of crafting a product nobody wants to use. Thankfully, this has not been the case for Nokero, and the company has seen many levels of success, thus far.

Nokero's successes

The greatest success of a company is to positively impact the lives of its customers. At the highest level, the million units of Nokero's solar light bulb have impacted millions of lives by influencing the users of kerosene lamps. Specifically, Nokero's light bulbs have solved many of the health, safety, environmental, and economic problems discussed earlier. Nokero's success can be attributed to several factors and strategies employed in the company's development, from the productive maintenance of key relationships, to strategic branding, and patent drafting.

Replacing kerosene lamps with solar light bulbs positively impacts the Energy Poor by reducing their susceptibility to health and safety risks. As discussed earlier, the burning of kerosene for lighting has been associated with various ailments connected to indoor air pollution, from cancer to cataracts. As solar light bulbs do not emit any chemicals or particulate matter, the end users are effectively protected from the indoor air pollution dangers they may face through kerosene lamp exposure. Additionally, kerosene lamps present great safety dangers, as people, particularly children, can suffer grave health consequences from accidentally ingesting kerosene. Fires from kerosene lamps tipping over and explosions from kerosene's volatile nature also comprise grave safety dangers for the Energy Poor. As solar light bulbs cannot be ingested or spilled, are not dangerous when dropped, and do not explode, Nokero's products also protect the Energy Poor from some of the most prevalent dangers in the developing world.

Replacing kerosene lamps with solar lamps improves the natural environment, too. Unlike kerosene lamps, which emit black carbon and carbon dioxide, solar light bulbs do not emit anything. Solar light bulbs do not require an unsustainable energy source for power. Indeed, these products exemplify the goals of sustainable development because the only input required for a solar bulb to generate light is sun exposure – a resource that is plentiful in many regions populated by the Energy Poor.

Finally, replacing kerosene lamps with solar light bulbs enhances families' long-term spending power. Kerosene lamps burn 30 liters of kerosene per year, costing users about $1.50 per liter (Mills, 2010). This aggregate running cost of a kerosene lamp, $45 per year, is a huge expense for the Energy Poor, who have very limited means. By displacing one kerosene lamp with a solar light bulb, the expense of acquiring the solar light ASET is a capital cost, but does not have the running cost (the constant need to refill with kerosene) as does a kerosene lamp. Nokero's rechargeable batteries last at least a year and a half before they require replacement. Accordingly, this allows for up to 20 percent of an individual's income to be available for other purposes, such as agriculture investments, education investments, health care, and clean water technologies.

Nokero's success as an ASET distributor can be attributed, first and foremost, to its establishing strong relationships and collaborations. Nokero's founder, Steve Katsaros, started manufacturing products eleven years ago, in China; ultimately, the people he worked with there became the co-founders of Nokero. Other relationships formed the basis of relationships with agents and reseller networks that bring the products to market. Additionally, Nokero collaborates with several parties, including their factories, quality control and logistics companies, importers, exporters, financial institutions, companies that purchase and resell its products, and, most importantly, the end users of the products. It is also incredibly important that Nokero collaborates with in-country partners, especially when aiming to sell products in rural locations. While Nokero has the sales tools for hand-to-hand sales, in-country partners are crucial for successful community-level engagements. Nokero also collaborates with intergovernmental agencies, such as the World Bank and International Finance Corporation, as their project, "Lighting Global," aims to support the sustainable lighting sector.

Beyond these relationships, the trustworthiness and clarity of Nokero's brand have helped Nokero to become a leader in the sustainable lighting sector. Nokero's mission, to create a world without kerosene, is the clear foundation of its status as a purpose-driven for-profit company. Accordingly, Nokero has successfully cultivated relationships with parties with no financial interest in Nokero's success, but who are committed to alleviating energy poverty through ASETs. Nokero's firm belief that everybody should have access to illumination has formed the basis for relationships with a large number of non-governmental organizations, companies, and governments.

Another factor supporting Nokero's success has been the company's carefully drafted patent portfolio. Infringers present a major threat to the stability of all companies, and thus pose a threat to sustainable development when they illegally infringe upon ASET-producing companies. Nokero has successfully utilized their patent portfolio to shut down two infringing factories, and procure monetary damages from them. With Nokero's products improving the quality of life for the end users so dramatically, the stakes are too high to allow infringers to destroy the brand integrity that Nokero has worked so high to achieve. This brand integrity is necessary to earn end-user trust, and ultimately, to alleviate energy poverty.

ASET distribution challenges

While a worthwhile and globally beneficial endeavor, Nokero's experience also illustrates that the business of distributing ASETs is fraught with challenges. These challenges include financial, behavioral, regulatory, and political challenges. However, Nokero's experience has also demonstrated some strategies for overcoming these challenges.

Financial challenges – specifically, the affordability of products – present the most daunting obstacle to distributing ASETs. When the target customers have limited financial means, it can be difficult for companies to establish the value of ASETs. The Energy Poor are some of the most economically disenfranchised people on Earth. Thus, regarding Nokero's solar bulbs, the company has found it difficult to convince people of the utility of solar energy, as well as to establish the value of their investing in a solar light bulb. When a customer has limited means, there is often no culture of saving money to purchase an item like an ASET; "investments" may be perceived as impossible, as even a small amount of money can wield a large impact on their quality of life. Even when an individual may possess the vision and desire to save money to purchase an ASET, urgent financial matters often take precedence over the investment (e.g. weddings, deaths, health care needs, school fees).

In conjunction with financial challenges, behavioral challenges present another major obstacle to ASET-producing companies. When Nokero first began, the staff believed that delivering high-quality products at a correct price point would suffice to create a vibrant market for Nokero bulbs among the Energy Poor. However, it soon became apparent that the distribution of ASETs often requires an inordinate amount of training and challenging existing behaviors before customers are willing to adopt them. When individuals in the developed world adopt new technology, there usually exists an analogous technology to aid with the acceptance of a new product. For example, before the advent of mobile phones, pagers were widely used, so users understood the value proposition of wireless communication devices. However, the Energy Poor often do not have access to analogous technology, so the distributors of ASETs must strive to establish that value independently. If potential customers cannot trust the technology, or they do not understand how it works, they will continue to utilize traditional methods to meet their needs.

Additionally, countries' regulatory policies can present a major challenge for ASET companies. Some countries with large Energy Poor populations also have very protectionist market policies. In these markets, the government places a high duty on imported products to "protect" domestic industries. In some of these markets, foreign-made products can be subject to a price increase of as much as 50 percent (United Nations Foundation, 2013). As the entire manufacturing base for solar energy, generally, is located in China, companies like Nokero can find it difficult to penetrate these markets. Such a price increase can prove prohibitive for the Energy Poor, who cannot absorb any additional cost.

Nokero and other ASET-producing companies have employed a number of strategies to address these challenges. Some ASET-producing companies have partnered with microfinance institutions to enable affordability; however, properly scaling microfinance programs can prove to be a challenge. A program may work in one village or region, but differing cultural and physical realities may render that program ineffective in another area. Some entities are testing electronic methods of payment, but this can often create a need for extended training time and efforts during the sales process.

To overcome behavioral and financial challenges, Nokero has created a large number of materials to help salespeople establish the value proposition for solar products and communicate compelling reasons to purchase them. Nokero has successfully recognized that it is crucial to establish that the buyer has the means to purchase the ASET, that they understand the value proposition, and that they understand the health and safety issues that are at stake if they continue utilizing kerosene. However, the method behind this process requires further explanation.

As Figure 15.1 illustrates, technology adoption commonly occurs along a "bell curve." Innovators and early adopters often comprise the first purchasers, and they instigate much of the behavior change associated with adopting the technology. In the context of the Energy Poor, these early adopters can and should be governments and agencies because they can demonstrate that these technologies are trustworthy. However, 70–80 percent of the market, the "early" and "late majority," purchase later, once the behavior has been established. In order to obtain these majorities, Nokero's success has demonstrated that companies must focus upon behavior change through the building of trust and integrity of the brand. Nokero notably achieves this through hand-to-hand field sales, which allow the customers to become familiar with, and learn to trust, the products.

Regarding regulatory challenges, Nokero has created products that are modular in design, and, thus, have enabled in-country assembly. While in-country assembly can be costly, providing this as an option can mitigate the potentially disastrous price increase associated with protectionist regulations; this often depends on the classification of goods at the time of import. Nokero's pilot programs with in-country assembly have, thus far, been greatly successful.

Lessons learned; moving forward

Nokero's experience in producing and distributing sustainable lighting products has imparted a host of valuable lessons that will benefit their company going forward, and may prove beneficial to other ASET-producing companies.

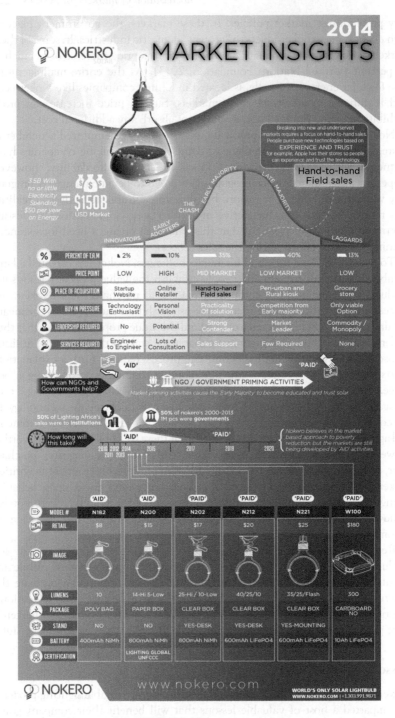

Figure 15.1 Market insights infographic

Firstly, mass communication on the value of ASETs and the behavioral changes needed to adopt them would prove useful for ASET producers. If communicated to the correct stakeholders, this communication could help to open markets to accept new technologies. Lighting Africa, a creation of the World Bank and the International Finance Corporation, is one such program (Lighting Africa 2014). Lighting Africa has created and piloted such programs to educate consumers about the products and steer them towards high-quality purchases. Programs such as this help to break down barriers that currently prevent people among the Energy Poor from adopting ASETs.

Secondly, entrepreneurs from the Energy Poor, who live among the Energy Poor, and who want to sell to their own counterparts and communities are crucially important to the alleviation of energy poverty. Steve Katsaros, Nokero's CEO, describes these "Energy Poor Entrepreneurs" as "the most important entrepreneurs." Unlike products distributed in the developed world, ASETs cannot simply be placed onto shelves in supermarkets in urban centers; to achieve their envisioned purpose, they must reach the peri-urban and rural locations of target countries. Energy Poor Entrepreneurs, by virtue of their understanding and engagement with target communities, are critical to fostering mass adoption. Solar Sister, a women-centered ASET sales network based in rural Africa, comprises one effort that is working in this manner (Solar Sister 2014).

All entrepreneurs – especially small ASET-producing companies – have an important role to play in alleviating energy poverty. As opposed to large, multinational corporations, small ASET producers are more nimble in developing countries. The resourcefulness and flexibility inherent in smaller, entrepreneurial companies is more compatible with the realities of developing countries than large corporations. For a century, large corporations have attempted to work in developing countries with small successes, but moreover, with overarching failures. Small entrepreneurial efforts can serve as a foundation upon which large companies can grow. However, the business practices of established companies from the developed world are incompatible with the conditions that exist in developing countries. History has demonstrated that it is impossible to force the business systems and ideologies of large, multinational corporations onto the Energy Poor; the market approaches practiced by small, sustainable entrepreneurial efforts are more compatible with the nuanced and often difficult realities of doing business in least-developed countries. This is why Nokero and its peers are seeing great success in bringing solar lights to the developing world, and why multinational corporations have not echoed this success.

Thirdly, in order to bring technologies to market, it is crucially important that the creators of ASET technologies and businesses carefully match customer needs to the features of the products they create. From a business perspective, entrepreneurs must exercise patience and frugality in bringing products to market. Indeed, while orders may often be foreseeable, orders are frequently delayed and many times more complicated than businesspeople from the developed world may expect. Accordingly, practicing patience and resourcefulness is critical to success.

Fourthly, Nokero believes that a blended distribution model will best cultivate a robust market for ASETs, and thus accelerate the alleviation of energy poverty. ASETs are delivered to end users vis-à-vis two mechanisms: one, through charitable gifts, is the "Aid Model." The other, distribution through purchases by end users, is the "Paid Model." At the time of this writing, Nokero's staff believes that a blended model is appropriate for this early stage in markets' development. Nokero's lower-end products are often purchased by entities practicing the Aid Model by distributing them at a subsidized rate or no cost. Some commentators argue that the Aid Model destroys a market opportunity; Steve Katsaros argues that the opposite is true, as it is impossible to destroy a market that does not exist.

While not a permanent solution, the Aid Model can create market awareness of the technology and train individuals on proper utilization of the products without forcing the end user to assume the risk. This can create a market space and demand for future sales activities. In the future, possibly as soon as five years from now, Nokero's staff believes that all sales of ASETs will be through the Paid Model, as customers will be familiar with the brands and the quality of product, and they will be comfortable with making an investment in the ASET. This belief is bolstered by Nokero's sales history, whereby aid agencies purchase their "entry-level" products, and subsequently, once the products are ingrained in communities and people are familiar with using them, paid channels increase because customers trust and value the product enough to invest. In short, the blended Aid Model forges the path for future dominance of the Paid Model.

To overcome the challenges in producing and distributing ASETs, Steve Katsaros believes that ASET companies could benefit from more communication. Currently, there is very little cross-communication between ASET companies. For example, clean cookstove initiatives do not necessarily communicate with solar lighting programs. Mr. Katsaros asserts that this should change, as lessons learned in one class of ASETs may be applied into another class.

Looking forward, laws and regulations could play a robust role in alleviating energy poverty, especially as they could reduce the use of kerosene for lighting. Proposing laws and regulations to encourage the distribution of ASETs or, alternatively, outlaw kerosene usage for lighting, will lift awareness to the dangers of kerosene vis-à-vis the accompanying public debate. Indeed, as kerosene is subsidized in many countries, presenting a change from subsidization to a ban would constitute a rapid progression in public policy. Whether such a law would pass or be enforced would be secondary to the marketing effect of a debate on the appropriateness of burning kerosene for light. Such a debate could serve as potent publicity for solar light companies, thus fostering the alleviation of energy poverty.

Finally, to conceptualize future markets after the alleviation of energy poverty begs a reflection on the operation of developed markets. Developed markets have known supply chains, reliable shipping companies to deliver goods, and customers have access to bank accounts and credit for making purchases. Future markets will ideally be equipped with reliable distribution, and governments will promulgate clear, non-protectionist rules about bringing products into a country. There will exist clear methods for transporting products, and customers will have the will and funds available to purchase products. Ideally, the future of markets in regions currently in the throes of energy poverty will resemble developed markets, but improved by virtue of their sustainable development.

Conclusion

Nokero's experience selling ASETs to the Energy Poor illustrates several truths. The burning of kerosene for lighting causes serious health, safety, environmental, and economic problems for the Energy Poor. These problems, however, are preventable when ASETs are made available. Nokero, through its unique story and strategy, has seen tremendous success, thus far, in alleviating these problems by distributing ASETs to the Energy Poor. The business of distributing ASETs can be challenging for companies, particularly companies unused to doing business in developing countries; however, Nokero has employed strategies to overcome these challenges, and continues to do so. Finally, many lessons learned from Nokero's experience can inform and ultimately improve the ASET industry, bringing the world all the closer to alleviating energy poverty, and providing a world where every man, woman, and child has access to safe, sustainable light after dark.

References

Bond, T.C., et al. 2013. "Bounding the role of black carbon in the climate system: A scientific assessment." *Journal of Geophysical Research Atmospheres* 118: 5380–5552. Accessed October 8, 2014. doi:10.1002/jgrd.50171.

Gengnagel, Tim, Wollburg, Philipp, and Mills, Evan. 2013. "Alternatives to fuel-based lighting for night fishing: field tests of lake and ocean applications in East Africa." *The Lumina Project, U.S. Department of Energy.* Accessed October 30, 2014. http://light.lbl. gov/pubs/tr/lumina-tr11-night-fishing.pdf.

Gupta, P., Singh, R.P., Murali, M.V., Bhargava, S.K., and Sharma, P. 1992. "Kerosene oil poisoning – a childhood menace." *Indian Pediatrics* 29(8): 979–984. Accessed October 8, 2014. www.researchgate.net/publication/21695438_Kerosene_oil_poisoning--a_ childhood_menace.

International Energy Agency. 2014. "About energy poverty." Accessed October 8, 2014. www.iea.org/topics/energypoverty/.

Lam, N.L., Chen, Y., Weyant, C., Venkataraman, C., Sadavarte, P., Johnson, M.A., Smith, K.R., Brem, B.T., Ellis, J.E., and Bond, T.C. 2012. "Household light makes global heat: high black carbon emissions from kerosene wick lamps." *Environmental Science & Technology* 46(24): 13531–13538. Accessed October 8, 2014. www.ncbi. nlm.nih.gov/pubmed/23163320.

Lam, Nicholas L., Smith, Kirk R., Gauthier, Alison, and Bates, Michael N. 2012. "Kerosene: a review of household uses and their hazards in low- and middle-income countries." *Journal of Toxicology and Environmental Health*, Part B (Critical Reviews): 396–432. Accessed October 8, 2014. www.ncbi.nlm.nih.gov/pmc/articles/ PMC3664014/

Lighting Africa. 2013. *Lighting Africa Market Trends Report 2012*. Accessed October 8, 2014. www.dalberg.com/documents/Lighting_Africa_Market_Trends_Report_2012.pdf.

Lighting Africa. 2014. "About us." Accessed October 8, 2014. www.lightingafrica.org/about-us/.

Mills, Evan. 2010. "From carbon to light: a new framework for estimating greenhouse-gas reductions from replacing fuel-based lighting with LED systems." *The Lumina Project, prepared for the United Nations Framework Convention on Climate Change*. Accessed October 30, 2014. http://cdm.unfccc.int/Panels/ssc_wg/meetings/025/ssc_025_an13.pdf.

Oludiran, O.O. and Umebese, P.F.A. 2009. "Pattern and outcome of children admitted for burns in Benin City, mid-western Nigeria." *Indian Journal of Plastic Surgery* 42(2): 189–193. Accessed October 8, 2014. www.ncbi.nlm.nih.gov/pmc/articles/PMC 2845362/.

Provost, Claire. 2013. "Energy poverty deprives 1 billion of adequate healthcare, says report." *The Guardian*, March 7. Accessed October 8, 2014. www.theguardian.com/global-development/2013/mar/07/energy-poverty-deprives-billion-adequate-healthcare.

Shepherd, Joseph E. and Perez, Frank A. 2007. "Kerosene lamps and cookstoves – the hazards of gasoline contamination." *Fire Safety Journal* 43(3): 171–179. Accessed October 8, 2014. http://shepherd.caltech.edu/EDL/publications/reprints/Kerosene LampCookstove.pdf.

Solar Sister. 2014. Home page. Accessed October 8, 2014. www.solarsister.org/.

Tedsen, Elizbeth. 2013. "Black carbon emissions from kerosene lamps. Potential for a new CCAC initiative." *Ecologic Institute*. Accessed October 8, 2014. www.ecologic.eu/sites/files/publication/2014/black-carbon-and-kerosene-lamps-brief_0.pdf.

United Nations. 1987. *Report of the World Commission on Environment and Development: Our Common Future*. Official Records, Annex to document A/42/427. Brundtland: United Nations.

United Nations. 1992. *The United Nations Framework Convention on Climate Change*. Rio de Janeiro: United Nations Conference on Environment and Development.

United Nations Environment Programme. 2013. *Off-grid Lighting Assessment: Kenya*. Accessed May 12, 2015. http://unep.org/pdf/OGL_KEN.pdf.

United Nations Foundation. 2013. "Tariff database." *Sustainable Energy for All Energy Access Practitioner Network*. Accessed October 30, 2014. www.energyaccess.org/resources/tariffs-database/search-tariff-database.

Webster, George. 2012. "Solar lamps replace toxic kerosene in poorest countries." *CNN*, February 1. Accessed October 8, 2014. www.cnn.com/2012/01/10/tech/innovation/solar-powered-led-lamps/.

World Health Organization. 2014. *Fact Sheet – Burns*. Accessed May 12, 2015. www.who.int/mediacentre/factsheets/fs365/en/</REFL>

16 Energy for rural women

Beyond energy access

Anoja Wickramasinghe

Introduction

For rural women, access to energy means access to lighting, economic advancement, lessening drudgeries, capacity development, food security, and other services (UNDP 2001, 2007; ESMAP 2005). This chapter argues that the best way to ensure energy access for women is a structured process that follows the principles of equality, social justice, women's citizenship rights, social inclusion, and human development.

Studies of the data have shown that the global Sustainable Energy for All initiatives have caused transitional effects for women (Wickramasinghe 2013a). This chapter begins by examining these transitional effects in the broader context of the discourse on energy for women. This discourse has expanded the meaning of "All" beyond energy access for *all people* to energy access for *all purposes* and this chapter's first half identifies several key aspects of what energy access for all purposes entails. By framing the *household* as the hub of energy use in rural communities, the role of women in manipulating energy use and demand is highlighted (Wickramasinghe 2012, 29). Women organize the intra-household energy-use demands, creating the opportunity to promote energy-use patterns that avoid peak-period exhaustion of energy services and reduce energy use. However, there is a crucial need to educate women on energy efficiency and conservation, particularly given that women are the change agents to demonstrate good energy practices to children.

The second half of this chapter is focused on the interrelationships between women's economic empowerment, women's health, and access to energy. These links are discussed by surveying data from a number of empirical studies from the nations of South Asia, which cumulatively demonstrate that women's custodianship over energy is an asset in need of recognition and investment. Thus, the chapter culminates in a set of recommendations for forward-looking development and empowerment of rural women and the communities they live in.

Energy for women – a reflection on the under-served

The Sustainable Energy for All initiative has made a progressive change in the ideology of energy, pushing it towards a humanitarian paradigm. The inclusion of women into energy decisions and policy, as well as financing for women, has become crucial. Women are crucial not only in ensuring energy justice but also in finding solutions to development problems. Women and men have different priorities on energy and energy policy formulation, planning, and management are not reflective of this (Cecelski 2005, 1–5). Women and men use and benefit from electricity differently and thus interact differently with conservation and efficiency efforts. Reports suggest that 40 percent of household electricity is wasted due to inefficient use, and lack of technical know-how (Wickramasinghe 2012, 29). Who is responsible for the use, intensity, and purpose of electricity is becoming increasingly important from several perspectives (Practical Action 2013, 55).

Still the key question of why energy for women is important has not been fully answered. The evidence illustrates some commonalities that justify investing in energy for women (Wickramasinghe 2010). Many studies indicate differences in the effectiveness of access to energy on gendered development (ENERGIA 2007, 128; Havet 2003, 75–79; UNDP 2001). A wealth of information is available on gender and energy, providing a valid basis for understanding the implications of energy on gender and how the gender-based socially structured issues are connected with energy (Wickramasinghe, 2006b).

Equality, social justice, and social inclusion are the guiding principles that should be followed in dealing with developing energy for women. The field-based experience, and research findings and evidence point out several key aspects:

1   Investing in energy for women leads to broader social inclusion in energy sector development (Wickramasinghe 2013c; Masse and Samaranayske 2002, 14–16).
2   To date the energy supply agenda has not been driven by the need to improve women's well-being (Wickramasinghe 2010; Practical Action 2013, 55).
3   Enhancing access to energy for women closes development gaps that are being induced partly due to the relegating of women's energy needs to the fringes of energy development. Energy access, which is often equated with electricity access, is seen as a means to eradicating women's subordination, their unequal access to and use of energy and energy technologies (Wickramasinghe 2012, 29; Heruela and Wickramasinghe 2009, 8–10).
4   Providing access to energy improves livelihoods through productive use of energy and technologies enabling women to comfortably engage in conventional field and home-based enterprises (Lallement 2009, 10–13; Practical Action 2012; Wickramasinghe 2009, 39).
5   Energy for women means reducing domestic burdens and household work. This requires access to different types of energy for different purposes (Wickramasinghe 2009, 39).

6   Energy for economic empowerment of women is crucial from several perspectives such as equality, income distribution, acquisition of assets, enhancing endowments, and changing their agency from subsistence to affluence (Wickramasinghe 2009, 39; Lallement 2009, 10–13).

7   The idea of energy for women should use modern energy solutions to reduce persistent inequalities in the stereotypical division of labour. Non-remunerative work in most societies and households is skewed towards women, while remunerative work and leisure time is skewed towards men. There is the potential to address these issues through providing modern energy solutions for women (Wickramasinghe 1999; 2011, 7567–7574).

8   Energy for women is a way to reduce energy-related health risks and hazards, increasing service access and personal safety, and also reducing violence against women. Energy is seen as a means to lighting the lives of women and children contributing to psychological and physical well-being and reducing their vulnerability to energy-based social exclusions, and marginalization (Wickramasinghe 2004a).

Energy for lightening the lives of rural women

Electricity is placed at the highest tier of the energy ladder. It is considered a gender neutral requirement with the potential to meet both women's and men's energy needs. However, women and men differ substantially in their use of electricity beyond illumination. For a majority of rural women electricity is a means to secure knowledge, information, education, technology, safety, and outmigration (ESMAP 2005; Masse and Samaranayake 2002, 14–16). Implications reported by women are reduced isolation by over 80 percent, increased external linkages by over 95 percent, personal safety by over 85 percent, personal skills and contacts by 52 percent, and outmigration by over 46 percent (Wickramasinghe 2009, 39).

Electricity access for women affects the day-to-day activities of women, such as doing laundry, dehusking paddy, and pounding grain. The demand for community grinding mills and water pumps powered by electricity has emerged as a means to save women's time and labour (Wickramasinghe 2009, 39). For example, solar-powered drip irrigation systems, introduced under the Matale Regional Economic Advancement Project in Sri Lanka, contributed to increase women's income by over 300 percent while saving 3 to 4 hours of time daily expended on field irrigation (Wickramasinghe 2005a).

However, the energy-use practices of women in rural areas demonstrate that multiple resources are currently filling household energy demand. The data on energy consumption by sectors in Sri Lanka in 2013 shows that there has been no significant change in the use of biomass, and a slight downward trend in petroleum and electricity consumption occurred between 2008 and 2013 (Ministry of Power and Energy 2013). The energy sector profile and the consumption show that electricity is not being used for cooking, but biomass is. In these circumstances, technologies such as gasifiers or improved cookstoves have the potential to provide significant improvements to the lives of women.

Household as hub of energy use

The household is the hub of energy use in rural life, bringing together disparate energy resources. People use multiple sources for meeting household energy needs (Practical Action 2010). For instance, in Sri Lanka, about 79 percent of the Sri Lankan population of twenty million people live in rural areas where agriculture remains as either the main source or a supplementary source of livelihood (Department of Census and Statistics 2012). Out of 4.5 million households reported in the national census in 2007, 75.8 units are male headed and 24.2 percent are female headed (Asian Development Bank 2008). These two types of functional organizations differ in energy management decision making, but play key roles in manipulating a demand (Wickramasinghe 2012, 29). Clearly defined gender targets for energy transition should be explored.

Household energy consumption profiles in South Asia reflect a low use of commercial energy (see Table 16.1). These fuel types differ in relation to the sources. For instance, types of biomass derived for energy varies: wood is tree based; other types include residues and waste which are mostly crop based, and dung is animal based so women tend to use various sources available at their access to meet the needs. Petroleum based types also include several types and vary in regard to their contribution to household energy. Energy derived through combustion of solid biomass – wood, dung, residues etc. – is extremely high, because it is affordable for individual households, for women in particular (Wickramasinghe 2012, 29). The data illustrates the common situation in these countries: biomass is the primary energy resource.

Table 16.1 Household energy consumption in 2005 (Terajoule) by fuel type in some selected countries in South Asia (% are given in brackets)

Country	Dung	Other	Wood	Kerosene	Natural gas	LPG	Electricity	Total
Bangladesh	27.2 (5.0)	106.6 (19.5)	271.1 (49.7)	30.3 (5.6)	75.2 (13.8)	0.93 (0.2)	34.1 (6.2)	545.43 (100)
India	589.1 (9.1)	1178.4 (19.6)	2993.7 (49.7)	404.3 (6.7)	26.4 (0.4)	448.2 (7.4)	421.1 (7.0)	6018.2 (100)
Nepal	13.2 (7.6)	21.4 (12.2)	124.4 (71.2)	11.2 (6.4)	–	1.6 (0.9)	3.0 (1.7)	174.8 (100)
Sri Lanka	–	–	54.7 (68.3)	8.7 (10.9)	–	5.1 (6.4)	3.0 (1.7)	80.1 (100)

Data sources: Nation Master (2011); FAO (2010)

The definition of energy access used by the IEA is "A household having reliable and affordable access to clean cooking facilities, a first connection to electricity and then an increasing level of electricity consumption over time to reach the regional average" (IEA 2011). It has further elaborated that access also involves a specified minimum level of electricity consumption which varies between urban and rural settings. The IEA estimated this threshold level of electricity consumption for rural households to be around 250 kilowatt-hours per year, and a growing pattern in the consumption over a period is considered as a reflection of eradication of energy poverty.

A noteworthy transition has occurred across regions with the adoption of household electrification policy. In Sri Lanka, the electricity for all initiative has reached almost 96 percent of the households in 2014 (Sugathapala 2013). However, biomass still provides nearly 52 percent of the energy demand, 38 percent is petroleum based, and 9 percent from electricity (Ministry of Power and Energy 2013). This policy had no women-targeted strategies but the benefits are reported high among women (Wickramasinghe 2013c). Self-reported changes include: increased labour efficiency, intra-household mobility, cleaner indoor environment, reduced risks, extended hours of work, convenience, cleanliness, leisure, and access to information and knowledge (Wickramasinghe 2005b, 2010). Women in isolated rural locations who had no access to the national grid electricity supply have made progressive changes through distributed energy development (Wickramasinghe 2012, 29). The benefits of expanded access go beyond kerosene elimination to helping women mobilize local capital for improving housing, household facilities and also in investing in property and education (Wickramasinghe 2005b, 9–10).

Energy, poverty, and economic empowerment

The nexus of energy and poverty illustrates the interrelationships between commodity markets and development. Access to energy contributes directly to development as a means to improve situations of poverty. For instance, one focus of the UNDP Millennium Goals is improving access to affordable and clean energy services for the poor as a prerequisite to achieving multiple development benefits, including economic, social, and environmental objectives (UNDP 2005a, 2005b). Situations of poverty are compounded where the poor spend a high proportion of their income on poor quality energy resources (UNDP 2008). Estimates indicate that poor families in the Asia Pacific region spend nearly 28 percent of household budgets on fuels, electricity, and transportation (UNDP 2007). The poor also devote a large portion of their time on energy-related activities; women and girls may spend many hours a day gathering firewood and water, and agro-processing. Women are impacted along multiple dimensions by poverty: through lack of income or low income; poor quality of occupational space and housing; and poor access to education, technology, and health (UNDP 2007; Cecelski 1995, 1–5; 2005, 1–5). Along each of these dimensions access to energy offers prospective solutions to tackle the causes of poverty.

Energy access (or lack thereof) is useful as a measure of poverty because lack of access to modern energy resources limits the economic options for the poor, and particularly for poor women (UNDP 2004; IEA 2010; Ramani and Heijndermans 2003; Lallement 2009, 11–13). It is estimated that out of the nearly 1.3 billion people living in poverty, 70 percent are women. Income earned by women is minimal when compared to the time and effort spent working (Wickramasinghe 2009, 39). This is influenced by the low efficiency of manual production, the prevalence of non-remunerative work, inefficient technologies, and wage disparities. Income poverty impedes women's access to energy, as well as their ability to purchase household appliances and machinery and to develop promising income generating avenues. Access to energy for poor women requires an integrated approach, especially from the perspectives of poverty alleviation and economic empowerment. The debate on poverty and defining poverty is ongoing (Cecelski 2002, 20–22). Most recently, the Open Working Group on the Sustainable Development Goals established under the Rio process has pointed out that there is a necessity to use a comprehensive definition of poverty because a metric focused on income alone does not capture all of the hardships that constitute poverty (Köhler et al. 2014, 1–3; Bessell 2014, 1–5).

The demand for energy-related solutions to poverty stems from the persistent disparities between the earned income of women and men. In Sri Lanka, women's share of earned income is closer to one-third while two-thirds is reported as the share earned by men (Wickramasinghe 2012, 29). A gender assessment in Sri Lanka carried out by the Asian Development Bank pointed out that gender difference in poverty is a consequence of gender inequality in the labour market (Asian Development Bank 2008). Labour is the major asset of women who lack access to other economic resources. There is a marked disparity between the rural and urban sectors in the labour force participation of women and their income. In rural areas women have a higher labour force participation rate but earn less income, whereas in urban areas women earn more income but have a lower labour force participation rate (Department of Census and Statistics 2011). These disparities in earned income are due to the poor capacity of rural women to enter and compete in the labour market, limited opportunities, and also the prevalence of low-paid casual work (CENWOR 2007). In these situations energy could be used for building capabilities and opening options in agriculture as well as non-farm enterprises for women. The stereotypical division of household responsibilities common to many rural households drives women to engage in non-remunerative household chores regardless of the lost opportunities for them to build their own capabilities to contribute to household income and the local economies (Wickramasinghe 2009, 39). Improved energy access and adoption of improved technologies, particularly electric appliances, kitchen utensils, improved cookstoves, and productive machineries, would enable women to undertake work for remuneration.

The connection between women's poverty and energy has been long recognized. Most of the women in poverty do not have access to clean energy options such as electricity or propane and technologies (Heruela and Wickramasinghe 2009, 8–10). Nor do they have access to technologies that would ease their day-to-day chores or by increasing the efficiency of available energy resources such as appliances for grinding and processing (Wickramasinghe 2009, 39). This situation is worsened by a lack of financial capacity to invest in energy resources and technology. The implication is that energy poverty and income poverty are interrelated and situated on the two sides of the same coin. Lack of income is a barrier for women to access clean energy resources and technologies. In the same manner lack of modern energy and technology is a barrier for women to develop economically.

Empirical evidence suggests that effects of energy poverty are felt stronger with lower income (Cecelski 2002, 20–22). Energy consumption by the women in poor households whose income is below the poverty line is much lower when compared to the energy consumption of women in middle class households. While the poorest households in Sri Lanka use less than 30 kWh per month, middle class households often consume three times that amount per month (Wickramasinghe 2013b). A similar situation is found with per capita consumption of firewood where the poor use less that 1 kg per day while the wealthier use around 2 kg per day. Hundreds of households living close to grid electricity supply lines are deprived of electricity because they cannot afford the cost of connection and house wiring. Strategies such as off-grid renewable energy development, elimination of kerosene lamp lighting, and state grants enhancing energy access have made transitional effects on the lives of women and the poor (Wickramasinghe 2013b). Investing in energy for women offers a fast track solution to reducing women's poverty.

Increased energy access and training help women to start new enterprises and economic activities and also increases per capita production output of ongoing work. The ways by which measures are being introduced with a focus on empowering women are rather diverse. There are no hard and fast rules on where to begin the process: whether to start by providing access to electricity, for example, or by building women's capacity to invest in skills and new technologies. In some cases, where access to electricity is provided by the state, women improve and expand conventional home-based production work such as food processing and sewing, eventually securing electric machinery for the production work (Masse and Samaranayake 2002, 14–16). Such initiatives enable women to increase their productivity by 200 to 300 percent (Wickramasinghe 2005a). What is more, such changes pave the way for women to earn recognition, enter business channels, and secure subcontracts from large agencies. Similarly women in the sesame sweet making industry in Matale have invested their earnings towards electricity access. By having electricity for illumination and partial mechanization of production, they were able to enter the market with products and to lead business enterprises (Wickramasinghe 2005a). In both cases, increased income reduced dependency on men's earnings and empowered women as decision makers.

Energy for improving health

It is widely recognized that lack of access to clean sources of energy leads to deterioration of human health (World Health Organization 2002, 2011). This is particularly true for those who are exposed to the by-products of incomplete combustion, which are often generated when using biomass as a fuel (Wickramasinghe 2004b, 18–34). Additionally, there are dangers to human health in securing and processing biomass for use as fuel. In-depth analysis of the differences between genders in engaging with energy resources through traditional roles is crucial. There are four sets of energy-related factors that impact women's health. The first set is the continuing uses of polluting sources of energy, such as kerosene for lighting, biomass for cooking, and biomass smoke for repelling insects. An extremely higher intensity of health risks is found in the biomass energy used for cooking. The second set includes the vast array of work related to collecting, harvesting, carrying, and processing of various types of solid biomass for fuel: wood, crop residues, dung, leaves, etc. The third covers the intra-household burning of biomass for generating energy for cooking where women often follow conventional practices and technologies. The fourth, but less explored, set is the health risks of production tasks handled by women in agriculture following conventional practices.

The links between energy and women's health are quite significant in developing regions, but they are often discussed in the global context rather than a local context. The effects of conventional cooking practices on women, in particular the implications of rudimentary cooking technologies, have been heavily discussed (Smith 1999; Global Alliance for Clean Cookstoves 2011, 50; Smith et al. 2004; World Health Organization 2002, 2007). Accessible, affordable, and clean energy access is crucial for delivering services (Practical Action 2013, 55). It is widely accepted that increasing access to clean energy is a means to improving women's health by reducing indoor air pollution (World Health Organization 2011). Empirical evidence of the detrimental effects of biomass cooking on health varies in relation to the context, physical status of the cooks, and patterns of exposure (Parik 2011, 7587–7594). The main issue affecting women's health is use of open fires and rudimentary cookstoves that are reported as inefficient, unsafe, unclean, inconvenient, drudgeric, and exhaustive (Wickramasinghe 2011, 7567–7574). During cooking women tend to inhale acrid smoke and fine particulates (World Health Organization 2006, 42). Cooking means several hours of exposure to harmful gases, intra-household pollution, and contact with fire, ash, soot, smoke, and particulates, which altogether causes serious physical and psychological stress. Recent estimates suggest that indoor air pollution causes nearly 4.3 million deaths per year due to chronic respiratory diseases, pneumonia, and lung cancer caused by household cooking over coal, wood, and biomass stoves (World Health Organization 2014). Research carried out in several areas found diseases such as asthma, bronchitis, tuberculosis, cataracts, blindness, and adverse pregnancy outcomes – in particular low birth weight (Parik 2011, 7587–7594; Laxmi et al. 2003, 50–68). Estimations done by Pachauri and others (2012) identified that improved access to modern cooking fuels has the potential to prevent 0.6 to 1.8 million premature deaths per year until 2030.

Research carried out in Sri Lanka investigating health problems experienced by women has illustrated that the entire biomass energy cycle, from collecting and harvesting, to burning and cleaning hearths, affects women's health (Wickramasinghe 2003, 51–61). Women in the study reported incidents of: injuries, snake bites, insect attacks, and poisoning while harvesting, collecting, and processing dead wood; repetitive strain injuries from carrying heavy loads of wood in head loads over long distances; and burns during combustion of biomass in kitchen hearths (Wickramasinghe 2003, 51–61; 2004b, 18–24; and 2006a). Comparing the findings from place to place makes it clear that detrimental effects are context specific and thus solutions need to not only be affordable but tailored to the specific context and acceptable to the women affected.

The effects of biomass-based cooking on women are exacerbated by the lack of suitable woody biomass. In India, Bangladesh, and Nepal, as well as other countries of South Asia, women use low-calorific materials such as residues, leaves, and dung for cooking. Field research carried out in Chalnakhel village in Nepal showed that women spent over 4 hours a day collecting forest leaves and rolling them to make fuel (Bhadra 1997, 74–87). In the Khanmohona village in Chittagong, Bangladesh women spend hours making straw sticks by wrapping straw in cow dung (Das 1997, 51–72). This series of work handled by women in securing solid material and then burning it in open hearths or rudimentary cookstoves is unhealthy. Women neglect the health repercussions of these activities in favour of family food security. They divert their productive time to undertake this stressful and unhealthy work over the course of their lives, ultimately leading them to physical and psychological disabilities during the later stages of their lives (Wickramasinghe 2004a).

There are multiple options for using energy to improve women's health. Discarding biomass-based cooking and adopting cleaner burning fuels such as propane or electricity are the best option. In the areas where biomass continues to be the only affordable source of energy the realistic option is gasification technologies and improved cookstoves which use complete combustion to reduce emissions of harmful particulates and gases. Research carried out in Sri Lanka suggests that adopting non-energy solutions or measures is also crucial in addressing these issues. These measures are kitchen improvements such as improved ventilation, cooking on elevated surfaces, and improved stoves with chimneys to release kitchen smoke (Wickramasinghe 2011, 7567–7574; Sugathapala 2010). Lessons learned from Sri Lanka also demonstrate the viability of growing sources of wood energy at the household using mosaics in the central hills (Wickramasinghe 1999). Such systems ensure the availability of woodfuel and reduce the burdens of collecting it from distant sources.

Agriculture is one of the less explored areas of links between women's health and production related work. Informally collected clinical records in the dry zone of Sri Lanka indicate that women who are engaged in post-harvest processing, particularly the winnowing of grain, suffer from a series of respiratory problems that become bronchitis. These epidemiological records also show that women who dehusk paddy, and who are engaged in grinding and milling, suffer from upper respiratory infections. Energy-based mechanical solutions are central to address these health problems, but most of the solutions are costly and beyond women's economic capacities.

Recommendations

Where do we go from here and what are the forward-looking strategies that countries and the global community could follow?

1   First and foremost is a commitment to "women-inclusive energy development." Prerequisite to this is the gathering of gender disaggregated data for energy policy makers, planners, and other stakeholders. This data will help point out the gaps in the ongoing process of development and the problems to be addressed through energy development and stakeholder engagement. It is also essential to map out the strengths and limitations of stakeholders.

2   Women-inclusive energy policy using special strategic instruments and set targets to address development problems and meet the needs and priorities of women. A favourable and conducive policy environment needs to be in place to work out strategies, actions, and budgetary allocations, and measure the effectiveness using indicators responsive to women.

3   A local mechanism and a national machinery accommodating women and recognizing women's agency in energy needs to be in place. Project-based solutions sought through externally driven mechanisms are limited to women in project areas and have proven unsuccessful in making change in the lives of women or in sustaining the systems.

4   Energy mixes and technologies that are suited to address women's multiple roles are promising options. Success cases and the lessons drawn from them should be made available not only for showcasing and replication, but also for framing national strategies and making institutional arrangements.

5   Rather than meeting women's energy needs using a piecemeal approach, a packaged approach is essential. Empirical evidence demonstrates that the benefits of increased production efficiency and production through solar-energy-based water lifting and drip irrigation are being fully realized with the introduction of micro-credit, knowledge on post-harvest processing technologies, storage and value addition, and access to market information and transportation.

6   In recognizing the prospects for using energy as a means to empowering women, a special energy tariff for women should be introduced, because expanding or improving their livelihood, increasing production and production efficiency, and enabling energy-based enterprises is crucial. Adoption of applications and machineries for economic activities are to be

recognized as pathways for adding value to energy beyond mere access. A new set of gender responsive indicators needs to be in place to enable the contribution of energy towards sustainable development.

7   Financing women, their organizations, and groups is crucial for them to get access to clean energy technologies and appliances. Women often lack the investment capacity to bear the cost of energy and other costs of enterprise development.

8   Capacity building is essential to realizing women-inclusive development targets into energy. Capacity building is crucial at three levels:

   a   Creating a favourable policy environment which is to be initiated with gender analysis of energy and gaps in the policy frameworks followed by integration of options for women.

   b   Enhancing institutional readiness and capacities to have mechanisms for implementing women-inclusive policies and strategies. This requires a process of institutional analysis through which strengths and limitations are to be identified and additional strengths are to be built to undertake these tasks.

   c   It is also crucial to developing capacities in women and their organizations to translate policies into action and for efficient use of energy, technologies, and services. Information, awareness, and skills are essential for women to make a progressive change.

References

Asian Development Bank. 2008. *Country Gender Assessment – Sri Lanka*. Manila: Asian Development Bank.

Bessell, Sharon. 2014. "The individual deprivation measure: A new approach to multi-dimensional gender sensitive poverty measurement." *CRO Poverty Brief* 20: 1–5.

Bhadra, C.K. 1997. "The land, forestry and women's work in Nepal." In *Land and Forestry: Women's Local Resource-Based Occupations for Sustainable Survival in South Asia*, edited by Anoja Wickramasinghe, 74–87. Sri Lanka: CORRENSA (Collaborative Regional Research Network in South Asia).

Cecelski, E. 1995. "From Rio to Beijing: Engendering the energy debate." *Energy Policy* 23(6): 567–575.

——. 2002. "Enabling equitable access to rural electrification: Current thinking on energy, poverty, and gender." *ENERGIA News* 5(3): 20–22.

——. 2005. "Gender energy and the MDGs: Towards gender-sensitive energy research and practice." *ENERGIA News* 8(2): 1–5.

CENWOR. 2007. *Gender Dimensions of the Millennium Development Goals in Sri Lanka*. Colombo, Sri Lanka: Center for Women's Research.

Das, Sharmila. 1997. "Women's contribution to homestead and agricultural production systems in Bangladesh." In *Land and Forestry: Women's Local Resource-Based Occupations for Sustainable Survival in South Asia*, edited by Anoja Wickramasinghe, 51–72. Sri Lanka: CORRENSA (Collaborative Regional Research Network in South Asia).

Department of Census and Statistics. 2011. *Household and Income Expenditure Survey, 2009/1010*. Colombo, Sri Lanka: Ministry of Financing and Planning.

——. 2012. *Sri Lanka Labour Force Survey, Quarterly Report – 2012 Third Quarter*. Colombo, Sri Lanka: Ministry of Financing and Planning.

ENERGIA. 2007. *Where Energy is Women's Business: National and Regional Reports from Africa, Asia, Latin America and the Pacific*. Edited by G. Karlsson. The Netherlands: ENERGIA Secretariat.

ESMAP. 2005. *Energy Services for the Millennium Development Goals* (UNDP/ World Bank Energy Sector Management Assistance Programme). Washington, DC: World Bank.

FAO. 2010. *What Woodfuel Can Do to Mitigate Climate Change*. FAO Forestry Paper. Rome Italy: FAO.

Global Alliance for Clean Cookstoves. 2011. *Igniting Change: A Strategy for Universal Adoption of Clean Cookstoves and Fuels*. Washington, DC: Global Alliance for Clean Cookstoves.

Havet, I. 2003. "Linking women and energy at the local level to global goals and targets." *Energy for Sustainable Development* 7(3): 75–79.

Heruela, Conrado and Anoja Wickramasinghe. 2009. "Energy options for cooking and other domestic energy needs of the poor and women in the era of high fossil fuel prices." *ENERGIA News* 12(1): 8–10.

International Energy Agency. 2010. *Energy Poverty – How to Make Modern Energy Access Universal?* Paris: International Energy Agency.

——. 2011. *World Energy Outlook: Energy for All, Financing Access for the Poor*. Paris: International Energy Agency.

Köhler, G., Pogge, T., and Sengupta, M. 2014. "Big holes in the SDG draft." *CRO Poverty Brief* 21: 1–3.

Lallement, D. 2009. "Energy options for livelihood needs of the poor and women." *ENERGIA News* 12(1): 10-13.

Laxmi, V., Parikh, J., Karmakar, S. and Dabrase. P. 2003. "Household energy, women's hardship and health impacts in rural Rajastan, India: need for sustainable energy solutions." *Energy for Sustainable Development* 7(1): 50–68.

Masse, R. and Samaranayake, M. R. 2002. "EnPoGen study in Sri Lanka." *ENERGIA News* 5(3): 14–16.

Ministry of Power and Energy. 2013. *National Energy Policy and Strategies of Sri Lanka*. Sri Lanka: Ministry of Power and Energy.

Nation Master. 2011. *Energy Statistics by Country*. Accessed February 2, 2015, www.nationmaster.com/country-info/stats/Energy.

Pachauri, S., Rao, N. D., Nagai, Y. and Riahi, K. 2012. *Access to Modern Energy: Assessment and Outlook for Developing and Emerging Regions*. Laxenburg: International Institute for Applied Systems Analysis.

Parik, J. 2011. "Hardships and health impacts on women due to traditional cooking fuels: a case study of Himachal Pradesh, India." *Energy Policy* 39: 7587–7594.

Practical Action. 2010. *Poor People's Energy Outlook, 2010*. Rugby, UK: Practical Action Publishing.

——. 2012. *Poor People's Energy Outlook, 2012*. Rugby, UK: Practical Action Publishing.

——. 2013. *Poor People's Energy Outlook 2013: Energy for Community Services*. Rugby, UK: Practical Action Publishing.

Ramani, K. V. and Heijndermans, E. 2003. *Energy, Poverty and Gender: A Synthesis*. Washington, D.C.: The World Bank.

Smith, K. R. 1999. "Indoor air pollution. Pollution management in focus." *The World Bank Pollution Management Discussion Notes* 8(4).

Smith, K. R., Sumi Mehta, and Mirjam Maeusezahl-Feuz. 2004. "Indoor air pollution from household use of solid fuels." In *Comparative Quantification of Health Risks: The Global and Regional Burden of Disease Attribution to Selected Major Risk Factors.* Edited by Majid Ezzati, Alan D. Lopez, Anthony Rodgers and Christopher J.L. Murray, 1435–1493. Geneva: WHO.

Sugathapala, A.G.T. 2010. "Indoor air quality due to use of biomass stoves – cases from the estate sector." Paper presented at the seminar on Policy Innovative Systems for Clean Energy Security, 23 December, 2010, Kandy, organized by Practical Action Consulting. Sri Lanka.

——. 2013. "Energy scenario of Sri Lanka." Paper presented at the National Level Knowledge Sharing Workshop on Gender Review of the National Level Energy Sector Policies and Programmes in Sri Lanka. 12 August, 2013. Organized by Practical Action Consulting and ADB, Colombo, Sri Lanka.

United Nations Development Programme. 2001. *Generating Opportunities: Case Studies in Energy and Women.* New York: United Nations Development Programme.

——. 2004. *World Energy Assessment.* New York: United Nations Development Programme.

——. 2005a. *Energizing Millennium Development Goals.* New York: United Nations.

——. 2005b. *The Energy Challenges for achieving the Millennium Development Goals.* New York: United Nations.

——. 2007. *Energy Access and Poverty Reduction: Synthesis of Country Level Gap Analysis.* Bangkok: United Nations Development Programme Regional Centre.

——. 2008. *Delivering Energy Services for Poverty Reduction: Success Stories from Asia and the Pacific.* Bangkok: United Nations Development Programme Regional Centre.

Wickramasinghe, Anoja. 1999. *Gender Aspects of Woodfuel Flows in Sri Lanka: A Case Study in Kandy District,* Regional Wood Energy Development Project [RWEDP], *Filed Document No. 55,* FAO Regional Office, Bangkok, Thailand, June 1999.

——. 2003. "Gender and health issues in the biomass energy cycle: impediments to sustainable development." *Energy for Sustainable Development,* VII (3): 51–61.

——. 2004a. "Gender and health threats related to energy: issues of women's rights to energy resources and services", Paper presented at the World Renewable Energy Congress (WREC-VIII), August 29–September 3, 2004, Denver, Colorado, USA.

——. 2004b. "Implications of biomass energy system for women in Sri Lanka." *Glow.* A Publication of the Asia Regional Cookstove Programme (ARECOP), 3: 18–34.

——. 2005a. "Evaluation study on micro-finance programme for women organizations, Matale Regional Economic Advancement Project (M-REAP)." Unpublished Research Report, M-REAP, Matale, Sri Lanka.

——. 2005b. "Gender, modern biomass energy technology and poverty," *ENERGIA News,* 8 (December): 9–10.

——. 2006a. "Women's work is never done." *The Health Exchange,* Magazine of REDR-IHE, 20.

——. 2006b. *Gender and Energy in Asia: Annotated Bibliography.* Netherlands: ENERGIA.

——. 2009. "Gender mainstreaming in micro-hydro in Rambukoluwa, Sri Lanka." Unpublished research report: 39. Report submitted to ENERGIA, Netherlands.

——. 2010. "Women and energy in Sri Lanka: emerging issues and responses." A paper presented at the WIE Conference on Energy Efficiency and Renewable Energy, 25–29 October 2010, Islamabad, Pakistan.

———. 2011. "Energy access and transition to cleaner cooking fuels and technologies in Sri Lanka: issues and policy limitations." *International Journal of Energy Policy* 39(12): 7567–7574.

———. 2012. *Gender and Household Energy: The Entry Points for Matching the Grassroots Needs with Sustainable Development*: 29. Colombo, Sri Lanka: CENWORR.

———. 2013a. *Household Energy Options and Technology in the Context of Sustainable Energy for All*, SAARC Workshop on Household Energy Efficiency & Conservation with Women Participation, 10–12 September 2013, Dhaka, Bangladesh.

———. 2013b. *Women in Household Energy Management and in Energy Governances Systems*, SAARC Workshop on Household Energy Efficiency & Conservation with Women Participation, 10–12 September 2013, Dhaka, Bangladesh.

———. 2013c. *Gender Review of the National Energy Sector Policies and Programmes in Sri Lanka*, Presentation at National Level Knowledge Sharing Workshop held in Colombo, 12 August 2013, organized by Practical Action and ADB.

World Health Organization. 2002. *Health Effects of Indoor Air Pollution Exposure in Developing Countries*. Geneva: World Health Organization.

———. 2006. *Fuel for Life, Household Energy and Health*. Geneva: World Health Organization.

———. 2007. *Evaluation of the Costs and Benefits of Household Energy and Health Interventions at Global and Regional Levels*. Geneva: World Health Organization.

———. 2011. *Indoor Air Pollution and Health*. Geneva: World Health Organization.

———. 2014. *Burden of Disease from Household Air Pollution for 2012*. Geneva: World Health Organization.

17 Lessons learned from six years of selling solar in Africa

Doug Vilsack

Elephant Energy is a non-profit organization that distributes solar-powered lights and chargers to off-grid customers via a network of shops and rural sales agents in Namibia, Africa. Its products, which include a battery-powered LED light charged by a solar panel the size of a notebook, cost between $10 and $50 and "pay for themselves" in a few short months by reducing expenditures on candles and kerosene. With modern lighting, children can study at night, shops can stay open later, and clinics can operate. Further, many solar lights charge cell phones, providing access to information in the most remote areas in Africa.

Elephant Energy has grown substantially over the past six years, distributing over 15,000 solar-powered products in Namibia. The solar lighting industry has grown in parallel, distributing 28.5 million solar lights in Africa (Lighting Africa 2014a). From its beginning in 2008, the personal testimonies of Elephant Energy's customers motivated its young staff and fueled its growth (Elephant Energy 2011). Examples of these inspirational stories include:

> I am very happy to use this product because now I'm not spending money to buy some needs like candles, matches and pay to charge cell phone each week. Now everything is possible.
>
> Susana Ndawedwa – Ohangwena, Ohangwena Region

> I am very proud for this solar product. The children are performing well now at school because of that.
>
> Teopolina Daniel – Ongha, Ohangwena Region

> It helped us to check our chickens during night when the wild cat wanted to eat our chickens. It also helped us to see where you walk in order to check for snakes.
>
> Lucious Mafwila – Kasika, Caprivi Region

But stories of individuals impacted by Elephant Energy's work will not lead to universal energy access in Namibia or elsewhere in the developing world. There are 1.2 billion people worldwide who lack access to electricity and 2.8 billion who rely on biomass for cooking and heating, despite the work of a growing army of solar light designers, manufacturers, distributors, and salespeople (Sustainable Energy for All 2013). Participants in the solar lighting industry must be open about the challenges faced in serving the masses still living without access to energy. Elephant Energy has many lessons to share after six years at the front lines of the energy access movement in Africa.

Namibia: the worst (and best) place to start a business

I did not intend to spend six years of my life building a solar light distribution business in rural Africa. As with many who set foot on the continent, I was inspired by the people I met on my first visit and appalled that many lacked the food, energy, water, education, and health care that I took for granted. Elephant Energy was the by-product of a transformational experience working in Namibia with the World Wildlife Fund paired with my imagination, some free time, and a good salary as a newly minted lawyer. It took over a year for me to realize that the organization could stand on its own and begin to consider it as a career path instead of a hobby.

Elephant Energy's initial approach utilized funds generated from community-based hunting and tourism businesses to purchase solar products for distribution to small farmers in northern Namibia. The idea was that farmers could protect their fields from elephants in the night with a solar light, which would charge during the day and run every night for years without needing new batteries. Poaching would decrease as farmers realized that they could benefit from a robust tourism industry. Many farmers did use solar lights to protect their fields from marauding elephants. However, setting up a solar product distribution business was a clear next step after many asked to purchase Elephant Energy's solar-powered products outright instead of waiting for local conservation organizations to appropriate funds.

On its face, Namibia is not a lucrative place to start and scale a distribution business for any product. It is the second least-populated country on Earth, behind Mongolia, with just over two million people spread over an area twice the size of Texas. Namibians live in isolated villages or homesteads in remote areas, and some groups remain semi-nomadic (Vilsack and Nania 2009). Katima Mulilo, where Elephant Energy got its start, is over 750 miles from the capital city, Windhoek, and 850 miles from Walvis Bay, the closest port. Shipping to Namibia is either via costly air freight or a long voyage that increases the risks of product theft and/or supply gaps.

However, these stark business challenges should not detract from the benefits of working in Namibia. Elephant Energy has few competitors, corruption is minimal, and the use of English facilitates business transactions. More importantly, Elephant Energy perseveres because of the deep connection its staff members and volunteers have with the country and its people. Perhaps Elephant Energy would have sold more products in the past six years if it focused its efforts on population centers in Kenya or India, but one million unelectrified Namibians would not have access to its life-changing products. Elephant Energy's goal is to develop a lasting solution to the energy access problem for the people of Namibia. That unwavering focus, despite the business case for chasing opportunities elsewhere, is the reason that the organization exists today.

Handouts: the illusion of impact

In 2008, I formed Elephant Energy as a Colorado non-profit organization, raised enough funds from family and friends to purchase 50 solar-powered flashlights, and carried them to Namibia in my backpack for distribution to farmers and community wildlife rangers. In 2009, two volunteers from the University of Colorado distributed 500 additional lights, including a subsidized sale of 100 lights at roughly $7 apiece to a local conservation organization ("conservancy") that distributed them to their members and another subsidized sale of 400 lights at $7 apiece directly to the members of another conservancy. These sales were accompanied by rigorous surveys that assessed the impact of the solar lights on individual households (Dill et al. 2009).

Survey results were promising: people avoided dangerous wild animals in the night; children studied into the evening; women felt more secure when traveling; and $7 was saved each month because candles were no longer necessary. But this non-profit "hand out" model caused problems. Some accused conservancy staff of only providing lights to their family and friends. While the subsidized sale resolved this problem, we quickly realized that our young organization would not be able to scale if we only recouped one quarter of the cost of each light. As a result, in 2010, Elephant Energy opened an energy shop in Katima Mulilo, selling 220 products, including solar-powered lights, cell phone chargers, and crank radios, in just over two months of operation (Murphy and Vilsack 2010). This business focus has been the core of Elephant Energy's work since that time, but donor preferences and the allure of a quick "success" story has distracted from this focus.

In July 2011, Elephant Energy was asked by an aid agency to provide solar-powered lights to flood victims living in camps in northern Namibia. The 2011 floods were unprecedented in their intensity and extent, displacing tens of thousands of people. While Elephant Energy submitted a plan to distribute products to flood victims, the bulk of the plan was focused on establishing a sales network after the floods receded. This part of the plan was rejected because available funds were earmarked for disaster relief. Despite reservations, Elephant Energy accepted the funds, which constituted its first major grant.

Elephant Energy distributed 2,280 solar products to flood victims in Namibia in September and October 2011, and it gathered important information about the energy access problem and the impact that its products had on people's lives. Product recipients no longer used candles and kerosene for lighting and were spending money they saved on other necessities. People also stopped walking long distances to charge their cell phones, and some were making money by charging their neighbors' phones.

While this project resulted in significant immediate impact, it distracted from Elephant Energy's long-term goal to build a sustainable distribution network for solar products in Namibia. In the nearly six months that Elephant Energy focused exclusively on handouts, it could have distributed thousands of products via an increased focus on rural distribution. Instead, after the floods receded, it took Elephant Energy two years to obtain the necessary funding and re-build its staff capacity to provide access to solar products in all of the areas that received donated products. In addition, because it did not have the capacity to maintain its presence in all areas impacted by the flood, a system was not in place to repair broken products, and the marketing opportunity generated by reaching so many unelectrified villages was lost.

On the other hand, Elephant Energy needed money in 2011 to purchase inventory and expand its reach across northern Namibia. The flood provided the organization with its first major grant and the experience to compete for and win larger grants aligned with its entrepreneur-focused mission. Since the flood, Elephant Energy has been faced with many other opportunities to obtain funding to hand out products to disaster victims, school children, churches, women's groups, etc. The organization is now in a better position to carefully weigh the positives and negatives of these projects, and whether they help reach the end goal of lasting energy access in Namibia.

Dreaming of dollars

Starting a solar distribution business in rural Namibia sounds exotic and exciting, but in reality, a tremendous amount of time is spent looking for funding. In the early years, I assumed that Elephant Energy would be funded by grants, and submitted dozens of applications. While the organization received some small grants, those funds barely covered plane tickets to Namibia. Instead, Elephant Energy was funded by donations from friends and family. While the organization started receiving significant grants three years later, the process and stipulations associated with these grants presented their own challenges.

Being creative in fundraising and doggedly pursuing every lead has been a key to Elephant Energy's growth. I signed up for Facebook in 2008 for the sole purpose of tracking down all of my friends and asking them for $10 to fund the first batch of 50 solar-powered lights I carried to Namibia. In 2009, Elephant Energy sent two recent law school graduates to Namibia with a $5,000 grant from the University of Colorado and the proceeds from a small fundraiser attended by my family and friends. The World Wildlife Fund provided housing for Elephant Energy's interns, and Elephant Energy paid for their plane tickets and gave them $600 per month to survive.

In 2010, Elephant Energy's fundraising took a more entrepreneurial tact. In addition to an annual fundraiser, the organization entered a contest to be listed on Global Giving, a leading crowd fundraising website. Elephant Energy would be listed on the site permanently if it raised $4,000 from 50 donors during one month. Bonus prizes were also available for the organizations that raised the most money and for the one organization with the most unique donors. Elephant Energy's newly formed board of directors spent the month reaching out to friends and family members to ask them to give $10 each. In the end, Elephant Energy raised funds from 356 unique donors, easily beating the other teams. In total, it raised $27,025.

Elephant Energy's victory on Global Giving helped the organization hire its first two full-time staff members in Namibia, Joseph Ziezo and Annah Simbilu, and its first full-time American staff member, Katie Murphy. But having staff also increased the urgency of the organization's fundraising efforts. Elephant Energy's staff depended on the organization for their livelihoods. The summer of 2011 was the first time I remember having trouble sleeping because of Elephant Energy. That became a common occurrence as the organization grew and more and more people began depending on the organization, not only for light, but to feed their families.

As Global Giving funds waned, Elephant Energy accepted a grant to focus on the floods in northern Namibia. This grant and funding to expand our rent-to-own model carried Elephant Energy into 2012 when it was awarded a significant grant to expand its distribution network across Namibia. But this grant presented its own unique risks and challenges. While the grant was written to begin in July, the review process dragged on. Suddenly, in October, Elephant Energy received an e-mail notice that the grant was starting. Instead of distributing funds beforehand, Elephant Energy had to pay its own way and then request reimbursement, which the staff was told would take a month to process. This meant that the organization had to locate up to $70,000 in operating funds to cover expenses between its three milestone reporting periods. We believed in our mission, and had staff to pay, so we accepted that risk.

However, Elephant Energy's grantor did not have the capacity to review detailed milestone and financial reports submitted by their numerous grantees. As a result, the first milestone payment took four months to process, pushing the organization's unreimbursed operating costs even higher and resulting in the retrenchment of some staff. The second milestone payment was similarly delayed because the grantor fired the contractor administering the milestone process and "went dark" for a period of three months. While Elephant Energy's relationship with this grantor improved dramatically after that, these financial difficulties dramatically impacted the organization's ability to meet its goals on the ground.

While Elephant Energy distributed thousands of lights, a granting process that took account of the organization's needs would have resulted in thousands more sales and fewer sleepless nights. Elephant Energy, like many other social ventures, struggles with the demands of grantors and investors that do not understand the challenges of working in Africa with innovative new business models and technologies. Elephant Energy now takes the time to consider the experience and expectations of donors before accepting their support, despite the organization's constant need for funds to support new staff and inventory. Elephant Energy's current major source of funding in Namibia understands the organization's business focus, and Elephant Energy's staff sleeps much better for it.

The price of innovation

I immediately recognized the transformative nature of the solar-powered light when a friend handed me one in the spring of 2008. I ordered three that night, and they worked beautifully. However, I would soon learn many lessons about the difference between a product on the shelves in the United States and an innovative new product that could change the world.

There were very few solar lighting products on the market in 2008. The products that existed were the result of recent advancements in three separate technologies, including inexpensive and efficient solar panels, LEDs, and rechargeable batteries. Suddenly, manufacturers in China could produce a solar-powered light at a cost that made sales in developing countries possible. But these early products were not without their faults, and many of them were produced by entrepreneurs with little manufacturing experience and little capital to expend on quality control. What's more, these untested products would be subjected to the most challenging conditions imaginable in Africa. They would be hung in the rain, bleached by the sun, laid on the dirt, dropped repeatedly, and even chewed on by mice.

Over the years, Elephant Energy has responded to dozens of quality control issues, the worst of which resulted from the organization's acceptance of refurbished or donated products from manufacturers. In 2009, Elephant Energy accepted hundreds of "free" solar-powered flashlights after being told that all they needed were replacement batteries to function. But after replacing the batteries, shipping them to Namibia, and distributing many of them, it became clear that the products had other defects. It took months to replace them, and many likely wound up in rubbish heaps in rural villages. In 2010, Elephant Energy accepted hundreds of solar chargers that were designed to be sold for $100 to customers in the United States. After shipping them to Namibia, staff realized that the products would not hold a charge and did not work with many local phones.

Despite extensive product testing on the ground in Namibia, Elephant Energy has also paid for thousands of products of dubious quality and spent months addressing warranty issues with its customers and suppliers. In 2009, an over-tightened screw inside a solar-powered flashlight resulted in the circuit board flapping loose. In 2010, the most common cell phone charging connector on Elephant Energy's most popular light was defective. While the piece likely cost less than five cents to produce, it took months to get replacement parts to Namibia and many more months to reach numerous rural customers. In 2011, Elephant Energy introduced a new inexpensive product and quickly learned that it would only run for an hour each night, far below the four to six hours advertised. Mice also loved to chew on the rubber switch.

Quality control issues have diminished as the solar lighting industry has matured, and Elephant Energy has developed relationships with the most quality-conscious suppliers. However, the industry is still young, and the organization is constantly at risk of receiving a large shipment of defective products. The stakes are also greater now, as a large shipment of defective products could result in a long stock outage that would jeopardize Elephant Energy's ability to pay, and thus retain, its best regional sales managers and sales agents.

The world is made in China

I have been asked hundreds of times why Elephant Energy does not manufacture solar-powered lights and chargers in Namibia. The answer is simple: Namibia, and even its industrialized neighbor South Africa, do not have the infrastructure to manufacture solar lighting products cheaply enough to make them affordable for the people that need them most. To generate local jobs in Africa, some non-profit organizations have attempted to construct solar-powered lights in rural settings, and some manufacturers have attempted to assemble their products in-country. While attempts continue, I am not aware of any successes to date (Lighting Africa 2014b).

The manufacturing efficiencies and scale that can be achieved in China are overwhelming, but logistics are a major challenge. In the early days, all of Elephant Energy's products were hand-carried to Namibia. As product demands grew, the organization was forced to balance shipping costs against the desire to maintain a healthy inventory. Shipping solar lights from China to Namibia via air generally takes three to four weeks from the first contact with suppliers, but shipping costs can be over $10 per product. Shipping via sea can take anywhere from three to four months, but costs $1 to $2 per product. Long shipping times have also resulted in significant stock outages, challenging the faith of Elephant Energy's regional sales managers and agents that depend on access to inventory for their livelihoods.

Importing products on its own also forced Elephant Energy to develop a closer relationship with the Namibian government. Non-profit organizations can operate as Trusts in Namibia with little oversight over their finances or operations by the government. However, importation requires setting up an account with the Ministry of Finance so that various duties and taxes can be collected. Elephant Energy's initial registration in 2011 resulted in a cascade of additional filings and reporting requirements. The most onerous requirements were associated with the convoluted value added tax (VAT) system, including payments of 16.5 percent of the value of products upon importation. While these funds are supposed to be returned, in part, Elephant Energy only just received its first reimbursement from the government after nearly four years of submitting VAT returns.

Setting prices as a non-profit organization

Elephant Energy is a non-profit organization, but it sells products. The organization does not have beneficiaries; it has customers. Elephant Energy's history with the World Wildlife Fund in Namibia and my experience setting up non-profit organizations are the reasons why it is a non-profit organization and not a for-profit company. However, Elephant Energy's corporate form is not merely an accident. Setting up a distribution network for solar-powered products in Namibia is tremendously challenging. While investors can sometimes be found to fund the development of a product that could impact the lives of millions of people, few are interested in funneling hundreds of thousands of dollars into a rural distribution network to ensure that this product makes it into the hands of the people that need it most. Charitable donations were necessary for Elephant Energy to build its distribution network in Namibia.

Being a non-profit has its challenges. The constant effort to raise funds from individual donors and grants distracts from Elephant Energy's goal to establish a truly sustainable distribution network. As the organization experienced in its early years, large grantors prefer organizations with history, even if that history has not resulted in significant impact. Elephant Energy has gained fundraising skills in the past six years, and could continue raising non-profit funds for years to support its work in Namibia. But while alluring, this is not the organization's goal.

The challenge for Elephant Energy is in pricing its products. In 2009 and 2010, pricing was largely based on recouping the amount paid to purchase and ship products to Namibia. In 2011 and 2012, as sales increased and the distribution network shifted towards a sales agent model, Elephant Energy began to internalize distribution costs at the agent level. In 2013 and 2014, the organization focused on setting prices and developing commission programs to cover staffing and distribution costs at a regional level – this work is still in progress. The last and most significant challenge will be setting prices at an appropriate level to cover the costs of Elephant Energy's management in Namibia, and even a portion of the cost to support administrative staff based in the United States.

Appropriately supporting marketing efforts and internalizing those costs is also necessary if Elephant Energy is to scale in Namibia and beyond. Elephant Energy has never invested sufficiently in marketing, including materials for sales agents, radio advertisements, promotions, and TV advertisements. This is because donors with limited business experience are hesitant to fund marketing costs. While Elephant Energy has developed quality marketing materials and radio advertisements, its ability to conduct marketing campaigns at the level necessary to introduce all Namibians to its products is limited. Elephant Energy's product line also competes with technologies like candles, kerosene, and even wood that have been used for lighting for hundreds of years.

In 2008, it would have been impossible for Elephant Energy to make a sound business case for developing a distribution network for solar-powered lights in Namibia. The establishment of a sustainable business may be possible after years of effort and product advancements. Elephant Energy's ability to make that transition depends on its capacity to set prices in a way that makes its products accessible to its customers while internalizing operating costs. Additional grant funds will help Elephant Energy scale its business into challenging new regions and counties and to develop new products in the absence of interested investors. But to truly scale, Elephant Energy must resist the temptation to perpetuate unsustainable distribution methods with grant funds.

The trouble with rural sales agents

Many organizations and businesses like Elephant Energy distribute solar lighting products and other appropriate technologies. Many of them were formed because of the clear impact that these products have on the lives of families in developing countries. Many also work with rural entrepreneurs or sales agents to distribute their products, and many list their number of agents as an indicator of their impact.

Elephant Energy has developed many different "sales agent" systems. The first, developed in 2011, involved loaning small batches of products to rural shops. The loans were necessary because few shops had the resources to purchase more than a few products at a time to put on their shelves. Elephant Energy staff surveyed every shop they could find in the Caprivi Region of Namibia in the spring of 2011 and selected a dozen that would receive product loans. Each month, a staff member would visit the "rural shops" to collect proceeds from sales, issue new inventory, and provide shopkeepers with their profit. While a few shops sold 10–20 products per month, most struggled to find customers that could afford to pay for the products up front. As a result, some shopkeepers would loan out products and struggle to collect payment, resulting in a loss for Elephant Energy. Most shops stopped participating when Elephant Energy staff members stopped their monthly visits and encouraged the shops to resupply at the major market town in the area. If a shop could make more money selling candles, then why would they switch to solar-powered lights?

Attempts to develop rural distribution networks via "traveling sales agents" in 2012 and 2013 faced similar challenges. While a small number of dedicated and successful agents emerged from each of these efforts, the costs to find these individuals and, more importantly, from training failed sales agents, were high. It is likely that the number of "agents" touted by many organizations is overstated. Some of these "agents" may not have sold a product for months, or perhaps only sold one or two products. Only a few highly skilled agents likely depend on solar light sales for their entire income.

Elephant Energy's approach to sales agents changed dramatically as the reality of the market in rural Namibia became apparent. Sales agents are now subject to a more rigorous vetting and training process administered by regional sales managers who understand the local context. Sales agents earn commission on their sales and are not paid a monthly salary. Products are never loaned to sales agents without a down-payment, and determinations about credit-worthiness are made by regional sales managers who know the reputations of their agents and are personally responsible for any losses that accrue as a result of unpaid loans. While Elephant Energy's sales agents have decreased in number, they are now each a useful part of the team, and not just a statistic.

Rent-to-own: a nice non-profit model

Even with a robust sales agent vetting, training, and monitoring process, it is clear that a distribution network of rural sales agents in Namibia cannot operate as a sustainable business if consumers are forced to pay full price up front for solar lighting and charging products. Namibians continue to purchase candles for lighting and pay to charge their phones, not because they do not want a solar-powered product, but because they can purchase these products and services in small amounts over time. Elephant Energy recognized the need for end-consumer financing in 2011 and began to develop solutions.

Many solar light distributors have experimented with rent-to-own systems. Some, in the urban or peri-urban context, have had limited success. However, rent-to-own systems in the rural context are extremely challenging. Elephant Energy's first rent-to-own pilot project in 2011 provided solar products to nearly 100 customers. A second rent-to-own project in 2012 distributed 129 solar-powered lights/chargers. These products changed the lives of hundreds of people, protecting them from snakes and wild animals, providing light for children to study, and improving communication, among numerous other benefits. The rent-to-own system also increased the incomes of 11 sales agents, including women who had little access to income-generating opportunities (Elephant Energy 2012).

However, these rent-to-own projects were, at most, extremely efficient non-profit distribution models. While revenue from sales compensated our agents and paid for inventory and other rural distribution costs, Elephant Energy's oversight costs, including staff to monitor the projects and manage complicated accounting systems, were not internalized. As opposed to electric power in Namibia, which is pre-paid and turns off when there are no more "units" on a home's power meter, there was no way to "turn off the lights" of a rent-to-own customer who did not pay on time. As a result, sales agents were forced to travel to customers' homes numerous times to collect rental payments. In addition, cultural barriers prevented some agents from repossessing lights when rental payments were past due. These realities greatly increased the amount of time required to collect payments and reduced the number of customers each sales agent could support. Elephant Energy's experience indicates that it is unlikely that even the best-run rent-to-own program for solar-powered lights in rural Africa is scalable as a business.

PAYGO technology is the answer, but technology takes time

John Steininger, a friend, entrepreneur, and genius engineer from Ft. Collins, and I founded a new company called "divi" to address Elephant Energy's consumer finance problem. The team that John built developed a new PAYGO solar light and cell phone charging technology that automates much of the rent-to-own process. The system allows customers to pay off a high quality, aspirational solar lighting product for a deposit of between $5 and $10 and weekly payments of between $3 and $5. This is made possible by inserting technology into a solar-powered light that allows it to link with a cloud-based payment system through a cell phone. If a customer has not paid for the next week of use, then the light shuts off until more credit is purchased. Each divi-enabled product comes with a week of use up front, and it unlocks and is free to the customer once paid off. As a result, customers visit sales agents to purchase credits when their lights turn off, eliminating the need to chase them to collect payments and repossess lights. All transactions and customer information are also stored in the cloud for analysis and accounting.

Elephant Energy conducted an extensive trial of the divi technology between July and December 2012. On average, lights were 69 percent paid off at the end of the trial, and 77.7 percent paid off in rural areas where the technology had the most value. In addition to data collected about payoff rates, the trial evaluated product and consumer preferences via three surveys. Customers provided valuable feedback concerning the design and function of the divi product. A total of 55 out of 57 respondents stated that the divi light was easy to use. "You just purchase credit and put solar to the sun and start using it," said one customer. Another stated that "[t]he divi light is flexible. I can pay when I am having money. It is safer than candles because it cannot burn the house." Total average savings accrued as a result of using the divi light in place of cell phone charging services and candles equaled $3.50 per week. Most importantly, 88 percent of customers surveyed wanted to purchase another divi light.

Despite the success of the initial trial and another trial with a diviLite study lamp in Uganda in 2013, the process of developing, financing, manufacturing, and marketing a new product is a challenge. Elephant Energy and its partners at divi are in a similar situation as Elephant Energy's suppliers were in 2008. They are developing a technology that could fundamentally change the lives of millions of people, but are wrestling with the realities of limited finances, quality control, manufacturing in China, and locating customers in new markets. The tragic loss of divi's founder and leader, John Steininger, in the fall of 2013 added tremendously to this challenge. However, divi persevered, distributing thousands of diviLite study lamps to Elephant Energy in Namibia and other distributors in Peru, Ghana, Uganda, Tanzania, Somalia, and other countries. At long last, a new game-changing divi-enabled lamp, available from January 2015, will vastly increase Elephant Energy's ability to operate a sustainable, and perhaps profitable, distribution network in rural Namibia.

Your people are your organization

Nothing is possible without a strong team. The origin stories of many international development organizations focus on the sacrifice of a lone savior with a good idea that could change the lives of the huddled masses. While the importance of leadership cannot be overstated, "savior" stories distract from the reality that building a sustainable project or business in rural Africa requires a team, and the most important members of that team are the people living in the communities where an organization works. I carried 50 solar-powered flashlights to Namibia on my back in 2008, but 50 of my friends paid for them, and Joseph Ziezo and Annah Simbilu, Elephant Energy's first paid staff members, and numerous other partners in Namibia were responsible for pushing the business forward. Elephant

Energy's successes can be traced to monumental efforts by its staff, and its failures can all be traced to staffing challenges.

Elephant Energy's first years were characterized by a parade of American "interns" in Namibia who were compensated via a round-trip plane ticket, a free place to stay on the banks of the Zambezi River, and $600 per month to cover living expenses. These "interns" stayed in-country for 3–4 months each, a limit resulting from visa restrictions that required a more robust process for stays in Namibia of over 90 days. Plus, many of these early "interns" recently graduated from college or graduate school, so school loans prevented them from undertaking such lightly compensated work for long. Carol Murphy, who had over twenty years of experience working in conservation in Namibia, looked after these interns and filled in the gaps when Elephant Energy could not afford or find new recruits. I also traveled to Namibia at least once a year to guide Elephant Energy's work. However, continuity of operations was difficult to maintain with so much transition. Elephant Energy's Namibian staff struggled with changing leadership, and institutional knowledge was lost each time an intern returned to the United States.

Katie Murphy became Elephant Energy's first paid American staff member in 2011 and first paid Executive Director in 2012 as I stepped back into a role as Chairman of the Board of Directors. As Elephant Energy's footprint in Namibia expanded, Katie inherited oversight of the entire Namibian operation and the stress that accompanied it. To manage our Namibian expansion, we spent months searching for a Namibian to manage our distribution network and for new regional sales managers. We thought we had found the perfect Namibian director, but he struggled to manage Elephant Energy's network of regional sales managers, keep track of inventory, and account for funds. As a result, regional sales managers struggled with their own finances, and some funds and inventory went missing. We were forced to look for a new director after only a few months, partially for performance reasons and partially because of delayed grant payments.

Elephant Energy has persevered because each challenge has been met by an American or Namibian staff member or intern who was willing to sacrifice enormously because they believed in our mission to bring energy to rural Namibians. We leaned on each other during the hardest of times and celebrated our successes together. Elephant Energy is not about the young man that carried the first 50 solar-powered lights to Namibia. It is about the team that worked and continues to work together to make life-changing solar products accessible to tens of thousands of Namibians.

The energy access problem in Namibia and throughout the developing world remains monumental. Elephant Energy has faced many challenges, and will undoubtedly face many more. By being open about these challenges, Elephant Energy will avoid repeating its mistakes and will help guide other organizations as they grow. And, hopefully, the individual stories of changed lives in Namibia will inspire hundreds more entrepreneurs to join the movement to energize the world.

References

Dill, Jennifer, Ryan Knight, and Doug Vilsack. 2009. *Caprivi Solar Light Project Summary & Operational Report*. Accessed January 27, 2015. www.elephantenergy.org/images/documents/EE_2009_Field_Report_(FINAL).pdf.

Elephant Energy. 2011. *Namibia Flood Relief Energization Plan Final Report*. Accessed January 27, 2015. www.elephantenergy.org/images/documents/Final_Report_-_Namibia_Flood_Relief_Energization_Plan__2011_.pdf.

Elephant Energy. 2012. *Women's Energy Project & Rent-To-Own Final Report*. Accessed January 27, 2015. www.elephantenergy.org/images/documents/WE_Project_Final_Report_(Elephant_Energy_2012).pdf.

Lighting Africa. 2014a. "Program Results as of July 2014." Accessed November 3, 2014. www.lightingafrica.org/results/.

Lighting Africa. 2014b. "Niwa Partners with Sun Transfer to Assemble Solar Products in Ethiopia." Accessed January 15, 2015. www.lightingafrica.org/niwa-partners-with-sun-transfer-to-assemble-solar-products-in-ethiopia/.

Murphy, Katie and Doug Vilsack. 2010. *Elephant Energy Shops Project Summary & Operational Report*. Accessed January 27, 2015. www.elephantenergy.org/images/documents/Elephant_Energy_Shops_Report_2010.pdf.

Sustainable Energy For All. 2013. "Tracking Progress." Accessed January 14, 2015, www.se4all.org/tracking-progress/.

Vilsack, Doug and Julie Nania. 2009. "Put Out the Fire: Developing A Sustainable Energy Policy for all Namibians." Accessed January 27, 2015. www.elephantenergy.org/images/documents/Namibian_Renewable_Energy_Policy.pdf.

18 Energy use and draft power in South Asian foodgrain production

Arjun Makhijani and Melissa F. Moore-Pachucki

Introduction

Draft animals are a primary source of mechanical energy for agriculture in much of Asia and Africa. The use of draft animals affects billions of people who are dependent on agricultural production for sustenance and income. Despite the increasing use of farm machines, draft animals remain a critically important energy input for agriculture and related rural activities in South Asia. Many studies have demonstrated the great importance of draft animals to agriculture and rural transportation.

There is only a modest amount of field data and practically no integration of the problems of traditional draft power with the rest of rural energy policy. Despite the fact that draft animals' feed is often the largest energy use in rural areas of South Asia, there has been no attempt to integrate this energy consumption into national and international energy data. Moreover, the data on land area requirements regarding both amounts and types of land needed are also similarly sparse and incomplete.

A corollary is that lack of official recognition of draft animals as an energy issue has meant a lack of resources devoted to its understanding. As a result, there are considerable uncertainties as to the numbers of draft animals, the total amount of draft power which they represent, the total amount of energy inputs which are required, and the total energy output which these animals provide to rural agriculture and transportation.

This chapter examines one major area of rural energy use – that of mechanical energy for agricultural production. Specifically, we focus on the use of draft animals in agriculture with specific reference to four countries in South Asia: Bangladesh, India, Nepal, and Pakistan. The provision of adequate mechanical power for agriculture in these South Asian countries might have possible broader application elsewhere in the developing world.

The principal food crops are rice, wheat, coarse grains, and pulses. The first three provide most of the caloric supply. The use of draft animals is prevalent in all three areas of foodgrain production.

Table 18.1 shows the total number of cattle in South Asia in the years 2000 and 2009.

Table 18.1 Cattle in South Asia

Country	Cattle & buffaloes per hectare (ha) of agriculture area head/ha		Total cattle, millions
	2000	2009	2009
Bangladesh	2.5	2.7	25
India	1.6	1.8	324
Nepal	2.5	2.8	12
Pakistan	1.7	2.4	63

Source: FAO (2013), Table 46 for cattle per hectare and Table 4 (for total agricultural land)

Not all of these cattle are draft animals, of course. Portions are milch animals, not used for draft purposes, and others are young animals not yet involved in fieldwork. As noted in Table 18.5, we assume that one-fourth of the total cattle in each of the South Asian countries are draft animals. This is evidently very approximate and should be refined by further research.

Part 1 of this chapter discusses the energy requirements or intakes for draft animals. There are considerable uncertainties in the energy intake and output of animals and, hence, in efficiency. We need to expand energy statistics to include the energy intakes of draft animals. Part 2 discusses energy outputs that can be inferred or derived from the available data. Part 3 deals with the land requirements for the draft animal system. Part 4 assesses the efficiency of the system and ways to increase it. Part 5 explores how natural farming and renewable energy could mitigate capital and financing requirements for farming, a major problem for poor farmers, while increasing yields and climate benefits. We present our conclusions in Part 6. In particular, we point out that the extent to which the benefits of renewable energy and natural farming are realized will depend on whether they can be practically extended to large numbers of farmers and areas of land in South Asia as well as other parts of Asia where draft power is an important issue.

Part 1: Energy inputs

A number of widely varying estimates of food intake per draft animal can be found in the literature. There are several sources of uncertainty including the average weight of draft animals and the distribution of weights of animals in various parts of South Asia. A considerable portion of the scientific literature on draft animals consists of measurements on a few tropical animals.[1] The relation of the weight and feed requirements of these laboratory animals to average draft animals has not been established, creating another source of uncertainty.

One reason for the uncertainties is the lack of adequate measurement-based field data on inputs required by the variety of draft animals found across South Asia. We have made a survey of the literature to come up with a plausible range to use for the purposes of this study. Table 18.2 shows some of them. It is evident that there is a wide divergence in the estimates, from an input of 14 gigajoules per year (GJ/y) to 40 GJ/y per animal. Some of these differences may be due to the differences in weight and type of cattle used as draft animals in different parts of South Asia. For instance, the use of cows as draft animals is common in Bangladesh, but this seems rather rare in India. Nepal uses buffaloes as draft animals, but in India they are mainly milch animals. A part of the range reflects the considerable uncertainties in the data. Parikh uses an equivalence of two bullocks = one buffalo (Parikh 1988, 333).

We will use a range of 20 to 40 GJ per year per draft animal as inputs, reflecting the use of cattle as draft animals for the vast majority of South Asian agriculture. There may be variations between countries, with lower inputs in Bangladesh and higher inputs in India and Pakistan; there may also be significant variations within countries. However, there are simply not enough measurement-based data points for a more refined approach. Policy in each country in South Asia would be well served by more refined regional data.

We also need to take into account the other animals that need to be maintained to reproduce the stock of draft animals. This consists of three components: animals must reach a minimum age before they can work; cows must be maintained to produce offspring that can work; and excess animals over these minimum requirements.

Rao has made estimates of the first of these three components. A 3-year old bullock will have consumed 54,666 MJ of feed and its caretaker 1,788 MJ of food for a total input of 56,454 MJ (before an animal can begin to provide work output). The scrap value of cattle slaughtered and fully used for meat, leather, bone meal, etc. has been estimated to be 18,300 MJ/ton of beast. Thus, a 400 kg bullock has a value of 7,320 MJ, reducing the fixed energy embodied in the

Table 18.2 Annual energy requirements of draft animals

Animal	Annual energy input estimate, GJ/y	Source and comments
Bullock	25	Makhijani and Poole (1975), for India
Cattle	16	Parikh (1988) for Bangladesh
Bullock	14	Calculated from Pimentel (2009, Table 4) by extrapolating to a total of 1,000 hours per year of work (Rao 1984, 541)
Bullock	30	Rao (1984) for India
Bullock	40	Calculated assuming a weight of 350 kilograms and an input of 2.5 kg of dry weight feed per day per 100 kg. This is closer to the input for a Brahma bull, which is larger than the typical South Asian draft animal.

Note: Only the energy inputs for the animals involved in the work are shown in this table.

bullock to 49,134 MJ. This fixed input will be spread over 10 years of working life. Thus, the embodied energy of a bullock will be used at the rate of 4,913 MJ per year (Rao 1984, 542).

An additional 5 gigajoule (GJ) energy input per year increases the range of energy inputs required per year from 20 to 40 GJ to 25 to 45 GJ/y. We have not come across any estimates of energy requirements for cows needed to maintain the system or cows that may be in excess of this number for cultural reasons. As a placeholder, we may assume that this is the same order of magnitude as the energy needed for young non-working animals – about 5 GJ/y per working animal. This number obviously needs to be firmed up or revised based on data and analysis.

In sum, the total energy input per working animal per year based on the above analysis is 30 to 50 GJ/y.

Part 2: Energy outputs

Here we take up the issue of energy outputs and efficiency of the draft animals individually and of the draft animal system as a whole. We also take approximate account of the energy recovered in the dung and reused as fertilizer or as a source of energy.

A typical bullock in South Asia is capable of producing about 300 to 400 watts of continuous power (about one-half horsepower) (Makhijani and Poole 1975, table 2-1). It is capable of several times this effort for a short period. On annual basis, the actual average power output is likely to be considerably below the capacity of the animal for continuous work, because animals work on light loads for a considerable portion of the time.

A thousand hours of work per year (about 6 hours per day for about 175 days), and 250 watts of average output, is about the maximum that such an animal will provide in energy output per year (Rao 1984, 541).[2] Under these assumptions, the annual output of energy amounts to 250 kilowatt hours or 0.9 gigajoules (GJ). This is *a practical upper limit* for the annual energy output of an average bullock.[3] Given that animals often do not have adequate feed and may work less than 175 days per year, a range of energy output per year may be taken as 0.5 to 1 GJ.

To get the upper limit of efficiency estimates, we take the input to be 20 GJ per animal per year, the lower limit of our estimates for energy intake (see Table 18.2). About 25 percent of the input energy can be collected as dung and used as fuel, so that the net energy input is about 15 gigajoules. For output at the higher end of the range of 0.9 gigajoules, we get an estimate of the efficiency of draft animals of 6 percent. If we ignore dung recovery, then the efficiency would be 4.5 percent. This is about the upper limit of a range of efficiencies which one might calculate for draft animal use in agriculture.[4]

The efficiency estimates of the system of draft animals are lower when the overall energy inputs are taken into account. Taking credit for dung used as fuel, the overall energy inputs are in the 25 to 45 GJ/y range; the outputs are in the 0.5 to 1 GJ/y range. This gives an efficiency range of 1 to 4 percent.

Finally, we note that while the total power on farms has gone up by about a factor of four, the total installed draft animal power has stayed about the same – range of 17 to 20 gigawatts (Singh 2006, 101–103).

Table 18.3 shows estimates of the contributions of various sources of energy in South Asian countries. As noted above, there is considerable uncertainty about energy intake per draft animal. We have used a range of 20 to 40 GJ per animal per year for feed requirements. Only direct food intake of draft animals is included in Table 18.3. We do not have updated data for all four countries.

Table 18.3 shows a wide variation among South Asian countries. In Nepal, the overwhelming majority of energy use (about 85 percent) consists of traditional domestic fuels like firewood and of draft animal feed. In India, traditional energy, including draft animals is about 30 percent.

With the exception of Nepal, the average per person energy use shown in Table 18.3 is not representative of rural people, and especially not of farming families in South Asia. Almost all traditional fuels and draft animal energy are used in rural areas, while most of the modern energy is consumed in urban areas.

Table 18.4 shows estimates of fuel use in rural areas on the approximate assumptions that 20 percent of modern fuels, 80 percent of traditional fuels, and all draft animal energy is used in rural areas. Table 18.5 shows the same data on the basis of energy use per person of the rural population.

Table 18.3 Per person energy use in South Asian countries, 2009, GJ/y

	Modern	Traditional fuels	Draft animals, low	Draft animals, high	Low total	High total
Bangladesh	6.3	2.5	0.8	1.7	9.6	10.4
India	19.8	6.5	1.4	2.7	27.7	29.0
Nepal	2.6	13.8	2.2	4.5	18.7	20.9
Pakistan	13.7	7.2	1.9	3.7	22.7	24.6

Source: IEA (2014)

Table 18.4 Rural energy use, total in petajoules/y and percent

	Modern energy PJ/y	Traditional fuels, PJ/y	Draft animal energy, (mean estimate) PJ/y	Total traditional plus draft animals, PJ/y	Total rural energy use, PJ/y	% traditional energy, including draft animals
Bangladesh	188	296	185	481	669	72%
India	4,712	6,191	2,430	8,621	13,333	65%
Nepal	14	293	89	382	396	97%
Pakistan	465	983	473	1,457	1,922	76%

Table 18.5 Rural energy use per person, GJ/y

	Per person modern energy GJ/y	Per person traditional fuel use GJ/y	Per person draft animal energy, GJ/y	Total per person energy use, GJ/y	% energy use draft animals	% traditional fuels plus draft animals
Bangladesh	1.7	2.7	1.7	6.1	28%	72%
India	5.6	7.4	2.9	15.9	18%	65%
Nepal	0.6	13.0	4.0	17.6	23%	97%
Pakistan	4.1	8.8	4.2	17.1	25%	76%

It is clear from Tables 18.4 and 18.5 that traditional energy forms predominate in rural areas of South Asia, most of all in Nepal. But even in India, where modern fuel use is the highest, traditional fuels and draft animal input energy account for almost two-thirds of all rural energy use.

Part 3: Land requirements for draft animals

The feed for draft animals comes from five sources:

1 Crop residues
2 Fodder grown on grasslands, grazing on grasslands and uncultivated marginal lands, such as hillsides
3 Grazing on fields which are fallow during the dry season
4 Fodder produced from trees and from forest areas generally
5 Grain: this is a small proportion of the total.

There is great uncertainty about the relative magnitude of these sources. J.K. Parikh has used an assumption that 25–30 percent of the energy requirements of draft animals come from grazing for Bangladesh (1988, 346). Some of this grazing occurs on cattle owners' land that is fallow during the dry season. However, much or most grazing may take place on common grasslands that have soils too poor to sustain the cultivation of crops.

We can make an order of magnitude estimate of the amount of uncultivated land involved in grazing draft cattle using available data from India. The middle estimate of the total feed for draft animals in India is in the range about 2,400 PJ/y. The total number of cattle is four times the number of draft animals (according to the assumptions used here to derive the numbers of draft animals).

Since grazing requirements of non-working cattle tend to be considerably lower than those for draft animals, the feed requirements for all cattle can be estimated as being on the order of 4,800 to 7,200 PJ/y. If we assume that one-fourth of the feed requirements come from grazing in fields and that half of these grazing requirements come from grazing on lands other than fields (including common lands), then the energy requirements met from land that serves as pasture can be estimated.

These assumptions lead to an estimate of energy needs from pastures of 600 to 900 PJ/y. Marginal lands, such as those on which cattle graze, are areas of low productivity. Assuming a figure of one ton of dry matter per hectare per year (which may be on the high side) and an energy value of 13 gigajoules per ton, we get an estimate of the amount of pasture land, including marginal land, needed to meet the energy requirements on the order of 50 to 70 million hectares (rounded).

The actual uncertainty is larger than indicated by the 50 to 70 million hectare range. However, the permanent pasture land in India is just a fraction of this area – about 12 million hectares, but the "other" category, including waste land, was about 49 million hectares (Makhijani 1990, table 9). A great deal of the land classified under this "other" category is truly waste land with little or no production; or it is marginal, uncultivable land that may provide some food for ruminants, but is unlikely to be productive at the assumed one ton of dry matter rate. Thus, while land in the other category may be used for grazing, the number of animals it could sustain even at a marginal level would be much smaller than that in our calculations. Or, conversely, the amount of land required to provide the 25 percent of the feed requirements would have to be considerably larger.

Much of the land needed for grazing is likely classified as "forests and woodland," which amounted to almost 70 million hectares in India in 2009 (FAO 2013, table 4). In India, as in Pakistan and Bangladesh, much of the land in the "forest" category is not dense forest; a considerable portion may actually serve functions such as grazing and even cultivation of food crops.

In conclusion, the total land available for pasture as such appears to be considerably short of the requirements, if one-fourth of the caloric requirements are assumed to come from this source. One may infer that a considerable amount of land in the "other" and "forests and woodland" categories are being used as grazing land.

In addition, if cattle are inadequately fed, this reduces the power availability for agriculture. It may also reduce the efficiency of the use of cattle in agriculture, since more of the energy intake is used for basic metabolic upkeep. This shortage of mechanical power, in part due to the unavailability of feed, is long-standing. What Marvin Harris noted in 1966, that cattle are fed largely according to season – on grass in the rainy season and half-starved in the dry season – still largely holds true today (Harris 1966, 55).

These facts have great bearing not only on agricultural policy, but also on other aspects of rural energy production and use. The land used for grazing and fodder production is often marginal land that could not sustain crop production, but may very well be suited to the planting of woodlots for fuelwood production. It is possible that such woodlots could serve the joint purposes of fuelwood and fodder supply.

Given the disparity between available grazing land and feed requirements, we may infer that it is likely that there are serious shortages of feed and hence of mechanical power for agriculture, especially at peak periods when adequate nutrition is required for good performance.

Part 4: Machines v. cattle

The draft animal versus farm machines issue has been a much-debated question but the debate has proceeded in the absence of any overall assessment of mechanical energy and land requirements for draft animals.

Let us first consider the advantages and disadvantages of draft animals. First, they reproduce and do not require large capital outlays if an appropriate stock of animals is maintained. Second, they provide cow-dung as fuel (or return nutrients to the soil), milk, meat, and leather. Third, they are flexible in that they can be used for many different purposes such as ploughing, threshing, irrigation, and transportation. Fourth, they can be obtained in small unit sizes (in terms of power per unit), a big consideration for small farmers. Fifth, they are not dependent on external supplies of fuel, so decreasing the risk in fuel cost is minimized. Sixth, they largely involve non-monetized energy sources, and use non-monetized labor that is even available in the off-season. Finally, they can provide peak power at several times the average power over short periods.

Yet the principal advantages of draft animals can accrue only to farmers already possessing cattle and an adequate amount of cultivated land to provide fodder and off-season grazing land. Initial capital outlays for acquiring cattle are substantial, and their maintenance can involve considerable monetary costs if the farmer does not possess enough land to produce the required fodder. Even in those cases where farmers do have cattle, their numbers frequently fall short of meeting the needs of present cropping intensity, much less increasing it.

One indicator of the difficulties of small farmers in acquiring sufficient draft power is the fact that in South Asia, the draft cattle population has been practically static, while human population and food requirements are increasing, creating the necessity of higher productivity per unit of land. Draft animal power in India has been static over about three decades; in contrast, machine power has increased rapidly and has provided the main energy to enable substantial increases in food production (Singh 2006, 101, 105).

The poor overall efficiency of draft animals and the substantial land requirements for maintaining them are largely responsible for the shortage of draft power in land-scarce situations. Of course, these shortages affect those who have small parcels of land more severely. This raises the question of a role for farm machinery for small farmers and others who need to increase mechanical energy inputs to agriculture but are restrained by the expense of feed or by shortages of fodder or grazing land.

The efficiency of modern energy use in farm machines is typically an order of magnitude greater than farm animals, even under conditions in the rural Third World where electricity distribution losses tend to be high and where machines tend to be old and inefficient.

But average efficiency does not tell the whole story. The system of draft animals exists and is the mainstay of agriculture in South Asia. Thus, a crucial question is: what is the marginal efficiency of feed? In other words, given that feed is insufficient, how much could energy output be expanded by increasing the quality and quantity of feed during the peak agricultural season?

Experimental work done at the Centre for Tropical Veterinary Medicine in Edinburgh, Scotland, indicates that the marginal efficiency of feed for an animal doing heavy work is about 18 percent (Lawrence and Smith 1988, 51).[5] In this calculation, energy intakes during non-working hours and non-working days are ignored. Thus, the output resulting from additional high-quality feed to existing animals can be obtained at marginal efficiencies comparable to farm machines. This indicates that the expansion of traction energy output by increasing feed availability to existing animals should be a much higher priority than expansion of energy output from draft animals by increasing animal population. This approach also reduces methane emissions per unit of useful energy output.

This addresses, to some extent, the problem of the poor peasant who does have some draft animals. However, it still begs the question of where the additional feed is to come from, especially if it is to be high-quality feed. It also leaves out the problems of those who have no animals, or where draft power is seriously inadequate for traction power, for irrigation, or for compressing work at peak time into fewer days to enable double cropping.

Let us first consider some aspects of farm machines before we address these issues. The difficulties with modern energy sources are well known. Farm machines require considerable monetary investment and are usually much larger than animals, though it is possible and often desirable to reduce the size of machinery. That is, while draft animal systems can be acquired half horsepower at a time, the smallest machines are typically several horsepower or even several dozen horsepower. It should be noted, however, that for specific applications, the price of horsepower of machines could be considerably lower than for draft animals. The price of oil is uncertain, and electricity is typically unreliable. In contrast, the exigencies of agriculture demand application of energy inputs at precise times.

Despite these disadvantages, modern energy sources have some powerful advantages: high efficiency and low land requirements at the point of use. The scarcity of grazing land and fodder means that modern energy sources can be used to increase agricultural productivity, especially for poor peasants who do not currently have adequate draft power and for those who need additional power for increasing cropping intensity and land productivity per crop.

Animals and farm machines can be used as supplements in a number of ways. Farm machines may be beneficial for farmers who do not have farm animals or can produce crop residues in excess of their animals' requirements. This would alleviate shortages of grazing land and of fodder for farmers who have larger numbers of farm animals, providing a reinforcing increase of energy output for this group as well. Moreover, shortages of adequate feed limit the cultivation of high-quality feed. The use of farm machines can substantially increase the total amount of draft power available in areas where such needs cannot be met by improvements in output per animals or modest increases in animal population.

The use of farm machines can also reduce peak labor requirements and therefore enable increases of cropping intensity.

An optimum strategy might be a mix of increasing feed for existing animals and increasing mechanization. The latter is occurring; the former has yet to receive due consideration in agricultural and energy policy.

Part 5: Looking forward

In truth, most poor farmers do not have the option of increasing draft animal power or acquiring machines and the fuel to run them. For them, the high cost of diesel fuel and the unreliable supply of electricity are major hurdles to making agriculture more productive and efficient in the manner that better-off farmers have been able to accomplish in the last several decades. But two developments, one dating back to the 1940s and the other much more recent, provide hope for a new path:

- The method of "natural agriculture" developed by Masanobu Fukuoka in Japan over many decades. He was able to dispense with chemical fertilizers and pesticides, machines, and even farm animals and still achieve very high productivity of land and reasonably high productivity of labor (Fukuoka 2001).
- The dramatic decline in the cost of solar photovoltaic panels that has made solar-generated electricity competitive with diesel-generated electricity and even diesel machines used for mechanical power functions such as irrigation.

We will consider each of these in turn.

Fukuoka's "natural agriculture"

Fukuoka was one of the pioneers of modern organic agriculture. He invented (or perhaps reinvented) agriculture with minimal and only natural inputs. The most unusual and important input was local knowledge acquired by observation of nature and the decision to work with it. The traditional "two crops per year system" in Fukuoka's area, which utilized careful planning and many people working together, allowed farmers to grow a crop of rice and a winter crop each year in the same field for centuries without reducing the fertility of the soil (Fukuoka 2001, xxvi). The traditional method involved a large amount of human labor as well as animal energy. In modern agriculture, machines would serve as substitutes for the animals and the chemical fertilizers, pesticides, and weedicides would be added inputs.

Fukuoka dispensed with all that, utilizing all natural materials and paying close attention to features of local ecosystems, especially rainfall. Despite this, Mr. Fukuoka harvested between 18 and 22 bushels (1,100 to 1,300 pounds) of rice per quarter acre (Fukuoka 2001, xxvii).

These are astonishing results. The mean yield of 1,200 pounds per quarter acre translates to over 5,400 kilograms per hectare (kg/ha). The average rice yield in India in 2010 was 3,400 kg/ha (FAO 2013, 160). While the Fukuoka farm produced 60 percent more rice, the net income would increase even more because Fukuoka eliminated most monetized inputs. Further, in contrast to land with chemical inputs, Fukuoka's land improved over the decades.

Fukuoka's methods have been tried in various places around the world, including in India. The Indian experiment over many years dispensed with chemical inputs and machines. It reduced but did not eliminate draft animals. The vagaries of rainfall made some irrigation necessary. But after some years, the land improved, the yields increased, and the farm that had not been profitable for decades began to have a surplus (Fukuoka 2001, preface by Pratap Agarwal).

While Fukuoka's book, *One-Straw Revolution*, does not discuss climate issues, natural farming raises a number of important and interesting possibilities for protecting climate by mitigating emissions. Almost all emissions of methane from rice cultivation are from rice fields where flooding is used for weed control. The mean emission rate is about half a metric ton per hectare with a range of one-sixth to one metric ton (Rev. 1996 IPCC Guidelines). South Asia has about 60 million hectares under rice cultivation (see Table 18.1), with most of it being under wet cultivation. The methane emissions would amount to 10 million to 60 million metric tons. The carbon dioxide (CO_2) equivalent amount depends on the average time used. On a 20-year averaging time, the range of emissions would be 800 million to 5 billion metric tons of CO_2. On the basis of 100-year average, these values would be 250 million to 1.5 billion metric tons of CO_2 eq.

The no-till feature of natural farming may also substantially increase the carbon stored in the soil, especially since the straw is returned to the fields as mulch. Implementing a no-till agriculture approach as opposed to conventional methods would result in decreased CO_2 (a greenhouse gas) emissions. The principal benefits of no-till agriculture are soil protection and increased soil carbon sequestration, which allow crops to remove carbon dioxide from the atmosphere during photosynthesis; non-harvested residues are then converted into soil organic matter (Marland et al. 2003; Huggins and Reganold 2008). However, this is not a technically established fact for Fukuoka's natural agriculture. If it proves to be correct, the method could lay a claim to credits for reducing atmospheric CO_2 concentrations; these credits would be applied to the promotion of natural farming.

Given that natural farming is in its essence oriented to local ecology, considerable effort will be needed to establish the patterns of cultivation to reach successful high yields. It should also be noted that the examples given by *One-Straw Revolution* indicate that considerable time and effort is needed before the benefits of the method are realized. This could mean a period of lost productivity that farmers, especially the poor among them, could not afford.

In sum, natural farming is one way in which the problem of insufficient draft power could be mitigated while addressing the need for increased agricultural productivity. However, the upfront effort and investment required will be considerable and significant uncertainties will remain until the method is more widely tested.

Renewable energy

Community-scale solar installations currently cost $2 per watt or less. In the high insolation circumstances of South Asia, the cost of solar electricity would, at that price, be roughly half of that generated using diesel as a fuel. Solar electricity cannot compete with heavily subsidized rural electricity; however, grid supply is often erratic, while the needs for power in agriculture are very time sensitive.

The government of India has embarked on a large program to replace diesel- and grid-powered pumps with solar-powered ones. As an initial step, it aims to install 200,000 solar pumps, with the eventual aim of replacing 26 million existing pumps. Replacing grid-powered electric pumps with solar-powered ones would also relieve pressure on the centralized electricity system, which suffers large transmission and distribution losses and chronic power supply deficits. Both diesel and electricity for irrigation are heavily subsidized – to the tune of $6 billion per year (Pearson and Nagarajan 2014). At $2 per watt, the subsidies alone would allow for 3,000 megawatts of solar electricity to be installed in rural areas each year. For comparison, the total cumulative installed solar power capacity in India as of March 2014 was just 2,647 megawatts. Of course, solar-powered pumps would not need electricity or fuel subsidies for at least two decades after that. This calculation does not include the cost of the pumps.

Solar-powered pumps have been in use for some time; the testimony of one Indian farmer provides an interesting glimpse of the benefits. With grid electricity, he often had to work at night, because that is when electricity was available, creating risks such as that of snake bites. Now he can work in the daytime and "without the fuel costs of a diesel generator" (Pearson and Nagarajan 2014).

Combining natural agriculture and renewable energy

Natural farming can, in principle, eliminate a large fraction or even most draft power requirements; renewable energy can supply the energy requirements where irrigation is needed. If solar electricity is used, the power can be used for a variety of other purposes when it is not used for irrigation. It is very difficult to evaluate the overall impact of various combinations of natural farming and renewable energy in the absence of demonstration projects. But we know that each method can work on its own. Together, they could form a significant part of the answer to the energy needs of poor farmers who cannot afford machines and even of wealthier farmers who could increase net revenues.

We should note here that Fukuoka's own approach to natural farming included a spiritual element. His farming was connected to an overall philosophy of living (Fukuoka 2001, 110). The adoption of this worldview by hundreds of millions of farmers in the near future is unlikely, given the enormous institutional and financial interests in the present arrangements. The question therefore arises whether Fukuoka's methods can be implemented through a framework of ecological agriculture that is scientifically oriented. It would not be a large-scale agriculture, since its essence depends on a deep understanding of local ecosystems and how agriculture can fit into and work with them. On the face of it, using machines such as tractors may be incompatible with no-till practices that depend on broadcasting seeds. A considerable amount of research and demonstration is needed to explore the ways in which Fukuoka's approach can be adapted to widespread adoption and to integration of renewable energy to supplement or complement human labor.

We should note here that the features of improving the soil, reducing energy use, and increasing yields (relative to present yields that poor farmers get) could add up to a resilient agriculture that presents the opportunity for adaptation to climate change, given that the present mode of agriculture may well be imperiled by the increasing frequency and intensity of extreme climate events. This would be in addition to the mitigation feature of reducing emissions. This collection of benefits indicates that considerable investment in exploring the potential of Fukuoka's methods is warranted. But nothing definitive can be said until serious efforts are made to widen the scope of the demonstrations to the economic and other vicissitudes in which middle income and subsistence farmers find themselves today.

Part 6: Conclusions

First, considerable effort needs to be put into expanding the amount of information and to improving existing estimates. Improvements are needed not only for average national statistics, but even more importantly for energy requirements for specific regions. Conditions vary enormously from one region to the next, by crop type, by varieties of soil, by topography and so on. Therefore, regional data are essential for sound policy here as with other traditional energy sources.

Second, if conventional agricultural policy is followed, increased use of farm machines is needed for: (i) small farms which have shortages of installed mechanical power which cannot be overcome by improving draft animal feed quantity and quality; (ii) irrigation; and (iii) meeting power needs not met by draft animals so as to enable increases in cropping intensity. This conclusion arises in large measure from two considerations. For one, the efficiency of modern energy sources is far higher than that of the draft animal system. Second, the constraints on land are so severe that it is unlikely that most small farmers could meet the mechanical power requirements by increasing draft animal population.

Third, our analysis indicates that the following should be investigated in more detail to address the problem of increasing the mechanical energy from draft animals on South Asian farms:

1   Increases in feed quantity and quality for existing draft animals, especially during the peak season to take advantage of the high ratio of marginal

efficiency to average efficiency of draft animals (in contrast to machines where this ratio is close to 1).

2   Increases in commercial production of high-quality feed for existing draft animals, so as to enable the efficiency increases.

3   Plantation of mixed forests to increase land availability for fodder production in ways compatible with other needs.

Fourth, a combination of natural farming complemented by solar and wind energy may provide an answer on numerous fronts, including reducing the need for draft animal or petroleum-fueled power. It could also be more accessible to cash-poor farmers since it requires far fewer continuing inputs.

The extent to which renewable energy and specifically solar energy can be combined with natural agriculture is unclear at present. But it is a matter of great importance, since it could address the needs of hundreds of millions of farmers who now must live with low labor and land productivity. It could also provide significant climate mitigation and adaptation benefits. The potential benefits indicate that substantial resources should be devoted to demonstrations of natural agriculture combined with renewable energy as well as to developing the intellectual foundation of the system that would lay out how it is to be adapted and applied.

Notes

1   For example, those studied by the Centre for Tropical Veterinary Medicine in Scotland.

2   Rao estimates that "[b]ullocks are used for about 176 days per year on bullock-operated farms and for about 80 days per year on tractorised farms" (1984, 541).

3   The power output may be somewhat higher in northwestern India and Pakistan where animals tend to be larger than the average (Lawrence and Stibbards 1990, 32).

4   Our estimate of efficiency is comparable to that provided by other sources. On a daily basis Rao estimates the efficiency of an adequately fed bullock as 8.6 percent (1984, 542). Taking into account that bullocks work about 175 days per year, this gives an efficiency estimate of 4 percent on an annual basis. Lawrence and Smith estimated the efficiency of draft animals on a daily basis as 10 percent, which gives an annual efficiency estimate of about 5 percent (1988, 51).

5   The authors cite measurements showing that during heavy work the energy inputs were 36,226 kilojoules and the output 6,400 kilojoules, for an efficiency of 17.7 percent. Light work required about as much energy input, but the output was only 1,955 kilojoules, for an efficiency of 5.4 percent.

References

Food and Agriculture Organization of the United Nations. 2013. *FAO Statistical Yearbook 2013*. Rome: FAO.

Fukuoka, Masanobu. 2001. *The One-Straw Revolution*. 8th edn. Translated by Chris Pearce, Tsune Kurosawa, and Larry Korn. India: Rodale Press.

Harris, Marvin. 1966. "The Cultural Ecology of India's Sacred Cattle." *Current Anthropology* 7, no. 1 (February): 51–66.

Huggins, D.R. and J.P. Reganold. 2008. "No-Till: the Quiet Revolution." *Scientific American* 299, no. 1: 70–77.

Intergovernmental Panel on Climate Change. 1996. *Revised 1996 IPCC Guidelines for National Greenhouse Gas Inventories.* Accessed December 1, 2014. www.ipcc-nggip. iges.or.jp/public/gl/invs6c.html.

Lawrence, Peter and Anthony Smith. 1988. "A Better Beast of Burden." *New Scientist* 118, April 21: 49–53.

Lawrence, P.R., and R.J. Stibbards. 1990. "The Energy Costs of Walking, Carrying, and Pulling Loads on Flat Surfaces by Brahman Cattle and Swamp Buffalo." *Animal Production* 50: 29–39.

Makhijani, Arjun. 1990. *Draft Power in South Asian Foodgrain Production: Analysis of the Problem and Suggestions for Policy.* Maryland: Institute for Energy and Environmental Research.

Makhijani, Arjun, and Alan Poole. 1975. *Energy and Agriculture in the Third World.* Cambridge: Ballinger.

Marland, Gregg, Tristam O. West, Bernhard Schlamadinger, and Lorenza Canella. 2003. "Managing Soil Organic Carbon in Agriculture: the Net Effect on Greenhouse Gas Emissions." *Tellus: Series B* 55, no. 2: 613–621.

Parikh, J.K. 1988. "Bangladesh: Agriculture, Biomass, and Environment." In: *Sustainable Development in Agriculture* 361–379. Dordrecht: Kluwer.

Pearson, Natalie Obiko and Ganesh Nagarajan. 2014. "Solar Water Pumps Wean Farmers From India's Archaic Grid." *Bloomberg,* February 8. Accessed December 1, 2014. www.bloomberg.com/news/2014-02-07/solar-water-pumps-wean-farmers-from-india-s-archaic-grid.html.

Pimentel, David. 2009. "Energy Inputs in Food Crop Production in Developing and Developed Nations." *Energies,* 2: 1–24.

Rao, A.R. 1984. "The Bioenergetics of Bullock Power." *Energy* 9, no. 6.

Singh, Gyanendra. 2006. "Estimation of Mechnisation Index and its Impact on Production and Economic Factors – A Case Study in India." *Biosystems Engineering* 93, no. 1: 99–106.

19 Sustainable energy for ICT

Sarah Revi Sterling and Matt Hulse

Introduction

In the summer of 2013, President Barack Obama announced the "Power Africa" initiative, intended to bring 10,000 megawatts of electricity to 20 million Africans by 2020. This US Agency for International Development (USAID) and Overseas Private Investment Corporation (OPIC) led effort would double access to power across sub-Saharan Africa. The initiative expects to leverage a nine billion dollar commitment from the private sector in addition to a seven billion dollar promise from the US government (White House 2013). The Obama administration is not the only entity concerned with bringing electricity – and thus progress – to developing regions. The World Bank Group's Energy Sector released their global priorities for electrification in the publication *Toward a Sustainable Energy Future for All*. A central focus for the publication discusses the role of energy in poverty alleviation, the need for hybrid energy solutions, and for financial support models resulting in doubled access to sustainable energy by 2030 (World Bank n.d.). By 2020, the Africa-European Union Energy Partnership intends to build 10,000 MW plus of new hydropower, wind, and solar facilities, and supply energy services to roughly 100 million Africans, for health, education, water, and communication initiatives (United Nations Foundation 2013). The Chinese government has pledged 20 billion dollars in energy infrastructure loans to "help African countries turn resource endowment into development strength" (Stoddard 2013).

With over six billion cellular phone subscriptions at the end of 2012 (ITU 2012), it seems that a subsection of the 10,000 MW of power will be used to power information and communication technology, via base stations or household chargers. Africa's mobile phone market is currently the fastest growing in the world (Agence France-Presse 2013), with the number of new mobile connections growing 30 percent annually over the last decade (GSMA 2011), with Latin American and Asian cell phone markets seeing similar growth (Epstein 2013). Mobile phones are considered an indisputable lifeline in the international development industry and are at the core of a growing subfield of development: Information and Communication Technology for Development, or ICTD. The GSM Association (GSMA), an alliance of worldwide mobile operators, predicates its ICTD work on the statement that "mobile is the predominant infrastructure in emerging markets," and a "transformative technology" to bring socioeconomic development to underserved communities around the world (GSMA 2013). Development economist and pundit Jeffrey Sachs states that mobile phones have "been a gift for development" and a major mechanism for achieving the UN Millennium Development Goals, covered in more detail in this chapter (Ford 2013).

This chapter demonstrates the inter-relatedness of energy and Information and Communication Technology (ICT) expansion in developing communities in the energy and ICT sectors. Energy access is a condition for technology use, and ICT is the mechanism driving and expanding the reach of energy systems. Energy and ICT push the adoption of each other and cannot be discussed as separate development sectors, although they are often treated as such in conferences and academic literature.

The relationship between ICT and energy

While cell phone markets in developing regions may be exploding, there are approximately 600 million people, mostly in rural communities, without access to the grid and consequently no local option to charge their cell phones (SunFunder 2014). Across the world, people rely on marketplaces and vendors, often hours away, to charge their phones and other electronic devices. Charging stations, powered by car batteries, are ubiquitous in commercial centers, but recharging costs can be prohibitive at USD 0.25 a charge. Mobile phones are easily stolen at charging centers, and car batteries need to be recharged. Often seen carrying their batteries from town to town, car-battery vendors not only charge phones, but also charge the batteries themselves. In one rural community where we have conducted research, car batteries were rolled into the embers of cooking fires to "boost" the battery to extend its charge. This was done within sight of a power line that runs along the Nairobi–Mombasa road; however, rural electrification was not an option. Even where power lines were present, a rural Kenyan household would pay around USD 500 for initial connection to the grid, not counting monthly use (Wyche and Murphy 2013). Kenya's grid, while woefully inadequate to meet demand, is not unusual for other African countries. Rwanda, one of the most technologically progressive countries in Africa – and one of the smallest – is stymied by electrical outages and a near-complete absence of electricity access outside the capital, Kigali – 95 percent of the country's 8.4 million people do not have electricity (Goering 2006). At the time of this research, the capital of Uganda, Kampala, was "electrified" every other day as a way to offset pressures on hydropower systems affected by drought and low water levels at Lake Victoria, the source of power for the major Nalubaale and Kiira Power Stations (Rugumayo 2006). This leads to the ongoing use of dangerous and unhealthy lighting options.

Rwanda and Uganda are not alone. The estimated economic value of power outages in Africa amounts to as much as 2 percent of GDP, and 6–16 percent in lost turnover for enterprises (Baziliana et al. 2011). The energy sector in sub-Saharan Africa is characterized not only by poor reliability of supply, but high electricity costs (approximately USD 0.50/kWh) and insufficient generation capacity to meet rapidly rising demand – a demand that will see a growth of 652 million more people by 2030. With current inadequate electrical grids, it is hard to imagine that expanding access to national energy systems is going to be effective and affordable (Baziliana et al. 2011).

Given the lag of conventional infrastructure development and the lack of cost-efficient electrical and communications systems it is evident that alternative energy sources must be used to facilitate access and use of ICT. The average revenue per user (ARPU) for infrastructure services, particularly telecommunications systems, is slow to increase in developing countries, and thus there is little incentive to improve services, especially when remote sites require high transport and operational costs (Fehske et al. 2011). As such, the market for alternative energy sources is immense. While providers such as MTN and Alcatel-Lucent plan to increase their number of Remote Base Stations (RBS), the transceivers connecting wireless devices to one another and with the larger network, there were a mere 300 solar-powered RBS sites globally in 2009 (Fehske et al. 2011). Basic electrical and communications infrastructure is absent and even as-yet-unplanned in many rural communities, making it near impossible to leverage technology to advance the Millennium Development Goals or any economic sector growth. According to Herselman in a review of ICT in rural South Africa, "without electricity, no industrial development beyond cottage industry can be started, and no agricultural activity beyond subsistence can be maintained. Without telecommunications, no current market information is available, and know-how cannot be transferred" (Herselman 2003).

These are not encouraging facts given both the global high demand for electricity and enthusiasm for Information and Communication Technology for Development (ICTD). Building on the ICT sector, ICTD focuses on the role of technology in poverty alleviation. A broad range of international or community development sectors have ICTD interventions, some of the more well known including the One Laptop Per Child initiative that began at MIT, and M-PESA, a mobile banking system that 75 percent of Kenyans use, although it was originally created for Bottom of the Pyramid (BOP) microloan recipients. General Electric has donated hundreds of millions of dollars to programs like its "India Rural Electrification Program," which provides energy and ICT infrastructure. GE's long-running program "Developing Health Globally" links ICT and telecom providers to health care worldwide (Lahiri and Pal 2009).

There are thousands upon thousands of mobile- and Internet-based health, education, agriculture, livelihood, and civil service applications. The major concern with so many ICTD systems and applications is sustainability; often, efforts do not take interoperability, scalability, financial viability, and upgrade and end-of-life considerations into design and deployment. Uganda has banned all new mobile health based projects, and South Africa has limited any new electronic health record systems until there is evidence that technology-based health (often called mHealth for *mobile*) interventions deliver on their promises of health and efficacy (Rosenberg 2013). Given the estimated spending on ICTD in developing countries at USD 840 billion (Heeks 2009) and the opening of industrial research labs (Microsoft, Google, and IBM among others) in developing countries, all with a focus on ICTD, these bans seem to be the only canaries in the coal mine, although critical reports have started to cast doubt on software and hardware as development panaceas (Rosenberg 2013; Setzer 2009).

ICTD and the Millennium Development Goals

It is important to ground this chapter in a brief historical context of ICTD. The combination of rapid technology innovation and adoption has led to exuberance about the transformative potential of technology in poverty alleviation, but also debates about "hope versus hype." When the United Nations Millennium Development Goals, or MDGs, were announced following the Millennium Summit of the United Nations in 2000, the ICTD community found support within the larger international development industry. There was much enthusiasm that ICT could help the MDGs "leapfrog" impediments to achieving the goals by enabling digital services that could bypass traditional development avenues. Much in the same way, many developing countries made the leap from no telecommunications infrastructure directly to cellular without first installing copper cables and following the industrial trajectories of developed countries. While mobile phones are one form of ICT, it is essential to remember that "Africa is not just a mobile-first continent – it is mobile only" (Shapshak 2012), thus the emphasis on mobile technologies as the leading ICT in developing regions.

While there are thousands of ICTD successes and failures to point to, the role of ICT in the UN Millennium Development Goals cannot be ignored. According to Denis Gilhooly, member of the United Nations ICT Task Force and United Nations Millennium Project,

> There is already a strong correlation between ICTs and the MDGs based on a mutually shared objective: namely, the efficient, scalable, affordable and pervasive delivery of goods, services and information flows between people, governments and firms. In addition, while ICT cuts across all seven Millennium Declaration goals targeted at specific objectives in promoting development and improving people's daily livelihoods – including income poverty, food security, healthcare, education, gender equity and environment – it also appears as an MDG itself within the eighth goal, "Develop global partnerships for development", focused on how to achieve the objectives themselves.
>
> (Gilhooly 2005)

ICT is specifically incorporated in *Goal 8: Develop a Global Partnership for Development*, under Target 18: "In cooperation with the private sector, make available the benefits of new technologies, especially information and communications technologies" (United Nations n.d.). Indicators for this target include cellular phone and broadband subscription numbers. To support these metrics, the Market Information and Statistics Unit of the International Telecommunications Union created the Digital Access Index (DAI) in 2003, a composite measure to track progress towards Target 18. The DAI is comprised of four vectors to determine a country's ability to support ICT access: infrastructure, affordability, knowledge, and quality and actual usage of ICT – and to compare themselves to other countries (ITU 2003a). ICT advocates also cited the utility of technology in achieving the other seven MDGs. The IUT's World Telecommunication Development Report 2003 published Table 19.1 to demonstrate the potential role ICT could play in contributing to global development (ITU 2003b).

Table 19.1 ICTs to support Millennium Development Goals

Goal/target	Role of ICTs
1. Eradicate extreme poverty and hunger *Halve, between 1990 and 2015, the proportion of people whose income is less than one dollar a day. Halve, between 1990 and 2015, the proportion of people who suffer from hunger.*	Increase access to market information and reduce transaction costs for poor farmers and traders. Increase efficiency, competitiveness and market access of developing country firms. Enhance ability of developing countries to participate in the global economy and to exploit comparative advantage in factor costs (particularly skilled labor).
2. Achieve universal primary education *Ensure that, by 2015, children everywhere, boys and girls alike, will be able to complete a full course of primary schooling*	Increase supply of trained teachers through ICT-enhanced and distance training of teachers and networks that link teachers to their colleagues. Improve the efficiency and effectiveness of education ministries and related bodies through strategic application of technologies and ICT-enabled skill development. Broaden availability of quality educational materials/resources through ICTs.
3. Promote gender equality and empower women	Deliver educational and literacy programs specifically targeted to poor girls and women using appropriate technologies. Influence public opinion on gender equality through information or communication programs using a range of ICTs.

Table 19.1 continued

Goal/target	Role of ICTs
4. Reduce child mortality 5. Improve maternal health 6. Combat HIV/AIDS, malaria, and other diseases *Reduce infant and child mortality rates by two-thirds between 1990 and 2015* *Reduce maternal mortality rates by three-quarters between 1990 and 2015* *Provide access to all who need reproductive health services by 2015*	Enhance delivery of basic and in-service training for health workers. Increase monitoring and information-sharing on disease and famine. Increase access of rural caregivers to specialist support and remote diagnosis. Increase access to reproductive health information, including information on AIDS prevention, through locally appropriate content in local languages.
7. Ensure environmental sustainability *Implement national strategies for sustainable development by 2005 so as to reverse the loss of environmental resources by 2015* *Halve, by 2015, the proportion of people without sustainable access to safe drinking water.* *Have achieved, by 2020, a significant improvement in the lives of at least 100 million slum dwellers.*	Remote sensing technologies and communications networks permit more effective monitoring, resource management, mitigation of environmental risks. Increase access to/awareness of sustainable development strategies, in areas such as agriculture, sanitation and water management, mining, etc. Greater transparency and monitoring of environmental abuses/enforcement of environmental regulations. Facilitate knowledge exchange and networking among policymakers, practitioners and advocacy groups.

Given the "accelerator" capabilities of ICT across development sectors, there has been a widespread call to "mainstream" ICT – to make it a dominant, normative component in international development. In a United Nations ICT Taskforce report, authors report:

> Since the MDGs are the key framework for development cooperation, there is a need to mainstream ICTs in all forms of assistance, including sector-wide approaches (SWAPs), and poverty reduction strategies (PRS) based budget support. Mainstreaming means that evaluating the ICT potential and incorporating ICT options is not left to the knowledge and preferences of individual desk officers (of government, donors or other organisations) but is built in at an institutional level.
>
> (Gerster and Zimmermann 2005)

For every case study that claims mobile phones *are* in themselves forms of development, or critical to any development success, there is a study that critiques the socioeconomic costs of mobile phones. Jeffrey Sachs has often argued that the mobile phone is the single most transformative development technology. At the same time, there is data that shows people in his Millennium Development villages spend money on mobile phone minutes rather than school fees, and that the price of mobile use feeds into poverty (Diga 2008; *Economist* 2012). The World Bank states that for every 10 percent increase of mobile phone penetration in a country, there is a corresponding 0.81 percent economic growth (Qiang 2009); there are also critiques of such studies that claim causal relationships between mobile penetration and growth rates, without accounting for other socioeconomic factors (Burrell and Toyama 2009).

ICTD has faced critical concern that the application of technology to development issues would not bring about the seamless "leapfrogging" prevalent in many hopeful predictions. According to a UN Task Force, "ICTs offer the developing world the opportunity to 'leapfrog' several stages of development by use of "frontier" technologies that are more practical, environmentally sound and less expensive" than traditional technologies (United Nations ICT Task Force 2003) This report states that "Countries such as Gabon, Uganda, Morocco, the Ivory Coast, Rwanda, and Tanzania have used ICT innovation to bypass barriers linked with fixed line infrastructure, making a quantum leap into the Information Age." The same task force also warns that, while mainstreaming is necessary, "further analysis of where ICT can have the greatest impact is required, rendering it even more important to develop appropriate tools for measuring, reporting and analyzing the real impact of ICT on development" (United Nations ICT Task Force 2005). Many ICTD interventions have a low success rate (Dodson et al. 2013), and researchers have stated that technology innovation "remains weak in forming convincing arguments about IT-enabled socioeconomic development" (Avgerou 2010). More critiques about the potential for ICT to "solve" development have emerged in reputable journals and conferences, as well as the blogosphere, with ICTD practitioners lamenting that the rush towards using mobile phones for development may be a bad idea in its current trajectory, due to the nature of "monolithic, tightly linked industries" that impede affordable access, no matter how useful mobile phones might be in individual pilot efforts (Song 2011).

However, the World Bank's *InfoDev* unit, concerned with "growing uneasiness about the lack of detailed information on the implementation of these (ICTD) projects, and rigorous evaluation of their impact," commissioned a 17-project assessment of ICTDs in MDG-focused projects around the world (InfoDev 2003). The findings and recommendations overall affirmed that technology contributed to the MDGs (InfoDev 2003). More recently, Linda Raftree of PATH presented a macro-level view of how ICT can support the MDGs. She posits that, through thoughtful and comprehensive application, ICT can: (1) engage children and youth in the development process; (2) identify resources and mapping patterns for better decision-making; (3) pull in quick information to guide further investigation, response, or advocacy, pushing out information for targeted actions; (4) support accountability and transparency; and (5) improve municipal services and information management. As Raftree states, "The MDGs are lofty, but informed local community participation and ownership is key in efforts to reach them and in ensuring that marginalized populations can also be included" (Raftree 2010).

Case studies: energy and ICTD collaborations

Travelers to the Global South are often impressed with the solar power infrastructure they come across in their travels, which seems to make sense given the number of sun-filled days. Experience has shown that most of the photovoltaic systems deployed in economically depressed communities are either not working to their full potential, or are not working at all. Many installations are left over from past development efforts that have long since been abandoned or turned over to the community for care and maintenance – albeit without a plan or funding for such upkeep. While solar panels and photovoltaic-powered devices offer a promise of cleaner, less expensive energy, they are often priced out of the range of poor communities. Many regions have long rainy seasons that lessen the utility of photovoltaic systems; panels are heavy and prone to damage and theft for resale value. Wiring is delicate, and battery life declines with use and over-use.

Meanwhile, kerosene, car batteries, and expensive diesel fuel provide sub-optimal energy. Yet the growing demand for energy to provide lighting and electricity means that many households rely on dirty, dangerous energy sources. The desire to educate one's children is a driving force behind many of the combination energy solutions being introduced in developing communities. Websites for products show children in remote locations doing homework on laptops and mobile phones under the light of a bulb or LED. With so much attention on the need to close the digital divide as a poverty alleviation strategy, just as many websites show farmers getting crop and market information on their mobile phones – phones that need to be charged at the end of the day. The growth of agriculture mobile applications, iCow, MFarm, Digital Green, Interactive Voice Recording (IVR) call-in hotlines, and educational mobile games for farmers such as Farm Game and Market Game, place heavier demands on cell phone use and charging than text or voice usage. Energy requirements increase with phone sophistication as well.

In a 2010 *Popular Mechanics* article, Michael Lin, founder of Fenix International, asks, "There are 500 million cellphone users worldwide who don't have access to the grid, so how in the world are they charging their phones?" (Goodier 2010). The ReadySet battery, by Fenix International, is a lead-acid battery encased in a heavy plastic enclosure that is meant to withstand the rough conditions of many regions. While it can be charged from a conventional grid, it can also be charged by a bicycle pedal generator or solar panel. In turn, ReadySet can charge phones, LED lanterns, and other small household devices. With the capacity to charge ten phones at a time, Fenix International is partnering with various savings and credit cooperatives to offer ReadySets on credit to spur micro-entrepreneurial efforts so that people with the charger can become a "micro-utility" (SunFunder 2013).

EGG-energy (Engineering Global Growth) in Tanzania aims to close the electricity gap. Stating that 80 percent of Tanzanians live within 5 km of the power grid, but 90 percent of that population does not have electricity, EGG-energy rents a "brick" of rechargeable batteries for a subscription fee, which lasts a household about 5–7 days. The batteries are returned for newly charged ones. The subscription service comes with an initial home visit by an EGG-energy technician to ensure the installation is correct and safely wired into the home. There are add-on applications that subscribers can buy optimized for use by the EGG system, including low-power lights, radios, and mobile chargers. The application sales model aims to incentivize the local creating of innovative add-on product (EGG-energy 2013).

M-KOPA is a service built on top of the highly successful mobile payment platform M-PESA, which enjoys near 75 percent adoption in Kenya. M-PESA and many copycat systems allow people to use their mobile phones not only to pay for items on the spot, but pre-pay for products and services, including energy credit strategies. M-KOPA is a home solar power system for lighting and charging that has a 2G mobile phone chipset embedded in it, so that users can pay for electricity as they go from their M-PESA mobile money accounts (Locke 2012). The M-KOPA system is comprised of a 4-watt rooftop solar panel, a control box, three lamps, and a mobile phone charger. The system is manufactured by the US company d.light. After a down payment, customers pay 40 Kenyan Shillings a day until the unit is paid off, and then the electricity is free. According to M-KOPA researchers, Kenyan families spend approximately 50 shillings a day on kerosene to light their homes and mobile phone charging stations (McGregor 2012). Other M-KOPA offerings in the wings include similar pay-as-you-go irrigation systems and appliances.

Azuri Technologies, of England, is a pre-paid solar power system, which uses SMS scratch cards that are entered into a mobile phone, returning a one-time code then entered into the Indigo unit. Each code provides electricity for two lamps and a cell phone charger for a week. Like M-KOPA, once the installation is paid off, the system operates for free. There are different levels of packages available for upgraded electrification services once the original cost is paid, enabling customers to make the jump from 3 watts of electricity to 10, 40, and finally 80 for small home businesses. The same model of SMS scratch cards, codes to unlock electrical access, and eventual ownership are also being tried in India by Simpa Networks and Mera Gao Power, both in rural India (Fehrenbacher 2013).

In addition to the efforts listed, myriad universities and development organizations have deployed energy interventions that do not make news in the trade press. Most of these efforts focus on mini- and micro-grids and are often coupled with ICTD initiatives including education or health. Many of these efforts involve photovoltaic energy generation to run an Internet lab in a school or offer a few hours of electricity and connectivity. Many of these installations face significant challenges often not integrated into the system design. Human behavior is also one of the major contributors to system downtime and power outages. In one community profiled in Buskens and Webb's "African Women and ICTs," a microgrid intended for school computer use was often overloaded with demand for electricity for radios, sewing machines, and small stoves. While stove use was "prohibited" on the system, and led to inevitable brown outs, women kept trying to use them to see if they would not cause outages, even though they were explicitly told not to plug in appliances (Muller cited in Buskens and Webb 2014). Likewise, in similar cases, outlets for school computers were being used for refrigerators, radios, and televisions. A DC-only charger for the computers was necessary to preserve electricity for the intended recipients (Hosman and Baikie 2013).

Another trend in ICTD and energy that involves human efforts directly demonstrates the sometimes difficult tradeoffs between energy and connectivity. In international development, there has long been the use of foot-powered treadle pumps for irrigation, which are made by several manufacturers globally, as well as other so-called "sweat equity" projects where people provide the labor to power devices or tools. In ICTD, there are several energy-producing systems that rely on human power. Idea Forge, an Indian company, has introduced the Roto Charger in local markets, a rotary device that requires one minute of rotation to supply three minutes of cell phone talk time. While this may not seem like much to ask, a thirty-minute conversation is only possible after ten minutes of physical effort. A study by Wyche and Murphy compares two commercial manual mobile phone charging products, the FreePlay Companion hand-crank powered cell phone charger (which comes with an integrated LED flashlight and radio) and the Nokia DC-14 Bicycle Charger Kit. While popular at first, the novelty of needing to exert energy to get energy soon wore thin. The FreePlay Companion devices studied had a 50 percent hardware failure rate within a few months (Wyche and Murphy 2013).

The Nokia system requires a sustained speed and time effort that is hard to achieve on congested or ill-maintained roads – people simply cannot maintain 10 km/hour and thus the system did not fit their lives and lifestyles (Wyche and Murphy 2013). This is not to say that "sweat equity" is not always inappropriate and in some cases necessary. There are several foot-based manual treadle pump manufactures that have been deemed successful by such organizations as the UN Food and Agriculture Organization (Kay and Brabben 2000). It is critical to remind implementers that using humans as an energy source comes with a set of serious considerations.

Energy innovation for ICT

Global demand for energy is constantly on the rise. Communities worldwide are facing exponentially increasing demand on their infrastructure. Energy access initiatives extend beyond global electrification, and the development of renewable sources as core pillars of a sustainable energy future. ICT technologies increasingly play a critical role in providing electricity, monitoring its usage, and optimizing service delivery. Technology not only fosters access, it increases efficiency. Using less energy to provide the same performance for services is an evolutionary necessity in energy.

Up to this point, this chapter has focused primarily on the energy requirements and challenges of ICTD. Innovation in the energy sector will be the gating or enabling factor in ICTD growth; yet, the energy sector itself is ripe with technological and policy challenges that are pushing the envelope of what is possible, from smart grids to Powerline energy. While smart grids often have been dismissed for use in the developing world due to cost and complexity, some countries have started to take the leap towards a smarter grid. South Africa's state-owned power utility Eskom has developed and deployed a hybrid smart grid that leverages its own communication system at the operational level. This deployment uses Internet Protocol (IP) packet communications to help with energy demand and metering, correct for system variability, and better utilizes renewable energy sources in order to reduce the current demand on coal.

Other research in smart grid technology focuses on "Smart and Just Grids" – systems that help electrification reach the poorest and most rural without economic or service marginalization (Baziliana et al. 2011). "Just Grids" are smart grids that support "equitable and inclusive global, economic and social development" while also supporting ecological goals (Baziliana et al. 2011). While smart grids in developing regions can mitigate loss reduction, manage peak demand loads, and increase the quality of energy supply, the "Just Grid" movement also highlights the ability of smart grids to mitigate climate change. This is a source of economic stress and migration, creates jobs in areas where job prospects outside major urban centers are scarce, and creates entrepreneurial spin-off opportunities for additional local income generation.

Looking ahead: the energy and ICT roadmap

Over 90 percent of urban growth is occurring in the developing world, adding an estimated 70 million new residents to urban areas each year. Tomorrow's energy and ICT infrastructure must be co-developed with the goal to meet new challenges that will inevitably involve energy as well as Information and Communication Technologies. ICT efforts continue to grow and connect development ideas, practitioners, and customers, as well as challenge traditional information networks by expanding access while decreasing latency in information exchange. As the world continues to connect, combining the relatively young practices of smart grids, open-data, and demand-side management, ICT will continue to positively influence access to electricity, increase service reliability, and provide development infrastructure.

The fostering of a strengthened partnership between ICT and energy development sectors will be critical in influencing the energy efficiency agenda as well as supporting the growing numbers of technology devices and services that are not only being exported to developing regions, but being produced within them. Successful application of energy-data projects will require knowledge sharing, cross-support, and leadership between leaders. ICT-enabled energy efforts will have a strong impact on the structure, operations, and management of the dozens of public administration agencies and industries involved in service delivery, from health care to transportation, from employment to social assistance, from water to energy supply and other human needs.

References

Agence France-Presse. 2013. "Mobile phone makers eye Africa as world's fastest-growing market." Accessed August 28, 2013. www.rawstory.com/rs/2013/02/27/mobile-phone-makers-eye-africa-as-worlds-fastest-growing-market/

Avgerou, C. 2010. "Discourses on ICT and development." *Information Technology for International Development*. 6(3): 1–18. Cambridge: MIT Press.

Baziliana, M. et al. 2011. "Smart and just grids: opportunities for sub-Saharan Africa." *Imperial College, London*. 2011. Accessed May 12, 2013. https://workspace.imperial.ac.uk/energyfutureslab/Public/Smart%20or%20Just%20Grid%20final_08Feb11.pdf.

Burrell, J., and Toyama, K. 2009. "What constitutes good ICTD research?" *Information Technology and International Development* 5(3): 82–94. Cambridge: MIT Press.

Buskens, I. and Webb, A. 2014. *Women and ICT in Africa and the Middle East.* London: Zed Books.

Diga, K. 2008. "Mobile cell phones and poverty reduction: technology spending patterns and poverty level change among households in Uganda." *Workshop on the Role of Mobile Technologies in Fostering Social Development*. Sao Paulo, Brazil. June 2008.

Dodson, L., Sterling, S.R., and Bennett, J. 2013. "Considering failure: eight Years of ITID research." *Information Technology for International Development* 9 (2): 19–34. Cambridge: MIT Press.

Economist. 2012. "Kenya's mobile telephones: vital for the poor." Online edition November 10. Accessed January 30 2013. www.economist.com/news/middle-east-and-africa/21566022-report-describes-sacrifices-poor-make-keep-mobile-phone-vital.

EGG-energy. 2013. Home page. Accessed June 15, 2013. http://egg-energy.com/.

Epstein, Z. 2013. "Sizing up the mobile handset market in Q2." Accessed August 15, 2013. http://bgr.com/2013/07/26/mobile-phone-market-share-q2-2013/.

Fehrenbacher, K. 2013. "British startup Azuri hits velocity with pay-as-you-go solar cell phone tech in Africa." Accessed August 10, 2013. http://gigaom.com/2013/07/17/british-startup-azuri-hits-velocity-with-pay-as-you-go-solar-cell-phone-tech-in-africa/.

Fehske, A., Fettweis, G., Malmodin, J. and Biczok, G. 2011. "The global footprint of mobile communications: the ecological and economic perspective." *IEEE Communications Magazine* 49(8): 55–62.

Ford, L. 2013. "Mobile phones have been a gift for development, says Jeffrey Sachs". *Guardian Online*. Accessed September 28, 2013. www.theguardian.com/global-development/poverty-matters/2013/sep/23/mobile-phones-development-jeffrey-sachs.

Gerster, R. and Zimmermann, S. 2005. "Up-scaling pro-poor ICT policies and practices." *Creating an Enabling Environment: Toward the Millennium Development Goals: Proceedings of the Berlin Global Forum of the United Nations ICT Task Force.* United Nations ICT Task Force.

Gilhooly, D. 2005. "Innovation and investment: information and communication technologies and the Millennium Development Goals." *Creating an Enabling*

Environment: Toward the Millennium Development Goals: Proceedings of the Berlin Global Forum of the United Nations ICT Task Force. United Nations ICT Task Force.

Goering, L. 2006. "Small generator aims to empower Africans." *Chicago Tribune online.* Accessed June 1, 2013. http://articles.chicagotribune.com/2006-07-03/news/0607030150_1_cell-phones-weza-battery.

Goodier, R. 2010. "How a new battery could charge Rural Africa." *Popular Mechanics.* Accessed June ,5 2013. www.popularmechanics.com/technology/engineering/gonzo/how-a-new-battery-could-change-rural-africa.

GSMA. 2011. *African Mobile Observatory 2011.* Accessed June 1, 2013. www.gsma.com/publicapolicy/wp-content/uploads/2012/04/africamobileobservatory2011-1.pdf.

GSMA. 2013. *Mobile for Development Overview.* Accessed August 10, 2013. www.gsma.com/mobilefordevelopment/overview.

Heeks, R. 2009. *Worldwide Expenditure on ICT4D.* Accessed September 20, 2010. http://ict4dblog.wordpress.com/2009/04/06/worldwide-expenditure-on-ict4d/.

Herselman, M.E. 2003. "ICT in rural areas in South Africa: various case studies." *Proceedings of the 2003 Informing Science + IT Education Conference.* Pori, Finland.

Hosman, L. and Baikie, B. 2013. "Solar-powered cloud computing datacenters." *IEEE IT Professional,* 15(2): 15–21.

InfoDev. 2003. "ICT for development: contributing to the Millennium Development Goals." Accessed May 1 2013. www.infodev.org/articles/ict-development-contributing-millennium-development-goals.

ITU. 2003a. *Digital Access Index.* Accessed May ,5 2013. www.itu.int/ITU-D/ict/dai/.

ITU. 2003b. *Telecommunication Development Report 2003.* Accessed January 30, 2013. www.itu.int/ITU-D/ict/publications/wtdr_03/.

ITU. 2012. "Measuring the information society." Accessed June ,1 2013. www.itu.int/dms_pub/itu-d/opb/ind/D-IND-ICTOI-2012-SUM-PDF-E.pdf

Kay, M. and Brabben, T. 2000. "Treadle pumps for irrigation in Africa." *Knowledge Synthesis Report No.1.* United Nations Food and Agricultural Organization.

Lahiri, A. and Pal, J. 2009. "ICTD in CSR: changing priorities in international development funding." *Proceedings of Second Annual SIG GlobDev Workshop,* Phoenix, AZ.

Locke, C. 2012. "The challenge of sustaining App entrepreneurs." *Innovations* 7(4): 21–26. Accessed August 2, 2013. www.omidyar.com/pdf/Innovations.pdf.

McGregor, S. 2012. "Kenya's M-KOPA gives phone-loans to put solar power in reach." *Bloomberg Online.* Accessed June 15, 2013. www.bloomberg.com/news/2012-10-04/kenya-s-m-kopa-offers-cheaper-solar-power-to-off-grid-villages.html.

Qiang, C. 2009. "Mobile telephony: a transformational tool for growth and development." *Proparco.* Accessed May 20, 2014. www.proparco.fr/jahia/webdav/site/proparco/shared/PORTAILS/Secteur_prive_developpement/PDF/SPD4/SPD4_Christine_Zhen_Wei_Qiang_uk.pdf.

Raftree, L. 2010. "5 ways ICTs can support the MDGs." Accessed May 21 2014. http://lindaraftree.com/2010/09/17/5-ways-icts-can-support-the-mdgs/.

Rosenberg, T. 2013. "The benefits of mobile health, on hold." *New York Times online.* Accessed March 15 2013. http://opinionator.blogs.nytimes.com/2013/03/13/the-benefits-of-mobile-health-on-hold/.

Rugumayo, A. 2006. "The electricity supply situation in Uganda and future direction." *Proceedings of the 2006 13 Sustainable and Energy Efficient Building in Africa workshops.* Accessed July 20, 2013. http://public.ises.org/PREA/3_Papers/16_ElectricitySupplySituationUganda_Rugumayo.pdf.

Setzer, V. 2009. "A critical view of the 'one laptop per child' project." *Proceedings of the IFIP World Conference on Computers in Education*. Bento Gonçalves, Brazil.

Shapshak, T. 2012. "Africa not just a mobile-first continent – it's mobile only." *CNN Online*. Accessed May 20, 2014. www.cnn.com/2012/10/04/tech/mobile/africa-mobile-opinion.

Song, S. 2011. "Three reasons why M4D may be bad for development." Accessed on May 3, 2013. http://manypossibilities.net/2011/11/why-m4d-may-ddardbe-bad-for-development/.

Stoddard, E. 2013. "Africa investment – can Obama's Africa Power plan hold a candle to China?" *Reuters online*. Accessed September 29, 2013. www.reuters.com/article/2013/07/02/africa-investment-idUSL5N0F821520130702.

SunFunder. 2013. "Solar powered phone charging: a game changer for rural farmers." Accessed June 1, 2013. http://blog.sunfunder.com/post/52911013639/solar-powered-phone-charging-a-game-changer-for-rural.

SunFunder. 2014. "SunFunder joins Power Africa's 'Beyond the Grid' initiative as a founding partner." Accessed on April 30, 2015. http://blog.sunfunder.com/post/87827909056/sunfunder-joins-power-africas-beyond-the-grid.

United Nations. n.d. *Goal 8: Develop a Global Partnership for Development*. Accessed May 11, 2013. www.un.org/millenniumgoals/global.shtml.

United Nations Foundation. 2103. "2020 targets of the Africa-EU Energy Partnership (AEEP)." Accessed September 3, 2013. www.sustainableenergyforall.org/actions-commitments/commitments/single/2020-targets-of-the-africa-eu-energy-partnership-aeep.

United Nations ICT Task Force. 2003. *Tools for Development: Using Information and Communications Technology to Achieve the Millennium Development Goals*. United Nations ICT Task Force.

United Nations ICT Task Force. 2005. *Creating an Enabling Environment: Toward the Millennium Development Goals: Proceedings of the Berlin Global Forum of the United Nations ICT Task Force*. United Nations ICT Task Force.

White House. 2013. *Fact Sheet: Power Africa*. Accessed August 15, 2013. www.whitehouse.gov/the-press-office/2013/06/30/fact-sheet-power-africa.

World Bank. n.d. *Toward a Sustainable Energy Future for All*. Accessed August 16, 2013. www.worldbank.org/content/dam/Worldbank/document/SDN/energy-2013-0281-2.pdf.

Wyche, S. and Murphy, L. 2013. "Powering the cellphone revolution: findings from mobile phone charging trials in off-grid Kenya." *Proceedings of the 2013 ACM SIGCHI Conference on Computer Human Interaction*. Paris, France. April 2013.

20 Model laws on cooking

Lakshman Guruswamy

Introduction to model laws

This chapter will canvass two premises of the concept of law.[1] The first premise is that law, as a normative construct, can and should respond to social problems. Second, the law can respond to a problem only after it understands the nature of the problem and the challenges raised by it. The jurisprudential foundation will be first discussed, followed by the bio-physical problem of indoor air pollution.

Jurisprudential foundation

The jurisprudential thesis underlying the assertion that law should be used for societal problems solving is that law is an "instrument," "tool," "machine," or "engine" for serving or achieving social objectives. Law in this sense is being used to achieve practical aims (Summers 1982, 20). Robert Summers, in discussing the use of the machinery of law to achieve socio-economic objectives, saw it as a particularly American form of legal theory spawned by theorists like Oliver Wendall Holmes, Roscoe Pound, John Dewey, John Chipman Gray, Karl Llewellyn, Walter Wheeler Cook, and Felix Cohen (Summers 1980, 11). Summers coined the phrase "pragmatic instrumentalism" to describe how these theorists created a theory of adjudication focused on the role of judges in shaping and molding law to achieve social means or ends (Moore 2000, 194). The pragmatic instrumentalists relied on courts as instruments or machinery for achieving their goals. Their attention was focused on what judges did when interpreting the written form of a legal text. They contended that judges engaged in interpreting a legal text to ascertain its true meaning cannot do so by a simple parsing of the plain words. Instead, judges should consider and construct their meaning in light of the context of the law as illustrated, for example, by the goals or objectives it was meant to achieve.

In addition to the pragmatic instrumentalists who charted a new theory of adjudication, and "a distinctive type of legal theorizing" (Summers 1982, 11) in the United States, the use of law for social engineering could trace its jurisprudential lineage to the British philosopher, jurist, and social reformer Jeremy Bentham (1748–1832). Bentham, perhaps best known for his utilitarian philosophy, was also an English legal revolutionary who re-drew the contours of law. In doing so, he recreated a vastly expanded domain of law in a way that had not hitherto been done. He called for a complete, comprehensive, and integrated legislative re-envisioning of the existing system of law and government. Bentham expounded the necessity for a new "form" of law that laid the foundations of a reformed society, in which the "whole of the community's social system no less than the community's legal system was to be located analytically within the province of legislation" (Lieberman 1989, 286). Moreover, he explicated how to design, draft, implement, and generally use legislation to achieve the social objectives of the new kind of law he was calling for. The vast and theretofore shapeless socio-political expanse envisioned by him had to be legislatively mapped and populated, and become part of a great reformist enterprise based on a new concept of law.

One of the major problems he confronted was that such an expansive concept of law flew in the face of the reality of his day, as reflected in the existing corpus of law, received orthodoxy, and extant legal theory. Legal theory of his time envisioned a minimalist state. For example, William Blackstone, in his masterly *Commentaries on the Laws of England*, first published in 1766, provided a complete overview of English law (Sprague 1915). Sections II and III of Blackstone's Introduction to the *Commentaries on the Laws of England*, "Of the Study, Nature and Extent of the Laws of England," offers an overview of the law in general. In this authoritative account of English law, Blackstone divides law into the unwritten common law and written or statutory law. According to Blackstone, "[s]tatutes are either declaratory of the common law or remedial of some defects therein" (Sprague 1915, 15). What is evident is that Blackstone treats the common law as the primary source of law and confines legislation to either declaring the common law or remedying its defects. While the latter conclusion may be interpreted as resembling the expanded concept of legislation called for by Bentham, that is not the case. It is clear from Blackstone's account of written (or statutory) law that it occupied an adjectival or minor position below the foundational common or unwritten law. Common law was primarily, and nearly exclusively, concerned about the private rights of person and property (Sprague 1915, 10). By contrast, the statute book (statutory law), except in the area of criminal law, was almost bereft of public law such as administrative law, regulation, or governance which dominates the statutory law of the modern state. Blackstone did not favor the creation of a new and expanded realm of statutory law, and neither did Edmund Burke, who was pleased that "the laws reach but a very little," and vehemently disliked expanding its province (Burke 1770, 69, 99). Law, clearly, was not seen as an instrument of social engineering as understood in today's terminology.

Bentham set his face to liberating existing law "from the trammels of authority and ancestor-wisdom on the field of law" and of modernizing the legal system through legislation (Bentham 1776). Bentham expressed contempt for the common law and English judges, and scorned at the idea that the judiciary could transform law and society (Bentham 1789). A distinguished English judge sums up Bentham's low opinion of judges and lawyers: "As he saw it, in order to enrich themselves, lawyers ensured that English civil justice was '... a system of exquisitely contrived chicanery which maximises delay and denial of justice'" (Neuberger 2011). In Bentham's view, the task of re-designing law was a task for the legislature, not the judges.

The following model laws are based on Bentham's jurisprudence. These model laws serve as blueprints for legislation that could be enacted by the legislatures of developed and developing countries. Legislatures enacting these model laws will be adopting problem solving legislative solutions that clearly fall within the compass of law envisioned by Bentham. For example, the model laws for developing countries are actually blueprints for the national dissemination of clean cookstoves. The model laws for developed countries provide a blueprint to legislate support for combating these issues through the common but differentiated responsibility for sustainable development accepted by developed countries.

Nations adopting these model laws, or variations of them, will be using the machinery of law to achieve the compelling social objectives of combating indoor air pollution, global warming, and gender inequality. Indoor air pollution is a global problem that could be addressed within the broad global enterprise of law that encompasses public international, as well as national, laws. The model laws can be adopted by municipal or national legislatures, as contrasted to treaties or other international law modalities. The main reasons for adopting such a course require explanation.

Public international law is the law that creates and governs inter-state (or country) relationships, primarily through contracts called treaties, conventions, and protocols. It is possible for the 192 countries in the world to come together as a lawmaking assembly with a goal of negotiating and drafting a global treaty to address issues associated with unsafe cooking. Under the international law approach, it is also possible for countries to enter into regional multilateral treaties restricted to regions identified by trade or geo-politics. It is also possible for one country to enter into a bilateral agreement with another country. Given the ubiquitous nature of indoor air pollution and the need for both developed and developing country responses, it is reasonable to conclude that the situation calls for a multilateral global treaty.

However, it is becoming evident that large international treaties or conventions of this kind are exceptionally difficult to negotiate, and even more resistant to implementation and enforcement. Despite tremendous diplomatic and media backing, the faltering negotiation of a treaty to replace the Kyoto Protocol is strong evidence of this retreat from large multilateral treaties. Additionally, the search for consensus between different legal traditions is not an easy enterprise. Some commentators claim that international treaties and conventions are drafted as multi-cultural compromises between different schemes of law. Consequently, they could be perceived as possessing less merit than the individual legal systems from which they have been derived (Hobhouse 1990, 530–533). Furthermore, if the United Nations Framework Convention on Climate Change (UNFCCC) is an example, it takes over a decade to advance from a framework agreement setting out the agenda to the negotiation of protocols requiring collective and specified action (Guruswamy 2012, 215–216).

Another way of looking at legal answers to a global problem is through the lens of domestic or municipal legal systems. The numerous developing countries actually afflicted by these issues could respond through domestic or municipal laws. Many of these countries have other laws dealing with differing aspects of pollution and hazardous waste. These laws are enacted by national legislatures, and the present model laws seek to expand the ambit of national pollution and health legislation by providing blueprint legislation on cooking that could be adapted and incorporated into domestic law.

A model law is a legislative text that is recommended to states for enactment as part of their national or state law, or tribal governance regimes. The United Nations Commission on International Trade Law describes model laws as "appropriate" vehicles "for modernization and harmonization of national laws when it is expected that States will wish or need to make adjustments to the text (...) to accommodate local requirements." The Commission further states that this flexibility makes a model law "potentially easier to negotiate," though it emphasizes that states are encouraged to change as little text as possible in adopting model laws (UN Commission on International Trade Law 2013, 14–15).

At a fundamental level, model laws use legislation to generate private and public action. For example, the model law uses a needs assessment to find out what people want and need; encourage different civil society entities, from entrepreneurs and business entities to non-governmental organizations ("NGOs"), to invest and trade in the fabrication, sale, and servicing of cookstoves; ensure that standards are set and enforced; and solicit international aid and assistance, while establishing a systematic use of monitoring that will ensure that standards are actually being met.

The socio-biological problem

The model law responds to specific problems of indoor air pollution, and in order to do so successfully it needs to understand the nature of the problem it confronts. This requires an appreciation of the socio-biological problem. The problem we are examining, implicated by biomass cooking, is the deadly phenomenon of indoor air pollution. The deadly impacts of indoor air pollution caused by biomass have been described in the Introduction to the volume.

Harmful cooking also implicates global climate change. It is well proven that the black soot, or carbon, found in the smoke generated by burning biomass and kerosene is the second largest contributor to global warming (the first being carbon dioxide) (Ramnathan and Carmichael 2008; Service 2008).

We need new laws because existing law and administration is either non-existent or unable to address this challenge. In creating new laws, it behooves us to understand that law is an existing, established social mechanism grounded in reality, and that it must command the acquiescence of the peoples it governs. It is not an idealistic and aspirational code of conduct, removed from social reality and actual human behavior. It tries to change behavior, but should not engage in flights of idealistic fancy.

A good law must satisfy some basic criteria. To begin, the law should be based upon a correct identification and diagnosis of the problem or issue that it purports to address (Guruswamy 2007). The model laws published herein present sets of Findings, which help in meeting the criteria of correct diagnosis.

Next, following the correct diagnosis, laws "should embody prescriptions aimed at the core of the problem, and deal with the sources of the malady" (Guruswamy 2007). They should accurately target the sources, and the substantial remedies they prescribe should include methods of implementation and compliance. Where behavioral changes are necessary, the law should be directed toward eliciting them. As Bentham has pointed out, prescriptions are only good if they are actually carried out. In order to secure the implementation of its prescriptions, legislation should set up concrete institutions, whether governmental or private, and contain details where necessary as to how the law should be administered. In the model laws published herein, we have tried to institute some of these social mechanisms.

Another criterion is that the remedies and methods employed by a law "should have a demonstrably beneficial impact on the problem" and help move the country or international community "toward the practical attainment of its goals and objectives" (Guruswamy 2007, 175–176). The extent of its beneficial impact will depend on the degree to which a law that may contain an accurate diagnosis and good prescriptions actually changes behavior and benefits people. Consequently, the impact of a law will depend on the nature of its goals or objectives, its methods, and the extent to which it succeeds in changing behavior. That is why the model laws for developing countries require extensive and continuous monitoring, not just of cookstoves but also of human health and behavior.

The model laws are accompanied by commentaries or "guides to enactment" setting forth explanatory information to assist governments and legislators in using the text. The guides include, for example, information that would assist states in considering what, if any, provisions of the model law might have to be changed to take into account particular national circumstances. The commentaries also include relevant discussions from the working/drafting groups and matters not addressed in the text of the model law that may nevertheless be relevant to the subject matter of the model law.

Adoption of the model laws by a significant number of countries will draw national and international attention to the problems caused by the burning of biomass for cooking and use of kerosene for lighting and constitute an effective and much needed legal response to these problems.

Model law on Cookstoves for Developing Countries

A BILL To promote the development and deployment of clean cookstoves to save lives, improve livelihoods, empower women, and combat global warming by creating a thriving global market for clean, affordable, and efficient household cooking solutions, and for other purposes.

Be it enacted by the [legislative organ] of the [country] assembled,

Short Title

This Act may be cited as the ***Development and Dissemination of Clean Cookstoves:*** Act of [*year*].

Effective Date. This Act becomes effective on [*date*].

§1. Findings

(a) [*Name of country*] is a member of the community of nations that has accepted well-recognized principles of international law and policy establishing the right of developing countries to sustainable development.

(b) [*Name of country*] seeks to support sustainable development pertaining to energy poverty and access to safe and sustainable cooking technologies through this Act.

(c) According to the World Health Organization, approximately 3 billion people – nearly half of the world's population – cook their food over open fires or with inefficient, polluting, and unsafe cookstoves that use firewood, dung, or coal as fuel.

(d) Nearly 2 million people each year die prematurely from illnesses attributable to indoor air pollution resulting from inefficient, unsafe cookstoves. Indoor air pollution accounts for more deaths yearly than malaria, tuberculosis, or human immunodeficiency virus infection/acquired immunodeficiency syndrome (HIV/AIDS).

(e) [*N, number of people*] in [*name of country*] cook their food over open fires or with inefficient, polluting, and unsafe cookstoves that use firewood, dung, or coal as fuel.

(f) It is estimated that smoke from cooking accounts for nearly [*N, number*] deaths annually in [*name of country*], which is more than the deaths from malaria, tuberculosis, or human immunodeficiency virus infection/acquired immuno-deficiency syndrome (HIV/AIDS). [*N, number*] are sickened by the toxic smoke and [*N, number*] suffer burns annually from open fires or unsafe cookstoves. Smoke from these traditional cookstoves and open fires is associated with a number of chronic and acute diseases, including respiratory illnesses, such as pneumonia, heart disease, and cancer. Women and young children are affected disproportionately.

(g) Women and children disproportionately shoulder the burden of collecting and managing biomass fuel for cooking. As nearby fuel supplies dwindle, women are forced to go farther to find fuel to cook their families' meals. In some regions, women and girls risk rape and other forms of gender-based violence during the up to 20 hours per week they spend away from their communities gathering firewood.

(h) Recent studies show that black carbon created by biomass cookstoves significantly contributes to global warming and climate change. Black carbon emissions from residential cookstoves in developing countries account for an estimated 21 percent of the total global carbon inventory and mitigation of black carbon is a cost-effective way of addressing global warming.

(i) Clean cookstoves positively impact the quality of life and the environment by:

> (i) Freeing women and children to engage in educational and economic endeavors;
>
> (ii) Promoting gender equality and women's empowerment;
>
> (iii) Improving child and maternal health and safety;
>
> (iv) Advancing environmental stability by reducing reliance on biomass; and
>
> (v) Reducing contributions to global climate change.

§2. Policy

The House of Parliament hereby declares it is the national policy of [*name of country*] to:

(a) Appropriate financial resources towards the research and development of the most appropriate and sustainable energy technologies for improved cookstoves that advance the objectives of this Act in [*name of country*];

(b) Encourage the growth of a domestic cookstove manufacturing industry by supporting entrepreneurs through tax incentives, loans, and micro- and other forms of financing that advance the objectives of this Act;

(c) Standardize, test, and certify all cookstoves based on ambient and durability standards;

(d) Distribute cookstoves in a manner that emphasizes accessibility while encouraging the recipient to contribute to the cost in currency, exchange, and/ or sweat equity;

(e) Encourage community participation in financing, manufacturing, distributing, and promoting the objectives of this Act;

(f) Seek the assistance, expertise, guidance, and experience of non-governmental organizations (NGOs) and faith groups in all aspects of the implementation of the Act;

(g) Promote awareness and education about indoor air pollution;

(h) Promote the involvement of cookstove users, *inter alia*, in the research, design, development, manufacturing, distribution, monitoring, maintenance, evaluation, and marketing of cookstoves; and

(i) Conduct training on use and maintenance to cookstove users and community members.

§3. Definitions

For the purposes of this Act:

(a) "Administrator" means the Administrator of the Cookstoves for the Reduction of Energy Poverty Agency (CREPA).

(b) "Agency" means the CREPA.

(c) "Cookstove" refers to a cookstove that:

(i) Employs appropriate sustainable energy technologies; and

(ii) Has been prototypically demonstrated, tested, and certified as meeting the emission and durability standards set out in Section 4.

(d) "Certification" or "certified" refers to certification by an entity or organization authorized by the CREPA.

(e) "Local conditions" means the holistic assessment of economic factors (ability to pay), cultural factors (willingness to change cooking patterns and behavior), and social factors (who the primary decision-maker in the household is, who is affected most by indoor air pollution, and who the primary social agents in the community are).

(f) "Organization" means an entity other than a governmental body, which was established or organized for any purpose relevant to this Act. This term refers to, *inter alia*, a corporation, company, guild, association, partnership, NGO, faith-based organization, trust, or trade union.

(g) "Endangerment" means the exposure, whether consented, voluntary, knowing, or without consent and involuntary, of individuals to conditions harmful to their physical health or the misrepresentation that certain harmful effects will in fact be reduced or removed by the actors' conduct.

(h) "Micro-financing" refers to loans which are granted for design, production, marketing, distribution, sale, maintenance, and repair of cookstoves.

(i) "Sweat equity" refers to the labor, skill, goods, or community services offered by recipients, in part or in full, for cookstoves. Sweat equity shall be transferable among households. The following activities shall qualify as sweat equity under this Act:

(i) Labor provided in building or retrofitting cookstoves;

(ii) Transportation of materials for new or retrofitted cookstoves; and

(iii) Participation in public education and community outreach.

§4. National Minimum Standards and Certifications

(a) Indoor Ambient Air Quality Standards

The term "indoor ambient air quality standards" means airborne pollution measurements that do not exceed the following:

(i) For particulate matter of 10 μm (PM_{10}) –

(1) A 24-hour mean of 50 μg/m³; or

(2) An annual mean of 20 μg/m³.

(ii) For particulate matter of 2.5 μm ($PM_{2.5}$) –

(1) A 24-hour mean of 25 μg/m³; or

(2) An annual mean of 10 µg/m³.

(iii) For carbon monoxide (CO) –

(1) 100 mg/m³ during any 15-minute period and not more than 1 time per day;

(2) 35 mg/m³ during any 1-hour period and not more than 1 time per day;

(3) An 8-hour mean of 10 mg/m³; or

(4) A 24-hour mean of 7 mg/m³.

(iv) For nitrogen dioxide (NO_2) –

(1) A 1-hour mean of 200 µg/m³; or

(2) An annual mean of 40 µg/m³.

(b) Interim Standards

The Administrator, acting upon reasonable grounds, may determine that the standards in Subsection (a) above cannot be achieved, and s/he may create interim standards that improve existing air quality, even if they are unable to meet the standards in Subsection (a). Such interim standards may be in force for 2 years, provided they are no longer in force 5 years after the coming into force of this Act.

(c) Durability Standards

The Administrator shall establish minimum durability standards based on needs and conditions of the country, taking into account standards stipulated by the Global Alliance for Clean Cookstoves when available.

(d) Testing and Certification

(i) All new cookstoves and/or component parts, including combustion chambers, chimneys, and cooking tops sold and/or marketed under this Act in [*name of country*] shall be tested and certified.

(ii) Testing and certification will be undertaken by approved private, public, or NGO owned and operated laboratories. Certification will attest that the products are capable of achieving the ambient air quality and durability standards referred to in this Section.

(iii) The Administrator will approve such laboratories based on relevant criteria to be determined after a public hearing, and shall publicly announce and publicize such standards.

§5. Administrative Discretion

The Administrator, acting on reasonable grounds, which shall be determined after public hearing, may postpone and/or phase in the implementation of this and other provisions of the Act for a period that shall not exceed 5 years.

§6. Establishment of Agency

The Cookstoves for Reduction of Energy Poverty Agency (CREPA) is hereby established to implement the provisions of this Act. The Administrator of the Agency shall administer this statute by, *inter alia*:

(a) Conducting Needs Assessments and Developing Specifications

Within 120 days of the adoption of this Act, the CREPA shall deploy [N *(the number of provinces or sub-national governments)*] provincial assessment officers (PAOs), one in each of the country's [N] provinces. PAOs shall, in collaboration with [*name of appropriate NGO*] and local health personnel, conduct needs assessments that will identify and investigate:

(i) Types of fuel and cookstoves being used in their respective region for cooking;

(ii) Local exposure to indoor air pollution from existing cookstoves;

(iii) The needs and receptivity of the population to new cookstoves;

(iv) Possible cultural or geographical barriers to the adoption of new cookstoves;

(v) Environmental degradation and challenges to community;

(vi) The infrastructure of the areas assessed;

(vii) The financial status of the communities;

(viii) The high density of children; and

(ix) Provincial targets for the combustion efficiency of cookstoves, based on the minimum standards in Section 4(a) and local conditions.

(b) Cookstove Selection

CREPA, in collaboration with the Minister of Energy and the PAOs, will select cookstoves that culturally and economically suits the [*name of country*] and the type of biomass fuel used.

(c) Targeted Installation of Cookstoves – Pilot Projects

The PAOs, under the direction of the Administrator of CREPA, shall carry out pilot projects in each province, which can be replicated in the rest of the country for the purpose of identifying the challenges of creating a stove selection process, and implementing a national cookstove program. The communities selected for the pilot projects by the Agency shall be ones in which:

(i) Biomass is the sole method for cooking;

(ii) Surveys and Needs Assessments, which are carried out by the PAOs, reveal that a large majority in the community want to participate in the Pilot Project;

(iii) There are between 100 and 500 homes;

(iv) Individuals are willing and able to provide sweat equity, currency, or exchange for the cookstoves; and

(v) The population is demographically representative of the [*number of people in the country*] people who rely on biomass for cooking and are representative of the varying types of biomass fuel used in the region.

(d) Completion and Review of the Pilot Projects

(i) At least two Pilot Projects shall be completed within targeted communities for each province or biomass fuel type region before the widespread installation of cookstoves among the rest of the province population. The data revealed by each Pilot Project and the lessons learned shall be analyzed and reviewed in a Pilot Project Report.

(ii) If there is different fuel use or cooking methods in the province, separate Pilot Projects will be constructed and implemented in the areas to accurately determine the best clean cookstove.

§7. Implementation and Administration

(a) Implementation

The Administrator shall use the information revealed by the Pilot Projects to inform and implement this Act by:

(i) Consulting and collaborating, with the Ministers of (1) Health and Human Wellness, (2) Energy, (3) Environment & Natural Resources, (4) Education, and (5) Industry & Commerce, and within reasonable time constraints, receive their inputs.

(ii) Encouraging public participation in the implementation of the provisions of this Act, by incorporating:

(1) Notice and comment prior to the adoption of any major rules implementing the provisions of this Act, as governed by the [*name of country's administrative procedure act*];

(2) Open meetings whenever the CREPA has a quorum present for a meeting in which the CREPA discusses any regular business of the agency concerning this Act; and

(3) A community liaison in all aspects of implementation of the Act.

(iii) Where appropriate, seeking international aid and assistance in the form of technological assistance and expertise for monitoring and evaluation from, *inter alia*, intergovernmental organizations, other states, NGOs, faith-based organizations, corporations, private individuals, and charitable trusts.

(iv) Establishing a nationwide program to train the citizenry on the design, production, marketing, distribution, sale, maintenance, and repair of cookstoves.

(v) Using innovation, appropriate sustainable technologies, and/or techniques that provide greater economic benefits, all at a limited cost to the end-user.

(vi) Utilizing technologies and organizational methods, which have been successfully tried, tested, and demonstrated by other developing countries.

(vii) Using sweat equity or exchange as a method for paying for the cookstoves.

(viii) Using comprehensive, holistic, cross-sectorial planning to capture the complexity of the cookstove initiative.

(ix) Seeking to establish in-country networks for the design, manufacture, marketing, and technological assistance of the cookstoves.

(b) Strategic 5-Year National Cookstove Plan (5-Year Plan)

After a widespread, open, and public consultation process, the CREPA shall draw up renewable strategic 5-Year Plans with annual targets and objectives that shall be publicly announced and publicized. The first Plan shall be completed within one year of the coming into operation of this Act. Once a 5-Year Plan has been completed, the CREPA shall issue annual reports that are announced and publicized on the actions taken pursuant to the 5-Year Plan and the extent to which the targets or objectives have or have not been met. The annual reports will be reviewed annually by the Parliament of [*name of country*].

(c) Stimulate the Cookstoves Industry and Markets

The CREPA shall stimulate and encourage the creation of a robust domestic cookstove industry, by engaging, *inter alia*, in the following:

(i) Improving access to capital by providing tax incentives and loans and removing restrictions on foreign investment in the cookstove industry;

(ii) Establishing certification and standardization protocols for cookstove parts and equipment; and

(iii) Collaborating with the Ministry of Energy to disburse grants for research and development to qualified universities in [*name of country*], which are able to undertake research and development.

(d) Monitoring and Inspection

Through collaboration with PAOs, the Administrator shall, with immediate effect, begin the following activities towards implementation of this Act:

(i) *Assessment.* Quantitative monitoring of the ambient air quality of representative samples of existing homes before the installation of improved cookstoves.

(ii) *Post-Installation Air Quality Monitoring.* Quantitative monitoring of the ambient air quality of the homes referred to in Section 6(c) above after improved cookstoves are installed within the following time-frames:

- Phase 1 – within 1 year of installation;
- Phase 2 – within 18 months of installation;
- Phase 3 – within 3 years of installation; and
- Annual monitoring once every year, thereafter.

(iii) *Use Monitoring.* Inspecting installed cookstoves to ensure they are being used and are working properly.

(iv) *Reporting.* Submitting to Parliament a report (Administrators Report) on the findings of the monitoring and inspection efforts under this Section, 2 years after this Section comes into force and annually thereafter.

§8. Authorization and Appropriations

[*Appropriated amount (USD or national currency)*] shall be authorized and appropriated every year, beginning in 20[__], continuing for the next 5 years, and allocated as follows:

(a) [*Appropriated amount (USD or national currency)*] to the Administrator for the administrative costs of implementing this Act.

(b) [*Appropriated amount (USD or national currency)*] to a grant and loan mixed funding mechanism, which is administered by the CREPA and encourages entrepreneurship and creates new markets by stimulating the large-scale manufacture and distribution of improved cookstoves.

(c) No grant shall be made under this Section unless 75 percent of the products, materials, and supplies have been mined or manufactured in [*name of country*]. This Section shall not apply where the Administrator, after reasonable consideration of relevant factors, including cost, efficiency, availability, and international agreements, determines that it is in the public interest to waive this requirement, either generally or with regard to specific materials.

(d) [*Appropriated amount (USD or national currency)*] for NGOs, such as, but not restricted to [*Appropriate NGO*], if they can provide matching funds on a 1:4 ratio (match 1 USD provided in this Section with 4 USD of their own) for carrying out education and awareness campaigns and monitoring of indoor air pollution.

(e) [*Appropriated amount (USD or national currency)*] to the Ministry of Energy to administer a program for the research and development of appropriate cookstoves. The appropriated amount shall remain available until expended.

(f) [*Appropriated amount (USD or national currency)*] to the Ministry of Health on an established needs basis.

§9. Research and Development

The Minister of Energy is authorized to conduct, promote, coordinate, and accelerate research, development, studies, surveys, experiments, demonstration projects, and training related to:

(a) The development and application of cooking technologies that provide effective and efficient alternatives to open-fire biomass, including alternative fuels and efficient cookstoves that meet and exceed the minimum standards set out in Section 4 and which maximize the use of local materials; and

(b) Health and safety in the application of such technologies, methods, and means.

(c) The Minister of Energy will actively solicit foreign aid, assistance, and collaboration in carrying out research and development from other governments, intergovernmental organizations, multinational corporations, NGOs, scientific bodies, and any other entities that will support objective scientific research and development.

(d) Prioritization

In conducting the activities authorized by this Section, the Minister of Energy may enter into contracts with and make grants to, qualified institutions, agencies, organizations, and persons. Priority shall be given to:

(i) The [*appropriate scientific or academic institution in country*];

(ii) Other public or private institutions that are scientifically equipped to conduct the required research; and

(iii) Other organizations that are equipped to create appropriate educational campaigns and workshops to engage communities and individuals.

(e) Availability of Information to the Public

Subject to the patent provisions of the [*name of country's patent act or other intellectual property law*], all discoveries, inventions, innovations, information, and data resulting from any research studies, surveys, experiments, assessments, or demonstration projects conducted or financed under this Section shall belong to the public domain and be available to the public for their use without charge.

§10. Education and Information

(a) The Ministry of Health shall be responsible for educating the public on the dangers of indoor air pollution. The Ministry of Health shall utilize existing health education channels to inform the public, including, but not limited to: (1) rural and urban hospitals and clinics; (2) school health awareness programs; (3) churches and other places of worship; (4) community leaders, including chiefs, faith leaders, and mid-wives; and (5) mass media forums, including radio, television, and cellular phone messaging.

(b) The Minister of Health shall have final authority over all private programs for the dissemination of information to the public and shall exercise discretion in determining the appropriateness of the message communicated under programs governed by this Act.

(c) The Minister of Health shall approve the health-science aspect of marketing materials to ensure that only verifiable findings of Parliament are used to convey the nature of the problem.

§11. Public Health

The Minister of Health shall encourage early treatment of signs and symptoms of respiratory problems. To this end,

(a) Health care workers will report specific cases of respiratory illnesses, by creating individual records of patients and monitoring their treatment;

(b) Data on respiratory illnesses will be shared with the Administrator in accordance with the mandate of this Act under Section 10; and

(c) The Minister of Health will enlist the help of NGOs.

§12. Enforcement

(a) Civil Remedies

Non-compliance order. On the basis of information available to him/her, if the Administrator finds violations of this Act, s/he may issue a non-compliance notice to the identified party. Non-compliance orders may be issued by the Administrator for violations of this Act in accordance with [*name of country's administrative procedure act*]. In addition, the Administrator must:

(i) Issue a notice of the alleged violation to the offending party within 15 days of discovery of a violation;

(ii) Allow the offending party 10 days to rebut the evidence against him/her and submit to agency-inspected corrective measures; and

(iii) Institute immediate suspension of activities that have or are reasonably expected to impose a grave health risk to the population.

(b) Citizen Enforcement

(i) Any citizen or resident of [*name of country*] may seek judicial remedies under this Section for violations of any mandatory provision of this Act. These citizen suits may be lodged in any District Court against any government agency, department, or private party that violates or fails to carry out any mandatory provisions of this Act. Prior to bringing an action, a citizen shall:

(1) Give notice to the defendant agency, department, or private party about the alleged violation(s) of this Act; and

(2) Allow a period of 2 months after receipt of notice to enable the defendant to rectify the alleged violation(s) of this Act before filing a lawsuit.

(ii) If the Plaintiff is successful, the court may order the defendant to comply with the Act and award damages. A successful litigant is entitled to recover full costs and the court shall include and order such costs in its judgment.

(iii) In the event an action is dismissed, the court may, in its discretion, order the citizen plaintiff to pay the defendant such costs as it deems reasonable and necessary.

(c) Criminal Penalties

(i) *Violation of Non-Compliance Order.* Any person who fails to comply within 3 months of receipt of a non-compliance order issued pursuant to Subsection (a) shall, after due inquiry by a District Court, be punished by a fine of not less than 250 USD [*or other typical fine in national currency*] nor more than 2,500 USD [*or other typical fine in national currency*] per day per violation, or by imprisonment for not more than 1 year, or by both.

(ii) *Negligent Misrepresentation.* Any person who negligently represents that cookstoves meet the minimum national standards of Section 4 or regional standards established pursuant to Section 4(a)(viii) shall be punished by a fine of 1,000 USD [*or other typical fine in national currency*] per cookstove sold under negligent misrepresentation.

(iii) *Knowing Endangerment.* Any person who knowingly endangers another person or community of persons by manufacturing, marketing and/or distributing cookstoves, and/or other cookstove parts that do not conform to the provisions of Section 4 (or regional standards established pursuant to Section 4(a) (viii)) shall be subject to a fine of not more than 25,000 USD or imprisonment of not more than 15 years. An organization shall be subject to a fine of not more than 100,000 USD.

COMMENTARY

Section-by-Section Analysis

Section 1: Findings

The model legislation provides a series of findings and lays the foundation for establishing the programs described in the following sections. The findings are based on generally and internationally available evidence.

Section 2: Policy

The policy articulated here is based on the premise that a solution to the problem of inefficient cookstoves must be comprehensive. It also involves public expenditures, as appropriated under this Act.

Section 3: Definitions

Many of these definitions simply explain terms and concepts in the model law. The adopting country will only use the definitions if the terms defined form part of the law being enacted by the adopting country.

Section 4: National Minimum Standards and Certification

Actual ambient air quality minimum standards under Section 4 will be country specific, based on what the adopting country determines is achievable. The World Health Organization (WHO) ambient air quality standards should serve as a guide/goal. In this context, it is important to emphasize the crucial importance of these standards. The ambient emission standards relating to indoor air pollution require improvement in air quality by reducing the emissions from cookstoves.

Section 4 also deals with certification. Product certification, undertaken by independent entities, is the process of certifying that a certain product has passed performance and quality assurance tests or qualification requirements and standards.

Section 5: Administrative Discretion

This Section grants discretion to the Administrator, after due process and public inquiry, to adapt the standards and regulations to the compelling conditions of the country.

Section 6: Creating an Agency

The choices of whether to establish a new agency for the reduction of cookstove pollution or create a new cadre of provincial assessment officials clearly fall within the administrative governance of each adopting country. However, some of the other substantive goals set out in Section 6 are to be institutionalized as law.

Needs assessments are necessary to avoid a cookie-cutter approach to the promotion of cookstoves. Local needs asssessments help to discover the local needs and conditions, and craft an area specific, bottom-up, rather than a top-down, cookstove program that addresses particular community needs.

Pilot programs are mini or scaled-down versions of a full-scale program. Pilot programs help to identify logistical problems, which might occur using proposed methods; estimate variability in outcomes; collect preliminary data; determine what resources (finance, staff) are needed for the full program; and assess the proposed programmatic techniques to uncover potential.

Section 7: Administration and Implementation

This Section refers to implementation by the Administrator of the new cookstove agency under Sections 6 and 7. The administration and implementation by the Ministers of Energy and Health are referred to in Sections 9, 10, and 11. As noted earlier, the adopting country does not need to create a new cookstove agency and could implement and administer this Act through its existing legal and administrative structures.

The Strategic Plan envisioned in Section 7(b) institutionalizes the need for the responsible agency to define its strategy or direction and make decisions on allocating its resources to pursue this strategy. In doing so, the strategic planning process should keep in mind the pivotal objective of encouraging the creation of markets for cookstoves and ensure that planning is an instrument for generating cookstove markets.

Section 8: Authorization and Appropriations

This Section deals with authorization and appropriations for three administrative/governmental units: the new cookstove agency and the Departments of Energy and Health. The adopting country could change this to suit its own administrative structures.

What is critical is that the legislature authorizes and appropriates funds for the purposes referred to in Section 8, enabling the policy and purposes of the Act to be achieved.

The incorporation of NGOs into the administration and implementation of the Act is based on compelling evidence that NGOs and other non-governmental entities are in many cases more effective and efficient distributors of goods and services than government agencies. They are, thus, a resource that should be utilized.

The dangers of indoor air pollution are often unknown and cookstove programs should be premised on awareness and information. As a result, the public health dangers of indoor air pollution must systematically and continuously be publicized, hence the appropriation.

Section 9: Research and Development

The design and manufacture of cookstoves has attracted very little scientific funding. The developing world would be in a much better position to attract scientific attention and funding by showing its own commitment and resolve to address this problem.

Section 9 places the prime responsibility for research and development on the Ministry of Energy and emphasizes the importance of soliciting and attracting foreign funds and assistance. As in every other administrative allocation of duties, the adopting country is free to make its own arrangements, provided that the substantive importance of research and development is in fact institutionalized.

Section 10: Education and Information

This model law places primary responsibility on the Health Ministry to educate the public about the dangers of indoor air pollution and the availability of remedies like cookstoves. The adopting country can make its own administrative arrangements, provided it commits to promoting awareness and education.

Section 11: Public Health

This Section requires public health officials to be aware of the health impacts of indoor air pollution and that such conditions need to be treated. In doing so, Section 11 attempts to integrate the largely ignored health hazards of indoor air pollution with other more recognizable ailments and conditions.

Section 12: Enforcement

Judicial and administrative enforcement is a necessary facet of the broader implementation of the Act. While civil and criminal enforcement by public officials is a familiar feature of the laws of many developed countries, the citizen suit provisions may need some explanation in the context of developing countries. In essence, a citizen suit is a form of private enforcement whereby the private litigant calls for enforcement against the official enforcers or government agencies. For a variety of reasons, government agencies are often unable or unwilling to enforce regulatory laws. When armed with citizen suit authority, private citizens are enabled to take over the enforcement of such laws, free of some of the bureaucratic and political constraints that can hobble government enforcers.

Any government that enacts this statute, seeking to address the problems of indoor air pollution, should not try to cover up the poor conduct of their agencies. Bringing questionable conduct into the light of judicial scrutiny will help governments meet the challenges they seek to address through this Act.

Model Law on Cookstoves for Developed Countries

A BILL to promote the development and deployment of clean cookstoves to save lives, improve livelihoods, empower women, and combat global warming by creating a thriving global market for clean, affordable, and efficient household cooking solutions, and for other purposes.

Be it enacted by the [legislative organ] of the [country] assembled,

§1. Short Title

This Act may be cited as the "Clean Cookstoves Support Act of [year]."

§2. Findings

[*Legislative organ*] finds that:

(1) [*Name of country*] is a member of the community of nations that has accepted well-recognized principles of international law and policy establishing –

(A) the right of developing countries to sustainable development; and

(B) the common but differentiated responsibility of [*name of country*] and other developed nations to institutionally, financially, and technologically support sustainable development among developing countries by alleviating energy poverty and providing access to safe and sustainable cooking technologies.

(2) [*Name of country*] seeks to support sustainable development and carry out its common but differentiated responsibility pertaining to energy poverty and access to safe and sustainable cooking technologies through this Act.

(3) According to the World Health Organization, approximately 3 billion people – nearly half of the world's population – cook their food over open fires or with inefficient, polluting, and unsafe cookstoves that use firewood, dung, or coal as fuel.

(4) An estimated 2 to 4 million people each year die prematurely from illnesses attributable to indoor air pollution resulting from inefficient, unsafe cookstoves. Indoor air pollution accounts for more deaths yearly than malaria, tuberculosis, or human immunodeficiency virus infection/acquired immunodeficiency syndrome (HIV/AIDS).

(5) Particulate matter, heavy smoke, and carcinogens created by inefficient cookstoves and open fires can cause chronic and acute illnesses, such as pneumonia, heart disease, and lung cancer. There also is evidence linking indoor air pollution to low birth weight, tuberculosis, and other types of cancer. Women and children are disproportionally affected because they are the main household members regularly breathing cooking smoke.

(6) Open fires and unsafe cookstoves lead to hundreds of thousands of burn deaths each year, and burn survivors often sustain permanent injuries ranging from debilitating scarring to loss of movement.

(7) Open fires are extremely inefficient at converting energy from biomass, so the amount of biomass required as fuel for cooking can reach up to 2 tons per family each year. Collecting this amount of fuel is time-consuming and environmental problems may result where demand for biomass exceeds the natural regrowth of resources.

(8) Women and girls disproportionately shoulder the burden of collecting and managing biomass fuel for cooking. As nearby fuel supplies dwindle, women and girls are forced to travel farther to obtain fuel, increasing their risk of injuries from carrying heavy loads long distances and of sexual harassment and assault. Furthermore, women and girls may spend 20 or more hours a week collecting fuel, leaving them with less time to attend school, fulfill domestic responsibilities, earn money, engage in public activities, learn to read, acquire other skills, or simply rest.

(9) Inefficient cookstoves contribute to global warming and environmental decline through deforestation and the release of black carbon, methane, nitrous oxide, and carbon dioxide into the atmosphere. Although biomass is primarily a renewable energy source, harvesting of unsustainable levels of biomass can lead to pressure on natural resources and eventually cause deforestation. Black carbon, methane, and nitrous oxide, produced through incomplete biomass fuel combustion, not only are dangerous when inhaled, but also are principal agents of global warming. Black carbon warms the atmosphere by decreasing the reflectivity of the earth's surface and has a significant impact in areas close to ice and snow accumulations. Additionally, black carbon contributes to extensive brown haze that can affect temperature and precipitation.

(10) The development and deployment of clean cookstoves is essential for achieving the United Nations Millennium Development Goals to reduce child mortality, improve maternal health, eradicate poverty, promote gender equality, and create environmental sustainability.

(11) Clean cookstoves positively impact the quality of life and the environment by –

   (A) freeing women and children to engage in educational and economic endeavors;

   (B) promoting gender equality and women's empowerment;

   (C) improving child and maternal health and safety;

(D) advancing environmental stability by reducing reliance on biomass; and

(E) reducing contributions to global climate change.

§3. Policy

It is the policy of the [*name of country*] to create programs and policies to –

(1) encourage manufacturing industries for clean cookstoves in developing countries by supporting international partnerships and local entrepreneurs with financial, institutional, and technological assistance;

(2) encourage the promotion, distribution, and maintenance of clean cookstoves for individuals in developing countries;

(3) provide funding for research, development, and deployment of clean cookstoves and the necessary air quality monitoring systems for developing countries; and

(4) support and disseminate research and monitoring of the adverse human health and environmental effects associated with the black carbon and other pollutants emitted by inefficient cookstoves.

§4. Definitions

In this Act:

(1) CLEAN COOKSTOVE. – The term "clean cookstove" means a cookstove that –

(A) employs appropriate sustainable energy technologies;

(B) has been prototypically demonstrated, tested, and certified as meeting–

(i) indoor ambient air quality standards; or

(ii) if a developing country determines that indoor ambient air quality standards cannot be achieved, the reasonable interim air quality standards established by the developing country that improve existing indoor ambient air quality; and

(C) meets minimum durability standards based on the needs and conditions of such developing country and its peoples, taking into account the available standards established by the Global Alliance for Clean Cookstoves.

(2) INDOOR AMBIENT AIR QUALITY STANDARDS. – The term "indoor ambient air quality standards" means airborne pollution measurements that do not exceed the following:

(A) For particulate matter of 10 μm (PM_{10}) –

(i) a 24-hour mean of 50 μg/m^3; or

(ii) an annual mean of 20 μg/m^3.

(B) For particulate matter of 2.5 μm ($PM_{2.5}$) –

(i) a 24-hour mean of 25 μg/m^3; or

(ii) an annual mean of 10 μg/m^3.

(C) For carbon monoxide (CO) –
    (i) 100 mg/m^3 during any 15-minute period and not more than 1 time per day;
    (ii) 35 mg/m^3 during any 1-hour period and not more than 1 time per day;
    (iii) an 8-hour mean of 10 mg/m^3; or
    (iv) a 24-hour mean of 7 mg/m^3.
(D) For nitrogen dioxide (NO$_2$) –
    (i) a 1-hour mean of 200 µg/m^3; or
    (ii) an annual mean of 40 µg/ m^3.

§5. Clean Cookstove Manufacturing, Promotion, and Distribution

(a) IN GENERAL. – There is established within the [*ministry or agency for international aid*] a Clean Cookstove Manufacturing and Distribution Program.

(b) PURPOSE. – The purpose of the program established by subsection (a) is to provide international partnerships and local entrepreneurs with financial, institutional, and technological assistance to develop, manufacture, promote, distribute, and maintain clean cookstoves in developing countries.

(c) FUNDING. –
    (1) IN GENERAL. – The program established by subsection (a) shall be funded in the amount of $15,000,000 each year for 10 years.
    (2) CRITERIA. – The administrator of the program established by subsection (a) shall establish criteria for the use of funds provided by paragraph (1) to carry out the purpose of the program.
    (3) CONSULTATION. – The criteria established under paragraph (2) shall be developed in consultation with –
        (A) governmental and community leaders in developing countries;
        (B) non-governmental organizations working to promote clean cookstoves;
        (C) [*other relevant ministries or agencies within the developed country*]; and
        (D) the interested public.
    (4) NOTICE AND COMMENT. – The administrator of the program established by subsection (a) shall provide public notice and an opportunity for any interested government, business, organization, or individual to comment on any proposal to establish criteria under paragraph (2) or amendments thereto.
    (5) AVAILABILITY OF FUNDS. – The funding provided by paragraph (1) shall be available to any offices or programs within the [*appropriate agency or agencies within the ministry for international aid*] in accordance with –
        (A) the criteria established under paragraph (2); and
        (B) such other rules as are established by the [minister or agency head].

(6) GRANTS AND OTHER AID. – The program established by subsection (a) may, in accordance with the criteria established under paragraph (2) and without the need for any matching or base funds, use up to 20 percent of the funding provided by paragraph (1) to provide grants, loans, or other methods of financial support to businesses and other non-governmental organizations working to develop, manufacture, promote, distribute, or maintain clean cookstoves in developing countries.

(a) MONITORING; REPORTING. – The administrator of the program established by subsection (a) shall –

(1) monitor the effectiveness of the program; and

(2) report every 5 years after the date of enactment of this Act to the [*appropriate developed country officials and entities*] and the public on the effectiveness of the activities supported by and carried out under the program.

(b) ACCOUNTING. – The administrator of the program established by subsection (a) shall account for the funds it receives and distributes. The accounting shall comply with generally accepted accounting principles and shall be made available to the [*appropriate developed country officials and entities*] and the public within 90 days of the end of each fiscal year.

§6. Applied Research and Development

(a) IN GENERAL. – There is established within the [*ministry or agency for applied energy research and design*] a Clean Cookstove Research, Development, and Demonstration Program.

(b) PURPOSE. – The purpose of the program established by subsection (a) is to enable and facilitate the research, development, testing, and demonstration of –

(1) effective and efficient appropriate sustainable energy technologies that provide alternatives to the use of damaging biomass cooking;

(2) alternative fuels; and

(3) efficient and effective clean cookstoves.

(c) FUNDING. –

(1) IN GENERAL. – The program established by subsection (a) shall be funded in the amount of $15,000,000 each year for 10 years.

(2) CRITERIA. – The administrator of the program established by subsection (a) shall establish criteria for the use of funds provided by paragraph (1) to carry out the purpose of the program.

(3) CONSULTATION. – The criteria established under paragraph (2) shall be developed in consultation with –

(A) domestic and international businesses, academic institutions, and non-profit institutions that are developing or are interested in the research, development, testing, or demonstration of clean cookstoves;

(B) [*other relevant ministries or agencies within the developed country*]; and

(C) the interested public.

(4) NOTICE AND COMMENT. – The administrator of the program established by subsection (a) shall provide public notice and an opportunity for any interested government, business, organization, or individual to comment on any proposal to establish criteria under paragraph (2) or amendments thereto.

(5) AVAILABILITY OF FUNDS. – The funding provided by paragraph (1) shall be available to any offices or programs within the [*ministry or agency for applied energy research and design*] in accordance with –

(A) the criteria established under paragraph (2); and

(B) such other rules as are established by the [*minister or agency head*].

(6) GRANTS AND OTHER AID. – The administrator of the program established by subsection (a) may, in accordance with the criteria established under paragraph (2) and without the need for any matching or base funds, use up to 80 percent of the funding provided by paragraph (1) to provide grants, loans, or other methods of financial support to academic, business, and other non-governmental entities for research, development, testing, or demonstration of clean cookstoves.

(d) MONITORING; REPORTING. – The administrator of the program established by subsection (a) shall –

(1) monitor the effectiveness of the program; and

(2) report every 5 years after the date of enactment of this Act to the [*appropriate developed country officials and entities*] and the public on the effectiveness of the activities supported by and carried out under the program.

(e) ACCOUNTING. – The administrator of the program established by subsection (a) shall account for the funds it receives and distributes. The accounting shall comply with generally accepted accounting principles and shall be made available to the [*appropriate developed country officials and entities*] and the public within 90 days of the end of each fiscal year.

§7. Health and Environmental Research

(a) IN GENERAL. – There is established within the [*ministry or agency for health or environmental research*] a Clean Cookstove Health and Environmental Research Program.

(b) PURPOSE. – The purpose of the program established by subsection (a) is to –

(1) conduct and support research and monitoring on the household, local, and global production of black carbon and other pollutants emitted by inefficient cookstoves;

(2) conduct and support research and monitoring on the adverse human health and environmental effects associated with the black carbon and other pollutants emitted by inefficient cookstoves;

(3) research and develop best practices and programs to reduce the adverse human health and environmental effects associated with black carbon and other pollutants through the use of clean cookstoves; and

(4) inform governments, researchers, and the public of the research, monitoring, best practices, and programs developed under paragraphs (1) through (3).

(c) FUNDING. –

(1) IN GENERAL. – The program established by subsection (a) shall be funded in the amount of $15,000,000 each year for 10 years.

(2) CRITERIA. – The administrator of the program established by subsection (a) shall establish criteria for the use of funds to conduct the research, monitoring, and other activities described in subsection (b).

(3) CONSULTATION. The criteria established under paragraph (2) shall be developed in consultation with –

(A) domestic and international businesses, academic institutions, and non-profit institutions that are interested in reducing the adverse health and environmental effects of inefficient cookstoves;

(B) domestic and international businesses, academic institutions, and non-profit institutions that are developing or are interested in the development of clean cookstoves;

(C) the [*other relevant ministries or agencies within the developed country*]; and

(D) the interested public.

(4) NOTICE AND COMMENT. – The administrator of the program established by subsection (a) shall provide public notice and an opportunity for any interested government, business, organization, or individual to comment on any proposal to establish criteria under paragraph (2) or amendments thereto.

(5) AVAILABILITY OF FUNDS. – The funding provided by paragraph (1) shall be available to any offices or programs within the [*ministry or agency for applied energy research and design*] in accordance with –

(A) the criteria established under paragraph (2); and

(B) such other rules as are established by the [*minister or agency head*].

(6) GRANTS AND OTHER AID. – The administrator of the program established by subsection (a) may, in accordance with the criteria established under paragraph (2) and without the need for any matching or base funds, use up to 80 percent of the funding provided by paragraph (1) to provide grants, loans, or other methods of financial support to academic and other non-governmental entities for the health and environmental research, monitoring, and other activities described in subsection (b).

(d) MONITORING; REPORTING. – The administrator of the program established by subsection (a) shall –

(1) monitor the effectiveness of the program; and

(2) report every 5 years after the date of enactment of this Act to the [*appropriate developed country officials and entities*] and the public on the effectiveness of the activities supported by and carried out under the program.

(e) ACCOUNTING. – The administrator of the program established by subsection (a) shall account for the funds it receives and distributes. The accounting shall comply with generally accepted accounting principles and shall be made available to the [*appropriate developed country officials and entities*] and the public within 90 days of the end of each fiscal year.

COMMENTARY

Section-by-Section Analysis

Section 1: Short Title

Section 1 provides the short title for the model legislation.

Section 2: Findings

The model legislation provides a series of factual findings and lays the foundation for establishing the programs described in Sections 4 through 6.

Section 3: Policy

Section 3 describes the basic policies generated by the model law.

Section 4: Definitions

Section 4 provides important definitions for a "clean cookstove" and "indoor ambient air quality standards." Paragraph (1) includes three important components of the definition of a "clean cookstove." Of note, the definition references "appropriate sustainable energy technologies" ("ASETs"). ASETs "seek to bridge the gap between the capital-intensive advanced technologies of the developed world and the traditional subsistence technologies of the [Energy Poor]" (Guruswamy 2011, 141). In the context of cookstoves, ASETs include relatively simple technologies that satisfy basic cooking needs through sustainable engineering tailored to the particular needs of the intended community (Guruswamy 2011, 146).

Second, the definition emphasizes the importance of testing, demonstrating, and certifying cookstoves as meeting or exceeding indoor ambient air quality standards to ensure that the cookstoves developed countries support will achieve the intended benefits in developing countries. In some cases, achieving the specified standards may not be immediately achievable, so the definition recognizes the need to tailor the standards to best serve the developing country and its communities.

Third, the definition provides for the establishment of minimum durability standards. Experience has demonstrated that cookstove durability is a critical component for the long-term success of any clean cookstove deployment program.

Paragraph (2) defines "indoor ambient air quality standards," setting forth standards recommended by the World Health Organization.[2]

Section 5: Clean Cookstove Manufacture, Promotion, and Distribution

Section 5 establishes a program to support the development, manufacturing, promotion, and distribution of clean cookstoves in developing countries.

The model legislation recommends $15,000,000 annually to carry out the Clean Cookstove Manufacturing and Distribution Program. The adopting country may consider more or less funding; this amount provides a realistic example of the amount of funding that is needed to address the challenge, assuming that it is multiplied both by numerous developed countries and through the multi-program approach envisioned by this model law. In establishing criteria for the use of the funds, the model law calls for opening the process to the participation of all interested persons and entities, regardless of nationality.

The model law also calls for significant and transparent monitoring, reporting, and accounting. Such practices are important for establishing and maintaining an effective and efficient international aid program.

Section 6: Applied Research and Development

Section 6 establishes a program to support applied research and development of effective, efficient, and affordable clean cookstove technologies. There is a critical need for significant advancements in appropriate and sustainable clean cookstove technologies.

Unlike the program established under Section 5, the program established by Section 6 contemplates that a large portion of the research and development funding will be used to support non-governmental efforts. This recommendation is based on the recognition that the most common structure for carrying out such research and development efforts is through public-private partnerships, which often provide the most efficient and effective approach to the kind of program that is contemplated here.

Section 7: Health and Environmental Research

Section 7 establishes a program to: (1) conduct and support research and monitoring on the pollutants that are produced by inefficient cookstoves; (2) conduct and support research and monitoring on the adverse human health and environmental effects associated with such pollution; (3) research and develop best practices and programs to reduce those adverse human health and environmental effects; and (4) inform governments, researchers, and the public of the research, monitoring, best practices, and programs developed through the program established by this section.

Notes

1   This chapter reproduces parts of, and is based on, the author's *Dissemination of Clean Cookstoves: Model Laws for Developing and Developed Countries 24*, Colorado Natural Resources, Energy and Environmental Law Review 319 (2013)
2   See *Air Quality and Health Fact Sheet No. 313*, World Health Organization (September 2011), www.who.int/mediacentre/factsheets/fs313/en/index.html.

References

Bentham, Jeremy. 1776. *A Comment on the Commentaries and a Fragment on Government*. Edited by J.H. Burns and H.L.A. Hart. 1977. London: Athlone Press.
——. 1789. *An Introduction to the Principles of Morals and Legislation*. Edited by J.H. Burns and H.L.A. Hart. 1996. Oxford: Oxford University Press.
Burke, Edmund. 1770. "Thoughts on the Cause of the Present Discontents." In *Select Works of Edmund Burke*. 1999. Indianapolis: Liberty Fund.
Guruswamy, Lakshman. 2007. "Judging Treaties." *American Society of International Law Proceedings* 101: 175–176.
——. 2011. "Energy Poverty" *Ann. Rev. Envt. And Resources* 36: 139–161.
——. 2012. *International Environmental Law in a Nutshell*. West Academic Publishing. Fourth edition.
Hobhouse, J.S. 1990. "International Conventions and Commercial Law: The Pursuit of Uniformity." *Law Quarterly* 106: 530–533.
Lieberman, David. 1989. *The Province of Legislation Determined: Legal Theory in Eighteenth-Century Britain*. New York: Cambridge University Press.
Moore, Michael. 2000. *Educating Oneself in Public: Critical Essays in Jurisprudence*. Oxford: Oxford University Press.
Neuberger, David. 2011. "Swindlers (Including the Master of the Rolls?) Not Wanted: Bentham and Justice." Paper presented at the Bentham Lecture 2011, University College London, UK, March 2, 2011.
Ramanathan, V. and G. Carmichael. 2008. "Global and Regional Climate Changes Due to Black Carbon." *Nature Geoscience* 1: 221.
Service, Robert F. 2008. "Study Fingers Soot as Major Player in Global Warming." *Science* 319: 1745.
Sprague, William. 1915. *Blackstone's Commentaries Abridged*. Chicago: Callaghan and Co.
Summers, Robert. 1982. *Instrumentalism and American Legal Theory*. Ithaca: Cornell University Press.
United Nations Commission on International Trade Law. 2013. *A Guide to UNICITRAL: Basic Facts About the United Nations Commission on International Trade Law*. Vienna: United Nations Office.

Conclusions

The emerging contours

Lakshman Guruswamy

It is evident that energy poverty is a complex, multivariable, multi-dimensional, non-linear issue with implications for human rights, international development, the environment, health care, the global economy, and more. Solutions will require a commitment to addressing energy poverty at all levels, spanning individual, community, national, and international decision making. These decisions might range from the practical introduction of Affordable Sustainable Energy Technologies (ASETs), to Sustainable Energy for ALL (SE4All) at the international level, but it is crucial that these decisions and underlying policies be situated within an integrated framework of multivariable socio-economic, political, cultural, and ecological requirements. The present chapter will attempt to weave together conclusions about energy poverty, and will do so within the organizational structure and rubrics of this book.

The phenomenon of the Energy Poor

The phenomenon of the Energy Poor is indisputable. Almost every chapter of this book confirms, in differing ways, that between 1.7 to 3 billion peoples, sometimes described as the Other Third, are subject to one or more dimensions of energy deprivation. The lack of access includes energy for cooking, lighting, sanitation, drinking water, and motive or mechanical power.

As substantiated by chapters throughout the book (particularly Chapters 2, 3, 4, 10, 11, and 16), the burdens of energy deprivation and lack of access to energy are carried preponderantly and disproportionately by women. The harm and hardship inflicted on women may amount to silent violence that contravenes their human and natural rights and negates their right to sustainable development.

The chapters in Part 1 on the phenomenon of the Energy Poor illustrates the pivotal importance of energy for human (male and female) progress and development. Chapter 1, by David Stern, explores the importance of energy in economic growth and this theme is also considered in later chapters. Chapter 4 by Lakshman Guruswamy argues that energy is a primary determinant of economic, social and environmental progress. Chapter 11 by Simon Trace delineates how energy is essential for domestic, livelihood or commercial as well as community purposes, while Anoja Wickramasinghe explains in Chapter 16 why energy is a priority for rural women.

Conceptual foundations

Part 2 deals with emerging philosophical, political, and theoretical concepts forging the conceptual foundations for addressing energy poverty. In his seminal contribution in Chapter 5, Christian Brugger reflects on the moral foundations of a right to energy. He discusses energy within a right–duty nexus, and concludes that the Energy Poor possess a natural right to energy, accompanied by the correlative duty of developed countries to honor this right.

Dr. Guruswamy in Chapter 4 on energy justice deals with the international dimensions of energy poverty, relying on Rawls rather than natural law. He argues that the Energy Poor could be analogized and even equated with the "burdened peoples" referred to by Rawls in his *The Law of Peoples*. The Energy Poor as burdened peoples are owed a duty of assistance by the other peoples of the world. Though approaching it from different predicates, both Brugger and Guruswamy make the case for a right to energy and the duty to honor that right.

In this context it is very significant, that at the highest level of international governance, international law, and policy is moving toward recognizing an institutionalized right to energy. The right to energy is either explicitly or implicitly referenced by Ved Nanda in Chapter 6 on sustainable development, as well as in Chapter 7 by Murodbek Laldjebaev et al. on energy security, and Chapter 8 by Carmen Gonzales on energy poverty and the environment.

In Chapter 6 Professor Nanda sketches how the United Nations (UN) declared 2012 the "International Year of Sustainable Energy for All (SE4All)" and declared the entire decade of 2014–2024 the "Decade of Sustainable Energy for All." Moreover, in creating SE4All, the UN announced a goal of universal, primarily electrical energy access by 2030, that is being echoed in potential Sustainable Development Goals (SDGs).

Nanda proceeds to show how "Access to affordable, reliable, sustainable, and modern energy for all" comprises one of 17 potential SDGs proposed at the United Nations' Open Working Group. The SDGs are a set of universal goals designed to build upon the prior Millennium Development Goals (MDGs), that were fashioned as a blueprint by all the world's countries and leading development institutions, in 2000 to meet the needs of the world's poorest. They did not however, institutionalize a right to energy in the way the potential SDGs seek to do.

Assessing the various challenges

Part 3 deals with a representative sample of the wide and varying obstacles confronting access to energy. Chapter 9 by Mark Safty analyzes various challenges to project financing addressing energy poverty and makes suggestions about how they can be met. His ideas will be dealt with more fully when discussing the way forward.

Margaret Matinga et al. in Chapter 10 deal with behavioral challenges and present an array of reasons as to why ASETs are not adopted. They argue that energy use is a practice of culture, not just a matter of technological adoption and change. They refer to the techno-centric view claiming that it is irrational to reject cookstoves because they are technically able to reduce indoor air pollution, and point to its shortcomings. They call attention to the fact that in making a decision to transition from traditional fuels to ASETs like cookstoves, potential adopters must compare benefits that are often unknown and uncertain at the initial stages of adoption, with known benefits and (often hidden) costs of their current technologies and practices. Such changes can provoke fears of uncertain costs, whether monetary or non-monetary, including costs related to cultural capital. By cultural capital they refer to the particular attributes of taste, and the use of fire in the preparation of food, that is peculiar to each culture. It is difficult to resist their conclusion, drawn from differing cultures within multiple countries, that there is a need to increase understanding of these behavioral challenges, and the logic of practices that underpin such behaviors.

In Chapter 11, Simon Trace offers a synoptic and revealing account of why the sometimes diverse needs of the Energy Poor give rise to different types of access to energy. There are variances between the household (domestic), enterprise (livelihood or commercial) and community needs. Energy for households include lighting, cooking, water and space heating, cooling, and information. For billions among the Energy Poor the ability to earn a living depends on access to energy. He states, "[H]aving lighting after dark to keep a shop open longer, or fuel for an engine to mill grain or a pump to irrigate land, can be the difference between earning a decent livelihood and remaining at or below the subsistence level and in poverty..." Additionally, community services provided by hospitals, schools, and street lighting require energy. He demonstrates why the goals of SE4All require a better definition and understanding of what constitutes access for different purposes and services.

In moving forward, it is important that access to electricity remain the immediate, future, and final objective of access to energy for all. But, as Simon Trace points out, it is necessary to better define what we mean by access to energy. The US consumes about 13,400 kWh per year per person of electricity while the consumption in Bulgaria and South Africa who are at the bottom of the energy consumption ladder, is about 4,500 kWh (Bazilian and Pielke 2013). In calculating the energy required to provide access to energy for all, the International Energy Agency defines an initial threshold for energy access to be 250 kWh per year for rural households and 500 kWh per year for urban households, assuming five people per household (International Energy Agency 2012). This equates to 50 to 100 kWh per year per person, or about 0.5 percent of that consumed by the average American and 1.7 percent of that of the average Bulgarian and South African.

According to work done by Bazilian and colleagues it would cost about one trillion dollars to achieve the total global access rising to 750 kWh per capita for new connections by 2030 – and 17 times more ($17 trillion), to achieve a level of worldwide access equivalent to that in Bulgaria (Bazilian and Pielke 2013). The Global Tracking Framework of the IEA and World Bank has estimated the cost of achieving the three SE4All goals of electricity for all, doubling energy efficiency, and doubling the use of renewable energy by 2030. Doing so will cost at least $600–800 billion per year over and above existing levels, entailing a doubling or tripling of financial flows over current levels (Banerjee et al. 2013). The daunting additional costs, and the time it will take to do so – realistically 2045–2050 – will shunt the Energy Poor into limbo unless intermediate energy sources are also provided.. Therefore, a number of authors suggest, it is also important to create a parallel track based on Affordable Sustainable Energy Technologies (ASETs).

The way forward

Beneficial energy, based on ASETs, can provide intermediate energy pending the arrival of electricity. ASETs alone cannot extract a country from poverty, but they can play a critical role in boosting economic development and improving the livelihoods of hundreds of millions of the Energy Poor. Some ASETs – such as improved cookstoves, portable water filtration systems, solar-charged illumination, and better mechanical and agricultural technologies – are already being distributed by a constellation of projects around the world.

ASETs bridge the gap between capital-intensive electricity, and the traditional subsistence technologies of the Energy Poor. ASETs include: clean fuels, clean cookstoves, illumination by photovoltaic lights, decentralized mini grids based on solar, wind, and biomass-generated electricity, treadle pumps, improved harnesses and yokes which boost the performance of draft cattle, better axles for transport by cart, simple windmills for pumping water, grain grinding appliances, and low-cost bicycles.

Several companies and NGOs design, manufacture, and distribute ASETs to the Energy Poor. Chapters 4, 11, 12, 14, 15, 17, and 20 illustrate how ASETs might be globalized. It is not enough or sufficient for ASETs to be disseminated among just a segment of the Energy Poor. The challenge is enormous and calls for the dissemination of hundreds of millions of ASETs. The Global Alliance for Clean Cookstoves has set a target of 100 million households by 2020 (Global Alliance for Clean Cookstoves 2010). The Global Alliance for Clean Cookstoves is a truly laudable and important international alliance or partnership addressing indoor air pollution and the need for cookstoves. But, among the ASET needs of the Energy Poor for cooking, lighting, sanitation, clean water, and mechanical power, only cookstoves have received international recognition. Unfortunately, the other needs of the Energy Poor have not received global recognition or institutional support. The challenge lies in globalizing ASETs that reach out to the unmet and relatively unacknowledged needs of the Energy Poor for lighting, sanitation, water, and motive or mechanical power.

The response to this challenge, can benefit from a few clear lessons. First, it is crucial that NGOs and companies manufacturing, and marketing ASETs understand their markets and communities, and act with the awareness that the Energy Poor are not a homogenous group. This underlying theme is articulated in Chapters 7, 9, 10, 11, 14, 15, 17, and 18.

In this context, Chapters 2, 10, and 16 stress the importance of recognizing that the lack of access to energy most seriously impacts women and children. In promoting ASETs it is necessary to design gender and child specific policies that are alive to the greater risks confronting women and children.

Second, what constitutes access to energy will depend on whether energy is required for domestic, commercial or livelihood, and/or community purposes. In Chapter 11, Simon Trace illuminatingly describes the differing energy needs of the poor, and the importance of not restricting access to domestic needs. It is imperative that energy be available for commercial or livelihood purposes so that the Energy Poor can earn a living, just as it is important to offer access to energy for schools and hospitals that serve the community. It is encouraging that the Global Tracking System (Banerjee et al. 2013) of SE4All has begun taking the right approach to this question.

Third, these energy needs, as well as cultural customs, gender norms, and community expectations vary widely among the Energy Poor. As Dr. Matinga et al. demonstrated in Chapter 10 on "behavioral challenges," preexisting cultural behaviors, norms, and traditions can inform whether and how an ASET will be accepted or rejected by a target community. She perspicaciously points out how these cultural norms are critically important regarding gender roles. To be aware of gender norms and behaviors of a community, particularly where cultural capital is concerned, can prove to be of critical advantage in the adoption of ASETs. There are also valuable opportunities, within ASET companies and organizations, to contribute to the empowerment and education of women, and these groups would be well advised to include women where feasible.

Fourth, active interaction and engagement with target communities can provide economic benefit, and subsequent improvement in quality of life, to these communities. The chapters detailing the experiences of Elephant Energy (Chapter 17), a non-profit organization, and Nokero (Chapter 15), a for-profit company, demonstrate how company interaction and engagement with their communities benefit both product distribution and provide economic opportunities for local entrepreneurs and agents. In order for both of these benefits to be realized to their full potential, ASET companies must heavily engage with their target communities and make an effort to employ individuals familiar with the customs and people of the communities.

Fifth, it is necessary to offer practical and pragmatic examples of integration. One way of doing so is to promote collaboration among multiple stakeholders involved in the design, fabrication, funding, marketing, deployment, and adoption of ASETs. Such collaboration could be achieved within sectors and regions, through voluntary alliances, such as, for example, solar bulbs in South Asia, or clean drinking water in East Africa.

One objective of such ventures should be to understand and flag the life cycle of an ASET from its conception, through design and manufacture, to marketing, service, impacts both positive and negative, and its final disposal. Where possible this requires tracking and tracing the product chain of each ASET in a manner that will offer private and public investors a better understanding of every significant link.

Once established, an alliance faces the crucial question of how to promote viable business enterprises that design, manufacture, market, and deploy ASETs in developing countries. This calls for entrepreneurship. Entrepreneurs in developing countries, as well as those in developed countries who wish to set up their enterprises in developing countries, face a host of daunting economic, political, and regulatory risks not encountered in developed countries. Even though flourishing entrepreneurship may be the key to the success of ASETs, the challenges and promises of entrepreneurship in developing countries has been inadequately explored. In Chapter 9, Mark Safty rejects the idea of "barriers" that need to be overcome in infrastructure and project financing. Instead, he explores ways of circumventing, working around and addressing the risk factors posed by infrastructure and project financing.

There are a number of questions pertaining to the kind of ASET enterprise that will best promote sustainable development among the Energy Poor, while others arise about the start-up or development, completion and operational costs of financing ASET enterprises. With regard to the first question, to what extent should we be looking at medium to larger growth-oriented enterprises rather than microenterprises? Most of the specialist research and attention in this field has concentrated on microenterprises and low-growth lifestyle businesses. Traditionally micro-firms impact on the larger population purchasing inclinations have not been significant. Large-scale product adoption usually is dependent on successful marketing strategies and reasonable product price points, which traditionally have not been a strength of micro-firms. It has been suggested that these micro-firms do not contribute in a meaningful way to the sustainable economic growth needed to reduce poverty in developing countries (Hanpongpandh et al. 2004; Chowdhury 2009).

Recent research strongly suggests that new and growth-oriented firms employing between 5 and 250 people, and seeking between $20,000 and $2 million in investment capital, are more likely to contribute to economic growth and provide important new sources of higher quality employment (Aspen Network of Development Entrepreneurs 2012, 1). In Chapter 9, Mark Safty deals with new and growth-oriented enterprises, and suggests ways in which they can succeed.

However, micro-firms tend to be more sensitive to their cultural milieu, and the impact of coordinated micro-firms collaborating with a central distribution and marketing enterprise by way of business linkages may offer benefits unmatched by growth-oriented larger firms (Jenkins et al. 2008, 1–36). Admittedly, most of the ASET enterprises in developing countries will function in economies dominated by subsistence agriculture, which relies heavily on labor and natural resources, in contrast to technological and financial innovation. However, in order to become regional, national or global enterprises will need to look for increased economies of scale and become more capital-intensive. A number of obstacles arise.

The first of these is start-up capital. Privately owned local enterprises (POEs), particularly in Asia, have been more innovative and enterprising than wholly owned subsidiaries of foreign firms and hold the greatest promise for promoting ASETs. This statement underscores the importance of small business in the creation of jobs and in the development of innovations. However, POEs still face great obstacles. They include the odds that the survival rate of a new enterprise in its first five years is less than 50 percent (Linglebach et al. 2005). This fact is compounded by the absence of financial innovation. Access to finance is often viewed as the most significant obstacle, coming out as the top constraint in World Bank Enterprise Surveys of over 45,000 enterprises in 196 countries (International Finance Corporation 2013). The very limited role played by banks and venture capital severely reduces the prospects of external financing and raises the question of how they obtain start-up capital. In Chapter 9, Mark Safty addresses many of these issues, and concludes they are not as formidable as sometimes made out.

Second, it appears that internal finance comprises the majority of start-up financing for small and medium enterprises in developing countries (Abdulsaleh and Worthington 2013). Much of this comes from savings and micro lending but we know little about personal finance rates and the critical intra-familial financial linkages. The question remains: How best might new ASET enterprises obtain start-up capital? The suggestions made by Mark Safty in Chapter 9 attempt to answer this question.

Once established, the enterprise needs to obtain early stage financing. Again, there is a scarcity of external risk capital financing because of the low rate of return among start-up enterprises in developing countries. This return is often estimated as break even for the first generation and is insufficient to attract risk capital.

It has been pointed out that risk capital finance is particularly important for growth-oriented entrepreneurs in the developing world, because it aligns the incentives of entrepreneurs and outside investors. In contrast to commercial bank lending, both the enterprise and the risk capital financier is properly motivated to maximize economic value of the enterprise (Ody and de Ferranti 2007).

What type of financial innovations might overcome these hurdles? Suggestions include commercial banks moving "down-market," micro-credit institutions moving "up," and creative application of venture capital investing ideas (Ody and de Ferranti 2007). Mark Safty (Chapter 9) suggests that where local conditions allow, the use of agreements or memoranda among governmental actors, communities, and specific project developers may be an effective way of doing so.

Given that many of the ASET developers will be interested in two aspects – societal impact and return on investment – perhaps a new perspective on capital acquisition is required. One way forward may be to develop financing structures that provide the ASET developer with the necessary capital to franchise local regions for the production, distribution, and service of the ASETs. The other consideration is to attract micro-lenders in a highly coordinated way so as to pool assets and create capital lending entities that not only understand the risk climate at the local level, but also are nimble enough to make the necessary adjustments to ensure market development in that area.

An important goal of an alliance will be to convene groups of committed individuals with experience ranging from bankers, regulators, developers, CEOs, and CFOs, to brainstorm on creating the most appropriate capital markets for ASET adoption.

Chapter 20 deals with model laws as blueprints for the dissemination of cookstoves. These model laws would be publicly available, and downloadable free of cost. In this chapter Lakshman Guruswamy makes the case for using law as an engine or mechanism for advancing the use of ASETs for cooking, lighting, sanitation, clean water, and motive power. The particular model, illustrating how this might be done, focuses on cookstoves. One model law applies to developing countries and a different law applies to developed countries.

The introduction to Chapter 20 underscores that indoor air pollution, resulting in around four million premature deaths of women and children, is an international problem, and needs an international response. It then discusses the formidable complexities and obstacles in drafting an international treaty, and looks for other ways of using laws, based on principles of sustainable development, common but differentiated responsibility and SE4All, to reduce indoor air pollution. Model laws are presented as vehicles for doing so. The central idea is that both developed and developing countries should accept their common but differentiated responsibilities for indoor air pollution by enacting model laws.

For their part developing countries adopt legislation for the development and dissemination of cookstoves, based on the model law for developing countries. The illustrative national law on the dissemination of clean cookstoves contains a variety of legislative prescriptions that create a blueprint for adopting clean cookstoves. They include legislative findings about energy poverty and silent violence on women, policies articulating what actions need to be taken, National Minimum Standards and Certifications, Indoor Ambient Air Quality Standards, Interim Standards, Durability Standards, Testing and Certification. The model law recognizes the need for administrative discretion, and the establishment of an agency if necessary. The law requires needs assessments, and specifications, in making cookstove selections. It also provides for targeted installations and pilot projects, completions and review of pilot projects, and the implementation mechanisms and administration required. These include the strategic five-year cookstove plan, and the stimulation of cookstove markets. It also embodies sections dealing with monitoring and implementation, authorization and appropriations. In dealing with Research and Development it covers R&D for cooking technologies, health and safety, foreign aid, public information, education, and public health. Finally there are articles dealing with enforcement by way of civil remedies, citizen enforcement, and criminal penalties.

Developed countries would adopt a different law for the dissemination and development of clean cookstoves. They contain policies and provisions that encourage manufacturing industries for clean cookstoves in developing countries by supporting international partnerships and local entrepreneurs with financial, institutional, and technological assistance. The statute also promotes the distribution and maintenance of clean cookstoves by differing entities, including individuals in developing countries, and provides funding for research, development, and deployment of clean cookstoves and the necessary air quality monitoring systems for developing countries. It also deals with the support and dissemination of research and monitoring of the adverse human health and environmental effects associated with the black carbon and other pollutants emitted by inefficient cookstoves.

Toward these ends each developed country will established within the ministry or agency for international aid a Clean Cookstove Manufacturing and Distribution Program. The purpose of the program will be to provide international partnerships and local entrepreneurs with financial, institutional, and technological assistance to develop, manufacture, promote, distribute, and maintain clean cookstoves in developing countries. The program shall be funded in the amount of $15,000,000 each year for ten years.

If a significant number of developing and developed countries adopt and enact these model laws as national legislation, they will create a critical mass of laws addressing indoor air pollution, and the adoption of clean cookstoves. These national laws will address the admittedly international problem of indoor air pollution by circumventing the intimidating and problem-ridden treaty making process.

The authors of this book – academics, practitioners, and business people – have sought to identify the emerging contours of global energy and poverty. Their conclusions often reflect an integrated, multivariable approach reaching beyond their own disciplinary, professional, and business perimeters. It is our hope that we have made a modest contribution toward sustainable energy for all.

References

Abdulsaleh, Abdulaziz M. and Andrew C. Worthington. 2013. "Small and medium-sized enterprises financing: a review of literature." *International Journal of Business and Management* 8(14): 36–54. doi:10.5539/ijbm.v8n14p36.

Aspen Network of Development Entrepreneurs. 2012. "Small and growing businesses: investing in the missing middle for poverty alleviation." Accessed February 17, 2015. www.aspeninstitute.org/sites/default/files/content/docs/ande/ANDE%20 Literature%20Review%20-%20FINAL.pdf.

Bazilian, Morgan, and Roger Pielke. 2013. "Making energy access meaningful." *Issues in Science and Technology* 29(4): 74–79.

Banerjee, Sudeshna Ghosh, Mikul Bhatia, Gabriela Elizondo Azuela, Ivan Jaques, Ashok Sarkar, Elisa Portale, Irina Bushueva, Nicolina Angelou, and Javier Gustavo Inon. 2013. *Executive Summary. Sustainable Energy for All.* Washington DC: World Bank. Accessed February 27, 2015. http://documents.worldbank.org/curated/en/2013/01/

17747194/global-tracking-framework-vol-1-3-global-tracking-framework-executive-summary.

Chowdhury, Anis. 2009. "Microfinance as a poverty reduction tool—a critical assessment." DESA Working Paper No. 89. Accessed February 16, 2015. www.un.org/esa/desa/papers/2009/wp89_2009.pdf.

Global Alliance for Clean Cookstoves. 2010. "About." Accessed February 16, 2015. http://cleancookstoves.org/about/.

Hanpongpandh, Somporn, Libardo Ochoa García, Diana Alarcón González, Octavio Damiani, Felipe Portocarrero Maisch, Albert Berry, Sumantoro Martowijoyo, Nohra Rey de Marulanda, and Abdul-Muyeed Chowd. 2004. *Priorities and Strategies in Rural Poverty Reduction: Experiences from Latin America and Asia.* Edited by Diana Alarcón González. Inter-American Development Bank: IDB Publications.

International Energy Agency. 2012. *World Energy Outlook 2012.* Paris, France: International Energy Agency.

International Finance Corporation. 2013. "Assessing private sector contributions to job creation and poverty reduction." IFC Jobs Study (January). Accessed February 17, 2015. www.businessenvironment.org/dyn/be/be2search.details2?p_phase_id=250&p_lang=en&p_phase_type_id=6.

Jenkins, Beth, Eriko Ishikawa, Emma Barthes, and Marisol Giacomelli. 2008. "Business linkages: supporting entrepreneurship at the base of the pyramid." Report of a Roundtable Dialogue June 10–12, 2008, Rio de Janeiro, Brazil. Washington, DC: International Finance Corporation, International Business Leaders Forum, and the CSR Initiative at the Harvard Kennedy School. Accessed February 16, 2015. www.hks.harvard.edu/m-rcbg/CSRI/publications/report_31_Business%20Linkages%20Rio.pdf.

Linglebach, David, Lynda de la Viña, and Paul Asel. 2005. "What's distinctive about growth-oriented entrepreneurship in developing countries?" UTSA College of Business Center for Global Entrepreneurship Working Paper No. 1. Accessed February 27, 2015. http://ssrn.com/abstract=742605.

Ody, Anthony J., and David de Ferranti. 2007. "Beyond microfinance: getting capital to small and medium enterprises to fuel faster development." The Brookings Institute Policy Brief #159 (March). Accessed February 17, 2015. www.brookings.edu/research/papers/2007/03/development-de-ferranti.

Index

For Product Safety Concerns and Information please contact our
EU representative GPSR@taylorandfrancis.com Taylor & Francis
Verlag GmbH, Kaufingerstraße 24, 80331 München, Germany